I0868922

Impacts of Online Advertising on Business Performance

Tereza Semerádová
Technical University of Liberec, Czech Republic

Petr Weinlich
Technical University of Liberec, Czech Republic

A volume in the Advances in Marketing, Customer Relationship Management, and E-Services (AMCRMES) Book Series

IGI Global
DISSEMINATOR OF KNOWLEDGE

Published in the United States of America by
IGI Global
Business Science Reference (an imprint of IGI Global)
701 E. Chocolate Avenue
Hershey PA, USA 17033
Tel: 717-533-8845
Fax: 717-533-8661
E-mail: cust@igi-global.com
Web site: http://www.igi-global.com

Copyright © 2020 by IGI Global. All rights reserved. No part of this publication may be reproduced, stored or distributed in any form or by any means, electronic or mechanical, including photocopying, without written permission from the publisher.
Product or company names used in this set are for identification purposes only. Inclusion of the names of the products or companies does not indicate a claim of ownership by IGI Global of the trademark or registered trademark.

Library of Congress Cataloging-in-Publication Data

Names: Semerádová, Tereza, 1989- editor. | Weinlich, Petr, 1976- editor.
Title: Impacts of online advertising on business performance / Tereza Semerádová and Petr Weinlich, editors.
Description: Hershey, PA : Business Science Reference, an imprint of IGI Global, [2020] | Includes bibliographical references and index. | Summary: "This book examines online advertising activities and their connection to business performance in online environments. It also explores online communication channels including website presentation, social media, advertising platforms, and e-mailing"-- Provided by publisher.
Identifiers: LCCN 2019031665 (print) | LCCN 2019031666 (ebook) | ISBN 9781799816188 (hardcover) | ISBN 9781799816195 (paperback) | ISBN 9781799816201 (ebook)
Subjects: LCSH: Internet advertising. | Electronic commerce. | Success in business.
Classification: LCC HF6146.I58 I54 2020 (print) | LCC HF6146.I58 (ebook) | DDC 659.14/4--dc23
LC record available at https://lccn.loc.gov/2019031665
LC ebook record available at https://lccn.loc.gov/2019031666

This book is published in the IGI Global book series Advances in Marketing, Customer Relationship Management, and E-Services (AMCRMES) (ISSN: 2327-5502; eISSN: 2327-5529)

British Cataloguing in Publication Data
A Cataloguing in Publication record for this book is available from the British Library.

All work contributed to this book is new, previously-unpublished material.
The views expressed in this book are those of the authors, but not necessarily of the publisher.

For electronic access to this publication, please contact: eresources@igi-global.com.

Advances in Marketing, Customer Relationship Management, and E-Services (AMCRMES) Book Series

ISSN:2327-5502
EISSN:2327-5529

Editor-in-Chief: Eldon Y. Li, National Chengchi University, Taiwan & California Polytechnic State University, USA

MISSION

Business processes, services, and communications are important factors in the management of good customer relationship, which is the foundation of any well organized business. Technology continues to play a vital role in the organization and automation of business processes for marketing, sales, and customer service. These features aid in the attraction of new clients and maintaining existing relationships.

The Advances in Marketing, Customer Relationship Management, and E-Services (AMCRMES) Book Series addresses success factors for customer relationship management, marketing, and electronic services and its performance outcomes. This collection of reference source covers aspects of consumer behavior and marketing business strategies aiming towards researchers, scholars, and practitioners in the fields of marketing management.

COVERAGE

- Ethical Considerations in E-Marketing
- Cases on Electronic Services
- Mobile Services
- Text Mining and Marketing
- Telemarketing
- CRM and customer trust
- Database marketing
- Legal Considerations in E-Marketing
- Online Community Management and Behavior
- Relationship Marketing

IGI Global is currently accepting manuscripts for publication within this series. To submit a proposal for a volume in this series, please contact our Acquisition Editors at Acquisitions@igi-global.com or visit: http://www.igi-global.com/publish/.

The Advances in Marketing, Customer Relationship Management, and E-Services (AMCRMES) Book Series (ISSN 2327-5502) is published by IGI Global, 701 E. Chocolate Avenue, Hershey, PA 17033-1240, USA, www.igi-global.com. This series is composed of titles available for purchase individually; each title is edited to be contextually exclusive from any other title within the series. For pricing and ordering information please visit http://www.igi-global.com/book-series/advances-marketing-customer-relationship-management/37150. Postmaster: Send all address changes to above address. Copyright © 2020 IGI Global. All rights, including translation in other languages reserved by the publisher. No part of this series may be reproduced or used in any form or by any means – graphics, electronic, or mechanical, including photocopying, recording, taping, or information and retrieval systems – without written permission from the publisher, except for non commercial, educational use, including classroom teaching purposes. The views expressed in this series are those of the authors, but not necessarily of IGI Global.

Titles in this Series

For a list of additional titles in this series, please visit:
http://www.igi-global.com/book-series/advances-marketing-customer-relationship-management/37150

Handbook of Research on Contemporary Consumerism
Hans Ruediger Kaufmann (University of Applied Management Studies Mannheim, Germany & University of Nicosia, Cyprus) and Mohammad Fateh Ali Khan Panni (City University, Bangladesh)
Business Science Reference • ©2020 • 361pp • H/C (ISBN: 9781522582700) • US $285.00

Improving Marketing Strategies for Private Label Products
Yusuf Arslan (Sakarya University, Turkey)
Business Science Reference • ©2020 • 383pp • H/C (ISBN: 9781799802570) • US $195.00

Digital Marketing Strategies for Tourism, Hospitality, and Airline Industries
José Duarte Santos (Instituto Superior Politécnico Gaya, Portugal) and Óscar Lima Silva (Instituto Superior Politécnico Gaya, Portugal)
Business Science Reference • ©2020 • 267pp • H/C (ISBN: 9781522597834) • US $225.00

Exploring the Power of Electronic Word-of-Mouth in the Services Industry
Sandra Maria Correia Loureiro (Instituto Universitário de Lisboa, Portugal) and Hans Ruediger Kaufmann (University of Applied Management Studies, Germany)
Business Science Reference • ©2020 • 463pp • H/C (ISBN: 9781522585756) • US $265.00

Green Marketing as a Positive Driver Toward Business Sustainability
Vannie Naidoo (University of KwaZulu-Natal, South Africa) and Rahul Verma (Department of Training and Technical Education, India)
Business Science Reference • ©2020 • 356pp • H/C (ISBN: 9781522595588) • US $225.00

Strategies and Tools for Managing Connected Consumers
Ree C. Ho (Taylor's University, Malaysia)
Business Science Reference • ©2020 • 365pp • H/C (ISBN: 9781522596974) • US $275.00

For an entire list of titles in this series, please visit:
http://www.igi-global.com/book-series/advances-marketing-customer-relationship-management/37150

IGI Global
DISSEMINATOR OF KNOWLEDGE

701 East Chocolate Avenue, Hershey, PA 17033, USA
Tel: 717-533-8845 x100 • Fax: 717-533-8661
E-Mail: cust@igi-global.com • www.igi-global.com

Editorial Advisory Board

Marián Lamr, *Technical University of Liberec, Czech Republic*
Ladislava Míková, *Technical University of Liberec, Czech Republic*
Jan Mrázek, *Deloitte, Czech Republic*
Lenka Suková, *Technical University of Liberec, Czech Republic*
Pavla Švermová, *Technical University of Liberec, Czech Republic*

Table of Contents

Detailed Table of Contents

Dynamic Product Ads (DPAs) and Dynamic Search Ads (DSAs) represent a type of online advertising primarily used for remarketing purposes. However, more and more advertisers can use DPA for acquisition campaigns as well. Dynamic ads are an integral part of the marketing strategies of all large e-shops and companies that have a product or service catalog. Dynamic advertising reduces the time and effort put into the creation of online advertisements and provides the highest level of personalized targeting possible. With a product catalog and a properly set pixel or tracking code, it is possible to create individually customized ads within seconds. This chapter tests the effectiveness of DPAs and DSAs within the context of the two greatest advertising platforms, Facebook and Google ads, and compares their performance against the manually optimized ad sets.

Video represents the most shared type of online content. The ability of this media to capture and convey a message in an interactive and informationally rich format has captivated both users and advertisers. Advertising platforms are trying to expand the offer of the tools that would help the advertisers to reach their potential customers. Therefore, many new video-based advertising formats are being introduced including ads with experimental length or dimensions. However, the increasing quantity of online advertisements the users have to face is raising questions about their actual marketing effectiveness. To provide relevant answers, authors examined the performance of 13 types of video ads that were implemented for a 30-day period and that generated 1 155 EUR overall profit. The advertising results are analyzed from three perspectives: financial, behavioral, and reactional. The main emphasis is put on the study of the video effectiveness depending on different viewing contexts with respect to the potential phenomenon of advertising blindness.

Preface

The digital advertising has become a key instrument for reaching marketing and business goals of many companies. This sector is rapidly growing reaching 281.407 billion USD in 2018. Even though the Search advertising still represents the largest segment with a market volume of 127.546 billion USD, Social media advertising is not far behind. With the annual growth of 10.5% this segment is expected to reach a market volume of 76.561 billion USD in 2022. Ad revenues of Facebook, the leading company on the field of social media advertising, stood at more than 39.9 billion USD in 2017 which is almost a 22 billion increase in comparison to 2015. In addition, the current statistics imply another potential for expansion for mobile advertising. According to Statista, mobile advertising seems to be the most promising form of revenue generation for the company. It is expected that Facebook mobile advertising revenues will reach 60.68 billion USD in 2021. One of the biggest issues in terms of assessing the effectiveness of online marketing efforts is the quantification of the achieved results. Only some of the advertising efforts may be directly expressed as revenues. The remaining processes such as raising awareness and community building, contribute to the generation of profit indirectly. However, companies invest significant amounts of money in order to expand their fan bases, promote their company culture or engage in communication with their current customers. All of these partial steps contribute to creating the brand´s image and finally selling the promoted products. These activities, in particular, are causing considerable problems when it comes to calculating their contribution to the final revenues. Nevertheless, knowing the performance of all the marketing efforts helps to effectively allocate the marketing resources.

The main objective of this publication is to merge the theoretical background presented in the scientific research with practical experience and real-life data originating from real advertising campaigns and website traffic. Thanks to the sophisticated tracking systems offered by advertising platforms such as Facebook or Google Adwords and their connection to website analytical applications such as Google Analytics, the companies have numerous possibilities how to monitor the impact of their advertisements on their business goals. It is important to understand the advertising system and the metrics related to it. Choosing the right metrics and interpreting them correctly with regards to the marketing goals is the only way how to assess the effectiveness of online activities and optimize the settlement of online advertisements. In this book, we comprehensibly focus on online advertising activities and their connection to business performance in online environment.

We believe that this book will provide valuable insights for professionals, researchers and executives concerned with the management of online marketing activities, return of online marketing investments and business activities using Internet environment as the main source of competitive advantage.

This publication contains eight chapters that are organized as follows:

- **Chapter 1:** What Do Facebook Users Feel About Facebook Advertising? Using an Experience Sampling Method (ESM) to Explore Their Digital Advertising Experiences
- **Chapter 2:** Employer Branding in the Digital Era
- **Chapter 3:** A Relationship Marketing Strategy in Brand Communication: Influencer Marketing Strategy
- **Chapter 4:** Customer Engagement Strategies of China's E-Commerce Industry and Their Impact on China's Economy Transition
- **Chapter 5:** Online Purchase and Advertising in Latin America: A Consumer Comparison Among Mexico and Colombia
- **Chapter 6:** Optimization Models in Google Ads Campaigns
- **Chapter 7:** Reaching Your Customers Using Facebook and Google Dynamic Ads
- **Chapter 8:** The (In)Effectiveness of In-Stream Video Ads: Comparison of Facebook and YouTube

Chapter 1 will help online advertising researchers to better understand the feasibility of using Facebook as a potential advertising medium through a non-survey-based method to better assess potential impacts on businesses. The chapter reports the findings from a qualitative study using the Experience Sampling Method (i.e., ESM) after recruiting Facebook college participants in a large university in the Southwest U.S. The ESM technique is a powerful tool to collect data to demonstrate participants' actual experiences and reflections when using Facebook and Facebook advertising. The authors use a signal contingent protocol to record participants' experiences in using Facebook and Facebook advertising after prompting participants to record their using experiences randomly.

Organizations are embracing employer branding now more than ever as a tool to retain, motivate and attract a valuable competitive asset, namely talented employees, as they play a vital role in organizational success. Recently, new digital technologies, particularly social media have replaced the traditional communication channels and made is less effortless for companies to achieve their employer branding objectives. Most organizations are now employing digital technologies at a great extent to get in touch with all their key stakeholders. Chapter 2 initially provides an overview of research on employer branding and its long-term strategic benefits to organizations. Next, it discusses the use of digital technologies, particularly social media, for employer branding purposes. And finally, a framework is introduced covering all the topics mentioned and providing insights to organizations on how and in what form employer brand value should be communicated within the digital media.

In the Chapter 3, the authors mainly focus on the subject of influencer marketing and its connection with relationship marketing. Influencer marketing is about to increase the awareness on the brand by generating appropriate contents that can attract the attention of consumers in virtual environment in accordance with the brand texture. The main purpose of this book chapter is to make an exploratory research to figure out the importance of influencer marketing in brand communication area which is based on relationship marketing. The authors also described the constituent parts of the topics and illustrate them with the case studies and several statistical facts. The authors strongly claim that influencer marketing is sharing the similar variables with relationship marketing and they are related with the basic keywords.

Chapter 4 helps readers understand how various customer engagement strategies of China's e-commerce companies have facilitated the change of their consumers' shopping habits - switching from offline shopping centers to online marketplaces and switching from cash-based payment to credit-based payment. In the past 15 years, China's e-commerce industry has grown tremendously. It is now world's largest e-commerce market. This chapter studies some popular e-commerce companies of China, including Alibaba, JD, and Pindoudou. Specifically, the customer engagement strategies of these companies are described and analyzed. The success of these customer engagement strategies have contributed to the performance improvement of e-commerce companies and could ultimately assist China to transfer from a production economy to a consumption economy. Moreover, these customer engagement strategies developed in China might also be applied to other e-business or marketplaces of different regions, especially developing countries that have similar economy structure as China.

Using a survey applied to samples in Mexico and Colombia, Chapter 5 analyses different online purchase behavior and advertising perceived usefulness and preferences. Online advertising has become an important part of marketing investment for firms around the globe. With the increasing use of these tools, concerns have arisen around their effectiveness. For that reason, during the last years, some research has focused on measuring online advertising effectiveness with different metrics and for different markets and categories, with a focus on the profitability of advertising. However, only a few intend to understand advertisement usefulness for consumers. Particularly, in Latin America, not many studies measure the usefulness or preferences of advertising. Research presented in the chapter tries to close that gap. The results have implications for improving the firm´s online advertising strategy and for future research, which aims to conduct comparative studies in the field of advertising usefulness.

Google Ads is a powerful tool for companies wishing to gain visibility on Google searches, as it offers impression privileges for advertisers, by featuring the ad above the natural results listing. Chapter 6 aims to contribute to the optimization of Google Ads campaigns. It includes an empirical study with a sample of marketing professionals, exploring their views on the challenges of Google Ads as a digital marketing tool. According to the participants in this study, Google Ads campaign profitability depends, largely, on the ability to choose a keyword pool that achieves the company's goals. Moreover, the complexity of these pay-per-click decisions, the costs involved and its business implications demand more reasoned, quantified and, if possible, optimized solutions. The chapter develops linear programming optimization models based on impressions, clicks, conversions and billing. The models are tested on a real example using Excel optimization add-ins.

Nowadays, dynamic ads are an integral part of the marketing strategies of all large e-shops and companies that have a product or service catalog. First, it helps to reduce the time and effort put into the creation of online advertisements. Second, dynamic advertising provides the highest level of personalized targeting possible. Dynamic Product Ads (DPAs) and Dynamic Search Ads (DSAs) represent a type of online advertising that is primarily used for remarketing purposes. However, more and more advertisers can use DPA for acquisition campaigns as well. With a product catalog and a properly set pixel or tracking code, it is possible to create individually customized ads within seconds. In Chapter 7, the authors test the effectiveness of DPAs and DSAs within the context of the two greatest advertising platforms, Facebook and Google ads, and compare their performance against the manually optimized ad sets.

Video represents the most shared type of online content. The ability of this media to capture and convey a message in an interactive and informationally rich format has captivated both users and advertisers. Advertising platforms are trying to expand the offer of the tools that would help the advertisers to reach their potential customers. Therefore, many new video-based advertising formats are being introduced including ads with experimental length or dimensions. However, the increasing quantity of online advertisements the users have to face, is raising questions about their actual marketing effectiveness. In order to provide relevant answers, Chapter 8 examines the performance of 13 types of video ads that were implemented for a 30 days period and that generated 1 155 EUR overall profit. The advertising results are analyzed from three perspectives: financial, behavioral and reactional. The main emphasis is put on the study of the video effectiveness depending on different viewing contexts with respect to the potential phenomenon of advertising blindness.

This publication contributes to the current knowledge about online advertising by providing valuable findings based on applicational experiments and local case studies using real advertising data and user experience. The knowledge areas covered by this book include direct insights regarding online advertising tools such as Facebook Ads and Google Ads, but also the extended topics such as strategic use of online advertising in building employer brand, the role of influencers in the product value creations, or the impacts of personalized advertising on the Facebook users.

Chapter 1
What Do Facebook Users Feel About Facebook Advertising?
Using an Experience Sampling Method (ESM) to Explore Their Digital Advertising Experiences

Yowei Kang
https://orcid.org/0000-0002-7060-194X
National Taiwan Ocean University, Taiwan

Kenneth C. C. Yang
https://orcid.org/0000-0002-4176-6219
The University of Texas at El Paso, USA

ABSTRACT

Because of its popularity and rapid growth, Facebook has become a viable advertising medium for corporations to communicate with their consumers. The experiences of Facebook users are important to ensure the success of any Facebook advertising campaign. This chapter reports the findings from a qualitative study using the Experience Sampling Method (ESM) after recruiting Facebook college participants in a large university in the Southwest U.S. The ESM technique is a powerful tool to collect data to demonstrate participants' actual experiences and reflections when using Facebook and Facebook advertising. The authors use a signal contingent protocol to record participants' experiences in using Facebook and Facebook advertising after prompting participants to record their using experiences randomly. The findings will help online advertising researchers to better understand the feasibility of using Facebook as a potential advertising medium through a non-survey-based method to better assess potential impacts on businesses.

DOI: 10.4018/978-1-7998-1618-8.ch001

Copyright © 2020, IGI Global. Copying or distributing in print or electronic forms without written permission of IGI Global is prohibited.

INTRODUCTION

Facebook as a Social Media Platform

Globally, there are 2.94 billion monthly social media users (*eMarketer.com, 2019*). Among them, Facebook has the largest number of social media users (*eMarketer.com,* 2019). Facebook is a social networking site that was founded in 2004 by Marc Zuckerburg (Facebook, 2004) and has about 169.5 million users in the U.S. (*eMarketer.com*. 2018a). Facebook is conceptualized as "a social utility that helps people communicate more efficiently with their friends, family and coworkers" (Facebook, 2004, n.p.). Like other social networking sites, Facebook was originally developed to target teen and adolescent users (MacMillan, 2009). However, recent statistics have shown that less than half of the U.S. Facebook users are between 12 to 17 years old (*eMarketer.com*. 2018a). The number of Facebook users in the U.S. below 11 years old is expected to decline by 9.3% (*eMarketer.com*. 2018a). An estimate of 2 million users (below 24 years old) is expected to quit Facebook (*eMarketer.com*. 2018a). Presently, Facebook has 1,755.1 million users in 2019 and is expected to grow to 2,023.7 million users in 2023 (*eMarketer.com*. 2019; Enberg, 2019). Other social media platforms have trailed behind Facebook, with Instagram (106.7 million users), Twitter (53.2 million users), Pinterest (78.7 million users), Snapchat (77.5 million users), and Tumblr (18.8 million users) (*eMarketer.com*. 2019) (Refer to Figure 1).

Figure 1. Social network users, by platform, in the U.S.
Source: (eMarketer.com. 2019)

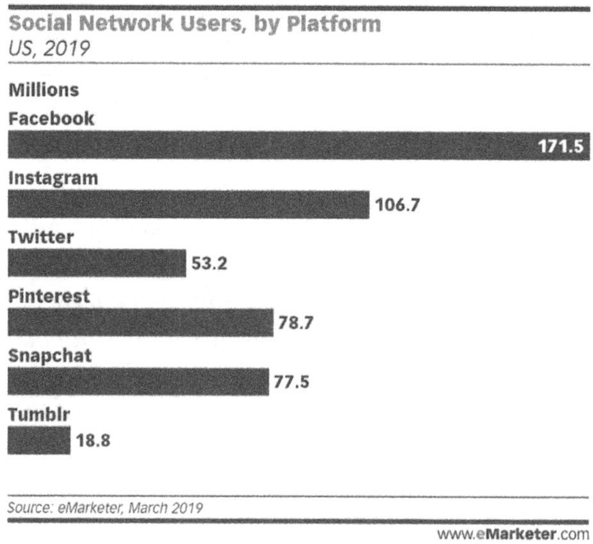

Figure 2. Facebook Users in the U.S., by Device
Source: (eMarketer.com, 2019)

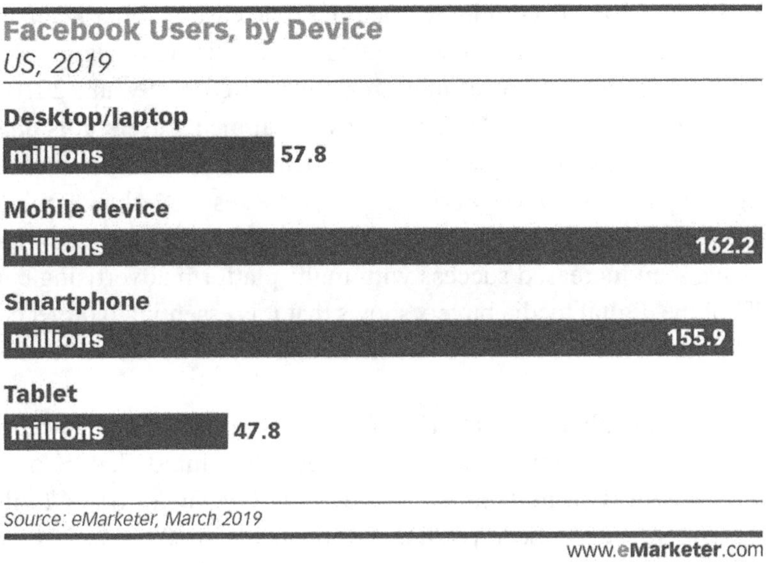

According to *eMarketer.com* (2019), the majority of Facebook users have accessed to this social media through their mobile devices (162.2 millions) or smartphone (155.9 millions), followed by desktop/laptop (57.8 millions) and tablet (47.8 millions) (Refer to Figure 2). The similar heavy reliance on mobile and smartphone devices is found among Twitter users as well (*eMarketer.com*, 2019).

Because of its popularity and rapid growth, Facebook has now been as a viable advertising medium for corporation to communicate with consumers (Yarmis, 2009). Some industry pundits have claimed "Facebook advertising is the most powerful marketing opportunity online" (Carter, 2014, p. 137). Recent statistics in digital advertising seem to support the rosy prediction. According to *eMarketer.com*'s prediction (2018b), the global digital advertising is expected to grow to USD$327.8 billion in 2019, a rapid increase of 17% from 2018, Facebook is the second largest advertiser with $67.2 billion, lower than Google's $102.4 billion, but higher than Alibaba's $30.5 billion (*eMarketer.com*, 2018b). Actual statistics confirms that Facebook has generated about $63.37 billion advertising dollars in 2019 (*eMarketer.com*. 2019; Enberg, 2019).

Facebook advertising has played an increasingly important role in today's multi-platform advertising ecosystem among advertisers and advertising agencies (*eMarketer.com*, 2016). Practitioners and researchers have attributed these dramatic changes to shifting consumer media consumption behaviors (Swant, 2016a; Yang,

2019). The popularity of multi-platform advertising is because of the evolving practices in today's advertising landscape. According to Joe Laszlo, VP of Industry Initiatives at IAB, "[i]t's becoming less and less the case that marketers or brands are just looking to reach their chosen audience on a single device or screen at a time—they're looking to get a lot more holistic" (cited by Swant, 2016a). Given the large percent of Generation M (65.6%) as social media users, it is unavoidable that marketers and advertisers will employ social media in their multi-platform advertising campaign (*eMarketer.com*, 2019). As a result, ValueClick Media and Greystripe (Tode, 2013) also reports that, 75% of 201 media buyers in the survey, said they have seen increased success with multi-platform advertising campaigns. About 89% of the digital media buyers shows that it is essential to target consumers across multi-platforms (Tode, 2013) by including social media platforms such as Facebook.

As a social media platform that offers free access to its service, Facebook relies solely on advertising revenues to support its operation. In 2017, 42% of Facebook operating revenue was from its annual advertising revenue of $18.42 billion (He, 2019). The percentage has been predicted to decrease to 20.6% in 2019, to 18.2% in 2020, and 17.0% in 2021, while Facebook decides to diversity its profile to profit from its new cryptocurrency venture (He, 2019) (Refer to Figure 3). As a viable media platform to deliver advertising to the target audience, Facebook advertising

Figure 3. Facebook Ad Revenues (2017-2021) in the U.S.
Source: (eMarketer.com, 2019)

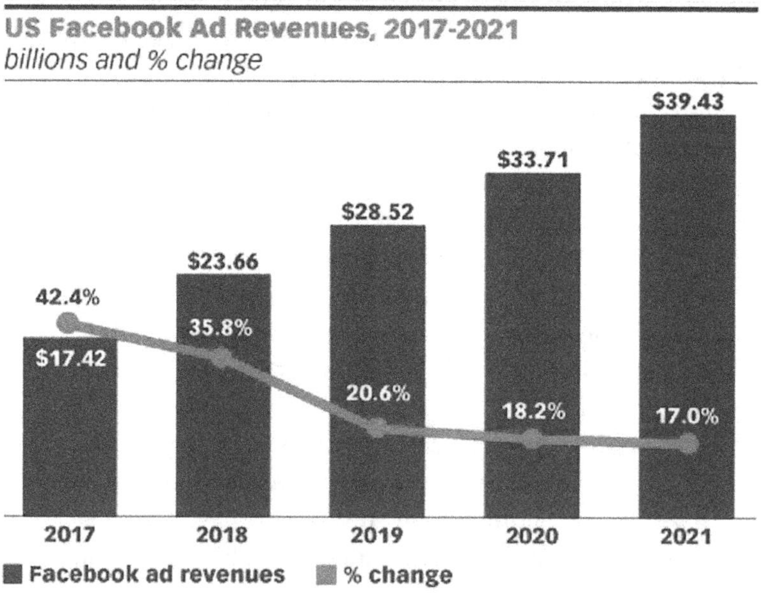

has a competitive CPM with that of other platforms. For example Facebook has an average of $5.14 to $9.64 CPM worldwide in the fourth quarter of 2018 (Fisher, 2019b). Facebook's News Feed ads have an average CPM of $8.35 in the fourth quarter of 2018 (Fisher, 2019b). In terms of its non-video ads, Facebook US CPMs for buy-side companies range from $2.44 to $22.87 in the fourth quarter of 2018, when compared with that of video ads, ranging from $16.27 to $24.87 in the same quarter (Fisher, 2019b).

BACKGROUND

The Growing Importance of Social Media Advertising

The popularity of social media has also led to the emergence of social network advertising as part of the digital advertising ecosystem, which, according to *eMarketer.com* (2015b) and Cohen (2015), global ad spending on social network will reach $35.98 billion in 2017, and accounts for 16% of overall global ad spending. The most-populated Asia-Pacific region has reached about $7.4 billion in social network advertising in 2015, followed by Western Europe ($4.74 billion) and Latin America ($680 million) (*eMarketer.com*, 2015b). It is estimated that the overall social network advertising expenditure will reach $35.98 billion in 2017 (*eMarketer.com*, 2015b). Middle East and Africa have the highest growth rate in social network advertising spending, estimating 33.9% in 2016 and 27.4% in 2017 (*eMarketer.com*, 2015b). The share of social network advertising as part of the global digital advertising expenditure also reflects differences in the diffusion of these platforms across regions. *eMarketer's* data (2015b) also predicts that social network ad spending in North America (18.7%) and Western Europe (16.8%) are expected to have the highest shares of advertising dollars in 2017 (Refer to Figure 4).

An average of $15.45 per social network users is dedicated to social network advertising (*eMarketer.com*, 2015b). However, country variations are noteworthy among economically advanced versus less developed countries. For example, in North America, social network ad spending per social network user is $71.37 and $34.40 per user in Western Europe (*eMarketer.com*, 2015b). Among less developed countries in Latin America and Middle East & Africa, the ad spending per user is about $3.61 and $ $0.90 in 2017, respectively. There exists a close relationship between a region's technology advancement level and the amount of advertising dollars as seen in Figure 5 that shows per social network users' ad spending is predicted to be the highest in North America ($71.37) and Western Europe ($34.40) in 2017 (*eMarketer.com*, 2015b) (See Figure 5).

Figure 4. Social Network Advertising Spending (2013-2017)
Source: (eMarketer.com. 2019)

	2013	2014	2015	2016	2017
Social network ad spending (billions)					
North America	$4.94	$7.71	$10.10	$12.67	$15.15
Asia-Pacific	$3.25	$5.18	$7.40	$9.66	$11.91
Western Europe	$2.34	$3.68	$4.74	$5.82	$6.85
Latin America	$0.35	$0.54	$0.68	$0.85	$1.00
Central & Eastern Europe	$0.41	$0.52	$0.61	$0.70	$0.79
Middle East & Africa	$0.07	$0.11	$0.16	$0.22	$0.28
Worldwide	**$11.36**	**$17.74**	**$23.68**	**$29.91**	**$35.98**
Social network ad spending growth (% change)					
Middle East & Africa	68.0%	63.9%	52.4%	33.9%	27.4%
Asia-Pacific	60.7%	59.4%	42.7%	30.6%	23.3%
North America	46.3%	55.9%	31.0%	25.5%	19.6%
Western Europe	49.8%	57.1%	28.9%	22.8%	17.7%
Latin America	58.2%	55.6%	24.2%	25.0%	17.9%
Central & Eastern Europe	38.5%	27.0%	18.0%	14.4%	13.0%
Worldwide	**51.1%**	**56.2%**	**33.5%**	**26.3%**	**20.3%**
Social network ad spending share (% of total)					
North America	43.5%	43.5%	42.6%	42.4%	42.1%
Asia-Pacific	28.6%	29.2%	31.2%	32.3%	33.1%
Western Europe	20.6%	20.7%	20.0%	19.5%	19.0%
Latin America	3.1%	3.1%	2.9%	2.8%	2.8%
Central & Eastern Europe	3.6%	2.9%	2.6%	2.3%	2.2%
Middle East & Africa	0.6%	0.6%	0.7%	0.7%	0.8%
Social network % of digital ad spending					
North America	10.5%	14.0%	15.9%	17.4%	18.7%
Western Europe	8.0%	11.4%	13.5%	15.3%	16.8%
Asia-Pacific	9.3%	11.4%	12.9%	13.8%	14.3%
Latin America	8.5%	9.9%	10.0%	10.4%	10.4%
Central & Eastern Europe	9.0%	9.3%	9.4%	9.5%	9.7%
Middle East & Africa	4.9%	5.8%	6.8%	7.2%	7.4%
Worldwide	**9.4%**	**12.2%**	**13.9%**	**15.1%**	**16.0%**

Note: includes paid advertising appearing within social networks, social network games and social network apps; excludes spending by marketers that goes toward developing or maintaining a social network presence; numbers may not add up to total due to rounding
Source: eMarketer, April 2015

Figure 5. Social network ad spending per social network user worldwide by region (2013-2017)
Source: (eMarketer.com, 2019)

Social Network Ad Spending per Social Network User Worldwide, by Region, 2013-2017

	2013	2014	2015	2016	2017
Social network ad spending per social network user					
North America	$26.87	$39.98	$50.42	$61.35	$71.37
Western Europe	$13.71	$20.40	$25.26	$29.97	$34.40
Asia-Pacific	$4.45	$6.27	$8.04	$9.46	$10.54
Central & Eastern Europe	$2.65	$3.08	$3.41	$3.71	$4.00
Latin America	$1.87	$2.58	$2.84	$3.26	$3.61
Middle East & Africa	$0.35	$0.47	$0.64	$0.77	$0.90
Worldwide	**$7.02**	**$9.82**	**$11.96**	**$13.87**	**$15.45**
Social network ad spending per social network user growth (% change)					
Middle East & Africa	36.6%	36.8%	36.2%	19.0%	16.9%
Asia-Pacific	39.1%	41.1%	28.2%	17.6%	11.4%
North America	38.9%	49.8%	26.1%	21.7%	16.3%
Western Europe	40.5%	48.9%	23.8%	18.7%	14.8%
Central & Eastern Europe	26.5%	16.3%	10.5%	8.7%	7.9%
Latin America	37.3%	37.7%	10.1%	14.8%	10.6%
Worldwide	**33.1%**	**39.8%**	**21.8%**	**16.0%**	**11.4%**

Note: includes paid advertising appearing within social networks, social network games and social network apps; excludes spending by marketers that goes toward developing or maintaining a social network presence
Source: eMarketer, April 2015

MAIN FOCUS OF THE CHAPTER

Emerging Issues Related to Facebook Advertising

At the macro-level, consumers have increasingly asked for transparency and accountability in the advertising industry as a similar trend found in other digital advertising platforms (Fisher, 2019a). Consumers continue to have concerns over their own privacy protection, resulting in strong demand on proper advertisers' data collection and management procedures to meet pending regulatory requirements (such as California Consumer Privacy Act) (Fisher, 2019a). As early as 2010, Facebook has been criticized for allowing 3rd app companies, data brokers, and advertisers to track and record the identities and usage behaviors of its users and their friends to develop more targeted ads (Worley, 2010). Facebook's recent privacy scandals with *Cambridge Analytica* demonstrate the potential problems when it comes to the monetization of consumer privacy data in the digital advertising marketplace (Kang & Yang, 2019). Despite Facebook's reactive responses to change its privacy policies as well as to allow its users to change their own privacy settings much easier, critics have pointed out that consumers still lack the full access to the data Facebook has collected (Corcoran, 2018). While social media users' own privacy concerns, government's regulatory regimes, and advertisers' own industry standards are expected to play very important role in determine the success of Facebook advertising, academic researchers are more interested in users' characteristics, their attitudes and feelings, message factors, among others on the effectiveness of Facebook advertising.

On the other hand, academic researchers have focused on factors affecting the success of integrating Facebook into an advertising campaign (Anastasiei & Dospinescu, 2017; Baglione, Amin, McCullough, & Tucci, 2018). For example, Baglione et al. (2018) examined the influence of personality, perceived importance of Facebook, users' reference groups, and their perceptions of the ethics of targeted advertising on social media on users' own attitudes toward Facebook advertising. Baglione et al. (2018) empirically confirmed users' personality and reference groups significantly predict their feelings about Facebook advertisements. Anastasiei and Dospinescu (2017) studied whether the lack of trust in online brands, the perceived purchase risk of online shopping, and the perceptions of promotional message types will influence brand image and brand trust in a paid or unpaid Facebook advertising campaign. Their experimental study confirmed that the types of promotional message (paid or unpaid) do not influence any study variables. Duffett (2015) studied whether Facebook advertising has effectively reached Generation Y users in South Africa to influence their cognitive attitudes and subsequent buying behavior. Duffett (2015) confirmed that Facebok advertising has an overall favorable effect on the awareness and knowledge of Generation Y consumers, according to the hierarchy-of-effects model.

While these studies are interesting, an area that has not been fully explored in the extant literature is what Facebook users have actually experienced when using Facebook and advertising delivered through this social media platforms. This study attempts to answer the following questions:

RQ1: What are the overall experiences users have when using Facebook and Facebook advertising?

RQ2: What are the emotional responses users have when using Facebook and Facebook advertising?

Research Method

Because the experiences of Facebook users are important to understand if placing advertising on this social medium will be a feasible option, the authors used an experience sampling method (i.e., ESM) to collect data among Facebook college student users in the U.S. The ESM technique is a powerful tool to collect data to demonstrate participants' experiences (Khan, Markopoulos, & IJsselsteijn, 2007). The benefits of applying ESM are its methodological advantages to "examine fluctuations in the stream of consciousness and the links between the external contents and the contents of the mind" (Csikszentmihalyi, Hektner, & Schmidt, 2006, p.6). Because of the dynamic interactions when users interact with Facebook and its advertisements, ESM allows us to capture not only what Facebook users think of advertising placed on the Facebook when they encounter the messages. To follow ESM protocols, we use signal contingent protocols to record participants' experiences in using Facebook (Conner, Barrett, Bliss-Moreau, & Lebo, 2003). The signal-contingent protocols refer to "reporting on experience in responses to a signal at various times throughout the day" (Conner, Barrett, Bliss-Moreau, & Lebo, 2003, p. 60). The method is appropriate for observing on-going behaviors that are likely to be occurring when prompted (Conner, Barrett, Bliss-Moreau, & Lebo, 2003).

Research Procedure

The authors prompted participants to record their experiences using Facebook and Facebook advertising randomly. Signals were provided to users to prompt them to record their experience using Facebook and its advertising placements. The authors expected the large amount of experience data provided by these participants helps the authors to understand what users think of advertising on the Facebook. The empirical findings help online advertising research to understand the feasibility of using Facebook as a potential advertising medium through a non-survey-based method to better assess potential impacts on businesses.

Data were collected from 26 students who took part in this study for extra credits at a university computer lab where access to Facebook and Facebook advertising is possible. Four research sessions were scheduled for student participants at a large Southwest university and students were requested to take one hour to take part in this IRB-approved study.

Students were first briefed before the study to explain the purposes of the study, the procedures, and the time required to complete, using the following slide presentation.

- Thank you for participating in this study that will collect data on your experiences when you use Facebook and advertising that comes with Facebook
- The study will take about 1 hour to complete
- To take part in this study, you need to have a Facebook account
- Before you begin your study, please read the booklet in front of you. Read the consent agreement (pp. 1-3) and sign the form first before you proceed
- "STOP" after you sign the consent form

Students were asked to log in their Facebook account and use the Facebook for 10 minutes. Afterwards, they were asked to "complete pages 4-5 of the booklet" (as the first prompt).

Participants were asked to skim the ads on Facebook and feel free to click on any ad if they want to brose the advertising contents. As the second prompt to collect experiential data, student participants were asked to "complete pages 6-7 of the booklet."

More specifically, student participants are asked to take 5 minutes or more to browse one Facebook ad of their choice. As part of the 3rd prompt to collect experiential data with Facebook advertising, students were asked to "complete pages 8-9 of the booklet". Once students have completed all booklets, they were thanked and were free to leave the research laboratory.

Findings

Among the recruited participants (N=26), seven of them were male, while 19 were females. Participants' age ranges from 20 to 28 years old, partially reflecting the age bracket of the current social network users (about 27.3% falls between 18 to 24 years old) (*eMarketer.com*, 2019). Their time spent on Facebook ranges from 0.5 hour (2 participants), 1-2 hours (11 participants), 2-3 hours (7 participants), and between 5 to 8 hours (4 hours).

Main Reasons to Use Facebook

When asked about the main reasons to use Facebook, participants have responded by emphasizing the social interaction functions with their friends and family members. For example, Participant 3-6 responds by "Social interaction with my friends and sisters", while Participant 3-5 says, the main reason to use Facebook is to "Keep in touch with friends that I went to school with or ...... in the military with". Participant 4-3 says "Stay in contact with friends, and see what they are up to", while Participant 2-6 indicates, "To stay in touch with friends that have moved away."

Obtaining information about friends, family members, and recent events has been the main reason to use Facebook. For example, Participant 3-4 says, "I like to see what my friends are doing. I work and go to school full-time so sometimes it's hard for me to go out", while Participants 4-5, 4-4, and 4-2 have similar reasons to use Facebook: "For upcoming events and interest on my friends" (4-5), "To keep in touch with friends that I do not see often" (4-4), "Networking, keep in touch, events" (4-2). Some other examples include "I like to read what people post/pictures sometimes play Farmville" (Participant 3-3) or "To socialize & see what everyone is up to" (Participant 2-8).

The rise of Facebook has replaced traditional communication methods as two of the participants suggest. For example, Participant 2-2 says, "It's my only way to communicate because I don't have cell phone." Another participant has used Facebook to "advertise an organization I lead on campus" (Participant 2-10).

Participants are also using Facebook for relaxation and fun. For example, Participant 2-5 says, they use Facebook to "Get distracted. When bored I like to see what everyone else is doing even if I am not talking to them" or to "[i]nteract with my friends and family, entertainment, to relax" (Participant 2-11). The convergence of social and game media has allowed some participants to express their main reason to use Facebook to have "Conversations w/ friends & playing games" (Participant 2-9).

WHAT PEOPLE THINK OF DIGITAL ADVERTISING?

When asked about what they think of advertising on the Internet, participants have in general held positive views, despite many have criticize its intrusiveness. For example, Participant 3-6 says, "It's very useful, while Participant 4-4 says, "I think it's a great way to learn & see new ideas and products." The same favorable views are held among Participant 2-11 ("It must reach a lot of people because I think the Internet is one of the most used medias"), Participant 2-10 ("It's the best way to advertise"), "Great source! It is very useful" (Participant 4-2). One of the participants have mentioned "convenience" as one of the main benefits of digital advertising: "Sometimes is convenient" (Participant 1-2).

Most participants who have reservation about this advertising format have raised concerns about the annoyance or intrusiveness of digital advertising. For example, Participant 3-5 says, "Some times they are good advertising pieces but other times some are annoying", while "I think that advertising is pervasive and somewhat annoying. Often it is selling something I don't want or need (Participant 3-4), " Good resource for advertisers, but sometimes annoying and repetitive & in the way of what I'm trying to look at (Participant 3-3), and "Some is annoying others interesting" (Participant 3-2). One of the participants have raised the question of trust as the drawback of digital advertising: "I don't' trust it" (Participant 1-3).

To prevent the perceptions of intrusiveness, participants have emphasized the importance of relevance of the message and product to consumers. For example, Participant 4-5 says, "It could be bad and good. Advertising can benefit the company into promoting their product but the message can be bad for the consumers" (Participant 4-5), while Participant 4-3 says, "It should be more directed to the product itself" and Participant 2-9 thinks, "Sometimes it's annoying, other times it catches my attention. Depends what it is."

1ST PROMPT (AFTER USING FACEBOOK FOR 10 MINUTES)

Upon asking what users are thinking about, most people have begun to think about behaviors related to Facebook. For example, Participant 3-6 says, "How fast I needed to finish typing a wallpost on one of my ...... sisters facebook walls", while Participant 3-2, says they are "Checking my updates". Similarly, Participant 3-4 says, "I was thinking about what I should put as my new status on Facebook. The last time I uploaded it was 2 days ago, so I wanted to change it", while Participant 3-3 indicates, "I was thinking about my Farmville on Facebook and whose been working on it."

A majority of the participants have been exploring various functions that Facebook has provided. For example, Participant 3-1 is using Facebook to "See what's new with my friends" and to examine "I was thinking about checking my messages and wondering what to respond to on Facebook" (Participant 4-5). As updates of friends are critical to many Facebook users, participants in this study have expressed their need to check most up-to-dated information about their friends. For example, Participant 2-9 says, "I was thinking of the updates my FB friends were making", while Participant 2-2 says, "To have communication with my friends and to see something new (updates about my friends)."

Several participants were thinking about this study about Facebook. For examples, Participant 4-3 says, "Finish this and go back to Facebook", while Participant 4-2, says "I was thinking how fun! I get to be on Facebook for a study" and "I did not know how the questions in the survey were going to be because I felt that with 10 minutes on Facebook we could not get enough information" (Participant 4-1).

To better understand the emotional experiences that users have experienced after using Facebook for 10 minutes, participants' responses suggest positive emotional responses after social interactions with their friends and family members. For example, Participant 2-1 says, that they are "happy... a get to talk with friends, I not always see", Participant 2-6 says, he/she was "excited... my friend was coming to town", while Participant 2-9 also says, she/he was "excited... I was allowed to be on FB no questions asked." Several of the participants have generated emotional experiences related to this study. For example, emotions such as calm or excited were found in the participants' narratives: "calm.... This is an easy task" (Participant 2-3) or "excited... I get to take a survey using something fun that I like to do on my leisure time" (Participant 2-8).

2ND PROMPT AFTER USING FACEBOOK ADVERTISING

After using Facebook advertising for about 10 minutes, participants were prompted to ask what they were thinking about to share their experiences with Facebook advertising. Most have generated thoughts related to their exposure to Facebook advertising and have developed advertising-related thoughts. For example, Participant 3-6 thinks, "The ads weren't good enough" and Participant 3-2 says, "That the ads are completely false, and non-beneficial", while another Participant (3-4) thinks the lack of ad relevance to them, "I was thinking that there were not a lot of ads and that none of them are relevant to me. So that I don't even want to see them."

Similar to exposure to advertisements delivered through other platforms, characteristics of a good ad are still important to attract people's attention. For example, Participant 3-1 says," That there are some interesting ads, although they are not true, but they do catch the eye." Participant 2-2 expresses that she/he will be attracted by an ad related to their own interest, by saying "Well I was interested in the image I saw because they used a common board game as advertising." This suggests the importance of using consumer behavior data to develop Facebook ads relevant to the target audience. The image of an ad will be an attention-getting tool to attract users to use Facebook advertising, as express in Participant 2-1's narratives, "the image of the ad had to be attractive xxx it had to fulfill my interest."

Contextual relevance of an ad is also important, just like any other ads. Participant 4-4 says, "Thinking about the ads I would see on the right of the screen." For example, Participant 2-5 has doubt about the relevance of the Facebook ad he/she just saw, "I click on ad about photography. I need to find a photographer but their ad is sending me to a photography school. Now I'm thinking ...... is not what I wanted." Ad-generated emotions and thoughts were also elicited were reported among Participant 3-3 who are "Thinking about food because I'm hungry and just look at food ad/discount." Similarly, Participant 4-1 also reported the same process, as seen in the following experiential narratives, "Was thinking about the clothes I was looking. I went to that webpage because I clicked in one of the ads from my Facebook profile."

Macro-level issues about the appropriateness of Facebook advertising also emerge as users were exposed to Facebook advertising. For example, Participant 3-5 says, "I was thinking would some of the ads be appropriate for some of the younger children who have a Facebook page." Similarly, Participant 1-1 says, "I wonder if Facebook is making us weaker as a society because XX no longer enhancing ourselves with face to face communication." Some participants have also questioned the ethics of current digital advertising practices as part of their overall experiences. For example, Participant 3-4 says, "I think that a lot of the ads are a scam, they request your e-mail address, and if you register you get non-stop e-mails about things you don't want. It's very hard to get removed from those lists." Participant 3-1 criticizes the intrusiveness of many pop-up ads, "Honestly, ads on the side do not bother me, what bothers me the most are pop up ads or the ones they show when you're watching videos." 2-9: I was thinking that since I was interested to look for advertisements on FB I would look for some that were interesting. I also …… that if I got a notification & I answered it I would get in trouble since I was told to look for advertisements.

To understand Facebook's overall emotional responses about Facebook advertising, all participants were asked the following question, "If you felt a strong emotion since the last prompt, what did you feel and why did you feel that way?" While many have expressed their heightened interest in Facebook advertising by using the words, "interested" (Participant 1-4, Participant 2-2, Participant 4-2), "happy" (Participant 2-6), and "excitement" (Participant 2-1, Participant 2-7). The positive emotions were elicited after exposure to Facebook advertising because users are "interested… I felt identifying with the picture (the gameboard)" (Participant 2-2), or "ads were useful" (Participant 4-2). Some participants felt excited because "a found an ad that was promoting a game that I use to play when I was little) (Participant 2-1).

However, the majority of participants has expressed negative emotions as a result of exposure to Facebook advertising. For example, Participant 1-3 says, he/she is "bored" because of "tedious ads" or "I was finding more and more interested things" (Participant 1-4). Participant 3-6 is "annoyed…. The ads were boring." Ad clutter could also lead to negative feelings after exposure to Facebook advertising. For example, Participant 3-2 says, he or she is "annoyed… the adds are cluttering the screen." Participant 3-4 is "irritated… I don't like dealing with the ads."

The circumstance where Facebook advertising exposure occurs may also play a role in determining the effectiveness of Facebook advertising. For example, one participant (Participant 2-5) says, she/he is afraid… I don't like browsing with other people next to me. I don't like to be judge based on what's on my screen." Similarly, Participant 2-9 says, she/he is "slightly anxious…. I wanted to answer my notifications but I wanted to do so in a discreet manner so as to I wouldn't get on trouble."

3RD PROMPT AFTER USING A SPECIFIC FACEBOOK AD

The third part of the study involved the participants to watch a specific Facebook advertisement for 5 minutes before they were prompted to respond to the booklet. Participants need to write down what are in their mind when prompted. The experiential data the study has collected clearly indicate that exposure to Facebook advertising helps generate product-related thoughts. For example, Participant 3-5 says, "I was thinking about how funny some of the ads were." Participant 2-2 explained what make an ad attractive, "That I like the picture where I got to. The page on Facebook they had a lot of pictures, videos. It was very colorful." Participant 3-2 offered the most detailed description about what came to user's mind after exposure to a specific Facebook advertisement, as seen in the narrative below: "I found some clothes I would like to buy but the company is out of stock. If that's the case, they shouldn't be advertising what's not available." If the ad was not relevant to consumers, it is less likely to have a significant effect on consumers. For example, Participant 2-5 says, "I am looking for and ad I want to purchase something from and nothing appeals to me. Everything showing to me are not my interest. Only thing came close is a hot dog ad"; Participant 2-11 expresses something similar, "About the ads on the webpage, of something that would interest me, then I found the ad of a book."

The nature of interactive advertisements allows users to be the active seeker for information. Therefore, a successful Facebook advertising campaign needs to be attention-getting and interesting to generate stickiness before users move on to another ad. For example, Participant 2-9 says, "Finding an interesting advertisement" while Participant 2-8 expresses, "I've never clicked on an ad so this is going to be boring." Participant 2-4 opted to search for ads that would be interesting to him/her, "I was thinking about what pages to search that were of interest to me."

The ethics of existing Facebook advertising practices remain to be a concern among several participants, to the extent of questioning its effectiveness. For example, Participant 1-1 says, "The ads on Facebook are very direct and quick sells. I wonder how effective they are?" Another Participant (1-3) has doubt about the data collection process, by saying "The ad is useless and it's only a way to gather your email to send overloads of ads to that email."

In terms of participants' emotional responses, a mixture of emotions was elicited after they focused on one specific Facebook ad for five minutes. They were asked to complete the sentence below": **"**If you felt a strong emotion since the last prompt, what did you feel and why did you feel that way? I felt ________ ________________________________ because ______________". Compared with what happened after the second prompt, a higher percentage of negative emotions was generated. For example, Participant 1-3 says, **"**dissatisfied" and Participant 3-2 says, "dissatisfied.... I could not get the product I wanted.", while Participant

1-4 says, "disappointed.... I didn't see a lot of advertising." The lack of interest among participants may explain these negative emotions. For example, Participant 2-1 says, he or she is "a little bit bored... I couldn't actually found something really interesting" while Participant 2-7 expressed he or she was "bored... I want to finish already." Participant 2-8 also says, he or she was "bothered... I had to look a boring ads that I didn't want to."

Some participants have expressed very strong negative emotions because of the design of Facebook to make the platform difficult to use. For example, Participant 2-5 says, she/he was "Angry... the add section on facebook is so complicated. I couldn't find anything to ... appeal and it gets me mad that facebook can't read my interest right." The poor design of Facebook advertising can also generate negative emotions. For example, Participant 2-4 says, "disappointed... I clicked on an ad for shoes but I had to sign up for the site." Thoughts not related to the study or the advertising were found to affect the advertising communication process. For example, Participant 2-10 expressed that he or she was "sad/annoyed... sad b/c I will miss my family when I leave and annoyed b/c I don't want to go to work" or Participant 3-4 says "more irritated... my survey answers to the online ads got me nothing."

Positive emotional responses were often generated when participants found the Facebook ad to be relevant and well-executed. For example, Participant 2-9 says, "Interested... the pictures on the advertisement's website appealed to me. The sophistication of the product did to it almost made of feel tangible" while Participant 3-3 also says "interested; I want to learn more about the product I was looking at the ad" and Participant 4-4 says, "happy... I was looking at different products." Similarly, Participant 3-5 has enjoyed the favorable emotional response after seeing the Facebook ad, "humored by some good ads.... Some make me laugh." Reading a Facebook ad can be relaxing to some participants, "relaxed again..... I'm just browsing through ads" (Participant 2-3) and "relaxed... I was not worried about school or work" (Participant 4-5), while confusing to others, "confused... I didn't know if I should buy or not" (Participant 2-6).

CONCLUSION

As observed in the above qualitative study that collected Facebook users' actual experiences when using Facebook and Facebook advertising, the study concludes that the success of Facebook advertising depends on a set of similar mechanisms such as the message factors (Baglione et al., 2018). Attractive advertising layout and design elements will create similar positive effects and emotional responses as observed in the ESM study. As an empirical study, this research reports users' experiential data to help digital advertising practitioners and researchers to better investigate what people were thinking about when exposed to Facebook and Facebook advertising. As a qualitative study, it is not feasible to explore causal relationships among these study variables. Furthermore, this study does not explore whether existing advertising regulatory regimes are likely to guide Facebook advertisers through the challenges and opportunities of this emerging advertising practice around the world. However, because Facebook advertising campaigns will rely heavily on knowledge about consumer behaviors and data to make the best use of Facebook advertising to complement cross-platform efficiencies, this type of heavy data-driven advertising and marketing campaigns may face similar privacy-related concerns in real-time bidding advertising (Yang & Kang, 2016),or programmatic advertising (Wood, 2015). Similar to other advertising campaigns delivered through other platforms, transparency and accountability are also required for many data brokers who gather and examine consumer data to produce market insights to develop a more effective multi-platform advertising campaign (Wood, 2015).

One of the urgent concerns about the practices of Facebook advertising is consumer privacy. At the local/state level, the California Consumer Privacy Act (CCPA) will become effective as of January 1, 2020 and is expected to raise the stakes for marketers to comply with the protection of consumer privacy. At the federal level, since 2009, Federal Trade Commission in the U.S. has been observing how marketers use consumer data for behavioral targeting advertising. FTC (2012) has focused on how to safeguard consumer privacy in the digital age through measures such as privacy by design, simplified solution to discourage consumer privacy infringement (such as *Do Not Track* mechanism), and greater transparency in consumer data gathering and usage. In Europe, *The ePrivacy Directive (Directive 2002/58/EC)* focuses on the regulation of storing and accessing data on a users' mobile device (The European Parliament and of the Council, 2002). IAB UK (2011) has also proposed a self-regulatory structure for online behavioral advertising practices and to establish seven principles to increase transparency mechanisms, user choice, sensitive segmentation, enforcement compliance, and review for users within the EU countries.

In addition to government's pro-active actions to defend consumer privacy, industry self-regulation such as those proposed by IAB's *Self-Regulatory Principles for Online Behavioral Advertising* (2009) put a great importance on the advertising professionals to abide by seven principles when developing online advertising campaigns (Refer to IAB, 2009 for detailed discussions).

In conclusion, the emergence of Facebook and its advertising practice have evidently become a global phenomenon that have seen its impacts on the advertising and marketing industry. To plan and implement a successful Facebook advertising campaign, advertising and marketers not only need to understand consumer consumption behaviors of different media platforms, but they also need to make the best use of the platform's strengths, while factoring into their existing weaknesses.

REFERENCES

Anastasiei, B., & Dospinescu, N. (2017). Facebook advertising: Relationship between types of message, brand attitude, and perceived buying risk. *Annals of 'Constantin Brancusi' University of Targu-Jiu. Economy Series*, *6*, 18–26.

Baglione, S. L., Amin, K., McCullough, A., & Tucci, L. (2018, Winter). Factors affecting Facebook advertisements: Empirical study. *International Journal of Business, Marketing, & Decision Sciences*, *11*(1), 124–140.

Carter, B. (2014). *The like economy: How businesses make money with Facebook* (2nd ed.). Indianapolis, IN: QUE Publishing.

Castillo, M. (2017, Oct. 13). Facebook is under fire from advertisers, highlighting a wider industry issue. *CNBC*, Retrieved from https://www.cnbc.com/2017/2010/2013/facebook-under-fire-from-advertisers.html

Cohen, D. (2015, April 20). Study: Global social media ad spend to reach nearly $36b in 2017. Retrieved from http://www.adweek.com/digital/emarketer-global-social-media-ad-spend/

Conner, T. S., Barrett, L. F., Bliss-Moreau, E., & Lebo, K. (2003, February). A practical guide to experience-sampling procedures. *Journal of Happiness Studies*, *4*(1), 53–75. doi:10.1023/A:1023609306024

Criteo. (2014, September). *Cross-device advertising: How to navigate mobile marketing's next big opportunity*: Retrieved from http://www.criteo.com/media/1036/cross-device-advertising-criteo-sep-2014.pdf

Csikszentmihalyi, M., Hektner, J. M., & Schmidt, J. A. (2006). Experience sampling method: measuring the quality of everyday life (1st Ed.).Thousand Oaks, CA: Sage.

CTAM. (n.d.). Multiplatform definition. Retrieved from https://www.ctam.com/strategic-collaboration/advanced-cable/pages/multiplatform-definition.aspx

DeLuca, J. (2013, May 8). The new opportunity in cross-platform advertising. Retrieved from http://www.imediaconnection.com/articles/ported-articles/red-dot-articles/2013/may/the-new-opportunity-in-cross-platform-advertising/

Doyle, G. (2010). From television to multi-platform less from more or more for less? *Convergence: The International Journal of Research into New Media Technologies*, *16*(4), 431-449. doi:10.1177/1354856510375145

Duffett, R. (2015, June). The influence of Facebook advertising on cognitive attitudes amid Generation Y. *Electronic Commerce Research, 15*(2), 243–267. doi:10.100710660-015-9177-4

Dutta-Bergman, M. J. (2010, June 7). Complementarity in consumption of news types across traditional and new media. *Journal of Broadcasting & Electronic Media, 48*(1), 41–60. doi:10.120715506878jobem4801_3

eMarketer.com. (2014, May 9). Cross-device advertising a hot topic in 2014. Retrieved from https://www.emarketer.com/Article/Cross-Device-Advertising-Hot-Topic-2014/1010824

eMarketer.com. (2015a, April 2). Mobile ad spend to top $100 billion worldwide in 2016, 51% of digital market. Retrieved from https://www.emarketer.com/Article/Mobile-Ad-Spend-Top-100-Billion-Worldwide-2016-51-of-Digital-Market/1012299

eMarketer.com. (2015b, April 15). Social network ad spending to hit $23.68 billion worldwide in 2015. Retrieved from https://www.emarketer.com/Article/Social-Network-Ad-Spending-Hit-2368-Billion-Worldwide-2015/1012357

eMarketer.com. (2016, Oct. 11). *Multiplatform video ad buying is emerging as the new normal.* Retrieved from https://www.Emarketer.Com/article/multiplatform-video-ad-buying-emerging-new-normal/1014576

eMarketer.com. (2018a, Feb. 12). Facebook losing younger users: But not all are migrating to Instagram. *eMarketer.com*, Retrieved from https://www.emarketer.com/content/facebook-losing-younger-users-at-even-faster-pace

eMarketer.com. (2018b, Nov. 20). Global ad spending update: Alibaba, Facebook and Google to capture over 60% of digital ad dollars in 2019. *eMarketer.com*. Retrieved from https://www.emarketer.com/content/global-ad-spending-update

eMarketer.com. (2019, March). Social network users, by platforms. *eMarketer.com*. Retrieved from https://forecasts-na2011.emarketer.com/2584b26021403070290f26021403070293a26021403070291a/26021405851918b26021400626310a26021403070292c26021403070186b26021403070291b

Enberg, J. (2019, June 23). Q2 2019 social trends: Facebook continues to diversify its revenue streams, Snapchat holds first partner summit, and Twitter targets political tweets. *eMarketer.com*, Retrieved from https://content-na2011.emarketer.com/q2012-2019-social-trends

Enoch, G., & Johnson, K. (2010). Cracking the cross-media code. *Journal of Advertising Research, 50*(2), 125–136. doi:10.2501/S0021849910091294

Erdal, I. J. (2009). Cross-media (re)production cultures. *Convergence: The International Journal of Research into New Media Technologies, 15*(2), 215-231. doi:10.1177/1354856508105231

Federal Trade Commission (FTC). (2012, March). *Protecting consumer privacy in an era of rapid change: Recommendations for businesses and policymakers*. Retrieved from https://www.ftc.gov/reports/protecting-consumer-privacy-era-rapid-change-recommendations-businesses-policymakers

Fisher, L. (2019a, Jan. 22). Nine trends to know for this year's media plan. *eMarketer.com*. Retrieved from https://content-na2011.emarketer.com/digital-display-advertising-2019

Fisher, L. (2019b, April 18). Digital display ad pricing StatPack: Banner, video, mobile and native CPMs, and pricing trends to watch for in 2019. *eMarketer.com*. Retrieved from https://content-na2011.emarketer.com/digital-display-ad-pricing-statpack

Havlena, W., Ardarelli, R. C., & Montigny, M. D. (2007). Quantifying the isolated and synergistic effects of exposure frequency for TV, print, and internet advertising. *Journal of Advertising Research, 47*(3), 215–221. doi:10.2501/S0021849907070262

He, A. (2019, June 24). Facebook's new libra cryptocurrency helps the company diversify away from advertising. *eMarketer.com*. Retrieved from https://content-na2011.emarketer.com/facebook-new-libra-cryptocurrency-helps-the-company-diversify-away-from-advertising

Hubbard, G. T., Kang, J.-A., & Crawford, E. C. (2016). Strategic communication and news disciplines. *Journalism & Mass Communication Educator, 71*(4), 453–469. doi:10.1177/1077695815598865

IAB. (2009, July). *Self-regulatory principles for online behavioral advertising*. Retrieved from https://www.iab.com/wp-content/uploads/2015/2005/ven-principles-2007-2001-2009.pdf

IAB UK. (2011, April 14). Europe commits to self-regulation; Europe's online advertising industry agrees online behavioural advertising guidelines. Retrieved from https://iabuk.net/news/europe-commits-to-self-regulation

Kang, Y. W., & Yang, K. C. C. (2019, Aug. 7-10). Will location privacy concerns influence location-based advertising effectiveness. Presented at the Competitive Paper, Advertising Division, 2019 AEJMC Conference, Toronto, Canada.

Khan, V. J., Markopoulos, I., & Jsselsteijn, W. A. (2007). Combining the experience sampling method with the day reconstruction method. In *Proceedings 11th CHI Nederland Conference*.

Lella, A., Lipsman, A., & Martin, B. (2015). The global mobile report: How multi-platform audiences & engagement compare in the US, Canada, UK and beyond. Reston, VA: com.Score.

Loras, S. (2016, July 18). What do China's new online advertising rules mean for marketers? Retrieved from https://www.clickz.com/what-do-chinas-new-online-advertising-rules-mean-for-marketers/103221/

Macdonald, C., Chapman, M., Naik, A., Fanno, M., & Beilis, T. (2016). *Cross-channel advertising attribution: New insights into multiplatform TV*. Accenture. Retrieved from https://www.accenture.com/us-en/~/media/PDF-18/Accenture-New-Insights-Into-Multiplatform-TV.pdf

Manafy, M. (2014, June 6). Five tips for cross-platform advertising success. Retrieved from http://www.thedrum.com/opinion/2014/06/06/five-tips-cross-platform-advertising-success

Marks, R. (2016, May). Challenges and opportunities in cross platform media measurement. *Research World, 2016*(58), 9–13. doi:10.1002/rwm3.20366

McIntyre, P. (2006). Cross-media deals expected to double to $600m a year; alliance mulls multi-platform package. *Australasian Business Intelligence,* 33. Retrieved from https://www.highbeam.com/doc/2001G2001-154865588.html

McNeal, M. (2013, Summer). Solving the multiplatform puzzle. *Marketing Insights,* pp. 41-47.

Monllos, K. (2016, Sept. 13). Carrie Brownstein made this brilliantly creepy short film about internet fandom for Kenzo. *AdWeek*. Retrieved from http://www.adweek.com/brand-marketing/carrie-brownstein-made-brilliantly-creepy-short-film-about-internet-fandom-kenzo-173453/

Neijens, J., & Voorveld., R. (2015). Cross-platform advertising: Current practices and issues for the future. *Journal of Advertising Research, 55*(3), 55-60. doi:. doi:10.2501/JAR-2016-2042

Nielsen. (2014, May 29). *The 8% unleashing the power of cross-platform advertising*. Retrieved from http://www.nielsen.com/content/corporate/us/en/insights/news/2014/the-8-percent-unleashing-the-power-of-cross-platform-advertising.html

Nielsen. (2016a, March 22). *On-demand demographics: VOD viewing across generations.* Retrieved from http://www.Nielsen.Com/us/en/insights/news/2016/on-demand-demographics-vod-viewing-across-generations.Html:Nielsen

Nielsen. (2016b, March 24). *Facts of life: As they move through life stages, Millennials' media habits are different and distinct.* Retrieved from http://www.nielsen.com/us/en/insights/news/2016/facts-of-life-as-they-move-through-life-stages-millennials-media-habits-are-different.html

Nielsen. (2017a, Jan. 30). Nielsen launches cross-device provider verification powered by digital ad ratings. Retrieved from http://www.nielsen.com/us/en/press-room/2017/nielsen-launches-cross-device-provider-verification-powered-by-digital-ad-ratings.html

Nielsen. (2017b, March 2). Millennials on millennials: A look at viewing behavior, distraction, and social media stars. Retrieved from http://www.nielsen.com/us/en/insights/news/2017/millennials-on-millennials-a-look-at-viewing-behavior-distraction-social-media-stars.html

Precourt, G. (2015, December). How does cross-platform advertising work? *Journal of Advertising Research*, 356-357. doi:10.2501/JAR-2015-2018

ResearchLive. (2017, Feb. 23). *com.Score launches multi-platform digital video measure in UK.* Retrieved from https://www.Research-live.Com/article/news/comscore-launches-multiplatform-digital-video-measure-in-uk/id/5018952

Robertson, M. (2014, April 29). Media buyers see big value in multi-platform advertising. Retrieved from http://tubularinsights.com/media-buyers-see-big-value-in-multi-platform-advertising/#ixzz4g3oWQRKh

Romaniuk, J. (2015, September). Coming in December: How cross-platform advertising works. *Journal of Advertising Research*, 353. doi:10.2501/JAR-2015-2014

Roper, P. (2014, Dec. 16). November best global digital marketing: Red Roof Inn's search campaign, Burger King's motel, Turkish shoppable soap opera. *Marketing.* Retrieved from http://shortyawards.com/category/2017th/multi-platform-campaign

Sharma, A. (2013, July 18). 'Mad Men' tops 'House of Cards' on Netflix. *The Wall Street Journal,* p. B3.

Swant, M. (2016a, Jan. 19). Why cross-device programmatic advertising is ready to take off in 2016. *Adweek.* Retrieved from http://www.adweek.com/digital/why-cross-device-programmatic-advertising-ready-take-2016-169025/

Swant, M. (2016b, Feb. 24). 6 ways Netflix viewing habits vary around the world. *Adweek,* Retrieved from http://www.adweek.com/digital/2016-ways-netflix-mobile-habits-vary-around-world-169848/

The European Parliament and of the Council. (2002, July 2). Directive 2002/58/EC of the European Parliament and of the Council of 12 July 2002 concerning the processing of personal data and the protection of privacy in the electronic communications sector (directive on privacy and electronic communications). Retrieved from http://eur-lex.europa.eu/legal-content/EN/TXT/?uri=CELEX:32002L0058

Tode, C. (2013, Aug. 16). Cross-device advertising commands growing portion of media spend: Report. *Mobile Marketer*. Retrieved from http://www.mobilemarketer.com/cms/news/research/15969.html

Twice. (2016, June 20). Millennials lead way among cord-cutters. *Twice,* p. 20.

Westcott, K., Lippstreu, S., & Cutbill, D. (2017). *Digital democracy survey: A multi-generational view of consumer technology, media, and telecom trends* (11th ed.). UK: Deloitte Development.

Wood, D. J. (2015, April 14). As marketers rush to programmatic, consumer-privacy rules still apply. *AdAge.com.* Retrieved from http://adage.com/article/digital/rush-programmatic-privacy-rules-apply/298060/

Yang, K. C. C. (2018). Multi-platform advertising as a global phenomenon. In Yang, K. C. C. (Ed.), Multi-platform advertising strategies in the global marketplace (pp. 1-28). Hershey, PA: IGI-Global. doi:10.4018/978-1-5225-3114-2.ch001

Yang, K. C. C., & Kang, Y. W. (2015). Exploring big data and privacy in strategic communication campaigns: A cross-cultural study of mobile social media users' daily experiences. *International Journal of Strategic Communication, Special Issue, 9*(2), 87–101. doi:10.1080/1553118X.2015.1008635

Yang, K. C. C., & Kang, Y. W. (2016, Oct. 15-16). Real-time bidding (RTB) advertising, programmatic advertising, digital advertising marketplace: Emerging policy and regulatory issues. Presented at Direct/Interactive Marketing Research Summit, Los Angeles, CA.

ADDITIONAL READING SECTION

Aronstam, S. (n.d.). Measuring the effectiveness of multi-platform advertising. Retrieved on July 7, 2016 from http://www.irisnetwork.org/media/work/SPA_Multi-Platform-Advertising.pdf

Assael, H. (2011). 50th Anniversary Supplement)). From silos to synergy: A fifty-year review of cross-media research shows synergy has yet to reach its full potential. *Journal of Advertising Research*, *51*(1), 42–58. doi:10.2501/JAR-51-1-042-058

Crain, R. (2001, May 21). Multiplatform buys can lead to disruption for buyer, seller. *Advertising Age*, *72*, 19.

eMarketer (2016, September 13). Us digital ad spending to surpass TV this year. Retrieved on January 10, 2017 from https://www.emarketer.com/Article/US-Digital-Ad-Spending-Surpass-TV-this-Year/1014469

Feit, E. M., Wang, P.-Y., Bradlow, E. T., & Fader, P. S. (2013, June). Fusing aggregate and disaggregate data with an application to multiplatform media consumption. *JMR, Journal of Marketing Research*, *L*, 34850–364.

Fulgoni, G. M. (2015, December). Is the grp really dead in a cross-platform ecosystem? In a cross-platform ecosystem? Why the gross rating point metric should thrive in today's fragmented media world. *Journal of Advertising Research*, *55*(4), 358–361. doi:10.2501/JAR-2015-019

Indian Investment News. (January 3, 2014). Research and markets: Cross-platform & mobile advertising market by solutions &advertising - worldwide market forecasts and analysis (2013 - 2018). *India Investment News*, Retrieved on June 1, 2016 from http://www.marketsandmarkets.com/ResearchInsight/mobile-advertising-market.asp

Kim, S. J. (2016). A repertoire approach to cross-platform media use behavior. *New Media & Society*, *18*(3), 353-372. *DOI*, *3*. doi:10.1177/1461444814543162

Ksiazek, T. B. (2011). A network analytic approach to understanding cross-platform audience behavior. *Journal of Media Economics*, *24*, 237-251. *DOI*, *2*. doi:10.1080/08997764.08992011.08626985

Nielsen. (2011, June 22). Innovating to keep up with the ever-changing consumer. Retrieved on December 10, 2016 from http://www.nielsen.com/us/en/insights/news/2011/innovating-to-keep-up-with-the-ever-changing-consumer.html

Parsons, R. (2014, January 28). Privacy concerns harming online advertising. *Marketing Week*, Retrieved on December 1, 2016 from https://www.marketingweek.com/2014/2001/2028/privacy-concerns-harming-online-advertising/

Phalen, P., & Ducey, R. (2012). Audience behavior in the multi-screen "video-verse.". *International Journal on Media Management, 14*(2), 141–156. doi:10.1080/14241277.2012.657811

Snyder, J., & Garcia-Garcia, M. (2016, December). Advertising across platforms: Conditions for multimedia campaigns a method for determining optimal media investment and creative strategies across platforms. *Journal of Advertising Research*, 352-367. *DOI, 3*. doi:10.2501/JAR-2016-2042

Taylor, J. R., Kennedy, C., McDonald, N., Haddad, Y., Ouarzazi, E., & Larguinat, L. (2013). Is the multi-platform whole more powerful than its separate parts? Measuring the sales effects of cross-media advertising. *Journal of Advertising Research, 53*(2), 200–211. doi:10.2501/JAR-53-2-200-211

Umstead, R. T. (2014, February 17). Hulu Latino adds exclusives, originals providers aim for keys OTT demographic. *Multichannel News,* p.10.

Varan, D., Murphy, J., Hofacker, C. F., Robinson, J. A., Potter, R. F., & Bellman, S. (2013). What works best when combining television sets, pcs, tablets, or mobile phones? How synergies across devices result from cross-device effects and cross-format synergies. *Journal of Advertising Research, 53*(2), 212–220. doi:10.2501/JAR-53-2-212-220

Winslow, G. (2014a, February 3). com.Score launches cross-platform ratings. *Broadcasting & Cable,* 4.

Winslow, G. (2014b, July 14). Race intensifies for multiplatform ad systems. *Broadcasting & Cable,* 27-28.

Zelenkauskaite, A. (2016). Remediation, convergence, and big data: Conceptual limits of cross-platform social media. *Convergence (London)*, 1–16. doi:10.1177/1354856516631519

KEY TERMS AND DEFINITIONS

Analytics: Consumer behavioral data related to their platform usage behaviors such as the number of visits to a platform, time spent on the platform, and actions when using the platform. Using these behavioral data, advertisers and marketers are able to segment target audience to increase their experiences and to improve campaign effectiveness.

Big Data: A term that defines a large dataset that produces in the size of collected data over time. It refers to the size of dataset that surpasses the capturing, storage, management, and analysis of traditional databases. The term refers to the dataset that has huge, more diverse, and multifaceted structure, accompanies by difficulties of data storage, analysis, and visualization. Big Data are characterized with the commonly known attributes: high-volume, -velocity, and –variety information assets.

Channel: In the advertising industry, the term refers to the platform or media to reach the target audience. Example of (advertising channels) include television, cable television, direct mail, outdoor, radio, etc. In the area of digital advertising, examples of channels include display, social, search, or mobile app advertising.

Consumer Behavior: The study of the decision-making processes to select, secure, use, and dispose of products or services by individuals, groups, or organizations. In the advertising industry, this term usually refers to how customers respond to advertising and marketing communications messages (such as in the information processing model) or how consumers decide to use multiple platforms in their daily lives. Consumer behavior aims to examine social, cultural, regulatory, and other ecological factors in affecting the decision-making process.

Digital Advertising: Used interchangeable with Internet or online advertising. This term covers a wide variety of online advertising formats, ranging from email, social media applications, search engine advertising, mobile advertising, video advertising, etc.

Digital Games: The terms, digital game or video game, often refers to a game which users play through audiovisual platform with contents on the basis of a story created from historical or fantasy themes. The concept of digital games as represented in existing game studies literature focuses on game itself, narrative (story), interactivity, and play.

Display Advertising: A type of digital advertising associated with and displayed on an Internet website. Its format ranges from audio, flash, images, text, and video.

Engagement: Also called consumer engagement, the term is a psychological concept that refers to how and whether users are satisfied with their experiences with advertising contents.

Mobile Advertising: An emerging platform of new digital media advertising formats that are delivered via consumers' mobile devices such as mobile phones, smartphones, tablets, etc.

Mobile Social Media: A term to refer to social networking media or applications such as Facebook, Foursquare, Instagram, Pinterest, Twitter, etc., that are often delivered via mobile devices such as smartphone, tablet, or laptop computer.

Multi-Platform Advertising: Also known as cross-channel, cross-media, cross-touchpoints, or multi-screen advertising, this term refers to advertising/marketing communications activities "that run during a similar timeframe across two or more screens including TV, computer, tablet, mobile phone and digital place-based media."

Programmatic Advertising: The term refers to an emerging advertising practice that relies on behavioral and Internet-based targeting to improve and implement highly computer-based advertising buying and placement.

Social Media: The term refers to a group of Internet-based applications that build on the ideological and technological foundations of Web 2.0. Social media include collaborative projects (such as Wikipedia), microblogs and blogs, contents (such as YouTube), social networking services (such as Facebook), virtual games, and virtual social life (such as Second Life).

Synergy Effect: In the context of advertising and marketing industry, this term refers to two or more advertising/marketing activities are able to generate a response that are greater than the total effects of these activities if conducted alone.

Chapter 2
Employer Branding in the Digital Era

Aslı Kuşçu
https://orcid.org/0000-0003-3856-8518
Yeditepe University, Turkey

ABSTRACT

Organizations are embracing employer branding now more than ever as a tool to retain, motivate, and attract a valuable competitive asset, namely talented employees, as they play a vital role in organizational success. Recently, new digital technologies, particularly social media, have replaced the traditional communication channels and made it harder for companies to achieve their employer-branding objectives. Most organizations are now employing digital technologies at a great extent to get in touch with all their key stakeholders. This chapter initially provides an overview of research on employer branding and its longterm strategic benefits to organizations. The author discusses the use of digital technologies, particularly social media, for employer branding. A framework is introduced covering all the topics mentioned and providing insights to organizations on how and in what form employer brand value should be communicated within the digital media.

INTRODUCTION

Times are tough, which is the case unfortunately for all businesses without any exemption. As competition increases, companies are struggling more to develop strategies to differentiate themselves from the competitors and to gain competitive advantage in the eyes of the consumers. Strategy researchers and more specifically the resource-based view (RBV) (Barney, 1991) for long define employees as one

DOI: 10.4018/978-1-7998-1618-8.ch002

Copyright © 2020, IGI Global. Copying or distributing in print or electronic forms without written permission of IGI Global is prohibited.

of the resources for competitive advantage that provide value to consumers, are superior to those of competitors, and are difficult to imitate or substitute (Barney, 1991; Dyer & Singh, 1998; Grant, 1991; Hunt & Morgan, 1995). This view is also in line with the internal marketing perspective, which argues that "the organization's personnel are the first market of any company, the rationale being that employees are internal customers" (Berthon, Ewing, & Hah, 2005). Thus, internal marketing constructs a workforce that is difficult for others to replicate. By systematically revealing employees the employer's brand value proposition, a unique "workplace culture" is created allowing the company to excel at its own business and thus achieve corporate goals through its unique way (Backhaus & Tikoo 2004). The value proposition of the organization perceived by the employees is enhanced through the prestige or image of the organization reflected to the society, which is termed as the employer brand (Barrow & Mosley, 2011). Employer branding generates a compelling image and positive associations not only among the current employees but also among other key stakeholders (Minchington, 2010) as well as among the prospective employees (Kuscu & Okan, 2010; Cappelli, 2001) and it is mostly shaped by the external organizational communication (Smidts, Pruyn, & van Riel, 2001).

The digital era is changing everything, and brands are also benefiting from the digital technologies as they enable brands to develop stronger bonds with their target audiences. Laswell (1948)'s traditional one-way communication model with a source and a receiver is now obsolete and has been replaced with two-way and many-to-many communication. Organizational processes such as attracting, selecting, recruiting and retaining talent are no exception. Recently, new digital technologies, particularly social media, which are defined by Kaplan and Hänlein (2010, p.101) as "a group of Internet-based applications that build on the ideological and technological foundations of the Web 2.0 and that allow the creation and exchange of user generated-content" have replaced the traditional communication channels and made is less effortless for companies to achieve their employer branding objectives. Most organizations are now employing digital technologies at a great extent to get in touch with all their stakeholders. Further, Dabirian et al (2016) suggest that employees' expectations with respect to employers and employer brand perceptions are shaped, when "work-related experiences" are shared over social media. Hence, not only do companies use these digital tools to communicate their value but they also encourage their employees to share their unique employer and work-related experiences with others.

The aim of this chapter is to highlight the importance of employer branding as a competitive asset and to provide insight on latest research about the use of digital technologies in establishing and maintaining a strong employer brand. With this aim, the chapter will initially concentrate on employer branding with its antecedents and consequences as well as on the development steps and discuss its role in business success. Following a review on previous research of digital technology use within organizations for employer branding purpose and taking all the topics discussed into consideration, suggestions on how and in what form employer branding should be communicated in digital media as well as a theoretical framework will be presented.

EMPLOYER BRANDING

According to the American Marketing Association, a brand is "a name, term, sign, symbol, or design, or combination of them, which is intended to identify the goods and services of one seller or group of sellers and to differentiate them from those of competitors." In a similar fashion, employer branding is defined by Backhaus and Tikoo (2004, p. 502) as "the process of building an identifiable and unique employer identity" emphasizing its differentiable characteristics. In other words, employer branding signifies how compelling an organization's reputation is and how valuable its value proposition is to its employees (Barrow & Mosley, 2011). As Ewing et al. (2002) elegantly summarize, employer branding can be termed as developing an image to convince labor markets that the organization is a "great place to work" to win in the competitive "war for talent" (Michaels, Handfiels-Jones, & Axelrod, 2001). However, employer branding does not only target prospective employees. According to Srivastava and Bhatnagar (2010) employer branding is the best help for best performing employees in the organization find their reason-to-exist because it reflects the unique attributes of the organization.

Employer branding was first used by Ambler and Barrow (1996, p. 187) as "the package of functional, economic and psychological benefits provided by employment, and identified with the employing company" and emerged under internal marketing which is "the relationship between the company and its employees" (Kotler 1994, 170) to create a customer-centric organization (Cahill, 1995). Internal marketing views employees as internal customers and values their perceptions and their experiences with the company as much as the ones by the customers (Berry, 1981). Thereafter, internal marketing as a philosophy helps companies to create a workforce that is hard for others to imitate. By systematically exposing workers to the value proposition of the employer brand, a workplace culture is developed that is gathered around the corporate goals. By this, the company achieves a unique culture focused on doing business "the firm's way" (Backhaus & Tikoo, 2004). Researchers in the area define culture as "the assumptions, beliefs, goals, knowledge, and values that are shared by organizational members" (Deal & Kennedy, 1983; Hunt, Wood, & Chonko, 1989; Schein, 1985). They further conclude that internal marketing is a comprehensive philosophy (Ahmed & Rafiq, 2003) that builds on the shared culture of the organization and transmitted to the employees (Reichenberg, 2009; Varey, 1995), particularly through the internal communication (Ahmed & Rafiq, 2003). If employees accept and adopt this culture, organizational commitment, organizational identification (Ashforth & Mael, 1989; Riketta, 2005), pride (Chatman & Jehn, 1994) and satisfaction (George, 1990) will follow, which altogether will enhance organizational performance (Backhaus & Tikoo, 2004).

There is vast amount of research over similar benefits of employer branding in the literature. It is reported that employer branding provides a competitive advantage for the organization by leveraging human capital (Dell et al., 2001). Human capital is a term used to denote the combination of knowledge, skills, and abilities that an organizations' employees possess (Coff, 2002), which contrary to other competitive assets is challenging to replicate (Coff, 2002), rare to find (Castanias & Helfat, 1991) and different in nature, as it cannot be purchased (Peteraf, 1993). Human capital is specifically found to enhance organization performance and Crook et al. (2011) in their meta-analysis on the human capital and company performance link further suggest that organizations must focus on activities that will preserve and enhance firm-specific human capital. Employer branding further creates public awareness and customer satisfaction (Barrow & Mosley, 2011; Sullivan, 2004). It is claimed that a successful employer branding leads to getting more skillful applicants without searching for them by creating desire on the potential employees and thus improves recruitment process (Dell et al., 2001; Heilmann, Saarenketo, & Liikkanen, 2013, Moroko & Uncles, 2008; Wilden, Gudergan, & Lings, 2010). Strong employer brands cut the cost of employee acquisition (Berthon, Ewing, & Hah, 2005), improves identification with organizational values, increases satisfaction, commitment, engagement and performance of employees and thus assist in employee retention and lower turnover costs (Backhaus & Tikoo 2004; Barrow & Mosley 2011; Dell et al., 2001; Moroko & Uncles, 2008, Sullivan 2004).

Organizational behavior researchers are concerned with all these outcomes since they all have many customer-related and company-related positive consequences like job satisfaction, work motivation, more frequent and more freely contribution to the organization, higher retention, higher performance, customer orientation and consciousness, and even customer-company identification (Dutton, Dukerich, & Harquail, 1994; Homburg, Wieseke, & Hoyer, 2009; Riketta, 2005; Wieseke, Ahearne, Lam, & Dick, 2009). Researchers have identified social identity theory (Tajfel & Turner, 1986) to play particularly an important role in explaining the reasons of these anticipated organizational outcomes. Organizational members who identify strongly with the organization consider the successes and failures of the organization their own (Ashforth & Mael, 1989; Riketta, 2005) and strive to achieve self-enhancement (Smidts, Pruyn, & van Riel, 2001) which mostly depends on the attractiveness (Dutton et al., 1994) and the perceived prestige or image of the organization (Mael & Ashforth 1992).

As can be seen there are various benefits of employer branding. Yet, to be able to understand how to build and keep a strong employer brand, initially what constitutes an employer brand needs to be understood.

Employer Brand Development Process

Ambler and Barrow (1996) point out the similarities between an employer brand and a traditional brand as both have personality and positioning, which make up the core of a brand together with differentiation. In traditional branding, companies try to differentiate themselves in the eyes of their target external audiences and employer branding is the extension of these efforts to the target internal audiences. Hence, the concepts of brand management and the rules that apply to create and maintain a strong brand reputation are easily applicable to employers from the employee branding perspective. Overall, employer branding is the process of developing a brand that is unique to the organization and targets not only job markets in order to attract and employ potential talents and retain and engage existing employees but also any external stakeholders (Minchington, 2010). As a result, employer branding principles are mostly based on a mixture of branding and human resources standards (Sivertzen, Nilsen, & Olafsen, 2013). As such, brand equity in employer branding as it is in branding refers to the brand knowledge both potential and current employees have with respect to the company (Backhaus & Tikoo, 2004). Brand knowledge is produced through strong forms of brand awareness and brand image (Aaker, 1996; Keller, 1993), with the initial one demonstrated by recall and recognition and the latter by the positive and differentiated associations, all of which are generated through consistent brand communications (Heckler, Keller, Houston, & Avery, 2012). These brand communications point out new points-of-parities (must-haves) and points-of-differences (unique differences) of the brand to the target customers and are designed in a way to also remind the customers of the previously established ones. Hence, brand communications that demonstrate that the brand can offer a bundle of benefits for the consumers are used in branding to generate a strong brand knowledge. With the same reasoning, the internal marketing process consistently informs employees about the promises of the employer brand such that the messages given by the organization are shared among employees. Therefore, this process is not a one-shot event but rather an ongoing process that needs to be frequently adjusted according to environment (Cascio & Graham, 2016). As employer branding is the product of the "sum of a company's efforts to communicate to existing and prospective staff that it is a desirable place to work" (Lloyd, 2002, p. 65), a strong employer brand should be unique, have better attributes than competitors and should communicate it with an authentic voice (Barrow & Mosley, 2011).

There are three steps in developing a compelling employer brand. The initial step involves fostering a "value proposition" for employees with the help of culture, management style and performance of the organization as well as with the image of the existing employees. The value proposition mainly contains the message of what specific value is given to employees and is transmitted through various types of communication. Berthon, Ewing, & Hah (2005) state that it is the combination of social, interest, economic, development, and application values, which is further enhanced by Dabirian et al. (2016) with the values of management and work/life balance. As within branding, the value proposition needs to be audience-centered, focusing on the main benefits and differentiating points of the organization, which generally lie in psychological factors instead of monetary ones because they are in fact the main drivers in choosing an employer (Barrow & Mosley, 2011; Sivertzen et al., 2013). Also, companies need to keep in mind that the importance of these values may differ among the audiences. Current employees may value one thing more than prospective employees such that there might be differences in terms of the weights put for each in generating the overall value. Nonetheless, the overall employer brand value is a non-written psychological contract between the employer and employee (Moroko & Uncles, 2008), which needs to be consistent across all the departments of the organization (Cascio & Graham, 2016) and if false promises are given by the organization, negative rather than positive employee reactions may be faced by the employer (Backhaus & Tikoo, 2004). It further should change continuously to meet and exceed the demands of the target audience (Sullivan, 2004). An employer brand should be attractive both to existing and potential employees (Maxwell & Knox, 2009). Therefore, an analysis of what both audiences find attractive is going to be highly helpful in setting the correct value proposition.

Next, the organization promotes and communicates its overall value proposition to the external audience to attract new talent. The influence of corporate communication on consumers has been documented widely in the literature (Men & Tsai, 2015). In a similar fashion, according to Sullivan (2004), a successful employer brand should obtain public recognition, inform not only the public but also potential employees about the practices of the organization and encourage employees to share their experiences both inside and outside the organization. Varey (1995) argues that internal marketing should be a two-way communication process between employees and management. However, it should be noted though that the employer brand and its marketing efforts need to be tightly aligned with other brands of the organization as they are supporting each other (Sullivan, 1999) and as the overall image of an employer is a combination of the overall perception in terms of the people, culture, career opportunities, job characteristics and employer reputation (Caligiuri, Colakoglu, Cerdin, & Kim, 2010).

In the third and final step, the organization fulfills its value proposition with existing employees and communicates it internally with the internal marketing purpose so that an aligned workforce that is highly engaged with the organization, identifies with the organizational values and goals and is willing to reach goals put by the organization is generated (Backhaus & Tikoo, 2004; Sharma & Kamalanabhan, 2012). This part of the employer branding process is a continuous process that needs to be frequently adjusted according to environment (Cascio & Graham, 2016). However, the perceived prestige or image of the organization which is what an employee believes how outsiders view the organization and consequently themselves as employees of that organization (Dutton et al., 1994), can be also shaped by the external organizational communication (Smidts, Pruyn, & van Riel, 2001). Hence, employees are not only informed about their employer's value proposition through internal communication but they just like consumers also come across with the advertisements of their employers and process and evaluate them, most likely in a more detailed and involved fashion than consumers. For instance, Drumwright (1996) has postulated how advertising with a social dimension is effective in employees by creating a higher degree of organizational identification. When employees perceive that the perceived external image of the employer is congruent with the image of the organization perceived by the internal audience, they start to identify themselves stronger with the organization.

Within the internal marketing literature, Berry (1981) appears to be the first to recognize the impact of advertising on both current and potential employees and it is perhaps the reason why the influence of ads on employees has been studied in literature mostly within service organizations. These papers are usually about advertisements that portray employees providing service to their customers and that have been suggested to help depict the kind of behaviors employees are expected to perform (Zeithaml, Berry, & Parasuraman, 1988), to communicate and reinforce brand values (De Chernatony, Cottam, & Segal-Horn, 2006) or even to train employees (Wentzel, Henkel, & Tomczak, 2010). However, in general, empirical and conceptual work investigating how employees respond and evaluate advertisements of their own employers is limited (examples include: Celci & Gilly, 2010; Hughes, 2011; Gilly & Wolfinbarger, 1998; Wentzel et al., 2010). Gilly and Wolfinbarger (1998) and Celci and Gilly (2010) define three criteria to be used by employees in their cognitive evaluation of the communication, which are termed as promise accuracy, value congruence, and effectiveness. According to Gilly and Wolfinbarger (1998), product and service advertisements should be accurate, not over- or under-promising and corporate advertisements should be depicting the organization's culture accurately in order to create positive outcomes. Other studies have also emphasized the importance of consistency messages (De Chernatony, Cottam, & Segal-Horn, 2006; Miles & Mangold, 2004). The second criterion used by employees to evaluate communications is value congruence, which is the similarity between personal values and the highlighted values of the employer. The final criterion, effectiveness of the communication specifically applies to ads and is evaluated by employees with respect to previous advertisements of the employer, of the competitor, or of other business units within their own company. However, effectiveness here is not used in terms of achieving organizational goals. It refers to the belief in employees that ads will be successful in gaining attention. Evaluation of each of the three criteria may lead to either positive or negative outcomes within employees. Positive evaluation of these criteria leads to commitment, pride, organizational identification (Drumwright, 1996; Gilly & Wolfinbarger, 1998), trust (Miles & Mangold, 2004), and customer-focus (Celci & Gilly, 2010) of employees. On the opposite, negative evaluation of these criteria creates perceived role conflict, employee frustration, lessened trust (Gilly & Wolfinbarger, 1998), and intention to leave (Edward & Peccei, 2010).

Overall, according to the typology developed by Moroko and Uncles (2008), "sustained success" in employer branding is achieved in" the case if an organization successfully attracts new talents and delivers the right employer value to employees. If on the other hand, the employer brand value is attractive to the talents but not to current employees a "strategy mismatch" may occur. Also, in the case that the organization delivers its value proposition inside but fails to attract talent due to reasons such that employer brand is not distinct from competitors or is not consistent with other brands of the organization a "communication breakdown" may follow.

DIGITAL ERA AND EMPLOYER BRANDING

Digital technologies are here to stay, and they are changing how individuals and organizations communicate with each other. The major change though has not been on the expectations of the consumers in terms of the brand promise, rather it happened on how it is communicated to the consumers (Edelman, 2010). It can take many forms like social networks, internet forums, weblogs, virtual communities, or social blogs; nonetheless with billions of active users (Osman, 2018), social media are the new phenomenon. Particularly social media have replaced the traditional communication channels and made is less effortless for companies to achieve their branding objectives. In addition, in all these forms, individuals are not passively receiving content anymore; on the opposite, millions of people interact with each other and with the companies and brands they like and follow and adopt increasingly active roles in co-creating content in a so-called "network co-production model" (Kozinets et al, 2010). As a result, individuals interact with, experience and co-create the brand (Schmitt, 2012), which contributes highly to the power of social media particularly in terms of branding (Hoffman & Fodor, 2010).

As mentioned earlier, "employer branding involves identifying the unique "employment experience" by considering the totality of tangible and intangible reward features that a particular organization offers to its employees" (Edwards, 2010, p.7). In addition, Born and Kang (2015) state that utilizing the right channels to communicate the "employer value" plays a significant role in employer brand management. With digital being used more extensively, Ewing et al. (2002) highlight the significance of employer branding in a highly information-based economy as skilled talent is becoming hard to attract and to keep.

Candidates try to gain information about a prospective employer through different channels and digital seems to be the easiest one they reach to. The digital human resources or company recruitment websites of organizations play a key role in attracting new talents (Williamson et al. 2010). The correctness, relevancy and the clarity of the information given in these websites affect the organization's ability to communicate its value proposition with potential employees. Hence, similar to branding, as more and more current and potential employees are using digital technologies, organizations need to incorporate them into their branding efforts at least from the perspective of increasing visibility and to develop a stronger employer brand presence among many others.

However, social media provide additional benefits. Kietzmann et al. (2011) identify identity, presence, conversation, relationship, reputation, sharing and groups as the seven "functional blocks of social media" and propose that different social media tools concentrate on different ones and are therefore beneficial for different purposes under the umbrella term of communication. For instance, LinkedIn is useful for identity development but also to some extent for relationships and for reputation. On the other hand, YouTube is more essential for sharing, but can also be used for conversations, groups and reputation building. It is a known fact that the interactive nature of social media not only allows companies to reach a higher number of talents more easily (Coon, 2010), but also to communicate the organizations' values in a more personal, targeted, cost-effective and efficient way (Men & Tsai, 2015). Then again, because of the complex and fragmented nature of information flow in social media, organizations need to more strategically manage their perceptions by deliberately developing, controlling, and nurturing a compelling and consistent employer value, that is developed around seven benefits (social, interest, economic, development, application, management, work/life balance) put forward by Dabirian et al. (2016).

First Step: Employer Brand Value Development

According to Kaplan and Hänlein (2010), social media are "platforms whereby content and applications are no longer created and published by individuals, but instead are continuously modified by all users in a participatory and collaborative fashion" (p.

61). It is vital to comprehend that thanks to interactive, open, and co-creative nature of various social media tools, the employer brand is not something that is built by the organization alone, rather it is co-created along with the organization and the external and internal audiences, impacting the knowledge of both and hopefully creating enhanced engagement. Within social media, all stakeholders' opinions on the values offered by the company are shared and influenced by each other (Vernuccio, 2014) and they form the core of the employer brand together (Einwiller & Will, 2008). In other words, as asymmetric flow of information is changed into a many-to-many form and anybody can collaborate in content creation in the form of comments, organizations no longer own the employer brand, they just "host" the brand. That does not mean organizations do not play a role in employer brand proposition development. The strategy beyond is still their responsibility. Hence, they still need to assess the expectations of their target audiences and enhance the value of their "offering". As Fichter (2007, p. 57) states ''social media are replacing traditional media in the eyes of the consumer by informing their views on brands, purchases and services offered." Therefore, the values that employees expect from employers are also shaped by the social media presence of organizations.

Social media further enable reverse information flow. Hence, organizations can also easily gain information in terms of their image and reputation in the public as an employer and what their target employees are expecting from them, which will also shape their employer branding efforts and enhance their effectiveness. Dabirian et al. (2016) discuss and provide examples on how social media can be used by organizations for crowdsourcing with respect to employer branding. The authors also suggest that this "intelligence" can be used for churn analysis in terms of human resources to help companies understand why employees leave and to improve their employer brand value so that they develop enhanced loyalty among their highly skilled employees. But, once different aspects that altogether make up the overall employer value proposition are communicated through social media, organizations are not in total control of them. Anyone can contribute to it. By this way, how much of the organization's planned employer brand positioning is achieved depends on a combination of what the company communicates, what current employees experience and articulate as well as what the overall public perceives.

Second Step: Communicating the Value to External Audiences

As can be seen, although initially social media may seem to be only useful for interpersonal and company-consumer communication, the usage of social media for employer branding purposes provides various benefits for employers.

Similar to communicating the value of a product or a service, communicating the value of an employer to the target audience is easier and more effective when organizations use social media as it is a medium where individuals can be addressed both personally and collectively (Simmons, 2008) and through mass customization as a combination of both. The values that altogether make up the employer brand value proposition are defined as follows. Interest value is the how interesting and innovative the products and services offered by the company are as well as how the company is perceived at these dimensions. Social value refers to the social relations between the employees. Economic value applies how economically rewarding it is for the employees to work in this organization. Development value signifies the opportunities an employee has within this organization to develop himself with respect to job opportunities, whereas application value represents how much what has been learned in this organization can be applied to other settings. And finally, management value denotes to the leadership qualities of the managers and work/ life balance represents the flexibility of the organization in terms of allowing its employees free time with their families. Within social media communication, content in other words how something is communicated plays a significant role (Kaplan & Hänlein, 2010). Therefore, the transmitted messages communicating or enhancing any of the values mentioned above need to be simple and direct, should consist of the whole or part of the employer value proposition and values of the company as well as the promise of the brand along with the reasons-to-believe that the company is a desirable place work. Further, the message should also be consistent, continuous and credible (Barrow & Mosley 2011). The language and the tone of the communication should be relevant to the audience and the channel or the communication platform.

As stated in Singh and Sonnenburg (2012), storytelling is the best method as it generates and strengthens the connections and creates context while making the individuals remember their similar experiences and evoking their affective and cognitive involvement. Therefore, similar to brands, companies also use stories in their social media accounts and try to match the job market's value expectations with the ones they offer through the stories that they tell. Hence, the total employer value generated through tangible and intangible benefits need to be translated into authentic stories as this type of content generates more engagement. Even posting videos on interesting and innovative products or aspects of the company while showing what current employees experience during the process might generate that effect. Not only does that type of content communicate the interest value that is part of the overall employer brand value proposition, but it also enhances the organizations reputation and may further generate engagement among the viewers. Nonetheless, as mentioned earlier different social media tools provide different benefits for individuals. Therefore, each individual might choose a different combination of social media. For instance, as demonstrated by Bondarouk et al. (2014), social networks or blogs are better areas to connect with external audiences. Owing to this fact, identifying which social media channels the organizations' target external audiences more frequently use may help companies to concentrate on these channels. A consistent and coherent voice through those identified channels, though providing different types of content, might enhance effectiveness. Consequently, from employer branding perspective, three aspects play a significant role in the effectiveness of using social media to target external audiences for employer branding purposes: (1) identification of the audience (2) identification of the social media tools that they use and finally (3) identification of the type of content.

However, as mentioned in Bondarouk et al. (2014), not all organizations are at ease with "a world where the consumers can speak so freely with each other and businesses have increasingly less control over the information available about them on the cyberspace" (Kaplan & Haenelein, 2010). In this co-created reality, companies do only have limited control over their image on social media. So, social media can generate not only opportunities but also threats to organizations. Framing effective and meaningful messages for digital content carries a number of challenges. The first one lies in developing a more substantial notion of value, which is followed by the constraints and opportunities of different social media tools as communication space and to communicate and manage the value in time. Previously employers had control over the content of information as well as over the flow of it. However, now social media facilitate co-created stories that matter more for most and challenge employers in that they lose control once it is distributed. Another threat lies in when the current employees share their own experiences with the company over social media. This type of content helps potential employees evaluate the attractiveness of the employer as they can understand if the company satisfies tangible and intangible demands (Lubecka, 2013). Nevertheless, unfortunately, as demonstrated in Bondarouk et al. (2014), most employers only allow their current employees to share their stories to some extent, which makes it less meaningful and relevant for the external audiences.

Third Step: Communicating the Value to Internal Audiences

It is through social media that organizations disseminate information related with them with external as well as with internal audiences. The way people process information depends on environmental, personal, and contextual characteristics (Lothia, Donthu, & Hershberger, 2003). It is obvious that employees are highly involved with their employers and therefore they will be more inclined to engage and interact with the company and with any content that communicates their employer's brand proposition on social media. Internal marketing suggests that communications by their own employers attract employees' attention the most and that they are highly influenced by them. Similarly, according to Rodgers and Thorston (2000), statements and promises in advertisements can also influence employees' cognitive processes and shape their perceptions. Moreover, existing employees are becoming more influential on the employer brand since they are equipped with new communication tools such as social media, web pages, blogs etc. With other stakeholders, they co-create the employer brand by providing constant and authentic feedback on the company. By being a target audience of the employer branding, they are better informed of their employer, as well. When it comes to the evaluation stage, as mentioned earlier, Celci and Gilly (2010) define three criteria to be used by employees. These are defined by the scholars as promise accuracy, value congruence, and effectiveness. Hence, current employees assess the truthfulness of the communications and as consumers they would value employers more when they see a match between themselves and what the company communicates. Moreover, Gilly and Wolfinbarger (1998) conclude that employees are consumers in their everyday lives, so that their persuasion knowledge also influences their judgments about the effectiveness of their employers' communication. Moreover, content shared over social media can also exemplify current employees expected behaviors towards customers and may enhance transparency and communication between the organization and themselves. Hence, a positive evaluation of the social media presence of the current employer will not only contribute to the overall value perception but also to the overall image and reputation of the company within the minds of current employees. Hence, any co-created content on social media is evaluated along these criteria mentioned and therefore, the subsequent involvement of the employee to cognitively process any corporate communication and the following consequences are the result of these various factors.

SOLUTIONS AND RECOMMENDATIONS

Kaplan and Hänlein (2012) mention that social media pose different directions in terms of creating connectiveness and relationships between consumers and brands and refer to it as bridging the gap between virtual and real as well as between future and past. Moreover, social media are the combination of owned, earned, and paid media, which increases its effectiveness with respect to company-consumer connectedness. The same is true for its effect on employer-employee relationships. Social media provide opportunities for employers that have not been possible before in that it initiates new relationships and strengthens old ones while linking virtual and real to the reputation of the organization. Further, enhancing this perspective, no longer are employees recipients of company communication but they can now rule recruitment trends and create an opportunity and a threat to employers as they can share literally anything to and with anyone. Hence, both from the theoreticians' and practitioners' perspective, once the employer value has been identified, it can now be more easily communicated through social media and the attractiveness of the employer brand can be more clearly enhanced and disseminated, whilst reaching a wider audience (Bondarouk et al., 2014) and increasing the visibility of the organization.

Figure 1 provides a pictorial summary on what has been discussed throughout the chapter and shows the use of social media with employer branding purposes to attract and keep talent and generate competitive advantage in the marketplace. As discussed before, employer branding starts with the identification of the value proposition that is unique and compelling to the talent pool. Next, it needs to be communicated to internal as well as to external audiences through the selection of channels and type of content. The cognitive processing of the content differs for internal and external audiences. Due the high involvement and knowledge about the employer, internal audiences are able to evaluate the company based on promise accuracy, value congruence and effectiveness. On the other hand, external audiences are simply just able to generate a positive or negative perception. Consequently, the expected organizational outcomes are different as well. Whereas internal audiences may develop commitment, identification or enhanced loyalty with their organization, the positive image and reputation may be advanced in external audiences. Nonetheless, as can be seen most of the proposed relationships are not linear, which is mainly because of the nature of the communication medium. Bondarouk et al. (2014) mention that human resources professionals are nowadays particularly confused on how to use social media at its best to create the intended positioning for their companies, or on how to respond to negative perspectives or crises. Therefore, now it is more about managing relationships and conversations around the organization, rather than just pushing messages to the external and internal audiences. Social media tools such as LinkedIn, Youtube or Facebook are perfect examples for this type of usage. For instance, they all can be used for reputation and identity development.

FUTURE RESEARCH DIRECTIONS

This chapter contributes to the conceptual understanding of the link between social media and employer branding and provides avenues for future qualitative and quantitative research that can generate insightful results for organizations and their digital agencies. Obviously although the practical world has already acknowledged the use of social media for employer branding purposes, the academic side falls behind, with a large scarcity of studies concentrating on this issue (Madera, 2012). As such, directions for future research are not limited to the issues mentioned throughout the chapter. The lack of studies on both employer branding and its relationship with social media provide extensive research opportunities.

Figure 1. Employer Branding in Social Media
Source: Author

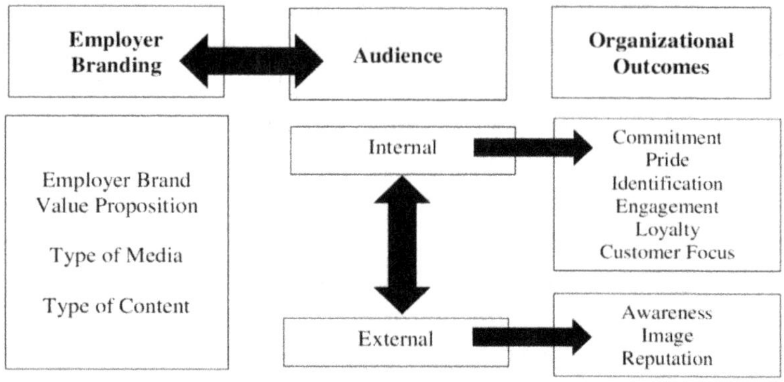

First of all, researchers may identify the most frequently used social media tools and type of content for employer branding through qualitative analyses. Only few studies have been able to delineate this issue providing a limited perspective. The findings might differ with respect to sector or even with respect to the demographics of the target audience. Further, how the employer brand is co-created by external and internal audiences is another fruitful research avenue in line with the analysis of the impact of the channel and the content. Here researchers may adopt the frameworks developed for company-consumer relationships and apply and test them for employer-employee (current/potential) relationships. Most of the scarce research on this topic is qualitative. As a result, quantitative studies are highly needed. And finally, the consequences of social media communication for both internal and external audiences in terms of organizational outcomes can be tested over quantitative or experimental designs.

CONCLUSION

Social media have become the new phenomenon. There is no individual or organization that can escape its influence, specifically on socialization and communication. According to Kozinets (2002) companies are interested in social media for two reasons. The first one is that the Internet has gained tremendous importance by allowing active consumers especially in online communities to foster company interest and second; social media enable marketers to be close to their consumers. Gillin (2007) further adds declining response rates of traditional marketing tools and low costs as two important reasons why companies are utilizing social media. Owing to the impact of social media on interpersonal and company-consumer relationships and its consequences, most research concentrate on these aspects (Kietzmann et al., 2011), nonetheless leave the interaction between companies and internal audiences aside. However, employees just as consumers also consume and co-create content of organizations and this influence is widely accepted by the practitioners. Particularly as stated by Vernuccio (2014), the interactivity and openness of social media aid dramatically to corporate branding approaches.

Henceforth, this chapter focuses on the use of social media for employer branding purposes and highlights the importance of social media-based communication in employee attraction and retention. Overall, the questions that are tried to be answered in this chapter are whether social media can be used by the companies for employer branding purposes and how companies can employ social media more effectively to reach their goals. The chapter highlights the importance of employer branding for organizational goals and suggests a conceptual framework while combining employer branding with the nature of social media.

REFERENCES

Aaker, D. A. (1996). Measuring brand equity across products and markets. *California Management Review*, *38*(3), 102–120. doi:10.2307/41165845

Ahmed, P. K., & Rafiq, M. (2003). Internal marketing issues and challenges. *European Journal of Marketing*, *37*(9), 1177–1186. doi:10.1108/03090560310498813

Ambler, T., & Barrow, S. (1996). The employer brand. *Journal of Brand Management*, *4*(3), 185–206. doi:10.1057/bm.1996.42

Ashforth, B. E., & Mael, F. (1989). Social identity theory and the organization. *Academy of Management Review*, *14*(1), 20–39. doi:10.5465/amr.1989.4278999

Backhaus, K., & Tikoo, S. (2004). Conceptualizing and researching employer branding. *Career Development International*, *9*(5), 501–517. doi:10.1108/13620430410550754

Barney, J. (1991). Firm resources and sustained competitive advantage. *Journal of Management*, *17*(1), 99–120. doi:10.1177/014920639101700108

Barrow, S., & Mosley, R. (2011). *The employer brand: Bringing the best of brand management to people at work*. John Wiley & Sons.

Berthon, P., Ewing, M., & Hah, L. L. (2005). Captivating company: Dimensions of attractiveness in employer branding. *International Journal of Advertising*, *24*(2), 151–172. doi:10.1080/02650487.2005.11072912

Bondarouk, T., Ruël, H., Axinia, E., & Arama, R. (2014). What is the future of employer branding through social media? Results of the Delphi study into the perceptions of HR professionals and academics. *Social Media in Human Resources Management*, *9*(5), 23–57.

Born, N., & Kang, S. K. (2015). *What are best practices in the space of employer branding that enable organizations attract and retain the best talent?* Retrieved from https://digitalcommons.ilr.cornell.edu/student/86/

Cahill, D. J. (1995). "We sure as hell confused ourselves", but what about the customers? *Marketing Intelligence & Planning*, *13*(4), 5–9. doi:10.1108/02634509510781298

Caligiuri, P., Colakoglu, S., Cerdin, J. L., & Kim, M. S. (2010). Examining cross-cultural and individual differences in predicting employer reputation as a driver of employer attraction. *International Journal of Cross Cultural Management*, *10*(2), 137–151. doi:10.1177/1470595810370890

Cappelli, P. (2001). Making the most of on-line recruiting. *Harvard Business Review*, *79*(3), 139–148. PMID:11246921

Cascio, W. F., & Graham, B. Z. (2016). New strategic role for HR: Leading the employer-branding process. *Organizational Management Journal*, *13*(4), 182–192. doi:10.1080/15416518.2016.1244640

Castanias, R. P., & Helfat, C. E. (1991). Managerial resources and rents. *Journal of Management*, *17*(1), 155–171. doi:10.1177/014920639101700110

Celsi, M. W., & Gilly, M. C. (2010). Employees as internal audience: How advertising affects employees' customer focus. *Journal of the Academy of Marketing Science*, *38*(4), 520–529. doi:10.100711747-009-0173-x

Chatman, J. A., & Jehn, K. A. (1994). Assessing the relationship between industry characteristics and organizational culture: How different can you be? *Academy of Management Journal*, *37*(3), 522–553. doi:10.5465/256699

Coff, R. W. (2002). Human capital, shared expertise, and the likelihood of impasse in corporate acquisitions. *Journal of Management*, *28*(1), 107–128. doi:10.1177/014920630202800107

Coon, M. (2010). *Social media marketing: successful case studies of businesses using Facebook and Youtube with an in-depth look into the business use of Twitter* (Unpublished Master's thesis). Stanford University, Stanford, CA.

Crook, T. R., Todd, S. Y., Combs, J. G., Woehr, D. J., & Ketchen, D. J. Jr. (2011). Does human capital matter? A meta-analysis of the relationship between human capital and firm performance. *The Journal of Applied Psychology*, *96*(3), 443–456. doi:10.1037/a0022147 PMID:21244126

Dabirian, A., Kietzmann, J., & Diba, H. (2017). A great place to work!? Understanding crowdsourced employer branding. *Business Horizons*, *60*(2), 197–205. doi:10.1016/j.bushor.2016.11.005

De Chernatony, L., Cottam, S., & Segal-Horn, S. (2006). Communicating services brands' values internally and externally. *Service Industries Journal*, *26*(8), 819–836. doi:10.1080/02642060601011616

Deal, T. E., & Kennedy, A. A. (1983). Culture: A new look through old lenses. *The Journal of Applied Behavioral Science*, *19*(4), 498–505. doi:10.1177/002188638301900411

Dell, D., Ainspan, N., Bodenberg, T., Troy, K., & Hickey, J. (2001, April). Engaging employees through your brand. In *Conference Board Report, Number R. 1288-01-RR. Canada*. Washington, DC: Conference Board.

Drumwright, M. E. (1996). Company advertising with a social dimension: The role of noneconomic criteria. *Journal of Marketing*, *60*(4), 71–87. doi:10.2307/1251902

Dutton, J. E., Dukerich, J. M., & Harquail, C. V. (1994). Organizational images and member identification. *Administrative Science Quarterly*, *39*(2), 239–263. doi:10.2307/2393235

Dyer, J. H., & Singh, H. (1998). The relational view: Corporative strategy and sources of interorganizational competitive advantage. *Academy of Management Review*, *23*(4), 660–679. doi:10.5465/amr.1998.1255632

Edelman, D. C. (2010). Branding in the digital age. *Harvard Business Review*, *88*(12), 62–69.

Edwards, M. R. (2009). An integrative review of employer branding and OB theory. *Personnel Review*, *39*(1), 5–23. doi:10.1108/00483481011012809

Edwards, M. R., & Peccei, R. (2010). Perceived organizational support, organizational identification, and employee outcomes. *Journal of Personnel Psychology*, *9*(1), 17–26. doi:10.1027/1866-5888/a000007

Einwiller, S., & Will, M. (2008). Towards an integrated approach to corporate branding-Findings from an empirical study. In *Kommunikationsmanagement im Wandel* (pp. 231–247). Gabler. doi:10.1007/978-3-8349-9772-2_13

Ewing, M. T., Pitt, L. F., De Bussy, N. M., & Berthon, P. (2002). Employment branding in the knowledge economy. *International Journal of Advertising*, *21*(1), 3–22. doi:10.1080/02650487.2002.11104914

Fichter, D. (2007). How social is your web site? Top five tips for social media optimization. *Onlinenmag*, 57-60.

George, W. R. (1990). Internal marketing and organizational behavior: A partnership in developing customer-conscious employees at every level. *Journal of Business Research, 20*(1), 63-70.

Gillin, P. (2007). *The new influencers: A marketer's guide to the new social media.* Sanger, CA: Quill Driver Books.

Gilly, M. C., & Wolfinbarger, M. (1998). Advertising's internal audience. *Journal of Marketing*, *62*(1), 69–88. doi:10.1177/002224299806200107

Grant, R. M. (1991). The resource-based theory of competitive advantage: Implications for strategy formulation. *California Management Review*, *33*(3), 114–135. doi:10.2307/41166664

Heckler, S. E., Keller, K. L., Houston, M. J., & Avery, J. (2014). Building brand knowledge structures: Elaboration and interference effects on the processing of sequentially advertised brand benefit claims. *Journal of Marketing Communications*, *20*(3), 176–196. doi:10.1080/17544750.2012.660766

Heilmann, P., Saarenketo, S., & Liikkanen, K. (2013). Employer branding in power industry. *International Journal of Energy Sector Management*, *7*(2), 283–302. doi:10.1108/IJESM-03-2012-0003

Hoffman, D. L., & Fodor, M. (2010). Can you measure the ROI of your social media marketing? *MIT Sloan Management Review*, *52*(1), 41–49.

Homburg, C., Wieseke, J., & Hoyer, W. D. (2009). Social identity and the service–profit chain. *Journal of Marketing*, *73*(2), 38–54. doi:10.1509/jmkg.73.2.38

Hughes, D. E. (2015). The indirect effect of advertising perceptions on salesperson effort and performance. In *Proceedings of the 2010 Academy of Marketing Science (AMS) Annual Conference* (pp. 235-235). Springer, Cham. 10.1007/978-3-319-11797-3_130

Hunt, S. D., & Morgan, R. M. (1995). The comparative advantage theory of competition. *Journal of Marketing*, *59*(2), 1–15. doi:10.1177/002224299505900201

Hunt, S. D., Wood, V. R., & Chonko, L. B. (1989). Corporate ethical values and organizational commitment in marketing. *Journal of Marketing, 53*(3), 79-90.

Kaplan, A. M., & Hänlein, M. (2010). Users of the world, unite! The challenges and opportunities of Social Media. *Business Horizons*, *53*(1), 59–68. doi:10.1016/j.bushor.2009.09.003

Keller, K. L. (1993). Conceptualizing, measuring, and managing customer-based brand equity. *Journal of Marketing*, *57*(1), 1–22. doi:10.1177/002224299305700101

Kietzmann, J. H., Hermkens, K., McCarthy, I. P., & Silvestre, B. S. (2011). Social media? Get serious! Understanding the functional building blocks of social media. *Business Horizons*, *54*(3), 241–251. doi:10.1016/j.bushor.2011.01.005

Kozinets, R. V. (2002). The field behind the screen: Using netnography for marketing research in online communities. *JMR, Journal of Marketing Research*, *39*(1), 61–72. doi:10.1509/jmkr.39.1.61.18935

Kuşçu, A., & Yolbulan Okan, E. (2010). An exploratory study on the dimensions of employer brandıng. *Öneri Journal, 34*(9), 119-130.

Lasswell, H. D. (1948). The structure and function of communication in society. In L. Bryson (Ed.), *The Communication of Ideas* (pp. 37–51). New York: Harper.

Lloyd, S. (2002). Branding from the inside out. *Business Review Weekly*, *24*(10), 64–66.

Lohtia, R., Donthu, N., & Hershberger, E. K. (2003). The impact of content and design elements on banner advertising click-through rates. *Journal of Advertising Research*, *43*(4), 410–418. doi:10.2501/JAR-43-4-410-418

Lubecka, A. (2013). Employer branding–a dialogistic communication tool of a competitive employer. *Journal of Intercultural Management*, *5*(2), 5–16. doi:10.2478/joim-2013-0007

Madera, J. M. (2012). Using social networking websites as a selection tool: The role of selection process fairness and job pursuit intentions. *International Journal of Hospitality Management*, *31*(4), 1276–1282. doi:10.1016/j.ijhm.2012.03.008

Mael, F., & Ashforth, B. E. (1992). Alumni and their alma mater: A partial test of the reformulated model of organizational identification. *Journal of Organizational Behavior*, *13*(2), 103–123. doi:10.1002/job.4030130202

Maxwell, R., & Knox, S. (2009). Motivating employees to" live the brand": A comparative case study of employer brand attractiveness within the firm. *Journal of Marketing Management*, *25*(9-10), 893–907. doi:10.1362/026725709X479282

Men, L. R., & Tsai, W. H. S. (2015). Infusing social media with humanity: Corporate character, public engagement, and relational outcomes. *Public Relations Review*, *41*(3), 395–403. doi:10.1016/j.pubrev.2015.02.005

Michaels, E., Handfield-Jones, H., & Axelrod, B. (2001). The war for talent. Brighton, MA: Harvard Business Press.

Miles, S. J., & Mangold, G. (2004). A conceptualization of the employee branding process. *Journal of Relationship Marketing*, *3*(2-3), 65–87. doi:10.1300/J366v03n02_05

Minchington, B. (2010). *Employer brand leadership: A global perspective*. Collective Learning Australia.

Moroko, L., & Uncles, M. D. (2008). Characteristics of successful employer brands. *Journal of Brand Management*, *16*(3), 160–175. doi:10.1057/bm.2008.4

Osman, M. (2018). *28 powerful Facebook stats your brand can't ignore in 2018*. Retrieved from https://sproutsocial.com/insights/facebook-stats-for-marketers/

Peteraf, M. A. (1993). The cornerstones of competitive advantage: A resource-based view. *Strategic Management Journal*, *14*(3), 179–191. doi:10.1002mj.4250140303

Reichenberg, N. (2009). Branding the government as an employer of choice. Retrieved from http://unpan1.un.org/intradoc/groups/public/documents/UN/UNPAN021819.pdf

Riketta, M. (2005). Organizational identification: A meta-analysis. *Journal of Vocational Behavior*, *66*(2), 358–384. doi:10.1016/j.jvb.2004.05.005

Rodgers, S., & Thorson, E. (2000). The interactive advertising model: How users perceive and process online ads. *Journal of Interactive Advertising*, *1*(1), 41–60. doi:10.1080/15252019.2000.10722043

Schein, E. H. (1985). Defining organizational culture. *Classics of organization theory, 3*, 490-502.

Schmitt, B. (2013). The consumer psychology of customer–brand relationships: Extending the AA Relationship model. *Journal of Consumer Psychology*, *23*(2), 249–252. doi:10.1016/j.jcps.2013.01.003

Sharma, N., & Kamalanabhan, T. J. (2012). Internal corporate communication and its impact on internal branding: Perception of Indian public sector employees. *Corporate Communications*, *17*(3), 300–322. doi:10.1108/13563281211253548

Simmons, G. (2008). Marketing to postmodern consumers: Introducing the internet chameleon. *European Journal of Marketing*, *42*(3/4), 299–310. doi:10.1108/03090560810852940

Singh, S., & Sonnenburg, S. (2012). Brand performances in social media. *Journal of Interactive Marketing*, *26*(4), 189–197. doi:10.1016/j.intmar.2012.04.001

Sivertzen, A. M., Nilsen, E. R., & Olafsen, A. H. (2013). Employer branding: Employer attractiveness and the use of social media. *Journal of Product and Brand Management*, *22*(7), 473–483. doi:10.1108/JPBM-09-2013-0393

Smidts, A., Pruyn, A. T. H., & Van Riel, C. B. (2001). The impact of employee communication and perceived external prestige on organizational identification. *Academy of Management Journal*, *44*(5), 1051–1062.

Srivastava, P., & Bhatnagar, J. (2010). Employer brand for talent acquisition: An exploration towards its measurement. *Vision*, *14*(1-2), 25–34. doi:10.1177/097226291001400103

Sullivan, S. E. (1999). The changing nature of careers: A review and research agenda. *Journal of Management*, *25*(3), 457–484. doi:10.1177/014920639902500308

Tajfel, H., & Turner, J. C. (1986). The social identity theory of inter-group behavior. In S. Worchel & W. G. Austin (Eds.), *Psychology of intergroup relations* (pp. 7–24). Chicago, IL: Nelson-Hall.

Varey, R. J. (1995). Internal marketing: A review and some interdisciplinary research challenges. *International Journal of Service Industry Management*, *6*(1), 40–63. doi:10.1108/09564239510078849

Vernuccio, M. (2014). Communicating corporate brands through social media: An exploratory study. *International Journal of Business Communication*, *51*(3), 211–233. doi:10.1177/2329488414525400

Wentzel, D., Henkel, S., & Tomczak, T. (2010). Can I live up to that ad? Impact of implicit theories of ability on service employees' responses to advertising. *Journal of Service Research*, *13*(2), 137–152. doi:10.1177/1094670510363304

Wieseke, J., Ahearne, M., Lam, S. K., & Dick, R. V. (2009). The role of leaders in internal marketing. *Journal of Marketing*, *73*(2), 123–145. doi:10.1509/jmkg.73.2.123

Wilden, R., Gudergan, S., & Lings, I. (2010). Employer branding: Strategic implications for staff recruitment. *Journal of Marketing Management*, *26*(1-2), 56–73. doi:10.1080/02672570903577091

Zeithaml, V. A., Berry, L. L., & Parasuraman, A. (1988). Communication and control processes in the delivery of service quality. *Journal of Marketing*, *52*(2), 35–48. doi:10.1177/002224298805200203

ADDITIONAL READING

Caligiuri, P., Lepak, D., & Bonache, J. (2010). *Global dimensions ofhuman resources management: managing the global workforce*. Hoboken, NJ: John Wiley & Sons.

Christopher, M., Payne, A., & Ballantyne, D. (2002). *Relationship marketing: creating stakeholder value (2nd press)*. Oxford, UK: Butterworth-Heinemann.

David, J. D. (2001). *Engaging employees through your brand*. New York, NY: Conference Board.

Davies, G. (2008). Employer branding and its influence on managers. *European Journal of Marketing*, *42*(5/6), 667–681. doi:10.1108/03090560810862570

Foster, C., Punjaisri, K., & Cheng, R. (2010). Exploring the relationship between corporate, internal and employer branding. *Journal of Product and Brand Management*, *19*(6), 401–409. doi:10.1108/10610421011085712

Leekha Chhabra, N., & Sharma, S. (2014). Employer branding: Strategy for improving employer attractiveness. *The International Journal of Organizational Analysis*, *22*(1), 48–60. doi:10.1108/IJOA-09-2011-0513

Martin, G. (2007). Employer branding - time for some long and 'hard' reflections? Chartered Institute of Personnel and Development Research Insight, Employer branding: the latest fad or the future for HR. London.

Mihalcea, A. D. (2017). Employer branding and talent management in the digital age. *Management Dynamics in the Knowledge Economy*, *5*(2), 289–306. doi:10.25019/MDKE/5.2.07

KEY TERMS AND DEFINITIONS

Competitive Advantage: Competitive advantages enables companies to gain a superior and therefore advantageous position than their competitors in the marketplace.

Digital Technologies: Technology, where information is coded in a binary form of digits of 0 and 1. Revolutionary devices such as computers, laptops, tablets, and mobile phones and the applications within them use digital technology.

Employer Branding: Employer branding is the combination of strategies used by organizations to develop and promote a distinctive and valuable employer image within the minds of both internal and external audiences.

Employer Value Proposition: The combination of tangible and intangible benefits developed, enhanced, and communicated by an organization. Employer value proposition is what makes an employer attractive to current and prospective employees and the public in general.

External Communication: External communication includes any communication between an organization and its stakeholders outside the company such as customers, suppliers, intermediaries, investors or society in general.

Internal Communication: Internal communication refers to the dissemination of information within the organization and among the members of the organization.

Internal Marketing: Internal marketing views employees as internal customers and states that they should be targeted in the same way as external customers. The major aim of internal marketing to enhance employees' engagement, identification and advocacy towards the overall goals of the organization. As these mostly appear to be important in services, internal marketing was initially termed within service industry.

Social Media: Social media use digital technologies and are a combination of interactive, interconnected, and interdependent networks to assist the creation and dissemination of information between individuals and organizations.

Chapter 3
A Relationship Marketing Strategy in Brand Communication:
Influencer Marketing Strategy

Bülent Özsaçmacı
https://orcid.org/0000-0001-9074-0149
Çankaya University, Turkey

Tolga Dursun
https://orcid.org/0000-0003-1235-1361
Abant İzzet Baysal Üniversitesi, Turkey

ABSTRACT

Influencer marketing increases brand awareness by generating appropriate content to attract the attention of consumers in a virtual environment in accordance with the brand texture. This chapter explores research to determine importance of influencer marketing in the brand communication area, which is based on relationship marketing. Authors mainly focus on influencer marketing and its connection with relationship marketing. They describe the constituent parts of the topics and illustrate them with the case studies and statistical facts. The authors strongly claim influencer marketing shares similar variables with relationship marketing and their basic keywords are related.

DOI: 10.4018/978-1-7998-1618-8.ch003

Copyright © 2020, IGI Global. Copying or distributing in print or electronic forms without written permission of IGI Global is prohibited.

INTRODUCTION

Today's digital technologies—the Internet and the surge in online, mobile, and social media—have profoundly changed the ways that people on the planet relate to one another. In turn, these events have had a huge impact on how companies and brands connect with customers, and how customers connect with and influence each other's brand behaviors (Kotler, et al., 2017). Developments in virtual / social media, in particular, have moved the concept of brand communication to a more personalized, mobile and interactive environment. Furthermore, the development and expansion of social media platforms leads to a change in the marketing industry. Businesses aims to adapt their dynamics according to changing conditions in order to understand the trends and expectations of consumers and meet them.

The main purpose of this book chapter is to make an exploratory research to figure out the importance of influencer marketing in brand communication area which is based on relationship marketing. On this proposed chapter we mainly focus on the subject of influencer marketing and its connection with relationship marketing. We also describe the constituent parts of the topic and illustrate them with the case studies and statistical information.

In the age of information and technology, the rapid penetration of the Internet into our lives and the expansion of various social media tools create new opportunities for the development of marketing techniques (Montgomery, 2001; Shukla, 2010). Currently, advertisers and marketers who use the Internet and mobile devices to deliver marketing messages often adopt more innovative tactics, such as, viral marketing is common to target consumers or their followers who feel less confident in traditional advertising.

BACKGROUND

The digital age has produced an impressive set of new customer relationship-building tools, from Web sites, online ads and videos, mobile ads and apps, and blogs to online communities and the major social media, such as Twitter, Facebook, YouTube, Instagram, and Pinterest. The old marketing involved marketing brands to consumers. The new marketing is customer-engagement marketing fostering direct and continuous customer involvement in shaping brand conversations, experiences, and community (Kotler, et al., 2017).

Technological innovations and cultural changes have a significant impact on the emergence of viral marketing. The word-of-mouth marketing (WOMM), is a marketing communication channel that is frequently preferred in traditional marketing periods, has influenced purchasing decisions before consumers purchase products, and shared experiences about the product has led to growth among consumers. People found this way quite reliable and started to do research without making a purchase decision.

It is important to point out that the transition from modern to postmodern approach is also effective in the emergence of these developments in the field of marketing and communication. Odabaşı (2017:67), while making the distinction between postmodern producer and consumer, he expresses postmodern producer; the image is presented as a product and the product is defined as a way of life or hope. On the other hand, the postmodern consumer defines as; daily pursuit of happiness, improved self-sense, hedonistic direction came forward, instant satisfaction and consumption instead of content as an individual who expressed emphasis on the form.

When the marketing literature is examined, it is possible to say that the determinants of consumer relations are based on the 1980s. The researchers (Berry, 1983; Magrath, 1986) argued that relationship marketing concept is needed to attract and retain customers more than the traditional marketing mix efforts. Magrath (1986) mentioned that building trust with prospective customer is vital when transforming them into a loyal customer. Morgan & Hunt (1994) also based their commitment and trust theory to relationship marketing concept and referred as the focal point to effectively reach the customer.

The brand, on the other hand, is the promise that the producer is committed to keep that is given to its target audience for long term regardless of the circumstances. Brand communication and tools are the most basic way to convey this promise to the other party. With the widespread use of social media, consumers have the opportunity to communicate with brands. It can be said that positive or negative consumer experiences about products / brands are shared through social media tools, and people influence purchasing decision processes. This situation can also be considered as an important source of data for the consumers in recognizing and solving the problems in terms of marketing managers while reducing the risk that consumers endure in the purchasing process.

The main purpose of influencer marketing is to increase the awareness on the brand by generating appropriate contents that can attract the attention of consumers in virtual environment in accordance with the brand texture. This enables the brand to be more visible in the virtual environment and allowing the consumer to touch and communicate with the brand. Basically, influencer marketing provides the consumer with a natural advertising mood and access to the content.

Businesses strategically networking influencers in a specific industry who have potentially larger audiences. By this way, businesses can market their brands directly to the influencers' followers. The importance of influencer marketing is that the audience is hearing the recommendation from a symbol that they trust. As a result, the authors strongly claim that influencer marketing is sharing the similar variables with relationship marketing and they are related with the basic keywords, such as, communication, commitment, trust and attention.

Relationship Marketing Concept

In today's intense competitive conditions, businesses that are aware of the fact that keeping their existing customers are less costly than finding new customers are in an effort to maintain long-term relationships with customers. However, it is quite difficult to keep the customer under intense competition. Arlı (2013), mentioned that in order to keep the customer in hand, it is necessary to enter into one-to-one and intimate interactions with them, to make them feel special.

Increasingly, a key goal of marketing is to develop deep, enduring relationships with people and organizations that directly or indirectly affect the success of the firm's marketing activities. Relationship marketing aims to build mutually satisfying long-term relationships with key constituents in order to earn and retain their business. Four key constituents for relationship marketing are customers, employees, marketing partners (channels, suppliers, distributors, dealers, agencies), and members of the financial community (shareholders, investors, analysts). Marketers must create prosperity among all these constituents and balance the returns to all key stakeholders. To develop strong relationships with them requires understanding their capabilities and resources, needs, goals, and desires (Kotler & Keller, 2012, pp. 20).

Kotler et al. (2003, p. 391), proposed the model for relationship marketing in the conventional market context which identifies five levels of supplier-customer relationship – basic, reactive, accountable, proactive, and partnership – based on the supplier's effort of maintaining its interaction with customers (Table 1). They argued that, at the basic level, there is little to no trust because of lack of communication. Trust and long-lasting relationships can be fully achieved only when the customer and seller are at the partnership level. As the relationship progresses up the scale, the more likely it is that the prospective customer will become a customer (Han et al., 2005).

Lenard Berry was the first scholar in service marketing field who firstly used the term "relationship marketing" as part of a marketing literature review (Table 2). He argued that "researchers and businessmen have concentrated far too much on attracting consumers to products and services than retaining them" (Harker & Egan, 2006). Berry (1983), claimed that the customer is an integral part of the marketing and service delivery process that demands a close relationship between the customer and the service provider. The principal concepts of relationship marketing prompt businesses to shift their marketing goals from share-of-market to share-of-customer through developing and maintaining profitable relationship with their customers (Gummesson, 1999).

Table 1. Five levels of relationship marketing

Relationship Marketing Level	Characteristics of Level
1. Basic	Does not really involve relationship building, but does feature positive interaction between the seller and customer when a product or service is sold.
2. Reactive	As above, but seller also suggests that the customer can contact them personally if they have any problems or queries.
3. Accountability	Here the seller actively contacts the customer after sale to check that the product is satisfactory and to receive feedback.
4. Proactive	At this level the seller continues to contact the customer and proactively attempts to understand and satisfy their needs.
5. Partnership	The ultimate form of relationship marketing, involving actually living with the customer. Usually confined to business-to-business relationships.

Source: Dibb & Meadows (2001)

Sheth (2002), explored that there were three antecedents responsible for the popularity of relationship marketing. First one is the energy crisis of the 1970s and the consequent economic stagflation resulted in excess capacity and high raw materials costs. This situation leads to business had a high competition on global scale. It became necessary to defensively focus on retaining customers and defocus customer acquisition related marketing expenditures and activities. In other words, customer retention became the corporate focus and this resulted in the emergence of ongoing relational exchange in contrast with the one-time transactional exchange (Sheth et al., 1988). The second antecedent is the emergence of service marketing which become as a popular new domain of research and understanding. Because of their nature services are generally direct offerings to the end users and direct record of transactions over time with each individual customer, enabling researchers to analyze and theorize about customer loyalty and personalized marketing. Emergence of Total Quality Management (TQM) philosophy was the last premise of relationship marketing. Businesses desired to reduce the number of suppliers in order to improve quality at a lower cost. This collaborative as opposed to combative attitude toward the suppliers further resulted in treating business exchanges as relational and interactive.

In addition to the antecedents described above Sheth (2002), proposed three more antecedents that could shape the course of relationship marketing. The first one is the impact of the internet and information technology (IT), especially in all situations where there is a direct account receivable (customer) relationship. Customer relationship management (CRM) become more important in developing loyalty programs, affinity marketing and campaign management. The second important factor is that a company must be selective in its use of relationship marketing and also should consider segmenting the market into relational and transactional markets.

Table 2. Definitions of relationship marketing

Researcher	Definition
Berry (1983)	Attracting, maintaining, and – in multi-service organizations – enhancing customer relationships.
Berry and Parasuraman (1991)	Relationship marketing concerns attracting, developing, and retaining customer relationships.
Gummesson (1994)	Relationship marketing is marketing seen as relationships, networks, and interaction
Morgan and Hunt (1994)	Relationship marketing refers to all marketing activities directed towards establishing, developing, and maintaining successful relational exchanges.
Sheth (1994)	The understanding, explanation, and management of the ongoing collaborative business relationship between suppliers and customers.
Sheth and Parvatiyar (1995)	Attempts to involve and integrate customers, suppliers, and other infrastructural partners into a firm's developmental and marketing activities.
Grönroos (1996)	Relationship marketing is to identify and establish, maintain, and enhance relationships with customers and other stakeholders, at a profit, so that the objectives of all parties involved are met; and that this is done by a mutual exchange and fulfillment of promises.

Source: Hunt, Arnett, & Madhavaram, (2006)

Therefore, unlike TQM movement, relationship marketing is likely to remain more selective and targeted (Sheth, 2002). The final antecedent is about outsourcing the customers. The major aim of the marketing is to create and retain customers. Ironically, many companies are permanently outsourcing their customers. Most customers do not provide enough purchasing power on an ongoing basis to justify the fixed cost of serving them (Sheth, 2002, pp. 591). Fundamentally, the logic of customer outsourcing is to make unprofitable customers profitable by making them apart of another company's more favorable cost structure (Sheth, Sisodia & Sharma, 2000, pp. 62).

The Forms of Relationship Marketing

Morgan & Hunt (1994), offered various forms of relationship marketing (Figure 1) which categorized with reference to a focal firm and its relational exchanges in supplier, lateral, buyer, and internal partnerships.

Morgan & Hunt (1994) propose that all ten of the exchanges relational in nature and they affect and influence with each other. For instance, relational exchanges involving service providers, as between advertising or marketing research agencies and their respective clients. The long-term exchanges between firms and ultimate

Figure 1. Forms of relationship marketing
Source: (Morgan & Hunt, 1994; cited by Hunt, Arnett & Madhavaram, 2006)

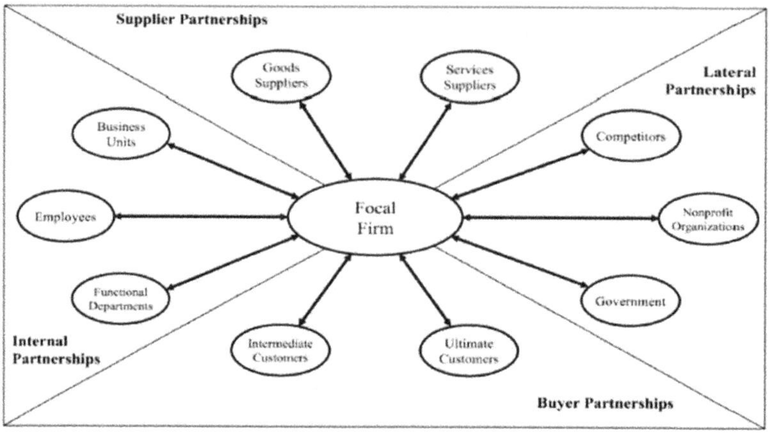

customers, as implemented in "customer relationship marketing" programs, affinity programs, loyalty programs, and as particularly recommended in the services marketing area. The within-firm relational exchanges, as those involving such business units as subsidiaries, divisions, or strategic business units (Hunt, Arnett & Madhavaram 2006: 72-73).

According to Christopher et al. (1991) relational marketing provides convenience in the several areas such as; focusing on customer retention, offering superior goods and services benefits, succeeding long-term vision, focusing exemplary customer service, forecasting customer connections/linkages and achieving totally desired quality (Balta 2006: 11).

Contemporary Relationship Marketing Perspective

How do you define relationship? How is this concept structured? Basically, at least, another person's presence is needed to relate as an individual. However, this might not enough. For the existence of a relationship, parties should able to communicate with each other. But this is not enough either. The priority of a healthy relationship is that a healthy communication which can be established between the parties. When it's considered one of the participants as a "Brand" and other participant as consumer, for a healthy relationship; factors such as trust, love, respect, appreciation, common understanding, awareness and loyalty is required. That is the reason why thousands of people gathering in a queue to get a new iPhone in front of an Apple store or for a promotion event of Coca Cola. This is the consequences of a healthy communication and relationship that these brands have established with their target audience.

When authors try to explain this situation within the framework of marketing science, it is necessary to accept that there are many subjects and variables that can be considered. In today's technological structure, brands use various communication mediums such as facebook, YouTube, instagram, twitter and other actors (such as youtubers, influencers or instagrammer) while establishing or developing long-term profitable relationships with their customers. One of them is the "Influencer Marketing" which can be evaluated within the context of relationship marketing.

Relationship marketing is less transactional than traditional marketing strategies. Basically, it's all about developing a long-term, strong relationship with customers that already exist. It has been suggested that the Internet is a proper platform to grow and sustain relationships to succeed competitive advantages over industrial players (Bauer, Grether, & Leach, 2002a; Tzokas & Saren, 2004; Wilcox & Gurau, 2003). Internet provides an innovative and strategic marketing mechanism and serves as a major distribution channel to conduct online relationship marketing and facilitates a sustainable e-relationship between online customers and consumer service providers in consumer markets (Bauer, Grether, & Leach, 2002b; Gilbert & Powell-Perry, 2002; Srirojanant & Thirkell, 1998). Bai et al. (2007) defines e-relationship marketing as a strategic marketing practice of establishing, maintaining, enhancing, and commercializing networked customer relationships through promise fulfillment communicated or implemented over certain electronic channels such as the Internet.

Global companies usually invest in operating elegant and effective relationship marketing campaigns. In some large companies, relationship marketing using as a strategic tool that affects related departments. In these departments manager or staff should interact with customers for daily operations such as, after sale services, maintenance services or satisfaction surveys.

One of the main reasons for the large-scale enterprises to be included in such strategic applications is to increase the satisfaction of the existing customer, to bring new customers to the business and finally to be the leader in the industry. For instance, American Airlines Company maintains a comprehensive frequent flyer program that rewards customer loyalty with the promise of free flights, upgrades, and discounts. Similarly, Dell computers created a special online store for high volume corporate customers. By tailoring the ordering process to the specific customer's needs, Dell was able to expedite many of the hassles corporate technology buyers face. Another case is about famous Swedish furniture company. IKEA changed the font in their ubiquitous catalog, Ikea lovers took to the Internet to air their complaints. Rather than alienate their customers for a trivial reason, Ikea changed the font back in the next catalog (Marketing-Schools, n.d., para. 11).

Founder and CEO of Ambassador software Jeff Epstein defines relationship marketing as creating positive brand awareness and growth for a business through understanding, fostering, and leveraging its relationships. He also claims that

Figure 2. Segments of relationship marketing
Source: (Epstein, 2018)

relationship marketing is a strategy, but not a tool. It's a way of looking at the relationship which the brand has with customers, and followers that parallels any other type of marketing tactic. According to Epstein (2018), relationship marketing is an all-encompassing term that personifies any effort to build long-term relationships with customers, rather than push for one-time sales. This strategy basically consists of 5 segments including influencer marketing, affiliate marketing, partner marketing, referral marketing and employee advocacy (Figure 2).

One of the interactive segments of relational marketing is referral marketing. Berman (2016), defines referral marketing by means of motivating current customers as a referral base, views customers as influencers and advocates, seeks out current customers that can provide referrals with high lifetime value, and uses referral-based marketing programs to augment traditional promotions on brands. The second one is affiliate marketing which represents something of an open marketplace in which innovative internet marketers can generate revenue by acting as free agent salespeople for thousands on on-line brands. Advertisers achieve the benefit of a predictable marketing cost as a percentage of sales. In other words, the affiliate offers to pay for its own marketing efforts aimed at generating orders for the brand and will motivate customers order these brands directly from the company (Duffy, 2005).

According to Epstein (2018), influencer marketing is a modern take on affiliate marketing, and financially incentivizes individuals with large, captive following in specific niches, empowering them to drive awareness and revenue for brands. In partner marketing, technically paying a commission or fee to companies such as distributors, resellers, agencies, and other third-party firms to promote leads and sales. The fifth segment in relationship marketing is the employee advocacy which is the self-promotion of a business by its team to generate positive exposure and raise awareness for their brand. Fullerton (2011), defines the concept as an endorsing or recommending the benefits of the products or services of their firm to others such as friends, relatives, acquaintances and co-workers. Employee advocacy technically represents the word-of-mouth communication of giving favorable recommendations.

Influencer Marketing Concept

Worldwide, 2.307 billion people are active social media users and the generation with the most purchasing power, millennials, is heavily active with 90% of U.S. 18- to 29-year-olds being on social media (Statista, 2017). According to these figures, it is obvious that visibility on social networking sites is important for the profitable up-to-date businesses. Today, the focus of influencer marketing shifted to online opinion leaders - active users of social networking sites with large amounts of followers. During the last five years, the spread of social media has further changed buying and selling techniques. With platforms like Facebook, Twitter and YouTube, consumers are able to comment on their experiences with products and companies and to share them with their friends. This has led to the growing need for companies to generate positive customer experiences in order to minimize negative word-of-mouth messages, which would easily be spread within the social media platforms to other, potential customers (Sudha & Sheena, 2017, p. 14).

Although influential marketing is conceptually new to the marketing world, it is possible to accept it as a part of daily life when we consider it as content. We've always learned from the experiences of our friends and family or looked to aspirational figures for inspiration on what to buy (Brooks, 2019). The first influencers in the history of influencer marketing can be traced back to the early 18th century. In 1760s, a potter by the name Wedgwood made a tea set for the Queen of England. Since the monarchy were the influencers of their time, his forward-thinking decision to market his brand as Royal-approved afforded it to the luxury status and the brand still enjoys today (Brooks, 2019). In the 1920s, there were only a few brands on the market shaping the product-centered marketing 1.0. Brands of this market created personas to trigger the purchase decisions of consumers emotionally (Ehrhardt, 2017).

A fashion icon "Coco Channel" has been credited as being the most transformative influences on fashion. In 1984, Michael Jordan signed with Nike which included custom design Air Jordans. In the nineties Loreal Elvive choose Jennifer Aniston to be the face of their hair products. In 2004 "Blog" named platforms popped up and make it easier for anyone to share their thoughts for their audience. After 2010 with the launch of instagram bloggers and brands find a new way to communicate and share their ideas. In 2019, the first influencers are given the power to sell directly through instagram and by 2020 its assuming that influencer industry will be worth $ 5-10 billion (Brooks, 2019).

The social science theorist Bandura (1971), explored the basics of influencer communication theories to understand how people react in social situations. Bandura (1971) stated that, in the social learning system, new patterns of behavior can be acquired through direct experience or by observing the behaviors of others. On the basis of informative feedback, they (consumers) develop thoughts or hypotheses about the types of behavior most likely to succeed. These hypotheses then serve as guides for future actions. To put this into simpler terms, people learn from example, and influencers lead by example for those who "follow" them. This explanation can help to understand why influencers are so influential (cited in Glucksman, 2017).

Influencer can be defined as a third-party endorser who significantly shapes the customer's purchasing decision, but may ever be accountable for it (Brown & Hayes, 2008, pp. 50). Influencer marketing is a relationship between a brand and an influencer. The influencer promotes the brand's products or services through various media outlets such as Instagram and YouTube (Mathew, 2018). Influencer marketing is a marketing practice based on influence theory, which advocates the idea that a small percentage of key individuals can be effective at persuading a great amount of others. Rather than marketing towards a large group of consumers, influencer marketing uses influential individuals to drive a brand's message to the larger market and influence buying decisions (Braatz, 2017, pp. 6). Hearn and Schoenhoff (2016) describe social media influencers as working to generate a form of celebrity capital by cultivating as much attention as possible and crafting an authentic personal brand via social networks, which can subsequently be used by companies and advertisers for consumer outreach. According to the another definition, influencer marketing is a process of identifying and activating individuals who have an influence over a specific target audience or medium, in order to be part of a brand's campaign towards increased reach, sales, or engagement (Sudha & Sheena, 2017, pp. 16).

Influencer marketing is the practice of identifying key decision makers among target audiences and encouraging them to take advantage of their influence and generate word-of-mouth messages (Thorne, 2008). Influencer marketing and Word of mouth marketing (WOMM) are both genuine and essential strategies in the marketing area. Although they differ in some titles, they basically serve the same purpose for brands and organizations. WOMM is a general term for marketing practices that aims to make consumers talk about a brand. Kirby & Marsden (2007) in their book defines the term WOMM as; the promotion of a company or its products and services through an initiative conceived and designed to get people talking positively about that company, product or service. The literature on WOMM describes multiple attributes of influencers. Influencers supply the authority that allows a message to be conveyed quickly and reliably through WOMM techniques. Schafer (n.d., para. 7) stated that one of the prominent differences between influencer marketing and WOMM are technically based on the relationship (emotional and financial) of organization and influencers who is designated to spread the story of the brand. This assures some measure of accountability and reliability on influencers. By contrast, WOMM is less dependent on relationships between a company and the people spreading a story. WOMM relies on seeding irresistible stories within relevant groups of strangers. In a study, Kirby & Marsden (2007) found that the mass-media messages do not directly influence the mass market. In fact, they influence a small minority of individuals (the so called "influencers" or "opinion leaders"), who then influence their peers through word of mouth. Keller & Berry (2003) argue that influencers have multiple interests, they tend to be early adopters in markets, they are trusted by others, and have a large social network (cited in Kiss & Bichler, 2008).

Brown & Hayes (2008, pp.50) mentioned (with examples) that influencers influence their audience in many different ways, sometimes at the emotional level ('You want to over-spec this project five-fold – you can't afford this one to fail!'), sometimes at the regulatory level ('You need the auditors' sign-off at every stage of this project – get their name on every decision'), sometimes at the strategic level ('Now that we're a public company we need to be seen to be partnering with the right kind of people – get Accenture to oversee this'). There can clearly be many other pressures – those that are tactical, résumé-minded, fueled by internal politics, cost based, etc.

Influencers are a late modern phenomenon; there has been a huge increase in their collaboration with marketing agencies over the past year. For instance, Content Agency (2018) divides influencers into four groups, as follows (Kadekova & Holiencinova, 2018, pp. 92):

- **Blogger:** The owner of a blog (website) aimed to share their thoughts and passions. A blogger creates authentic and unique content – photos, texts and comments – and displays them in chronological or alphabetical order by posting on the blogs. Such posts are often shared via social media.
- **YouTuber (Vlogger):** Interacts with audiences through their videos on YouTube, expressing own feelings and experiences and dealing with the most diverse topics one can imagine.

- **Celebrity:** Most often an actor, singer, presenter, athlete, but also a person who gets watched due to some extraordinary action or show. In other words, it is a person who has become widely known thanks to media. On Facebook, Instagram or YouTube, these celebrities have a number of followers to share their everyday Professional accomplishments and private 'secrets' with.
- **Instagrammer:** A person who, thanks to high-quality photo content, has been able to attract the audience to Instagram while gaining a large number of followers. This person is not a typical celebrity.

Taxonomy of Influencer Roles

When we examine the current literature sources, we can see that influencers are classified in different ways. Marketers generally divide influencers into the following categories: 1) celebrities; 2) industry experts and thought leaders; 3) bloggers and content creators; and 4), micro-influencers (Influencer Marketinghub, 2017). Izea (2017) uses size of the following to distinguish among micro- and macro-influencers, with micro-influencers having 500 to 10,000 followers. On the other hand, Influencer Marketinghub (2017) establishes another category, namely that of mega-influencers, with audiences of over 1 million. Morin (2016) advocates that there are also niche influencers that are focused on particular topics like gamers and mom bloggers who are focused on monetizing their social media activities while micro-influencers are often not primarily driven by monetary rewards (Gretzel, 2018).

Brown & Hayes (2008, p. 39) in their book, identified a number of roles that can be played by influencers based on various key points in the process. These roles are shown in Figure 3 (Brown & Hayes, 2008, pp. 40-43):

- **Idea Planters:** Idea planters are the thinkers in your industry. These people ask what if? They are the innovators. Typically, they provoke and challenge opinions and conventional wisdom, and raise questions that begin to break inertia.
- **Predictors:** Predictors tell us what (they believe) will be adopted soon. They ask what next? Much of the origination of this kind of influence comes from the supplier community, which is essentially telling us what's next in their product pipeline. But this market priming is held in check by third parties such as analysts (who sanity check the plans), financiers (who fund new product development) and other commentators such as bloggers and management gurus.
- **Trendsetters:** They are the early adopters. They set themselves as reference points and create the direction for the rest of the market. They are important because they not only validate the market but also communicate success to

the market. They are influential due to their early adoption, and the fact that they spread the news of their success. For example, Citigroup has become a trendsetter in homeworking policy, and Dell Company was a longtime trendsetter in supply chain management.

- **Proclaimers:** Some influencers just stand up and proclaim that the world will be how they want it to be. They mandate (as far as they can) what and how. They are therefore in a position to be listened to and acted upon. Sometimes this is due to their position (such as regulators), sometimes just down to the weight they carry in their market.
- **Aggregators/Communicators:** One of the most important roles an influencer can play is that of information gatherer and disseminators. It's where the media and analysts get the majority of their influence: their knowledge of the detail of the market allows them power as to who has access to that knowledge.
- **Scopers:** At some point a definition of the decision to be taken has to be made. That's the role of scopers, to map out the limitations, parameters and dimensions of the problem and its likely solutions. Scopers tell us what now. For example, a firm may have a problem with its customer service operation, but the scopers will determine whether the decision to be made is to outsource the operation, invest in training or implement a new customer relationship management (CRM) system.
- **Recommenders:** Recommenders suggest what you should do. They are sometimes, but not often, able to dictate a decision. Most often they will make their Professional judgment known, and then leave the final decision up to the ultimate decision-maker. They are therefore usually somewhat passive in their influence, which is advisory in nature.

Figure 3. Influencer Roles in Decision Process
Source: (Brown & Hayes, 2008, pp.40)

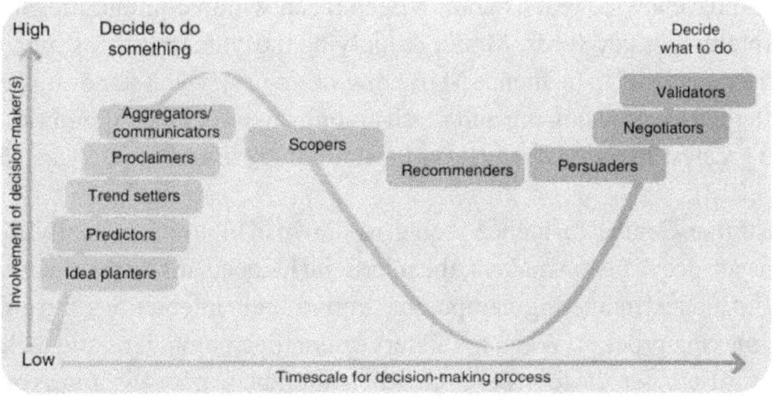

- **Persuaders:** Persuaders tell you what you must do. They are not passive at all, conveying precise direction rather than advice. They are the people who are able to make or break a decision.
- **Negotiators:** negotiators, who decide how and how much, advising on the financial elements of the deal, as well as the mechanics of how to construct a deal.
- **Validators:** Validators say its okay, and are the safety net for a decision-maker. Not the oft-perceived rubber stamp, they give any decision the health check, to make sure the decision-maker has covered all options. They can halt a deal, or send it circling back for additional scoping or negotiating. The best examples of validators are reference site visits. The decision-maker is using the validator to prove to his superiors that the decision is low risk.
- **Super-Influencers:** There are in some markets super-influencers, key individuals that command the highest respect and attention. Super-influencers are rare. These people typically influence macro industry directions, rather than purchase decisions within a market. For example, Steve Jobs is a super-influencer. His influence is immense at an industry level.

Marketing models and practices are constantly evolving to adapt to consumer needs and wants, technological improvements, and socio-economic changes. For the total growth of the company and the brand, it is vital to stay ahead of consumer preferences so the company may influence them to choose their products. Brown & Fiorella (2013), in their book, reposition the customers' role between influencers. Authors state that the current paradigm of influence marketing places the influencer at the center of the marketing universe and hiding the customer who makes the purchasing decision. From this point of view, researchers have developed two different models which are The Fisherman's Influence Model and Customer-Centric Influence Model.

The Fisherman's Influence Model as shown in Figure 4, marketers must identify people who have a wide reach and/or a deep reach within communities focused on specific interests or keywords. Model is applying the concept of "casting a wide net to catch the most fish" to Influence Marketing strategies, which stands for leveraging those with the largest following and reach among large social communities that will drive the greatest brand awareness and eventually result in a purchase (Brown & Fiorella, 2013).

In Customer-Centric Influence Model, as shown in Figure 5, basically identifying product or service decision makers, the micro- influencers in their social graphs, and aligning influence marketing campaigns around their interactions throughout the decision-making process. When marketers orient their campaigns and technologies around the influencer, the focus becomes their attempt to drive awareness or possibly

Figure 4. Fisherman's Influence Marketing Model
Source: (Brown & Fiorella, 2013, pp.77)

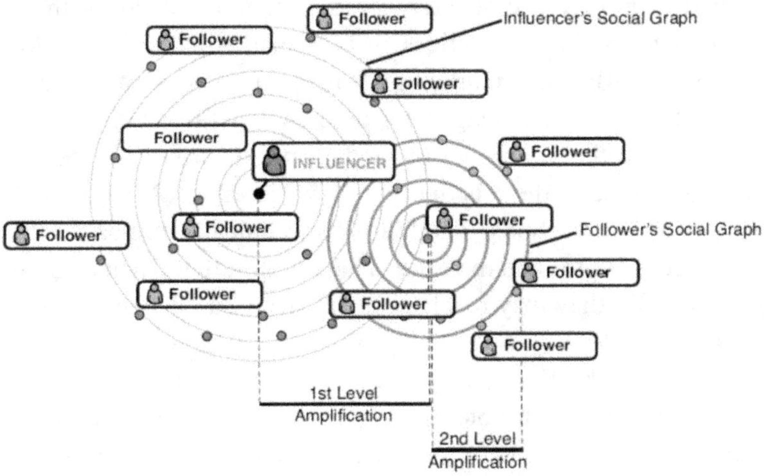

Figure 5. Customer-Centric Influence Marketing Model
Source: (Brown & Fiorella, 2013, pp.78)

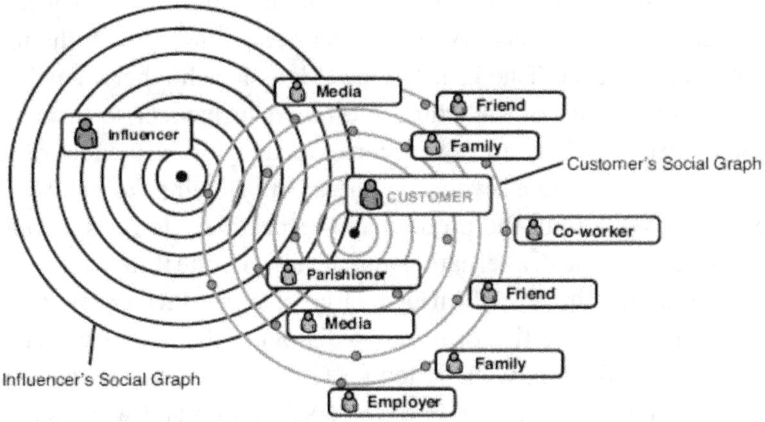

even sway purchase decisions, instead of addressing the decision-making process. Placing the customer at the center forces us to look at the decisions he or she makes and what impacts those decisions.

Phases of Influencer Marketing

Influencer marketing may one of the most important approach for the companies which conducting marketing practices in post-marketing era. The development of the concept of influencer marketing from past to present causes important decisions to be taken in the management process, whether earned or paid. In this context, it is inferred that a number of models and theories have been developed by the researchers. One of them is the Brown & Fiorella's (2013) Four M's model which is described in their book. The four M's technically comprises the concepts of; make, manage, monitor and measure. They suggest that when a company apply these stages correctly they may reach a crucial size of audience and this will have a positive effect on sales.

The first stage of the Four M's model is about making influencers. Finding the right influencers for each potential buyer and make them brand advocates to move companies toward a purchase decision. By creating brand advocates with those influencers leads to connect to potential customers by meeting them on their level through engaging marketing tactics. Once the company touched the related influencers for their target customer, they need to move into the managing stage. Companies should consider the impact of influencers on brands and what they may pass on to their superiors. Relationships with the influencers may continue for future outreach and promotions. By continuing a relationship with the influencers there are benefits like established trust, knowledge of each other, a ready customer base, and the opportunity of switching the brand influencer to brand advocate. Authors mentioned that there are seven steps to managing influencer relationships for all brands to follow. These seven steps are a path flowing from the brand to the influencer which starts with the product and respectively follows as, knowledge, calendar, message, platform, alternatives and feedback. The third stage of the model is dealing with the monitoring of influencer campaigns. Influencer monitoring is considered to gauge the positive or negative dialogues that exist around the brand. With the help of search analytics, listening tools, dedicated messaging, landing pages and more, marketers can begin to understand who and what is offering the greatest return on marketing investment (ROMI), where they need to adapt the brand message, and which influencer is influencing consumers and their decision process at any given time. The last stage of the four M's is the measure stage, For being able to replicate the success of a campaign in future campaigns, the brand need to measure why it happened and who created it. In this case, it's the ability to measure the ROMI from the influencer marketing efforts. According to Freberg et al. (2011), the success of social media influencers is extremely important to brands; therefore, technology has been developed to identify and track influencers' relevance to a brand or organization. This technology tracks the number of hits on a blog, times a blog is shared, likes and comments, and followers. All of these points are essential features of a social media influencer's success.

The influencers who change the trends and activate the minds about a certain thought, assume the activist role of the brand. Influencer marketing reaches its destination in 4 stages, which are access, action, convert and interaction (Erdensoy, 2018).

At the "*Access*" stage, brand manager chooses the right influencer to represent itself through social media distribution channels. At first the target audience does not aware and trust the brand, so traditional advertising and marketing methods cannot be use. However, the influencer is an expert in the field and have a reputation and credibility in the eyes of the followers. Brands access the target customer group with influencers, enabling them to realize the desired buying behavior of their products and services. Next stage referred as "*Action*". Brands create secondary marketing campaigns through influencers. Influencer asks them to comment from their followers while experiencing and honestly introducing brand products and services in problem solutions for real life scenarios. The interest of the target audience is drawn by the created discussion environment; they express only pure ideas about the product value of the brand that have not passed through any filter.

The third stage on influencer marketing phases is the "*Convert*". On this stage influencer transform their followers into customers who buy the brand's products. By using the consumer to consumer (C2C) marketing, the WOMM effect is generated and also the advertising revenue is doubled by the brand. This also contains the User-Generated-Content understanding. Consumers' wishes and excitement about the product are kept alive with the special discounts created by the person or a certain group (follower kit) created for instant use. Thus, the audience is transformed into active customers. At the final stage of "*Interaction*", it is important to build strong customer relationships. Influencers should transform their first customers into loyal customers of products and brands. The formation of a steadfast loyalty depends on the consumer's bond to the influencer. For this, it is necessary to define the prototype of the target audiences of the brands, to characterize it by creating a Persona as a result of the research and samples. The Influencer should be able to represent the desired Persona of the brand in a natural and passionate way, be transformed into a Superstar that shines in the consumer's eyes and reflect the brand's target audience. This will increase the interaction of the target audience and create a large customer group that is faithful to the brand through influencers.

SOLUTIONS AND RECOMMENDATIONS

According to Murphy & Schram (2014) influencer marketing comes with a variety of benefits for marketers: "unique branded social content from a trusted, influential source. It also gives them syndication of content through all platforms, the ability to target micro niches at scale, higher click-through rates (CTRs) and lower cost per clicks than traditional display, fresh and lasting content and loyal partners that care and share" (as cited in Hesse, 2015).

Tapinfluence & Nielsen Company (2016), collaborated together to measure the effects of influencer marketing campaigns on in-store sales based on purchased data from over 90 million U.S. households. According to results, 1000 people viewing content generated $285 of incremental sales over the control group. But display ads generated $16 of incremental sales. Study revealed that influencer marketing gives a "Return on investments" 11 times higher than traditional forms of digital advertising.

Linqia Company (2017), designed a study to understand how brands and agencies are using influencer marketing and how they plan to leverage the channel in 2018. 181 marketers and their agencies participated in survey. The study revealed that %92 of marketers who used influencer marketing in 2017 found it to be effective. Marketers believe that influencer marketing channel is becoming a significant part of the marketing mix. According to survey, %39 of participants plan to increase their influencer marketing budget. In addition, %92 of marketers believe that Instagram is the most important social media site to make influencer marketing campaigns.

A study by Berger and Keller Fay Group found that influencers have up to 22.2 times more conversations each week than regular users about purchasing recommendations. According to the study, 74 percent of the influencers encouraged someone to "buy it or try it," something only 66 percent of the general population did. Finally, Influencers were seen as more credible and believable, more knowledgeable, and better at explaining how the product works or could be used (Lafferty, 2016).

In 2017, PageFair reported that worldwide usage of ad-blocking programs had increased by a staggering 30% over the previous year. It means that 600 million devices have adblock software programs. Since influencer marketing campaigns do not have an adblock obstacles which provides a significant advantage. Brands which are using influencer on social medias, can avoiding ads in that way (Wang 2018). Linqia (2017) research also shows that %50 of survey participants' reason to use influencer marketing is to reach consumers and beats advertising blindness.

Influencer marketing connects with audiences where they spent the most time. Today, audiences spent much more time on social networks and it increases day by day. When influencers mention or feature a brand on one of these social media platforms, they allow the company to connect with audiences on the sites where they spend the most time (Kosaka, n.d.). Especially, if the aim of brand is to reach millennials and generation Z, it's most important tool to use influencer marketing. 85% of Generation Z use their social media accounts to learn and discover more about brands and products. Influencer marketing also has the ability to generate real results incredibly fast. If an influencer has followers from all over the world then, regardless of when they post something, it will be picked up by thousands of people straight away (Figueria, 2018).

Brands always strive to win the hearts of consumers and create a positive brand image. So it's no wonder they work with influencers to promote their brands because influencers can increase positive brand sentiment. According to a RhythmOne study, influencer marketing programs that lasted for two or more weeks resulted in an 8.73 percent lift in positive brand sentiment. This genuine positive sentiment the influencers have towards your brand can help portray your brand personality in a positive light (Barker, 2017).

Wallace (2017), mentioned that social media influencers tend to be more authentic, and people tend to trust them more than celebrities when they endorse a product. 84 percent of millennials don't trust traditional advertising and prefer more authentic endorsements, like that of a trusted blogger or fashion designer. According to AdWeek, marketers received $6.85 in earned media value for every $1 spent on influencer marketing. Statistically, user-generated content is 50 percent more trusted by internet users than traditional media, and consumers are 71 percent more likely to make a purchase based on social media referrals. There are many influencer marketing cases which includes success stories even on global brands. Such as, in 2016, influencer Lilly Singh was the highest-earning person on YouTube with 11.9 million followers. She creates and posts her own comedic videos, which eventually landed her a contract with Coca-Cola. Another case is about Fiji water. Danielle Bernstein is a popular influencer who partnered with Fiji water last year to encourage viewers to use Fiji water after workouts (Pinegar, 2018).

Another example of successful influencer marketing campaign is about a micro influencer Slava Daniliuk who takes photos in interesting locations. Sperry (shoes selling company) asked Daniliuk if it could share his content and enlisted him to continually post on the brand's social channels and website. Daniliuk produced Sperry's most engaged with Instagram photo of 2017, which features him atop a skyscraper looking down.

A Turkish origin platform INFLOW (Influencers of The World), actively brings together partner brands with leading bloggers, digital influencers, social media content creators and digital trendsetters from all over the world. INFLOW Summits hosted many organizations, such as INFLOW Travel Summit 2016 in Cappadocia and 2017 in Istanbul, INFLOW Meet-up & Workshop 2017 in Venice, Global Summit 2018 in Istanbul and 2019 in Qatar (Inflow, n.d.). The world's leading digital influencers in the travel industry came together with leading brands and participated in several activities including, keynotes, panels, networking get-togethers and structured 'matchmaking sessions' to share ideas, collaborate and engage in a unique style. More than 400 influencer addresses different interest groups from various parts of the world are listing on the INFLOW website. Combining Influencers worldwide with such organizations millions of followers engaging on social media, and events also reaches millions of people and gets millions of impressions on digital audience. Business-to-Influencer meetings are ultimate matchmaking opportunity for brands and influencers as brands seeking digital marketing partners have the chance to meet with the leading influencers of the world. Through this meetings, influencers get to know the industry professionals to explore sponsorship and collaboration opportunities (Inflow, n.d.).

FUTURE RESEARCH DIRECTIONS

Influencer marketing is spreading very rapidly on a global scale. With the rise of social media networks and performing influencers on these channels are attracting the attention of marketing managers. It will not be a mistake to say that it will be one of the beneficial marketing communication tool for businesses. Unfortunately, it's an inevitable fact that the number of people focusing on the same job upsurges, problems related to the quality of the work begin to emerge. At this point, different ones will come to the fore. In the coming period, marketing managers to stand out and to increase awareness of their brands they may want to employ authentic and niche influencers (also known as micro-influencers).

CONCLUSION

This study basically provides a better understanding the link between relationship marketing and influencer marketing with respect to brand communication. After the review of the literature, it was understood that relationship marketing is one of the premature stages of the influencer marketing on customer relations. It is important to understand the relationship marketing for a better understanding of influencer marketing. Influencer marketing is a growing trend on today's brand communication.

Reminding, persuading, informing and entertaining are the standstill valid factors of promotion and marketing communication. By the use these factors marketers hardly try engage and influence their target markets to purchase their brands. In today's new marketing world, influencer is an industrial expert who has a certain strength and popularity in social media channels and influences or changes the behaviors of the followers. As influencer marketing has matured as an industry, it has attracted support companies and apps to simplify the process for both brands and influencers. The main purpose of influencer marketing is to increase the awareness on the brand by generating appropriate contents that can attract the attention of consumers in virtual environment in accordance with the brand texture. This enables the brand to be more visible in the virtual environment and allowing the consumer to touch and communicate with the brand.

The Influencer MarketingHub (2019), conducted several surveys covers influencers, social networking sites, marketing agencies, brands, PR Agencies, and others in related fields which compares years 2017 to 2019. In their Influencer Marketing Report (2019) the outlook for influencer marketing is still extremely positive. 320 new influencer marketing focused platforms and agencies entered the market over the last 12 months. This grew to 335 in 2016 and 740 in 2018 more than twice the number that existed just two years previously. Influencer marketing has continued to grow as an industry over the last few years. It was a $1.7 billion industry in 2016, $4.6 billion in 2018 and is expected to continue its upward trajectory this year (2019) to potentially become a $6.5 billion industry. The most popular reason why respondents engage in influencer marketing is for the awareness purposes (37%); the second category, at 32%, has the more clear-cut objective of increasing sales. Slightly less popular, at 31%, is the group of respondents who engage in influencer marketing to build up a library of user-generated content (Influencer Marketing Report, 2019).

After all these literature review and statistical facts, influencer marketing progressing and becoming a healthier industry. As the increasing importance of customer relations and consumer behaviors are understood, the trustworthiness of advertising messages and advertising appeals used by the brands in communication has become more prominent. Therefore, it is to conclude that influencer marketing would most probably increase its popularity and more companies in local and global scale would try to use and implement it into their brand communication strategies. Companies should invest more on product development and also marketing research to identify their target audience in detail. This will enlighten them to arrange for an accurate match with influencers.

REFERENCES

Arlı, E. (2013). Marina işletmeciliğinde ilişkisel pazarlama uygulamalarinin tekrar satin alma niyeti, tavsiye etme niyeti ve memnuniyet üzerindeki etkisi. *Anadolu Üniversitesi Sosyal Bilimler Dergisi*, *13*(1), 61–75.

Bai, B., Hu, C., & Jang, S. (2007). Examining e-relationship marketing features on hotel websites. *Journal of Travel & Tourism Marketing, 21*(2–3), 33–48. doi:10.1300/J073v21n02_03

Balta, N. F. (2006). *Endüstriyel Pazarlama*. İstanbul, Turkey: Nobel Yayıncılık.

Barker, S. (2017). *Why influencer marketing has become a powerful weapon for brands: Find out some of the best ways influencers can help promote your brand.* Retrieved from https://www.inc.com/shane-barker/why-influencer-marketing-has-become-a-powerful-weapon-for-brands.html

Bauer, H. H., Grether, M., & Leach, M. (2002a). Building customer relations over the Internet. *Industrial Marketing Management, 31*(2), 155–163. doi:10.1016/S0019-8501(01)00186-9

Bauer, H. H., Grether, M., & Leach, M. (2002b). Customer relations through the Internet. *Journal of Relationship Marketing, 1*(2), 39–55. doi:10.1300/J366v01n02_03

Berman, B. (2016). Referral marketing: Harnessing the power of your customers. *Business Horizons, 59*(1), 19–28. doi:10.1016/j.bushor.2015.08.001

Berry, L. L. (1983). *Relationship marketing: Emerging perspectives on services marketing*. Chicago, IL: American Marketing Association.

Braatz, L. A. (2017). *#Influencer marketing on Instagram. Consumer responses towards promotional posts: The effects of message sidedness and product depiction* (Unpublished Master's Thesis). University of Twente, The Netherlands.

Brooks, A. (2019). *A brief history of influencers.* Retrieved from https://www.socialmediatoday.com/news/timeline-a-brief-history-of-influencers/554377/

Brown, D., & Fiorella, S. (2013). *Influence marketing: How to create, manage, and measure brand influencers in social media marketing (Que Biz-Tech).* Hoboken, NJ: Que Publishing.

Brown, D., & Hayes, N. (2008). *Influencer marketing: Who really influences your customers?* UK: Butterworth-Heinemann. doi:10.4324/9780080557700

Christopher, M., Payne, A., & Ballantyne, D. (1991). *Relationship marketing*. Oxford, UK: Butterworth-Heinemann.

Content Agency. (2018). Content Agency - Influencer marketing. Retrieved from https://contentagency.sk/

Dibb, S., & Meadows, M. (2001). The application of a relationship marketing perspective in retail banking. *Service Industries Journal, 21*(1), 169–194. doi:10.1080/714005011

Duffy, D. L. (2005). Affiliate marketing and its impact on e-commerce. *Journal of Consumer Marketing, 22*(3), 161–163. doi:10.1108/07363760510595986

Ehrhardt, J. (2017). *A brief history of influencer marketing*. Retrieved from https://blog.influencerdb.com/brief-history-of-influencer-marketing/

Epstein, J. (2018). *The importance of relationship marketing for ecommerce brands.* Retrieved from https://www.getambassador.com/blog/relationship-marketing-strategies-ecommerce

Erdensoy, D. (2018). *What is influencer marketing?* Retrieved from https://creatorden.com/en_us/what-is-marketing-influencia/

Figueria, F. (2018). *17 incredible benefits of influencer marketing in 2018.* Retrieved from https://anova.co/blog/17-benefits-of-influencer-marketing

Freberg, K., Graham, K., McGaughey, K., & Freberg, L. (2011). Who are the social media influencers? A study of public perceptions of personality. *Public Relations Review, 37*(1), 90–92. doi:10.1016/j.pubrev.2010.11.001

Fullerton, G. (2011). Creating advocates: The roles of satisfaction, trust and commitment. *Journal of Retailing and Consumer Services, 18*(1), 92–100. doi:10.1016/j.jretconser.2010.10.003

Gilbert, D., & Powell-Perry, J. (2002). Exploring developments in web-based relationship marketing within the hotel industry. *Journal of Hospitality & Leisure Marketing, 9*(3/4), 141–159.

Glucksman, M. (2017). Rise of social media influencer marketing on lifestyle branding. *Elon Journal of Undergraduate Research in Communications, 8*(2), 77–87.

Gretzel, U. (2018). Influencer marketing in travel and tourism. In M. Sigala & U. Gretzel (Eds.), *Advances in social media for travel, tourism and hospitality: new perspectives, practice and cases* (pp. 147–156). New York: Routledge.

Gummesson, E. (1999). *Total relationship marketing, rethinking marketing management: From 4Ps to 30Rs*. Oxford, UK: Butterworth Heinemann.

Han, Y., Hu, C., Bai, B., & Jang, S. (2005). Marketing hospitality and tourism education on the Internet: An analysis of e-relationship marketing features. *Journal of Hospitality & Tourism Education*, *17*(1), 11–21. doi:10.1080/10963758.2005.10696811

Harker, M. J., & Egan, J. (2006). The past, present and future of relationship marketing. *Journal of Marketing Management*, *22*(1/2), 215–242. doi:10.1362/026725706776022326

Hearn, A., & Schoenhoff, S. (2016). From celebrity to influencer. In P. D. *Marshall, & S. Redmond (Eds.), A companion to celebrity* (pp. 194–211). West Sussex, UK: John Wiley & Sons/Blackwell.

Hesse, N. (2015). *Influencer marketing: How companies can benefit from influencers to strengthen their brands.* Retrieved from http://www.brandba.se/blog/influencer-marketing-how-companies-can-benefit-from-it-to-strengthen-their-brands

Hunt, S. D., Arnett, D. B., & Madhavaram, S. (2006). The explanatory foundations of relationship marketing theory. *Journal of Business and Industrial Marketing*, *21*(2), 72–87. doi:10.1108/10610420610651296

Influencer MarketingHub. (2017). *What is an influencer?* Retrieved from https://influencermarketinghub.com/what-is-an-influencer/

Influencer MarketingHub. (2019). *Influencer marketing report.* Retrieved from https://influencermarketinghub.com/IM_Benchmark_Report_2019.pdf

Izea. (2017). *The power of your everyday influencer is stronger than celebrities.* Retrieved from https://izea.com/2017/02/03/micro-influencers/

Kadekova, Z., & Holiencinova, M. (2018). Influencer marketing as a modern phenomenon creating a new frontier of virtual opportunities. *Communication Today*, *9*(2), 90–105.

Keller, E., & Berry, J. (2003). *The influentials: One American in ten tells the other nine how to vote, where to eat, and what to buy.* New York: The Free Press.

Kirby, J., & Marsden, P. (2007). *Connected marketing: The viral, buzz, and word of mouth revolution.* Oxford, UK: Routledge.

Kiss, C., & Bichler, M. (2008). Identification of influencers: Measuring influence in customer networks. *Decision Support Systems*, *46*(1), 233–253. doi:10.1016/j.dss.2008.06.007

Kosaka, K. (n.d.). *7 overlooked benefits of influencer marketing. Influencer marketing benefit #5: Connects with audiences where they spend the most time.* Retrieved from https://blog.alexa.com/benefits-of-influencer-marketing/

Kotler, P., Bowen, J., & Makens, J. (2003). *Marketing for hospitality and tourism* (3rd ed.). Upper Saddle River, NJ: Prentice Hall.

Kotler, P., Kartajaya, H., & Setiawan, I. (2017). *Marketing 4.0: Moving from traditional to digital*. Hoboken, NJ: John Wiley & Sons.

Kotler, P., & Keller, K. L. (2012). *Marketing management*. New Jersey: Prentice Hall.

Lafferty, J. (2016). *Can influencer marketing really motivate purchases?* Retrieved from https://www.adweek.com/digital/can-influencer-marketing-really-drive-conversions-study/

Linqia Company. (2017). *The state of influencer marketing*. Retrieved from http://www.linqia.com/wp-content/uploads/2017/12/Linqia-The-State-of-Influencer-Marketing-2018.pdf

Magrath, A. J. (1986). When marketing services, 4 Ps are not enough. *Business Horizons*, *29*(3), 44–50. doi:10.1016/0007-6813(86)90007-8

Marketing-Schools. (n.d.). *Relationship marketing: Explore the strategy of relationship marketing*. Retrieved from http://www.marketing-schools.org/types-of-marketing/relationship-marketing.html

Mathew, J. (2018). *Understanding influencer marketing and why it is so effective.* Retrieved from https://www.forbes.com/sites/theyec/2018/07/30/understanding-influencer-marketing-and-why-it-is-so-effective/#1471884c71a9

Montgomery, A. L. (2001). Applying quantitative marketing techniques to the Internet. *Interfaces*, *31*(2), 90–108. doi:10.1287/inte.31.2.90.10630

Morgan, R. M., & Hunt, S. D. (1994). The commitment–trust theory of relationship marketing. *Journal of Marketing*, *58*(3), 20–38. doi:10.1177/002224299405800302

Morin, R. (2016). *The rise of niche and micro-influencers*. Retrieved from https://maximizesocialbusiness.com/the-rise-of-niche-and-micro-influencers-24286/#

Murphy, T., & Schram, R. (2014). What is it worth? The value chasm between brand and influencers. *Journal of Brand Strategy*, *3*(1), 31–40.

Odabaşı, Y. (2017). *Postmodern pazarlama: Tüketim ve tüketici (5. Baskı)*. İstanbul, Turkey: MediaCat Yayınları.

Pinegar, G. (2018). *What is influencer marketing? (+How to identify influencers in 2019)*, Retrieved from https://learn.g2crowd.com/influencer-marketing

Schafer, M. (n.d.). *Word of mouth versus influencer marketing.* Retrieved from https://businessesgrow.com/2018/11/12/difference-between-influencer-marketing-and-word-of-mouth-marketing/

Sheth, J. N. (2002). The future of relationship marketing. *Journal of Services Marketing, 16*(7), 590–592. doi:10.1108/08876040210447324

Sheth, J. N., Gardner, D. M., & Garrett, D. E. (1988). *Marketing theory: Evolution and evaluation*. New York: Wiley.

Sheth, J. N., Sisodia, R. S., & Sharma, A. (2000). The antecedents and consequences of customer-centric marketing. *Journal of the Academy of Marketing Science, 28*(1), 55–66. doi:10.1177/0092070300281006

Shukla, T. (2010). Factors affecting Internet marketing campaigns with reference to viral and permission marketing. *The IUP Journal of Management Research, 9*(1), 26–37.

Srirojanant, S., & Thirkell, P. C. (1998). Relationship marketing and its synergy with web-based technologies. *Journal of Market-Focused Management, 3*(1), 23–46. doi:10.1023/A:1009790421951

Statista. (2017). *Most famous social network sites worldwide as of January 2017, ranked by number of active users (in millions)*. Statista. Retrieved from https://www.statista.com/statistics/272014/global-social-networks-rankedby-number-of-users/

Sudha, M. & Sheena, K. (2017). Impact of influencers in consumer decision process: The fashion industry. *SCMS Journal of Indian Management*, 14-30.

Inflow Summits. (n.d.). *Influencers of the world.* Retrieved from http://inflowsummits.com

Tapinfluence & Nielsen. (2016). *Sales effect study: influencer marketing*. Retrieved from https://pages.tapinfluence.com/hubfs/Nielsen_WhiteWave_Study/1009_-_Nielsen_Study_Case_Study.pdf

Thorne, L. (2008). *Word of mouth advertising online and off: How to spark buzz, excitement, and free publicity for your business or organization—With little or no money*. Florida: Atlantic Publishing Group.

Tzokas, N., & Saren, M. (2004). Competitive advantage, knowledge and relationship marketing: Where, what and how? *Journal of Business and Industrial Marketing*, *19*(2), 124–135. doi:10.1108/08858620410524007

Wallace, B. (2017). *A complete history of influencer marketing and what it means for the future*. Retrieved from https://socialmediaexplorer.com/content-sections/tools-and-tips/complete-history-influencer-marketing-means-future-infographic/

Wang, A. (2018). *Approaching digital marketing in the era of adblock*. Retrieved from https://medium.com/the-qchain-blog/approaching-digital-marketing-in-the-era-of-adblock-909b2a896349

Wilcox, P. A., & Gurau, C. (2003). Business modelling with UML: The implementation of CRM systems for online retailing. *Journal of Retailing and Consumer Services*, *10*(3), 181–191. doi:10.1016/S0969-6989(03)00004-3

ADDITIONAL READING

Kaplan, A. M., & Haenlein, M. (2010). Users of the world, unite! The challenges and opportunities of social media. *Business Horizons*, *53*(1), 59–68. doi:10.1016/j.bushor.2009.09.003

Kim, S. S., Lee, J., & Prideaux, B. (2014). Effect of celebrity endorsement on tourists' perception of corporate ımage, corporate credibility and corporate loyalty. *International Journal of Hospitality Management*, *37*, 131–145. doi:10.1016/j.ijhm.2013.11.003

Litvin, S. W., Goldsmith, R. E., & Pan, B. (2008). Electronic word-of-mouth in hospitality and tourism management. *Tourism Management*, *29*(3), 458–468. doi:10.1016/j.tourman.2007.05.011

Neti, S. (2011). Social media and its role in marketing. *International Journal of Enterprise Computing and Business Systems*, *1*(2), 1–15.

Payne, A. (1994). Relationship marketing: Making the customer count. *Managing Service Quality*, *4*(6), 29–31. doi:10.1108/EUM0000000003939

Wasserman, T. (2013). *So your ad went viral-big deal*. Retrieved from https://mashable.com/2013/12/12/so-your-ad-went-viral-big-deal

Young, K. (2017). *Why influencer marketing works for generation z?* Retrieved from https://wearesocial.com/blog/2017/05/influencer-marketing-worksgeneration-z

KEY TERMS AND DEFINITIONS

Affiliate Marketing: A strategy that an owner of the product gets rid of the cost of advertising and marketing, and the sales partner earns money by advertising a product that does not belong to him/her.

Brand Communication: Using several marketing efforts such as, advertisements, launches and promotions to create and promote a brand image over the target group.

Employee Advocacy: Employees to add value to a brand with their own online assets. In other words, it is the brand's advocacy for employees by using digital tools.

Influencer Marketing: A business strategy through a person who has a certain strength and popularity that influences or changes people's purchasing behavior through social media channels.

Marketing Strategy: Business's overall marketing goals and objectives which designed to reach customers with goods & services for satisfying their needs & wants.

Partner Marketing: A business strategy that collaborates two or more parties (e.g. distributors, resellers, agencies) to develop long term relations for communicating the value of the company's goods and services.

Referral Marketing: A business strategy which also known as, Word-of-Mouth marketing or Viral marketing. A product or service related message, images or videos are transmitted to other consumers verbally or virally through consumers.

Relationship Marketing: A strategy that provides company to establish long-term interactive relationships with its target audience. Company continuously desires to generate value for the customers.

Chapter 4
Customer Engagement Strategies of China's E-Commerce Industry and Their Impact on China's Economy Transition

Liguo Yu
Indiana University South Bend, USA

Alok Mishra
Atilim University, Turkey

ABSTRACT

In the past 15 years, China's e-commerce industry has grown tremendously and become the world's largest e-commerce market. This chapter studies some popular e-commerce companies of China, including Alibaba, JD, and Pindoudou. Specifically, the customer engagement strategies of these companies are described and analyzed. This chapter helps readers understand how various customer engagement strategies of China's e-commerce companies have facilitated the change of their consumers' shopping habits—switching from offline shopping centers to online marketplaces and from cash-based payment to credit-based payment. The success of these customer engagement strategies has contributed to the performance improvement of e-commerce companies and could ultimately assist China to transfer from a production economy to a consumption economy. Moreover, these customer engagement strategies developed in China might also be applied to other e-businesses or marketplaces of different regions, especially developing countries that have a similar economy structure as China.

DOI: 10.4018/978-1-7998-1618-8.ch004

Copyright © 2020, IGI Global. Copying or distributing in print or electronic forms without written permission of IGI Global is prohibited.

INTRODUCTION

China is world's largest e-commerce market. In 2017, its online retail sales reached US $1.15 trillion (Tong, 2018). In comparison, the U.S. consumers spent US $453 billion on the web for retail purchases in 2017 (Zaroban, 2018). In addition, China's e-commerce grows at a much faster rate. In the past several years, it has maintained an average of over 33% annual growth rate on total spending (Tong, 2018). Researchers believe that this is just the beginning. With the extensive urbanization and digitalization throughout the country, in the next 10-15 years, we expect the e-commerce sales in China might surpass its traditional offline retail sales and become the national supporting business.

Looking back, it is worth studying this dramatic transition. Many factors have contributed to the growth of e-commerce in China, such as adoption of smartphones, utilization of 4-G network, growth of middle class, millennial generation becoming the major consumers, and so on. However, one factor should not be underestimated, which is the customer engagement strategies utilized by e-commerce companies to attract and retain customers and eventually to reshape their shopping habits.

Currently, China is undergoing a transition from a production economy to a consumption economy. This fundamental national plan is a critical effort in dealing with its economic challenges both domestically and internationally. During this transition, e-commerce, as a major component of consumption economy, will play a unique role.

This chapter studies the representative e-commerce companies of China. Specifically, we investigate how these companies' customer engagement strategies have helped them promote products and services, grow user base, and encourage user spending. We will also discuss how the booming of e-commerce industry might facilitate China's economic transition. The remaining of the chapter is organized as follows. We first present the background knowledge and methodology of this study, including a brief description of customer engagement and China's economy. Then we describe some representative e-commerce companies of China and their customer engagement strategies. Next, we discuss China's economy transformation. Finally, we conclude the chapter.

BACKGROUND KNOWLEDGE AND RESEARCH METHOLOGY

Customer Engagement

Customer engagement is to encourage customers to buy products or services and share their shopping experience with others to promote further buying opportunities

(Ference, 2017). Advertisement, free trial, and after-sale services are traditional customer engagement strategies, which have been proven effective for offline retail business. Because e-commerce is becoming a new business model built on top of the Internet and virtual market, new customer engagement strategies are introduced in this field. A healthy body of research has been done to study customer engagement in the e-business era, some of which is described below.

Sawhney et al. (2005) considered Internet as a platform for customer engagement. Specifically, they studied the efficiencies of using the Internet to engage customers, such as interactivity, enhanced reach, persistence, speed, and flexibility. Their results suggested that companies should use the capacity of online resources to engage customers.

Srinivasan et al. (2002) studied the antecedents and consequences of customer loyalty in an online B2C (business to consumer) platform. They identified some factors, such as customization, contact interactivity, care, community, and convenience. Some of these factors are unique to e-commerce business. Their study indicated that a well-structured customer engagement strategies could potentially improve customers' loyalty.

Customer engagement is even more important in the e-commerce era (Fang et al., 2014). Not like traditional offline stores that target at local customers, who usually have few choices, ecommerce companies target at customers around the country or around the world. Those remote customers have more choices and are more likely to switch to a different shopping platform. Therefore, it is even more critical for e-commerce companies to engage their customers. Extensive research has been done in this area. For example, Vohra & Bhardwaj (2019) described a conceptual framework for customer engagement in the context of social media for emerging markets. The proposed framework involves the constructs of active participation, community trust, and community commitment in order to engage customers. Bao et al. (2016) investigated the roles of computer-mediated communication tools, interactivity, trust, and other e-engagement mechanisms in influencing customers' repurchase intention.

Word-of-mouth (WOM) is a marketing strategy used to influence and engage customers (Le, Dobele, & Robinson, 2018). Common types of WOM marketing include social media, brand loyalty, and product/service review. WOM is undoubtedly an important customer engagement strategy for e-commerce. For example, Le (2018) studied the influence of WOM on online consumption communities. Lindgreen et al. (2008) studied viral marketing, which encourages customers to pass along a company's marketing messages to family, friends and colleagues for free. Viral marketing is a typical WOM marketing strategy for e-commerce.

Identifying an efficient customer engagement strategy is not easy. To quantitatively evaluate the efficiencies of a customer engagement strategy is even more difficult.

Bijmolt et al. (2010) discussed the state of the art of models for customer engagement. They also addressed the problems that are inherent to calibrating and implementing these models. They also discussed several organizational issues of analytics for customer engagement. These issues are certainly also applicable to e-commerce customer engagement.

China's Economy

Since 1978, China has gradually switched from a planned economy to a market economy, which significantly improved its GDP (Gross Domestic Product) in the following years (Chow, 1994). Especially after China joined WTO (World Trade Organization) in 2001, its GDP (Gross Domestic Product) grew even faster and China finally became the second largest economy next to USA in 2010 (Barboza, 2010). Although China has maintained a high annual GDP growth rate for quite long time, in recent years, its GDP growth rate has dropped significantly from the highest 14% in 2007 to 6.6% in 2018 (National Data, 2019).

The main challenge to China's continual development is its economy structure. In the past years, China's GDP growth is mainly contributed by real estate (Liu & Xiong, 2018), infrastructure development (Tsui, 2011), and manufacturing (Li, 2000). However, after twenty years' expansion, China's real estate and infrastructure development is peaked. Manufacturing industry is also facing difficulties due to trade disputes with other countries.

In order to maintain its economic growth, China must gradually switch from a production economy, which is characterized by real estate, infrastructure development, and manufacturing industry, to a consumption economy, which is characterized by retail, healthcare, entertainment, travel, and hospitality and catering industry (Kenessey, 1987). However, the transitions won't be easy. One of the challenges is customers' consumption habit. Traditionally, China's consumers would like to maintain a high monetary saving rate and if they want to spend money, they would like to purchase a bigger house or a new car, which are representative merchandises of a production economy.

Therefore, it is important for China's customers to change their spending habit so that its economy can successfully transformed to a consumption economy. Fortunately, e-commerce in the past fifteen years has played a significant role in reshaping China customer's shopping habits. In the remaining of this chapter, we will discuss in detail how various customer engagement strategies have been utilized by different e-commerce companies and how e-commerce industry has facilitated China's economy transition.

Table 1. China's e-commerce GMV year by year (in billions of USD)

2012	2013	2014	2015	2016	2017	2018
$157	$285	$420	$570	$705	$945	$1,333

Source: (author)

Research Methodology

The objective of this study is to describe customer engagement strategies utilized by various e-commerce companies of China and analyze their impact on China's economy transformation. Due to data limit, we are not able to perform quantitative analysis. Instead, our study presented in this chapter is based on qualitative analysis. For these successful e-commerce companies, we are going to identify their customer engagement strategies. Again, due to data limit, we are not able to rank these strategies or single out the most effective ones. Instead, all these strategies are treated equally important in this study.

CHINA'S E-COMMERCE COMPANIES

China's e-commerce, like other internet-based industry, has a relative short history (Greeven, & Wei, 2017). Since 2000, Internet has been widely used in China and e-commerce has gradually grown into a new business model. Table 1 shows China's e-commerce GMV (Gross Merchandise Volume) in the past seven years. In 2018, China's total retail sales is US $5,650 billion. Therefore, e-commerce accounts for about 24% of the total retail sales (CIW Team, 2019).

In comparison, consumers of the United States spent $517 billion online in 2018, which represents 14.3% of the total retail sales (Ali, 2019). It can be seen that China's e-commerce not only surpassed USA and became the largest marketplace, but also has a higher percentage of total retail sales. In this section, we will describe several representative e-commerce companies in China and explain how their customer engagement strategies have facilitated the expansion of e-commerce industry in China.

Alibaba

Alibaba is China's Internet giant. It has businesses in e-commerce, logistics, financial services, cloud computing, digital marketing, social media, travel, map, and digital entertainment. In all these businesses, e-commerce is the foundation and core business. In 2018, Alibaba's e-commerce sales reached US $840 billion, which is about 63%

of the total e-commerce sales in China. Alibaba's major e-commerce platforms include Tmall, Taobao, 1688, Aliexpress, and Lazada. Each of these platforms and their customer engagement strategies are described below.

Tmall

Tmall is Alibaba's online B2C (business to consumer) platform (tmall.com). Tmall was first launched in 2008 and as of February 2018, it has accumulated over 500 million monthly active users, 50 thousand stores, and 150 thousand brands. It is important to note here that Tmall stores are known for selling authentic goods from retailers that are authorized by the brand. Example official flagship stores on Tmall include *Kappa*, *Levi's*, *Disney*, *Uniqlo*. In addition, Tmall also provides marketplace for department stores, such as *Macys* and wholesale stores, such as *Costco*.

Tmall is one of the world's most visited websites according to Alexa. In fiscal year 2018, the total GMV (gross merchandise volume) transacted on Tmall reached US $340 billion. Tmall's success is closely tied to its customer engagement strategies as illustrated below.

First, Tmall promotes selling authentic goods on its platform. Only authorized retailers could open a store on Tmall. Once a retailer is reported selling counterfeit products, investigation will be taken immediately and the store will be closed for good if the allegation is confirmed. This strategy assures China's middle class about the product quality sold on Tmall. Therefore, products like baby formula and baby food are among the most in-demand merchandise on Tmall (Havingga et al., 2016).

Second, Tmall has a generous 7-day return policy. Returning a product and getting refund is not an easy thing in China, especially for offline shoppers. Tmall's return policy no doubt encourages customers to try different products online risk-free.

Third, Tmall's Singles' Day Shopping Festival is the most effective event to engage customers (Hu et al., 2014). On November 11 (11/11), the retailers on Tmall will lower their products' price in order to sell more goods. Due to the limited supply on most popular products, customers stay up past midnight to fight for good deals. At the same time, Alibaba will hold an hours-long fashion show to engage shoppers on site and in front of the television. Viewers can use their mobile phones to make immediate orders. Most amazingly, some products can be delivered to customers within several hours. In 2017, Tmall's Singles' Day shopping spree reached US $25.9 billion (Graziani, 2017).

Taobao

Taobao is Alibaba's online C2C (consumer to consumer) platform (taobao.com). Taobao was founded in May 2003. As of August 2018, it has 634 million mobile active monthly users and 576 million mobile active annual users. In addition, Taobao's GMV (gross merchandise volume) reached US $428 billion in 2018 fiscal year (DMR, 2018). It is not questionable that Taobao is the largest online marketplace worldwide (Ou & Davision, 2009). The success of Taobao is undoubtedly associated with its customer engagement strategies, which are detailed below.

First, Taobao transactions are supported by its unique communication App, *TradeManager*, which allows instant communications among buyers, sellers, and market managers (Cui et al., 2016). In addition, Taobao also supports direct chat room functions to allow easy communications between sellers and buyers.

Second, although most shops on Taobao have similar designs, personalized shop is also supported to allow sellers to customize their stores to attract certain customers. In addition, Taobao provides shopping trending data to its sellers through its Taobao Index service (Xu, 2013). This service allows sellers to better target specific consumers with specific products in specific periods or during specific events.

Third, in the past, conducting an online payment transaction in China is not an easy task. With the support of Alipay (Alibaba's payment system), the buyer's payment is transferred to a third party—Alibaba's account first. Once the product is delivered and confirmed by the buyer, the payment is then transferred from Alipay to the seller's account. This mechanism assures the buyers about the delivery of the product and quality of the product (Greeven, 2012). In case the order is not fulfilled or the product does not meet the specification, the consumer can easily get refund.

Taobao has also implemented other customer engagement strategies, such as collaborating with commercial TV channels to create programs to promote their shops and products to customers, introducing VR (virtual reality) shopping to some stores (Zeng & Richardson, 2017). These efforts effectively attracted and retained customers.

1688

1688 is Alibaba's B2B (business to business) platform (1688.com). 1688's main function is to support wholesale and industry level procurement. Products sold on 1688 include raw materials, semi-industrial products, clothing, apparel, and household commodities (Jun et al., 2015). It is important to know that 1688 buyers are mainly from overseas. Currently, products from 1688 have been sold to over 220 countries (Havingga et al., 2016; Sun & Bao, 2010).

The main customer engagement strategies employed by 1688 are described here. First, to improve the buyers' shopping experience, 1688 collaborates with Guangzhou (a major city of China) and hosts trade fairs to showcase the products to interested buyers regularly. Second, in order to provide more accurate information about the sellers, 1688 evaluates the sellers based on customers' feedback and the credit scores will be provided to potential buyers. Third, 1688 works closely with local factories to design and manufacture customized products for buyers. Fourth, buyer and seller networks are established by 1688 to allow participants to share their products and their shopping and consumption experience.

Aliexpress

Aliexpress is Alibaba's international online B2C (business to consumer) platform (aliexpress.com). It was launched in 2010 and the major sellers on Aliexpress are small businesses in China. The buyers are from over 220 countries, among which, Russia and Brazil have the most active consumers. Products sold on Aliexpress include computers, communications and consumer electronics, clothing, furniture, apparel, and automobile accessories (Shia et al., 2016).

The customer engagement strategies utilized on Aliexpress platform include translation service, online communication service, flexible return policy, free shipping for some small packages, and incentive registrations programs (Dehui, 2016). For example, during a holiday or some special events, a new registered Aliexpress customer could receive $5 credit and it can be used to make any purchases.

Lazada

Lazada (lazada.com) is a Southeast Asian e-commerce company founded in 2012. It was acquired by Alibaba Group in 2016. Lazada connects hundred of thousands of local and international sellers with hundred millions of consumers of Southeast Asia through its marketplace platform. Lazada offers a wide range of products in categories such as consumer electronics, toys, clothing, sports equipment and groceries (Sharuddin & Rajagderan, 2018).

Lazada's C2C model allows sellers to ship their products directly to the buyers. This approach is particularly effective for the delivery of food and fresh agricultural products. In addition, to encourage customer shopping, Lazada platform accepts various payment methods, including credit card, cash, Paypal, and Alipay. Furthermore, sellers on Lazada are provided with a wide range of tailored services, such as marketing and data analysis.

Discussions

It is worth to mention that Tmall and Taobao are Alibaba's domestic marketplaces while 1688, Aliexpress, and Lazada are Alibaba's international marketplaces. In 2018, Tmall's total merchandise sales is US $340 billion and Taobao's total merchandise sales is US $428 billion. Together, these two platforms account for about 93% of the totals e-commerce sales conducted through Alibaba. It can be seen that Alibaba's customer engagement strategies are very effective within China's marketplace. Outside of China, Alibaba has more growth potential.

JD.com

JD.com is China's second largest e-commerce company. It operates on a B2C (business to consumer) model. Similar to USA's Amazon, JD.com maintains its own warehouses. Products are ordered from the suppliers and stocked in its warehouses (Yang et al., 2015). In 2018, JD.com's GMV reached US $300 billion. As of August, 2018, JD.com has 314 million monthly active users. Customer engagement plays a central role in helping JD.com achieve its current e-commerce market share in China.

Tencent, an Internet giant of China, is one of the major shareholders of JD.com. Accordingly, *WeChat*, China's most popular social network app owned by Tencent becomes an important advertisement platform for JD.com. Because WeChat has about 1 billion monthly active users, it is easy for JD.com to promote its products to general internet users.

Because JD.com maintains its own warehouses, it can control the shipment of the products (Lu et al., 2016). Specifically, JD.com's warehouses are hierarchically structured. Six major logistics centers are established in six major cities of China across different regions. In addition, product delivery is carried out by JD.com itself. Therefore, free shipping had been a long policy of JD.com in order for it to attract and retain customers.

To compete with Tmall of Alibaba, JD.com implemented its *211 express delivery* policy (Wang & Xiao, 2015). In some cities, an order placed before 11:00am is promised to be delivered to the customer the same day; an order placed after 11:00am will be delivered to the customer before 15:00pm the next day. Similar to Alibaba Tmall's Single's Day Shopping Festival, JD.com has its own annual shopping festival, *618 (June 18) Shopping Festival*. In 2018, JD.com achieved record $24.6 billion in sales during this festival (Pymnts, 2018). In 2019's 618 Shopping Festival, JD.com registered US $31.53 billion worth of orders, representing a year-on-year increase of 26.57 percent (Zhang, 2019).

Last, but not least, JD.com utilizes GIS package tracking system, which allows customers to track their packages on the map in teal time (Li, 2018). This app can also inform customers the expected delivery time, improving their shopping experience.

JD.com customer engagement strategies are successful in supporting its business growth. In 2018, JD.com is ranked the 181th place on the Fortune Global 500 list.

Pinduoduo

Pinduoduo (pinduoduo.com) is China's third largest e-commerce platform. It also operates on a C2C (consumer to consumer) model. Different from JD.com, Pinduoduo does not maintain its own warehouses. It only provides a mobile app platform for sellers and buyers to reach a deal. Products listed on Pinduoduo include daily groceries and home appliances (Cedeno, 2018; Tan & Gao, 2017). The amazing achievement about Pinduoduo is that it was only founded in September 2015. In less than four years, its GMV (gross merchandise volume) reached US $20 billion in 2017 and US $68.6 billion in 2018. The unique success story of Pinduoduo is closely related to its unique customer engagement strategies.

First, Pinduoduo integrates shopping activities into social media. Tencent is also a major shareholder of Pinduoduo. Therefore, Pinduoduo's product information can be shared on *WeChat*, the largest social network in China, through which, customers can form a group to shop in order to get a good deal. Free products could be given to the buyer if he/she could bring some new customers to the platform and register the app. Pinduoduo implemented this strategy through encouraging buyers to share their shopping requests with their friends and their friends can help the buyers reduce the price from several cents to several dollars simply by just clicking the app and browse the advertisement. Because this is an effort-less action, most people do not mind participating in these promotion activities.

Another important feature of the products on Pinduoduo is that most of them are unknown brands or not branded. Often, these products have low qualities. However, because the price is really low (sometime as low as about 10% of similar products on market), the customers do have a low-quality expectation and they seldom complain and return the products.

It is worth noting that Pinduoduo's low price and low-quality products are targeted on low-income customers of small cities and rural areas. These customers account for about 65 percent of Pinduoduo's total user base (Lee, 2018). For them, low-price is a more important factor than high-quality when they make purchasing decisions. Another noticeable effect of Pinduoduo's customer engagement strategies is more and more senior citizen are becoming online shoppers on its platform. These senior citizens are more interested in buying groceries online if the price is attractive. Without promotions from Pinduoduo, they might stay with their offline shopping habit.

Different from Alibaba and JD.com. Pinduoduo also focus on helping farmers to sell their agriculture goods, such as fruit. In addition, using distributed AI algorithm and its *group purchase* model, Pinduoduo was able to identify the growing market demand and help farmers meet the demand (Pinduoduo, 2019).

Pinduoduo's customer engagement strategies are the key factors for its success. Without utilizing these customer engagement strategies, Pinduoduo, like many other startup e-commerce companies in China, would lose its completion to Alibaba and JD.com. For the same reason, Pinduoduo has become a national brand. In 2018, its GMV reached US$68.6 billion, representing an increase of 234 percent from 2017.

Other E-Commerce Companies and Their Customer Engagement Strategies

Besides the aforementioned three major e-commerce companies, there are some other medium scale e-commerce companies in China. In addition, some other internet-based companies, such as NetEase (163.com) also provide e-commerce marketplace services (Liu & Wang, 2018). The customer engagement strategies employed by some of these companies are described here.

Jumei (jumei.com) is a vertical B2C (business to consumer) e-commerce website (Zheng et al., 2017; Wang et al., 2014; Guo et al., 2013)). Its featured products include cosmetics, baby formulas, health supplements, and light luxury goods. One customer engagement strategy adopted by Jumei is to let the users to showcase the products through their social-media platform. For example, a girl could demonstrate lively how to use a beauty product, which could promote the viewers to order this product. Another strategy utilized by Jumei is to give out coupons to potential customers through Jumei's Weibo (micro blog). Weibo, the twitter-like social networking app of China, allows Jumei to reach millions of followers and encourage them to spend on its platform.

Vipshop (vip.com) is also a B2C (business to consumer) e-commerce platform (Lu, 2013; Tao, 2016). Vipshop features on-line discount brand sales. Over 20 thousand brands have cooperated with Vipshop to provide low cost genuine products to consumers. With this engagement strategy, Vipshop has attracted more than 300 million users across China.

Momo (immomo.com) is a location-based social-networking and entertainment app (Ma et al., 2017). No individual e-commerce advertisement is allowed on its platform. Instead, the company creates its own customized & branded products for the platform's cewebrities (celebrities on the web). The products are then promoted to the followers of the cewebrities (celebrities on the web). E-commerce is not the core business of Momo. However, this unique customer engagement strategy could help Momo to easily expand its business to e-commerce.

Table 2. Dominant China's e-commerce platforms and their adoption of major customer engagement strategies

	Tmall (Alibaba)	Taobao (Alibaba)	JD.com	Pinduoduo
Guaranteed authentic product	✓✓✓	✓	✓✓✓	
Generous return policy	✓✓✓	✓✓	✓✓✓	✓
Signature shopping festival	✓✓✓	✓	✓✓✓	
Personal loan	✓	✓	✓	✓
Low price		✓		✓✓✓

Source: (author)

Summary

In this section, we described various customer engagement strategies of China's representative e-commerce companies and analyzed their influential impact. The four dominant e-commerce platforms are Tmall (Alibaba), Taobao (Alibaba), JD.com, and Pinduoduo. In 2018, their total GMV sales is US $1137 billion, which accounts for over 85% of the total e-commerce sales in China. Table 2 illustrates these four platforms and their adoptions of major customer engagement strategies. The number of checkmarks (at most 3) indicates the implementation strength of a policy.

The customer engagement strategies employed by these e-commerce platforms are not exclusive. When a strategy is proved successful, it is quickly adopted by other e-commerce companies. For example, Alibaba Tmall's Single's Day (11/11) Shopping Festival is celebrated by all e-commerce companies in China, including JD.com and Pinduoduo, and JD.com's 618 (June 18) Shopping Festival is also celebrated on Alibaba and Pinduoduo's platforms.

It is worth noting that previously described e-commerce companies have a common property: they all survived the cruel competitions in China's e-commerce market. Without actively design, plan, and employ these strategies, an e-commerce company would not survive in China. Many start-up e-commerce companies were bankrupted due to many reasons and lacking a competitive customer engagement strategy is one of them. In the digital era, shopping is no longer the single goal of shopping online. Entertaining, socializing are among many other byproducts of shopping online.

CHINA'S ECONOMY TRANSFORMATION

As described in Section 2, in order to sustain its economy growth, China is gradually transforming from its previous production economy into a potential consumption economy. During this transition process, e-commerce industry plays a significant role, which is described in more detail below.

First, e-commerce or online shopping makes it so convenient for consumers to purchase their products in need. Supported by online payment system and door-to-door delivery service, e-commerce provides consumers unique shopping experience that cannot be obtained through offline shopping. Therefore, consumers are more willing to open their wallets online.

Second, the online shopping mall is arranged to attract customers for various products. Advertisement, recommended products, and various customer engagement strategies encourage customers to spend more and more. It is quite often that people buy something online that are not really needed, which are partially due to the success of product promotions.

Third, traditionally China is a cash-based economy and customers can spend at most what they have in their pocket. E-commerce, which is based on credit transactions, encourages people to spend using a personal loan even when they have no money in their pocket. China's rising consumer debt might not be good for individuals. However, it certainly benefited manufacture industry, retail companies, and financial institutions and contributed to the growth of consumer spending and national GDP.

Besides customer engagement strategies, there are other factors that have contributed to the growth of e-commerce in China. Some of them are describes below.

- **Urbanization:** Urbanization in China increased dramatically in the past 40 years (Kirkby, 2018). By the end of 2017, 58.52% of the total population of China lived in urban areas, a remarkable increase from 17.92% in 1978. Urbanization basically means that farmers who used to work in agriculture are now moving to cities. They could find a job in the factory. However, it is more likely for them to work in the service industry, such as hospitality and catering industry because of the low training requirement. When affordable and convenient services are available, urban consumers are willing to open their wallets and enjoy these services. At the same time, these new urbanizers could have changed their living style and joined the new generation of consumer groups.
- **Digitalization:** It is no doubt that Internet plays a fundamental role in e-commerce. However, the e-commerce booming in China largely happened after the wide adoption of smartphones. In 2018, the number of smartphone users in China reached 712.8 million, which is about 50% of its 1.42 billion

population. As smartphones are becoming indispensable to their users, shopping online is accordingly becoming a developed habit of them too. E-commerce, together with social networking, game, and media are the most popular mobile app categories in China. For example Alibaba's *Taobao* is among the top 3 most popular smartphone apps in China.

- **Millennials:** Millennials in China are not only willing to open their wallets to buy things online, they are even willing to purchase luxury goods online (Daily, 2019). Millennials in China are also the generation that outdated the concept of debt-free life. They are more willing to take personal loans to shop online. In fact, both Alibaba and JD.com provide personal loans to their customers. JD.com's *Jingdong White Strip* provides a 30-day interest-free loan while Alibaba's *Ant Financial Moonlight* program allows its customers to make the payment one month after they receive the orders.

Retail business is the core concept of consumption economy. The growth of retail business resulted the growth of logistics, financial services, and more. Besides e-commerce, there are also other service-based industries that have contributed to China's economy transformation. Entertainment, education, healthcare, and travel are some of these industries that are playing significant roles in this transformation. For examples, in 2018, entertainment and media industry of China generated US $228 billion sales (PWC, 2016) and healthcare industry of China generated about US $1 trillion sales. In comparison, retail industry of China generated US $565 billion sales. All these numbers represent a steady year to year growth and these industries are becoming the backbone of China's future consumption economy.

China's economy transformation is an ongoing process. There are many challenges and it may take decades for this transition to complete. Although e-commerce in China has expanded so dramatically in the past 15 years, it still has more potential to grow. For example, USA has a population of 320 million and 200 million of them are online shoppers in 2018, which represents a 62% e-commerce penetration rate while China has 1400 million population and 610 million of them are online shoppers in 2018, which represents a 44% e-commerce penetration rate. Accordingly, we expect more consumers in China will join the online shoppers and e-commerce in China could make further impact on its economy transition. In addition to e-commerce, many other domestic and international factors could also affect the success of this transformation. As discussed previously, e-commerce, especially customer engagement, could play a role in this transition.

CONCLUSIONS

This chapter discusses the customer engagement strategies of China's e-commerce industry. It is no doubt that customer engagement is one of the driving forces that have shaped China's e-commerce industry today and enabled China to surpass USA and become the largest e-commerce market in the world. This observation is evident by both transaction volume and buyer base.

Some of the customer engagement strategies described in this chapter could be introduced to other regions of the world. Having said that, we should keep in mind that some strategies are culture-based, which means although they worked well in China, they might not be feasible to other marketplaces.

In addition, some of these discussed customer engagement strategies could also be utilized in other online e-business, such as marketplace lending, peer to peer rental, and mobile payment, etc. For example, Pinduoduo's group shopping promotion strategy is an effective tool to attract new customers for many online businesses.

No consumers, no business; and no active consumers, no successful business. Since business activities are the catalyst of an economy, customers are the final determinant of an economy. Some of the customer engagement strategies described in this chapter could also be applied to other offline businesses. As offline businesses are facing fierce competitions from online businesses, it is even more critical for them to adopt new customer engagement strategies to maintain their market share. For example, a risk-free return policy would never be adopted by offline retail business in China without the competitions from e-commerce companies.

Customer engagement is a kind of advertisement approach. However, it goes beyond product promotion. The new customer engagement strategies are aiming at building a loyal customer base, attracting new members, and providing consumers an enjoyable shopping experience. Technology and Internet have revolutionized our business activities. Many ideas, which were hard to imagine and impossible to implement in the past are now transforming our business, society, and personal lives. It is reasonable to predict that e-commerce, which based on internet and mobile computing will have a dramatic impact on us. E-commerce-based shopping is no longer just a business activity, it is becoming a social activity. Eventually, it not only can contribute to economy transformation, but also can lead to social revolutions.

REFERENCES

AB, M. F., Sharuddin, S. H., & Rajagderan, S. (2018). E-commerce adoption and an analysis of the popular e-commerce business sites in Malaysia. *Journal of Internet Banking and Commerce*, *23*(1), 1–10.

Ali, F. (2019). US ecommerce sales grow 15.0% in 2018, Digital Commerce 360. Available at https://www.digitalcommerce360.com/article/us-ecommerce-sales/

Bao, H., Li, B., Shen, J., & Hou, F. (2016). Repurchase intention in the Chinese e-marketplace: Roles of interactivity, trust and perceived effectiveness of e-commerce institutional mechanisms. *Industrial Management & Data Systems*, *116*(8), 1759–1778. doi:10.1108/IMDS-07-2015-0296

Barboza, D. (2010). China passes Japan as second-largest economy. *The New York Times*, 15.

Bijmolt, T. H., Leeflang, P. S., Block, F., Eisenbeiss, M., Hardie, B. G., Lemmens, A., & Saffert, P. (2010). Analytics for customer engagement. *Journal of Service Research*, *13*(3), 341–356. doi:10.1177/1094670510375603

Cedeno, E. B. (2018, May). Formative model to determine intention to adopt mobile commerce. In *Proceedings of the 2018 International Conference on E-business and Mobile Commerce* (pp. 17–21). ACM. 10.1145/3230467.3230474

Chow, G. C. (1994). *Understanding China's economy*. World Scientific Publishing Company. doi:10.1142/2430

Cui, Y., Niu, J., & Yu, M. (2016). Effect of relationship benefits on satisfaction with an e-commerce communication tool. *Economic Management*, *5*(1), 1–8.

Daily, J. (2019). Why Chinese millennials are willing to max out their cards for luxury goods. *South China Morning Post*. Available at https://www.scmp.com/magazines/style/people-events/article/2178689/can-chinas-debt-ridden-millennial-and-gen-z-shoppers

Dehui, L. (2016). A comparative analysis of B2C cross-border e-commerce platforms: the AliExpress and the DHgate. In *Proceedings of the 2016 International Conference on Education, Management, Computer and Society*. EMCS.

DMR. (2018). 26 Amazing Taobao statistics and facts. Available at https://expandedramblings.com/index.php/taobao-statistics/

Fang, Y., Qureshi, I., Sun, H., McCole, P., Ramsey, E., & Lim, K. H. (2014). Trust, satisfaction, and online repurchase intention: The moderating role of perceived effectiveness of e-commerce institutional mechanisms. *Management Information Systems Quarterly*, *38*(2), 407–427. doi:10.25300/MISQ/2014/38.2.04

Ference, A. (2017). 7 customer engagement strategies that marketers can't ignore. Available at https://www.outbrain.com/blog/3-golden-customer-engagement-strategies-that-marketers-cant-ignore/

Graziani, T. (2017). 2017 single's day sales data, 39% YOY growth on Tmall. Available at https://walkthechat.com/2017-singles-day-sales-data-39-yoy-growth-tmall/

Greeven, M., Yang, S., Yue, T., van Heck, E., & Krug, B. (2012). How Taobao bested Ebay in China. *Financial Times, 12*.

Greeven, M. J., & Wei, W. (2017). *Business ecosystems in China: Alibaba and competing Baidu, Tencent, Xiaomi, and LeEco*. Routledge. doi:10.4324/9781315209142

Guo, Y., Yang, X., Ryabov, Y., & Liu, W. (2013). An empirical research on influencing factors of microblogging marketing effectiveness. *International Journal of u-and e-Service. Science and Technology*, *6*(4), 91–117.

Havinga, M., Hoving, M., & Swagemakers, V. (2016). Alibaba: a case study on building an international imperium on information and e-commerce. In *Multinational management* (pp. 13–32). Cham, Switzerland: Springer. doi:10.1007/978-3-319-23012-2_2

Hu, J., Marques, J., Holt, S., & Camillo, A. A. (2014). Marketing channels and supply chain management in contemporary globalism: e-commerce development in China and its implication for business. In Handbook of research on effective marketing in contemporary globalism (pp. 325–334). Hershey, PA: IGI Global. doi:10.4018/978-1-4666-6220-9.ch018

Jung, J. C., Ugboma, M. A., & Liow, A. K. (2015). Does Alibaba's magic work outside China? *Thunderbird International Business Review*, *57*(6), 505–518. doi:10.1002/tie.21739

Kenessey, Z. (1987). The primary, secondary, tertiary and quaternary sectors of the economy. *Review of Income and Wealth*, *33*(4), 359–385. doi:10.1111/j.1475-4991.1987.tb00680.x

Kirkby, R. J. (2018). *Urbanization in China: town and country in a developing economy 1949-2000 AD*. Routledge.

Le, T. D. (2018). Influence of WOM and content type on online engagement in consumption communities: The information flow from discussion forums to Facebook. *Online Information Review*, *42*(2), 161–175. doi:10.1108/OIR-09-2016-0246

Le, T. D., Dobele, A. R., & Robinson, L. J. (2018). WOM source characteristics and message quality: The receiver perspective. *Marketing Intelligence & Planning*, *36*(4), 440–454. doi:10.1108/MIP-10-2017-0249

Lee, E. (2018). The incredible rise of Pinduoduo, China's newest force in e-commerce. Available at https://techcrunch.com/2018/07/26/the-incredible-rise-of-pinduoduo/

Li, L. X. (2000). An analysis of sources of competitiveness and performance of Chinese manufacturers. *International Journal of Operations & Production Management, 20*(3), 299–315. doi:10.1108/01443570010294307

Li, X. (2018). Development of intelligent logistics in China. In *Contemporary logistics in China* (pp. 181–204). Singapore: Springer. doi:10.1007/978-981-13-0071-4_9

Lindgreen, A., Dobele, A., Beverland, M., & Vanhamme, J. (2008). Viral marketing. In *Marketing metaphors and metamorphosis* (pp. 102–117). London, UK: Palgrave Macmillan. doi:10.1057/9780230227538_7

Liu, C., & Xiong, W. (2018). *China's real estate market (No. w25297)*. National Bureau of Economic Research. doi:10.3386/w25297

Liu, H., & Wang, X. (2018, March). Study on the application of big data in accurate marketing of cross-border e-commerce in China. In *Proceedings of the 3rd International Conference on Big Data Analysis (ICBDA)* (pp. 24–27). IEEE. 10.1109/ICBDA.2018.8367645

Lu, L. (2013). The Chinese market layout and influence of international luxury e-commerce. *International Journal of Digital Content Technology and its Applications, 7*(4), 991.

Lu, Y., Liu, Z., & Ma, L. (2016). Competing through logistics management: Studies on e-retailing in China. In E-retailing challenges and opportunities in the global marketplace (pp. 256–275). Hershey, PA: IGI Global. doi:10.4018/978-1-4666-9921-2.ch014

Ma, M., Zhang, L., Liu, J., Wang, Z., Li, W., Hou, G., & Sun, L. (2017, June). Characterizing user behaviors in mobile personal livecast. In *Proceedings of the 27th Workshop on Network and Operating Systems Support for Digital Audio and Video* (pp. 43–48). ACM. 10.1145/3083165.3083169

National Data. (2019). Retrieved from http://data.stats.gov.cn/english/

Ou, C. X., & Davison, R. M. (2009). Technical opinion. Why eBay lost to TaoBao in China: The Glocal advantage. *Communications of the ACM, 52*(1), 145–148. doi:10.1145/1435417.1435450

Pinduoduo. (2019). Pinduoduo's AI-driven duo duo farm empowers farmers, helping to alleviate poverty in rural areas. Available at http://investor.pinduoduo.com/corporate-blog/pinduoduos-ai-driven-duo-duo-farm-empowers-farmers-helping

PWC. (2016). China entertainment and media outlook. Available at https://www.pwccn.com/en/entertainment-media/em-china-outlook-nov2016.pdf

Pymnts. (2018). JD.Com rakes in $24.6b during 618 shopping festival. Available at https://www.pymnts.com/news/ecommerce/2018/jdcom-618-shopping-festival-china/

Sawhney, M., Verona, G., & Prandelli, E. (2005). Collaborating to create: The Internet as a platform for customer engagement in product innovation. *Journal of Interactive Marketing*, *19*(4), 4–17. doi:10.1002/dir.20046

Shia, B. C., Chen, M., & Ramdansyah, A. D. (2016). Measuring customer satisfaction toward localization website by WebQual and importance performance analysis (case study on AliexPress Site in Indonesia). *American Journal of Industrial and Business Management*, *6*(02), 117–128. doi:10.4236/ajibm.2016.62012

Srinivasan, S. S., Anderson, R., & Ponnavolu, K. (2002). Customer loyalty in e-commerce: An exploration of its antecedents and consequences. *Journal of Retailing*, *78*(1), 41–50. doi:10.1016/S0022-4359(01)00065-3

Sun, X., & Bao, J. (2010, August). Research on the innovation and development of the third-party B2B e-commerce model of China. In *Proceedings of the 3rd International Conference on Advanced Computer Theory and Engineering (ICACTE)* (Vol. 4, pp. V4–317). IEEE.

Tan, L., & Gao, Y. (2017). The analysis of consumer behavior of fresh-products e-business—based on research in Chengdu. In *Proceedings of the 16th Wuhan International Conference on e-Business.*

Tao, Y. (2016). Survey on e-commerce development in areas inhabited by ethnic minorities of Qujing city, Yunnan province, based on computer data analysis. *Revista Ibérica de Sistemas e Tecnologias de Informação*, (E11), 239.

Team, C. I. W. (2019). China retail market overview 2018; rural areas grew by 10.1%, online retail up 24%, China Internet Watch. Retrieved from https://www.chinainternetwatch.com/28092/retail-2018/

Tong, F. (2018). Online retail sales in China soar past $1 trillion in 2017. Available at https://www.digitalcommerce360.com/2018/02/08/online-retail-sales-china-soar-past-1-trillion-2017/

Tsui, K. Y. (2011). China's infrastructure investment boom and local debt crisis. *Eurasian Geography and Economics*, *52*(5), 686–711. doi:10.2747/1539-7216.52.5.686

Vohra, A., & Bhardwaj, N. (2019). Customer engagement in an e-commerce brand community: An empirical comparison of alternate models. *Journal of Research in Interactive Marketing*, *13*(1), 2–25. doi:10.1108/JRIM-01-2018-0003

Wang, B., Li, S., & Liu, J. (2014). Assessing enterprise microblogging marketing communication effectiveness and improvement suggestions. *Journal of Chemical and Pharmaceutical Research*, *6*(6), 426–430.

Wang, J. J., & Xiao, Z. (2015). Co-evolution between retailing and parcel express industry and its geographical imprints: The case of China. *Journal of Transport Geography*, *46*, 20–34. doi:10.1016/j.jtrangeo.2015.05.005

Xu, W. J. (2013). Strategy study on China e-business service in big data era. Trans Tech Publications. *Advanced Materials Research*, *798*, 983–986. doi:10.4028/www.scientific.net/AMR.798-799.983

Yang, S., Chen, Y., & Wei, J. (2015). Understanding consumers' web-mobile shopping extension behavior: A trust transfer perspective. *Journal of Computer Information Systems*, *55*(2), 78–87. doi:10.1080/08874417.2015.11645759

Zaroban, S. (2018). US e-commerce sales grow 16.0% in 2017. Available at https://www.digitalcommerce360.com/article/us-ecommerce-sales/

Zeng, W., & Richardson, A. (2017). Using immersive virtual reality to create presence in online shopping. In *Australasian Conference on Information Systems.*

Zhang, J. (2019). Shopping festival '618' registers record-breaking numbers. Available at http://www.chinadaily.com.cn/a/201906/19/WS5d09d0cca3103dbf1432919b.html

Zheng, C., Yu, X., & Jin, Q. (2017). How user relationships affect user perceived value propositions of enterprises on social commerce platforms. *Information Systems Frontiers*, *19*(6), 1261–1271. doi:10.100710796-017-9766-y

ADDITIONAL READINGS

Cheung, K. W., Kwok, J. T., Law, M. H., & Tsui, K. C. (2003). Mining customer product ratings for personalized marketing. *Decision Support Systems*, *35*(2), 231–243. doi:10.1016/S0167-9236(02)00108-2

Elliott, S. (2002). *Electronic Commerce: B2C strategies and models*. John Wiley & Sons.

Goldfarb, A., Greenstein, S. M., & Tucker, C. E. (2015). *Economic Analysis of the Digital Economy*. University of Chicago Press. doi:10.7208/chicago/9780226206981.001.0001

Haig, M. (2001). *The B2B E-Commerce Handbook: How to Transform Your Business-to-Business Global Marketing Strategy*. Kogan Page Publishers.

Hashemi, S., & Hashemi, B. (2004). *Anyone Can Do It: Building Coffee Republic from Our Kitchen Table-57 Real-Life Laws on Entrepreneurship*. John Wiley & Sons.

Hunt, B. (2011). *Convert: Designing Web Sites to Increase Traffic and Conversion*. John Wiley & Sons. doi:10.1002/9781118255827

Kelly, K. (2005). We are the Web. *Wired Magazine, 13*(8), 113–123.

King, D., & Lee, J. (2000). *Electronic Commerce: A Managerial Perspective* (Vol. 1). Upper Saddle River, NJ: Prentice Hall.

King, K. A. (2015). *The Complete Guide to B2B Marketing: New Tactics, Tools, and Techniques to Compete in the Digital Economy*. Pearson Education.

Leeflang, P. S., Verhoef, P. C., Dahlström, P., & Freundt, T. (2014). Challenges and solutions for marketing in a digital era. *European Management Journal, 32*(1), 1–12. doi:10.1016/j.emj.2013.12.001

Liu, S., & Avery, M. (2009). *Alibaba: The Inside Story behind Jack Ma and the Creation of the World's Biggest Online Marketplace*. Collins Business.

Markoff, J. (2005). *What the Dormouse Said: How the Sixties Counterculture Shaped the Personal Computer Industry*. Penguin.

Milanovic, B. (1998). *Income, inequality, and poverty during the transition from planned to market economy* (p. p-237). Washington, DC: World Bank.

Mohlmann, M. (2015). Collaborative consumption: Determinants of satisfaction and the likelihood of using a sharing economy option again. *Journal of Consumer Behaviour, 14*(3), 193–207. doi:10.1002/cb.1512

Monteiro, J., Swatman, P. M., & Tavares, L. V. (2003). *Towards the Knowledge Society: Ecommerce, Ebusiness and Egovernment*. Springer. doi:10.1007/978-0-387-35617-4

Nahai, N. (2014). *Website Branding for Small Businesses: Secret Strategies for Building a Brand, Selling Products Online, and Creating a Lasting Community*. Skyhorse Publishing, Inc.

Palmer, C. (1988). Using IT for competitive advantage at Thomson Holidays. *Long Range Planning*, *21*(6), 26–29. doi:10.1016/0024-6301(88)90155-0

Plant, R. T. (2000). *Ecommerce: Formulation of Strategy*. Prentice Hall PTR.

Rayport, J. F., & Jaworski, B. J. (2002). *Introduction to E-Commerce*. McGraw-Hill/Irwin.

Roberts, M., & Zahay, D. (2012). *Internet Marketing: Integrating Online and Offline Strategies*. Cengage Learning.

Stone, B. (2013). *The Everything Store: Jeff Bezos and the Age of Amazon*. Random House.

Sung, T. K. (2006). E-commerce critical success factors: East vs. West. *Technological Forecasting and Social Change*, *73*(9), 1161–1177. doi:10.1016/j.techfore.2004.09.002

Tkacz, E., & Kapczynski, A. (2009). *Internet-Technical Development and Applications* (Vol. 64). Springer Science & Business Media. doi:10.1007/978-3-642-05019-0

Turban, E., King, D., & Wang, J. (2003). *Introduction to E-Commerce*. Upper Saddle River, New Jersey: Prentice Hall.

Watson, P. (2006). *Ideas: a History of Thought and Invention, from Fire to Freud*. Harper Perennial.

KEY TERMS AND DEFINITIONS

B2B (Business-to-Business): An e-commerce activity involves two business.

B2C (Business-to-Consumer): An e-commerce activity in which a product is sold by a business and to a consumer.

C2C (Consumer-to-Consumer): An e-commerce activity in which a product is sold by one consumer to another consumer.

Consumption Economy: The GDP (Gross Domestic Production) of a region or country is mainly contributed by service-based industry, such as retail, healthcare, entertainment, and hospitality and catering.

E-Commerce: An Internet-based trading activity.

E-Commerce Penetration Rate: The percentage of population that conduct online shopping on a region in a period of time.

GDP (Gross Domestic Production): The total a monetary value of all the products and services produced in a specific time period of a region or country.

GMV (Gross Merchandise Volume): The total sales of the values of products by a retailer in a specific period of time.

Market Economy: An economic system in which production and the pricing of goods and services are guided by the interactions of individual citizens and businesses.

Planned Economy: An economic system in which the government controls and regulates production and consumption.

Production Economy: The GDP (Gross Domestic Production) of a region or country is mainly contributed by agriculture, manufactory, and construction industry.

Social E-Commerce: An e-commerce built on top of social networking platforms, where products/services are sold to friends or followers in the social network.

Vertical E-Commerce: A website that sells a specific category of products.

Chapter 5
Online Purchase and Advertising in Latin America:
A Consumer Comparison Among Mexico and Colombia

Mauricio Sabogal Salamanca
https://orcid.org/0000-0002-2633-731X
Universidad EAN, Colombia

Carlos Hernán Fajardo-Toro
https://orcid.org/0000-0003-4596-9627
Universidad EAN, Colombia

Juan Carlos Renteria
https://orcid.org/0000-0003-1061-6039
Universidad EAN, Colombia

Yesica Mayett Moreno
Universidad Popular Autónoma del Estado de Puebla, Mexico

Laura Berenice Sanchez Baltasar
Universidad Popular Autónoma del Estado de Puebla, Mexico

ABSTRACT

Online advertising has become an important part of marketing investment for firms around the globe. With the increasing use of these tools, concerns have arisen around their effectiveness. For that reason, recent research has focused on measuring online advertising effectiveness with different metrics and for different markets and categories, with a focus on the profitability of advertising. However, only a few intend to understand advertisement usefulness for consumers. Particularly, in Latin

DOI: 10.4018/978-1-7998-1618-8.ch005

Copyright © 2020, IGI Global. Copying or distributing in print or electronic forms without written permission of IGI Global is prohibited.

America, not many studies measure the usefulness or preferences of advertising. This chapter tries to close that gap. Using a survey applied to samples in Mexico and Colombia, authors analyse different online purchase behavior and advertising perceived usefulness and preferences. The results have implications for improving the firm´s online advertising strategy and for future research, which aims to conduct comparative studies in the field of advertising usefulness.

INTRODUCTION

Advertising on the Internet allows segmentation of audiences in a way that was nearly impossible in the pre-Internet era. This is where the main advantages of online advertising reside. Chaffey & Ellis-Chadwick (2014) identifies several digital media communication channels, and among them, there are three specially devoted to communicating the firm's value proposition: (1) Search Marketing; (2) Interactive Ads, and (3) Opt-in E-mail.

Some studies (Hyejin & Huh, 2017; Rzemieniak, 2015; Wang & Sun, 2010) are trying to measure online advertising effectiveness, using the information of websites, mainly e-commerce platforms, that collects information of purchases, traffic sources such as banners, social media, e-mails and demographic profiles of buyers.

The effectiveness of advertising is measured as the percentage or ratio of success of each given advertising related to advertising investment, traffic generated or other similar metrics (De Haan, Wiesel & Pauwels, 2016). However, and mostly in Latin America, there are not so many studies that try to measure the usefulness or preferences of advertising for different markets or categories from the perspective of the consumer.

The aim of the chapter is trying to describe some of the existing relationships between the purchase process, the perceived usefulness and preferences for advertising in two Latin American countries, in order to understand if there is some advertising recognized as more useful, depending different aspects of the purchase decision. The study was conducted with 552 valid respondents at Bogotá (Colombia) and Puebla (México). This chapter starts with a background on the digital marketing and online advertising state of the art, including secondary sources information of both countries, in a following part are described the general results of the survey in terms of points of purchase, categories, frequency of purchase, influence of specific groups and advertising usage and preferences. Last part includes some conclusions and recommendations for future studies.

BACKGROUND

Digital Marketing and Online Advertising

Since 2017, the penetration of the Internet worldwide was 48,67% (The World Bank, n.d.), which proves the Internet is not a communication mean for a niche. It is broadly adopted now, and among the business processes, marketing might be the one that has been disrupted the most by it. At some degree, it is hard to imagine bringing something new to the market without considering using the Internet. This wide adoption of Internet brought the Digital Marketing, which Chaffey (2016) defines as using digital technologies to achieve marketing objectives such as the "profitable acquisition and retention of customers… within a multi-channel buying process and customer lifecycle" through a plethora of digital marketing tactics. In a more simplified way, one could say that Digital Marketing is the use of Information and Communication Technologies (ICT) to achieve marketing objectives. There are three main uses of the Internet on this regard:

- To promote the value proposition, better known as Online Advertising.
- To deliver the value proposition, better known as E-Commerce.
- To build strong relationships with customers, better known as Social Media Marketing

Online Advertising: Using the Internet to Promote the Value Proposition

Search Engine Marketing is the process to make products and services more easily "findable" online through search engines (Sen, 2005; Stokes, 2018). Google alone processes nearly 40,000 search queries every second and this number grows 10% annually (Internet Live Stats, n.d.). Search engine marketing is also "an effective means of encouraging website traffic and impacting important goals such as sales, inquiries, sign-ups, or conversion-oriented behaviors" (Clarke, Murphy, Wetsch, & Boeck, 2018). Furthermore, there is strong evidence on the correlation between sales and search traffic, especially in consumer durable goods (Jun & Park, 2016).

There are two ways that appear when searching in result pages: first using paid advertising with search terms, also called "keywords" to find something of interest, the advertiser then pays the search engine to show text adverts at the beginning of the search results. The second one is continuously improving the way search engines crawl one's website so, it appears on top of the search results, something that is better known as "Search Engine Optimization" or SEO(Sen, 2005).

Interactive ads include placing different advert formats in order "to increase sales, improve brand awareness, engage customers, and raise the share of voice in the marketplace" (Stokes, 2018). Interactive ads can be found anywhere on the web, on PCs and mobile devices such as tablets and smartphones. This kind of advertising follows web user behavior.

Among different types of advert formats there are the following: (1) display or banner ads that people can click on to get more information about the product or service advertised; they appear on content and social media sites; (2) video ads that a person can see when watching video content online on specialized sites as YouTube. Video ads are inserted at the beginning, during or at the end of the video content, but they are placed embedded in banner ads as well. Because of the connected nature of the Internet, online activities are highly trackable and measurable, which makes it possible to target adverts and to track and gauge the efficacy of the advertising accurately (Stokes, 2018; Tutaj & van Reijmersdal, 2012).

Opt-in E-mails and E-mail Marketing are electronic messages delivered to the user's inbox after his voluntary subscription to the corresponding distribution list. E-mail shares a particularly close relationship with the Internet, with most Internet sessions involving the use of e-mail (Reimers, Chao, & Gorman, 2016). There is a strong relationship between e-mail marketing and sales online; this is because both serve to drive website traffic, but they also influence impulse buying on online websites (Reimers, Chao, & Gorman, 2016). One aspect that makes E-mail so relevant in marketing is its reach and the possibility of personalization of the relationship with the recipient. However, finding optimal e-mail frequency is challenging for businesses because it "may differ across customers and over time" (Zhang, Kumar, & Cosguner, 2017). In 2018 global e-mail users amounted 3,800 million users and this figure is expected to grow to 4,400 million users in 2023 (Statista, 2019). Thus, it is not surprising why e-mail, which started alongside the Internet, is still one important tactical tool in digital marketing.

E-Commerce: Using the Internet to Deliver the Value Proposition

According to Laudon & Traver (2019), E-commerce is defined as "the use of the Internet, the web and apps to transact business. More formally, digitally enabled commercial transactions between and among organizations and individuals."

E-commerce have not stop growing since the first transaction in the mid 1990's. Even more, by 2022 global e-commerce is expected to reach USD $5.8 trillion growing globally at more than a 20% compound annual growth rate through 2022, of that amount, 17.3% is expected to come from B2C (Business-to-Consumer) E-Commerce in 2022 starting from 10.2% in 2018 (Forbes, 2018 citing 451 Research, 2018) as seen in Table 1.

Table 1. Digital commerce's share of global B2C sales 2018-2022

Year	B2C Expected Share
2018	10.2%
2019	11.7%
2020	13.5%
2021	15.3%
2022	17.3%

Source: Forbes, 2018 citing 451 Research, 2018

Using the Internet to deliver the value proposition is challenging for marketing professionals. The value proposition of the digital channel would be different from the traditional commerce activities, but there are other challenges in logistics, electronic payments, and direct sales process, which require the use of different tools, methods and strategies (Szymanski & Stanislawski, 2018).

The fact that in most online B2C transactions the consumer never meets his provider, it makes delivering value more difficult. However, business are transforming those challenges in opportunities through a new kind of commerce: Omnichannel commerce. Kaczorowska-Spychalska (2017) defines Omnichannel commerce as "a concept based on complementarity enabling to increase conversion as a result of the synergy of sales conducted in a number of channels". Meaning that business needs to integrate different channels to increase sales facilitating the experience when going from one channel to the other.

Another phenomenon drives faster adoption of Omnichannel strategies: the ROPO effect. ROPO stands for Research Online Purchase Offline. and it happens when consumers primarily surf the web for information on a product or service but make the purchase at a physical store (Szymanski & Stanislawski, 2018). Some ROPO effect studies show that as many as 77.11% of respondents in Poland (Szymanski & Stanislawski, 2018) and 76% in Colombia (The-Cocktail-Analysis, 2013) behaves as the ROPO effect suggests.

Social Media Marketing: Using the Internet to Build Strong Relationships With Customers

According to Hootsuite (2019), active social media users globally accounts for nearly 3.5 billion, meaning 45% of the population. This kind of penetration is difficult to see in other technologies; this is why social media has become cumbersome in marketing strategy. Social Media platforms such as Facebook, Instagram, or LinkedIn serve for two main purposes: (1) to communicate business' value proposition through advertising; and (2) to build strong relationships with customers. This way marketing professionals can and should use social media platforms to understand the customers´ needs and desires, which lead to "influence consumers to buy products" (Boon-Long & Wongsurawat, 2015; Bleier & Eisenbeiss, 2015).

Purchase Decision

According to Cheng and Chang (2003) interactivity, transactions, and accomplishment of the online sale are the main factors in the online shopping process for consumer's experience. Interactivity is characterized by its strong association with overall satisfaction, also the quality of Internet service providers has a significant effect in the Internet shopping experience; their convenience has a fundamental benefit. Finally, fulfillment (performance) is a factor that cannot be ignored, it is an important means to improve one´s confidence in online transactions. Furthermore, superior quality provides greater satisfaction for consumers.

Pentina, Amialchuk, and George (2011) studied five categories of online shopping experiences. They have applied a methodological triangulation approach in order to identify which online shopping experiences affect browser satisfaction as well as the store´s performance. They confirmed the main role that an efficient browser has in increasing sales and traffic in online stores. According to their results, improving relational and interactive/engagement experiences on a website will increase the satisfaction of visitors in webpages, as well as their shopping, but will not necessarily induce immediate purchases. Finally, satisfying experiences might intensify positive word-of-mouth and lead to repeated visits, thus increasing online sales by affecting both unique and traffic volume (Kasabov, 2016).

Types of Effects of Online Advertising in Different Types of Advertising

Many studies have centered in understanding the relationship between online advertising in several ways. Bruner & Kumar (2000) developed a study for webpages, suggesting a complex hierarchy of the impact in attitudes toward them, where complexity of the webpage plays an important role. Other studies analyses the effect of banner advertising. Finding out that the presence of animation, color, incentives and interactivity has positive and negative effects according click-through rates (CTR), depending of the type of business, B2C or B2B (Lohtia, Donthu, & Hershberger, 2003). Other studies have shown that banners have a positive effect on sales mediated by the number of exposures, with differences depending on if there are current or new customers ((Manchanda, Dubé, Goh, & Chintagunta, 2006). Studies with other different formats such as banners and skyscrapers are more related with the effect of animation in perception and memory, finding positive correlation but conditioned to ad format (Kuisma, Simola, Uusitalo, & Öörni, 2010). Lastly, some studies find that visual design of advertising, can have a positive effect on positive advertising and brand attitudes; however, they do not have a positive effect on the purchasing intention (Shaouf, Lü, and Li, 2016).

Interaction emerges as a strategic key in advertising of Internet 2.0. It is important to consider interaction´s theory needs, its structure, as well as its actor´s goals for engaging. In sum, to take interaction as a unit of analysis, and effectiveness of the communication metrics (Stewart & Pavlou, 2002). Social media studies also have focused in understanding YouTube, implying that entertainment, informativeness and customization are the strongest positive drivers, while irritation is negatively related to ads in this social media network (Dehghani, Niaki, Ramezani, & Sali, 2016). Studies for the Facebook platform have shown that advertising on that platform affects brand image and brand equity, both related to a positive change in purchasing intention (Dehghani & Tumer, 2015).

Web behavioral advertising, the one that shows the relate customer according their past Internet behaviors, is recently researched again, and reported as both useful and privacy-invasive by some attitude studies, influenced by previous beliefs of the type of data that is collected from the user (Ur, Leon, Cranor, Shay, & Wang, 2012).

Online Shopping Environment

Global Behavior

The expansion of the Internet has impacted the shop process worldwide. The complex technology of the Internet infrastructure gives new opportunities for different generations and products, in order to increase consumers´ satisfaction while they buy online. According to KPMG (2017), Generation X (born between 1966 and 1981) made more online purchases in 2016 and 2017 than any other generation (nearly an average of 19 transactions annually), and 20% more purchases than Millennials.

If we compare online global sales with traditional ones, we can observe that books, music, movies and video games are purchased online compared whit those bought in-store (60% versus 28%, respectively); this is the same with online toys acquisition on internet (39%). In other categories, store shopping is higher with percentages that range from 44% to 70% (Table 2.).

Internet Penetration and Online Profile in Colombia and Mexico

Table 3 shows some statistics related with Internet indexes, according internet growth and penetration. Population in Colombia is about 49,6 million, while its

Table 2. Online shopping compared with traditional shopping worldwide (percentages)

Category	Online	In-store
Books. music, movies & video games	60	28
Toys	39	37
Consumer electronics & computers	43	51
Sports equipment/outdoor	36	44
Health and beauty	37	47
Clothing and footwear	40	51
Jewelry/ watches	32	49
Household appliances	33	56
DIY/home improvement	30	52
Furniture & homeware	30	59
Grocery	23	70

Source: Global Ecommerce Report. Ecommerce Foundation, 2018.

Internet presence is near 68% in 2019. E-shoppers are about 10% of those people; and social media users are about 57%. Internet connections grew, as well as the use of smartphones, led to the increase of online transactions (Statista, 2018).

Regard the social media, in Colombia, is utilized to promote e-commerce websites and it is a very powerful communication tool. This trend is being capitalized by some companies who use social media to reach more customers in order to promote their brands. Facebook, Twitter, Instagram, Pinterest, and Youtube are the most popular social media platforms. On the other hand, Amazon has expanded its presence in South America, opening its first customer service center in Colombia. The favorite method of payment of online Colombian´s purchases is 2Checkout and DineroMail. Mercado Libre, which is the first established website and favorite shopping one (Minted, 2018).

In Mexico, whose population reached 131.5 million, the Internet presence is about 67% and 31% are considered e-shoppers (Marketing Society, 2018). The market will continue growing because its connectivity improvements, enhanced financial inclusion, more streamlined logistics, and increased digital literacy. Multichannel retailers have seen their online sales grew 25% of overall sales. Mexico has an important number of shopping events, where retailers offer special prices and promotions. The top international E-retailers or marketplaces in this country include Mercado Libre, Amazon, Liverpool, and eBay. Additionally, Mexicans prefer PayPal and Mercado Pago. A very important event in 2018 was Cyber Monday, with about US $7,800 million in sales (CNET, 2018).

Table 3. Different internet indicators – comparison between Colombia and Mexico

	Colombia			Mexico		
Population, Growth Rate (%) and Urbanization as a Percentage of Total Population	49,6 MM	0.8%	81%	131.5 MM	1.2%	80%
Mobile Subscriptions, Percentage of the Population and Growth (%)	57.4 MM	116%	1.5%	110,7 MM	84%	3.2%
Internet Users, Penetration (%) and Growth (%)	34 MM	68%	9.7%	88 MM	67%	6%
Active Social Media Users, Penetration (%) and Growth	34 MM	68%	9.7%	88 MM	67%	6%
Mobile Social Media Users, Penetration (%) and Growth	31	62%	6.9%	84 MM	64%	7.7%

All growth rates are annual, from January 2018 to January 2019. Penetration is the total type of users divided by the total population. MM = Millions

Source: (Hootsuite, 2019b) and (Hootsuite, 2019c)

RESULTS AND ANALYSIS

Description of the Survey

Two samples have been used for this study, one for each country, 295 in Colombia and 257 in Mexico. The sample size was defined non-probabilistically, a convenience sampling method but the sampling units were selected randomly. The two samples, as mentioned before, are from students, administrative staff and professors of Universidad EAN (Bogotá, Colombia), and Universidad UPAEP (Puebla, México). Demographic features are shown in Figure 1.

Figure 1. Descriptive statistics of demographic features

	GENDER			AGE RANGE				MARITAL STATUS					HAVE CHILDREN		
	N-A	M	F	10-19	20-29	30-39	40-49	0	1	2	3	4	N-A	YES	NO
COLOMBIA	2,0%	45,8%	52,2%	36,8%	52,8%	8,7%	1,7%	2,4%	88,1%	5,4%	3,4%	0,7%	4,4%	5,8%	89,8%
MEXICO	1,6%	52,9%	45,5%	17,9%	73,7%	6,4%	2,0%	1,9%	88,3%	7,0%	2,3%	0,4%	5,4%	5,4%	89,1%

	EDUCATION LEVEL								OCUPATION					
	0	1	2	3	4	5	6	7	0	1	2	3	4	5
COLOMBIA	2,0%	0,0%	0,7%	1,7%	57,6%	29,8%	7,5%	0,7%	15,3%	35,9%	14,9%	32,5%	1,4%	0,0%
MEXICO	3,1%	0,8%	0,4%	0,4%	49,8%	38,9%	3,5%	3,1%	15,6%	16,3%	15,6%	8,9%	1,9%	41,6%

Marital Status: 0= Don't Answer, 1 =Single, 2= Married, 3 = cohabitating, 4 = divorced, 5 = widow

Have children: 0 = don't answer, 1 = yes, 2=no

Education level: 0 = don't answer, 1= preschool, 2=elementary, 3= junior high, 4=high school, 5 = university, 6 = diploma or specialization, 7=master degree, 8= PhD

Occupation: 0= don't answer, 1= employee, 2= independent, 3=unemployed, 4= house work

Source: the authors

The first step was to establish differences between the samples of the two countries using the chi-squared test. Some statistically significant differences were found between the two samples. Mexican respondents are slightly older and there are more Mexican from graduate school compared to Colombians. Regarding the occupation, there are more Colombians working and studying than the Mexicans. All the statistics were performed using SPSS 25 Version.

Point of Purchase

Most Frequently Online Purchased Categories

Respondents were asked about their frequency of purchase online among 20 different categories (see table 4). The most frequent types for Colombia and Mexico are Clothes and Accessories, Airplane Tickets, Apps and Games, Events and Entertainment, Hotel Reservations, Public Services, Streaming, and Loans Payment. According to BlackSip.com, for Colombians the category Entertainment and Tourism (including Tickets for Airplanes, Events, and Entertainment, as well as Hotel Reservations) had participation of 27.48% of all online transactions in 2017, becoming the first category in importance (BlackSip, 2017). In Mexico, this category is also very important, given the fact that 35% of the online shoppers made a travel purchase in 2017 (Asociación de Internet, 2018).

According to a survey conducted by Hootsuite (2019a, 2019b), the average daily time spent listening to streaming music was of 1.02 hours for Colombia and 1.26 hours for Mexico, in 2018. The average daily time of broadcast, streaming and video on demand for Colombians was of 3.12 hours and 2.53 hours for Mexicans in the same year. For the total percentage of Internet users who stream different types of content monthly, 64% streamed TV content via the Internet in Colombia, and 79% in Mexico. Meanwhile 8,5% and 9,9% played games streamed live via Internet respectively in both countries, as well as 27% and 22% watched live streams of other playing games. This data also supports how important it is for both countries

Table 4. Frequency of online purchase by category and country and significance level differences (X2) by country

Category - % of More or Less Frequent Category purchased	Colombia			Mexico			X2
	Not Purchased	Less % (1 and 2)	More % (4 and 5)	Not Purchased	Less % (1 and 2)	More % (4 and 5)	
PC	26,4%	51,9%	7,8%	24,1%	54,1%	10,5%	0,216
Home and Garden	35,3%	44,9%	5,8%	40,5%	47,9%	3,9%	0,410
Clothe and Accessories	15,3%	31,9%	29,8%	16,3%	38,1%	24,1%	0,499
Cellphone and Telephone	31,5%	34,6%	14,2%	32,3%	40,1%	12,8%	0,250
Electronics	32,5%	38,3%	12,2%	31,5%	42,0%	11,3%	0,725
Vehicle Accessories	48,1%	42,4%	5,4%	44,7%	40,1%	8,6%	0,371
Airline Tickets	8,8%	20,7%	49,5%	11,3%	28,4%	43,2%	0,033
Apps and Games	13,6%	24,7%	44,7%	7,4%	21,0%	49,8%	0,108
Events and Entertainment	13,6%	26,8%	37,6%	16,7%	30,7%	35,8%	0,086
Sports	41,0%	37,6%	9,2%	41,6%	41,6%	8,6%	0,556
Restaurants	24,7%	34,9%	22,0%	35,8%	37,0%	13,2%	0,014
Supermarket Food	36,3%	43,4%	9,2%	47,5%	37,0%	5,1%	0,052
Other Supermarket Groceries	42,0%	40,3%	6,4%	46,3%	39,7%	7,0%	0,363
Hotel Reservations	14,2%	21,7%	44,7%	16,3%	35,8%	29,2%	0,000
Public Services	28,1%	24,1%	33,2%	25,7%	32,7%	24,1%	0,045
Personal Care Products	40,3%	41,0%	7,5%	43,2%	38,1%	8,6%	0,822
Books and Magazines	33,6%	36,3%	13,6%	28,0%	38,9%	19,1%	0,420
Streaming (Music and TV)	19,3%	27,1%	38,0%	14,4%	22,6%	43,2%	0,216
Education	24,7%	39,3%	15,3%	31,9%	37,4%	14,4%	0,346
Loans Payment	28,1%	25,1%	33,9%	31,1%	28,0%	23,0%	0,070

Frequency of Purchase: Likert Scale where 1=less frequent and 5=most frequent
Source: the authors

this type of entertainment, but also reflects how those activities are relatively more important in Mexico compared to Colombia.

According to the Chi-Squared test, some significant differences were found among countries. Airline tickets as well as Hotel Reservations categories are more frequent to be purchased online in Colombia, while restaurants are more common to be purchased in Mexico (See Table 3).

Table 5. Percentage of Respondents that Purchased or not Different Categories by Type of Channel used during the last Year and X2 Significance Level by Country

Categories / % of Respondents	Colombia				México				X2
	Not Purchased	Physical	Both	Online	Not Purchased	Physical	Both	Online	
PC	12%	72%	14%	2%	9%	60%	27%	5%	0,001
Home and Garden	15%	66%	16%	2%	11%	72%	17%	1%	0,154
Clothe and Accessories	2%	42%	53%	3%	2%	43%	51%	3%	0,971
Cellphone, Telephone	11%	58%	26%	5%	10%	60%	26%	5%	0,963
Electronics	16%	49%	29%	5%	11%	53%	29%	7%	0,335
Vehicle Accessories	23%	59%	13%	5%	12%	63%	18%	7%	0,009
Airline Tickets	7%	11%	32%	50%	7%	13%	40%	39%	0,069
Apps and Games	9%	13%	27%	51%	6%	7%	40%	47%	0,009
Events / Entertainment	11%	13%	41%	35%	9%	13%	42%	36%	0,824
Sports	18%	55%	23%	4%	13%	60%	25%	2%	0,166
Restaurants	3%	57%	37%	3%	4%	66%	28%	2%	0,093
Supermarket Food	4%	75%	19%	2%	5%	79%	14%	2%	0,313
Other Groceries	13%	62%	20%	5%	12%	63%	19%	6%	0,836
Hotel Reservations	15%	11%	27%	47%	11%	14%	33%	41%	0,112
Public Services	6%	40%	39%	15%	9%	27%	51%	14%	0,004
Personal Care Products	5%	75%	20%	1%	6%	69%	21%	3%	0,126
Books and Magazines	12%	48%	34%	6%	9%	44%	41%	7%	0,32
Streaming (music, TV)	12%	13%	31%	44%	9%	13%	31%	47%	0,711
Education	9%	39%	43%	9%	9%	37%	45%	9%	0,944
Loans Payment	10%	28%	42%	19%	14%	32%	40%	13%	0,105

Purchase by Category: 0=Not purchased at all, 1= only in physical stores, 2=both online and physical, 3=online only

Source: the authors

Preferred Type of Point of Purchase by Category

There was also asked about last year purchasing experience in a different type of channels among those categories. Options included purchase in a physical store, physical and online store, and online purchase only. (Table 5.). Both Colombia and Mexico have similarities in most of the categories in terms of purchasing online only or either online and physically. Airline Tickets, Apps and Games, Events and Entertainment, Hotel Reservations and Streaming are the ones with the highest preferences referring to use online or physical and online point of purchase. The categories with less frequency for online purchase at both countries are PC, Home and Garden, Vehicle Accessories, Cellphone and Telephone, Electronics, Sports, Market Groceries both food and non-food and Personal Care. Categories with significant differences between countries include PC, Vehicle Accessories, Apps and Games and Public Services.

Electronics, PC, and cellphones are categories with a high involvement, which indicates that consumers like to watch personally their performance and design, meaning that people buy less frequently those items online. In fact, in the case of the growth rate, for Colombia, personal electronics grew only 6,9% between 2015 and 2016, the only one digit growth for all the categories, and is expected to grow even less (3,2%) between 2016 and 2021 (BlackSip, 2017). For Mexico, the recurrence purchase of this type of electronics was of 19% in 2017 and occupied the 17th place among 20 categories that year (Asociación de Internet, 2018). This category, as well as other technology related such as Apps and Games, are statistically different among countries (with Colombians purchasing more physically related to Mexico).

In the case of groceries (also high in Physical purchase), it is possible that in these two countries there is a custom for going to offline providers, partly because of convenience because of organoleptic reasons. However, food as a category experienced an online growth rate of 17,8% between 2015 and 2016 for Colombia and is expected to grow 21,2% between 2016 and 2021. In the case of Personal Care is, even more, given the case that this category grew in the same period 48,9% and is expected to grow 15,5% in the next years (BlackSip, 2017). In the case of Mexico, consumer packaged goods had a recurrence of 19% in 2017, with a position in the ranking of 16 in importance (Asociación de Internet, 2018).

Relation Between Categories

Frequency of Purchase and Categories

There were found strong significant positive correlations in terms of frequency of purchase for some categories in both countries. As shown in Table 6, categories like Airline Tickets, Events and Entertainment, Hotel Reservations and Streaming Services are correlated for online purchase, meaning that if one category is purchased frequently the others too. This could be due to the fact that consumers that buy their tickets online also buy the rest of the package using that channel, even online entertainment services such as Netflix and Spotify.

A similar behavior can be shown in other categories such as Sports, that behaves similarly as Groceries and Personal care in both countries. Public Services behave similarly as Loans. Restaurants behave similarly to Groceries. In all the cases, the relation is positive (Table 7).

Table 6. Significant correlation coefficients among selected categories by country for online frequency of purchase

Country	Categories / Values	Airline Tickets	Event / Entertainment	Hotel Reservations
Colombia	**Event and Entertainment**	0,243		
	Hotel Reservations	0,509	0,426	
	Streaming Services	0,292	0,334	0,424
Mexico	**Event and Entertainment**	0,457		
	Hotel Reservations	0,531	0,492	
	Streaming Services	0,286	0,333	0,461

* All coefficients are significant at a level of 0.01, all the correlations used in this chapter are Spearman Range Correlations. Frequency of purchase measured for this question in terms of times a day, week or month.

Source: the authors

Table 7. Significant correlation coefficient among selected categories by country for online frequency of purchase

Country / Categories		Home and Garden	Telephone	Electronics	Vehicle Accessories	Sports	Restaurants	Food Groceries	Other Groceries	Public Services
Colombia	**Electronics**		,541							
	sports				,501					
	Food Groceries					,514	,604			
	Other Groceries						,525	,713		
	Personal Care					,514		,561	,544	
	Loans									,549
Mexico	**Vehicle Accessories**	,560	,515	,545						
	Sports	,510			,528					
	Restaurants					,599				
	Food Groceries					,680	,731			
	Other Groceries					,636	,634	,764		
	Personal Care	,522			,507	,523	,508	,634	,579	,525
	Loans									,554

Frequency of Purchase: Likert Scale where 1=less frequent and 5=most frequent

* Only significant (at a 0.01 level) coefficients above 0.5 are shown

Source: the authors

Table 8. Chi squared significance levels (X2) for person purchase by type of channel and by frequency of purchase online – comparison among countries

Categories / % by Country and X2 Significance Level	Colombia						México					
	% Purchase (online only, Physical and Online) and X2			% Most Frequent Purchase online (4 and 5) and X2			% Purchase (online only, Physical and Online) and X2			% Most Frequent Purchase online (4 and 5) and X2		
	X2	Women	Men	X2	Women	Men	X2	Women	Men	X2	Women	Men
PC	0,099	11,0	22,2	0,183	5,8	10,4	0,009	21,6	39,0	0,041	5,1	15,4
Cellphone Telephone	0,144	24,0	40,0	0,281	11,7	16,3	0,074	21,4	39,0	0,004	10,3	15,4
Electronics	0,107	27,3	43,0	0,108	7,8	17,0	0,003	22,2	47,8	0,000	6,8	15,4
Vehicle Accessories	0,015	18,8	16,3	0,609	3,9	7,4	0,614	22,2	27,2	0,058	5,1	11,8
Airline Tickets	0,548	78,6	85,2	0,661	46,8	52,6	0,215	85,5	74,3	0,026	51,3	36,0
Apps and Games	0,019	74,7	84,4	0,004	39,0	53,3	0,890	82,9	89,0	0,005	47.9	52.9
Sports	0,586	26,0	30,4	0,124	9,1	8,1	0,024	27,4	25,7	0,001	5,1	11,8
Other Groceries	0,005	27,3	23,7	0,781	7,8	5,2	0,000	28,2	22,1	0,000	8,5	5,9
Public Services	0,009	45,5	65,9	0,321	29,9	37,8	0,366	63,2	64,7	0,541	25,6	23,5
Personal Care	0,751	23,4	17,8	0,143	11,0	3,0	0,710	26,5	22,1	0,013	8,5	8,8
Streaming Services	0,015	71,4	77,8	0,365	33,1	44,4	0,279	77,8	83,1	0,465	40,2	46,3
Loans Payment	0,037	57,1	68,9	0,211	31,8	37,0	0,195	46,2	59,6	0,272	21,4	24,3

Frequency of Purchase: 1=less frequent and 5=most frequent
* There are only displayed the categories that are significant for at least one question
Source: the authors

Categories Related by Demographics

Gender Effect

For categories such as Vehicle Accessories, Apps and Games, Streaming, Loans and Electronics, men purchase more frequently online than women in both countries. In Groceries and Personal Care, online purchase is more relevant for women than for men in both countries. in the remaining categories, the results are mixed and depend on the country, being interesting the case of Airline Tickets, while in Colombia is more relevant the online channel for men than for women, in Mexico the case is the opposite (Table 8).

Age Effect

Were found some positive significant correlations between age and some categories in terms of the type of channel used for the purchase. In the case of Colombia, those are Loans, Public Services, Hotel Reservations, Sports, Events, Apps and Games and Airline Tickets. In the case of Mexico, the significant coefficients are Airline

Tickets, Events and Entertainment, Hotels, Streaming and Education. Both results are consistent with the intuition of that the older the person the higher the income and then more possibilities of purchase and access to online channels.

However, the sample included a low dispersion of age range surrounding the 22 years, and with a standard deviation is of 4,79 years for Mexico and 5.089 for Colombia. It could be possible that age could play a negative role in the online purchase of some categories, given that in this countries there is less adoption in higher range ages due to the lack of familiarity of older people with this media as well as their lower education level (Marketing Society, 2018; KPMG, 2017). According to Marchant (2015a) and Castro (2015), the percentage of persons that connected to the internet during 2015 was 48% in the age range of 15 to 34 years old and 52% for Mexico. In the age range of 55 years or more it was only 8% for Colombia and 5% for Mexico.

Education Effect

The other demographic factor that has significant, positive but correlations in terms of the type of channel used is the education level. Is positive in the case of Colombia for the categories Airline Tickets (0,168), Apps and Games (0,184), Events and Entertainment (0,204), Food Groceries (0,151), Hotels (0,201), Public Services (0,154) and Loans (0,182). In the case of Mexico, correlation was found for Restaurants (0,127) and Home and Garden (0,151). That means that the highly educated the person the more possible is that purchase online those given categories. That's could be due to the fact that the more educated the person the higher the income and their access to technology, but the sample has a concentration on upper graduate students, so future studies could be performed to confirm that results.

Monthly Expenditure

Lastly, there is a positive and significant correlation between monthly purchase and some categories in terms of the type of channel. For Colombia, 16 of the 20 categories has these correlations, with the highest being Events and Entertainment (0,26), Hotels (0,27) and Loans (0,36). In the case of Mexico, the relation is only significant for seven categories, with the highest values in the case of Loans (0,24), Public Services (0.20) and Electronics (0,21), meaning that the more the monthly online expenditure, the more likely are going to be purchased online. Those categories with the highest values also are higher average ticket and/or repeated online purchase categories, which could explain the relationship

Frequency of Purchase

Times per Week

There was also analyzed the relationship between frequency of purchase (times in a week or a month) and the type of day for making the purchase (Labor Day, Weekend, Everyday or with no specific choice). The results show that most of the respondents doesn't have a stablished frequent day of the week for purchasing or a frequency of purchase. (first column of Table 8). For those with a specific preference, Weekends are more frequent compared to Labor Days in both countries. The only significant difference is for once a month purchases. Most of the respondents are not so frequent buyers, as shown in Table 9.

There is no high significant relationship between frequency of purchase and a specific category for neither of the countries. However, there are low but negative and significant correlations between the answer No Specific Time and the purchase of specific categories, mostly for Colombia. In the case of Mexico, the results are negative and significant for only 2 categories, suggesting that persons that are more occasional online buyers are going to buy less online any given category, especially for Colombia.

Table 9. Frequency of purchase by country and type of day and X2 significance level

Frequency By Preferred Day of the Week, Country and Significance	Colombia				México				X2
	No Specific Day	Labor Days	Weekends Mainly	Everyday	No Specific Day	Labor Days	Weekends Mainly	Everyday	
Every Day	88,1%	1,7%	4,4%	5,8%	88,3%	3,1%	4,3%	4,3%	0,621
Three Times or More a Week	89,2%	3,1%	3,1%	4,7%	89,5%	0,8%	4,7%	5,1%	0,209
Two Times per Week	90,2%	2,0%	3,4%	4,4%	86,4%	4,3%	3,5%	5,8%	0,387
Once a Week	88,5%	3,4%	3,4%	4,7%	82,5%	4,7%	7,0%	5,8%	0,173
Three Times per Month	83,4%	3,1%	5,8%	7,8%	79,0%	4,3%	6,6%	10,1%	0,595
Two Times per Month	83,7%	3,4%	4,1%	8,8%	84,0%	1,6%	5,1%	9,3%	0,54
Once a Month	80,0%	5,1%	6,8%	8,1%	68,9%	7,4%	11,3%	12,5%	0,028
No Specific Frequency	46,1%	10,5%	11,2%	32,2%	58,4%	6,6%	12,5%	22,6%	0,011

Source: the authors

Hours Preferred for Doing the Purchase

For both countries, the most preferred time for doing the purchase is between 6 pm and Midnight, and the less preferred is between 6 am and 9 am. The more preferred hours increasing as the hour of the day increases until midnight as can been observed in Figure 2, which correspond to Colombia, and Figure 3 which, correspond to Mexico. The only significant difference between countries is at 9

Figure 2. Preferred time for doing the purchase, Colombia
Source: the authors

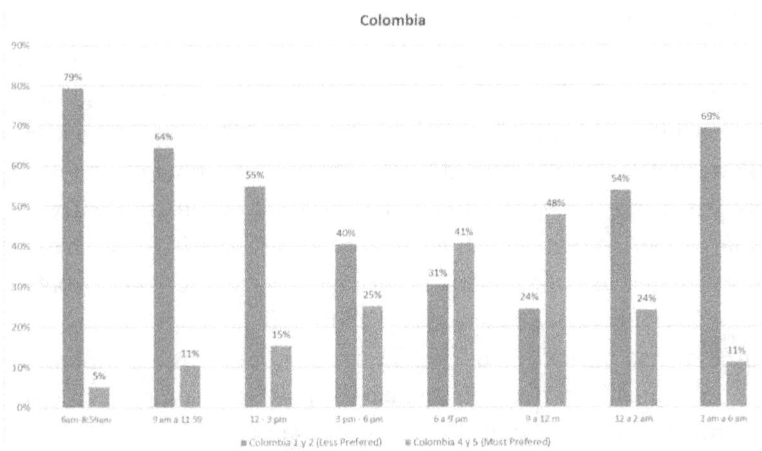

Figure 3. Preferred time for doing the purchase, Mexico.
Source: the authors

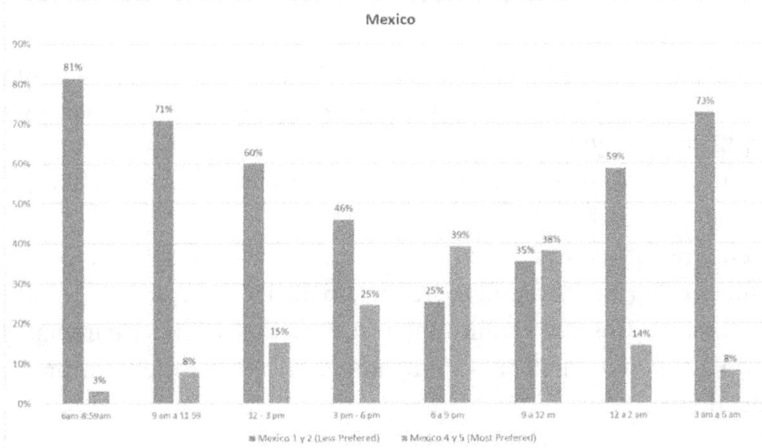

am, less preferred by Mexicans and more preferred by Colombians. This could be related to the average time of waking up in both countries. The results imply that persons in both countries could be more comfortable purchasing after they finish their labor day but before they go to sleep. Strategies could be used for encouraging purchasing on those hours, between 6 pm and before midnight.

Some other research also supports those findings. According to reports from the firm Comscore (Marchant, I. and Valencia, 2015; Marchant, 2015), for both countries, there is a differentiated behavior by the platform used to access to the internet and by type of device in the case of E-Commerce. During the day (office, work or study hours), between 8 am and 5 pm, there is a peak in the usage of desktop and laptop, but during the night (after 5 pm and until midnight) there is a peak in the usage of tablets and smartphones.

There is a significant (at a 0,05 level) but also low correlations between preferred day for doing the purchase and frequency of purchase. In the case of Colombia, most frequently preferred time for buying (Everyday, Three or More Times a Week and Two Times a Week), are related positively with the hours 9 am to 6 pm (with significant correlations between 0,141 and 0,260). There is also a positive correlation for night hours (3 am to 6 am) for Everyday buyers, Three Times a Week, and Two Times a Week. In the case of Mexico, the strongest correlation ranges between 0,161 and 0,220 for hours between 9 am, and 12 am and 12 am to 6 am and Everyday buyers, Three Times a Week and Two Times a Week. Results indicate that there is a positive relationship between frequency of purchase and preferred hour, in the case of Colombians during the day and in the case of Mexicans, the relationship is less frequent and more visible during the hours before sunset.

Influence of Specific Groups

Effects in Purchased Categories

There are significant correlations according the type of channel used to purchase and the different groups and countries. Table 9 shows the correlations between the type of group and the type of category, all them are positive, which means that the higher the influence of other groups for online purchase, the more likely the usage of this channel for purchasing.

The overall results confirm the intuition for purchasing specific categories; the mainly sources of influence are those related to the internet players (internet buyers and experts) as well as the family. Interestingly that friends, parents, and work colleagues play such a small part compared with other groups in the categories channel election.

Table 9. Number of categories with significant correlation with surrounding buyer potential influencers

Number of Categories with Significant Correlation Coefficient	Friends	Parents	Couple	Children	Work Colleagues	Social Media, Internet Buyers	Experts Opinion
Colombia	1* 2**	0	*3**2	*1	*1**1	*5**3	*4**6
Mexico	**1	*5**2	*4**6	*6**1	*3	*5**6	*2**11
Total (including both)	4	7	15	8	5	19	23

* Significant at 0,05 ** significant at 0,01.
Source: the authors

Despite these results are preliminary, they could help organizations´ marketing strategies for specific categories and specific groups of influence. In the case of Experts and Internet Buyers could be a relationship with higher average categories (Electronics, Education, Loans) but also for entertainment (Streaming, Games). In the case of a couple, could be more critical for long term decisions (Loans) and household activities (Public Services) but also group entertainment (Hotel Reservations).

Influence and Country

In terms of the group´s impact, it seems that purchasing is not the same for different countries. According to Table 10, meanwhile, for Colombian consumers, the power

Table 10 – Type of influences by degree of importance and significance

Type of Influence by Importance and Significance	Colombia			México			X2 Significance
	0 (No Response)	1 and 2	4 and 5	0 (No Response)	1 and 2	4 and 5	
Friends	2%	34%	39%	3%	41%	32%	0,285
Parents	3%	39%	36%	4%	50%	29%	0,002
Couple	5%	33%	42%	8%	47%	26%	0,001
Children	28%	61%	6%	25%	66%	5%	0,891
Colleagues at work	4%	48%	24%	8%	58%	14%	0,011
Online Buyers	3%	36%	40%	8%	37%	26%	0,003
Expert Opinions	4%	25%	49%	10%	27%	42%	0,015

Type of Influence: Likert Scale, 0 = Not answer, 1 = low influence, 5 = high influence
Source: the authors

of the partner, online buyers and expert opinions are the highest. In the case of Mexico, the highest proportion of influence comes from friends and expert opinions.

Influence and Demographics

There are some relationships between the importance of a particular group and the type of demographics. For both countries, there is a positive and significant correlation between age and couple influence (0,240 Colombia and 0,212 Mexico) meaning that higher the age, the more important is the opinion of the couple for making a decision.

There is also an influence in terms of gender, being different in both countries. In Colombia, the relationship is negative for Children (-0,15), and in Mexico is positive for Parents (0,12). It appears that for the first country, men are relatively less ready to receive advice from Children compared to women, and in the second, there are more women prepared to receive notice from Parents compared to men. These results are low but interesting for marketing specialists, and for both countries could mean that an excellent way to influence online purchases is by altering the surrounding members of the family differently.

Marital status has a relationship with the different groups of influence. In the case of Colombia, there is also a positive relationship with the impact of Children and marital status. That should be good advice for marketers, to influence the entire family group for the case of couples. This result is reinforced by the fact that having children has a negative correlation for receiving advice from Children.

Education is also related with the ability to receive advice; the more educated the person, the more eager to receive it from Couple and Experts in the case of Colombia and from Couple and Colleagues in the case of Mexicans.

Finally, there is a relation between monthly purchase and type of advice looked for, in the case of Mexico only, the more money spends online, more eagerness to receive notice from Couple and Expert's Opinions.

Advertising Usage and Preferences

Before analyzing the behavior consumers of the study in terms of means of access, the usefulness of advertising and preferred advertising, it is worth to highlight that most important E-Commerce activities are familiar to both Colombian and Mexican consumers. According to the survey of Hootsuite (2019a, 2019b), in 2018 at each country among adult population surveyed, the main E-Commerce tasks were: i) search online for a product or service to buy. ii) Visit an online retail store on the web by any method. iii) Purchase a product or service online by any device. iv) Purchase via laptop or desktop and, v) Make a purchase via a mobile device

Means of Access to a Webpage

Differences by Country

Respondents of both countries access to E-Commerce web page from Social Media Ads, typing the Webpage address or from the app of the Retailer or Brand (see Table 11). There are no significant differences between the two countries. The less used means by respondents in both countries are Banners in Apps, Webpage Banners, and QR Codes. According to the survey of Hootsuite (2019a, 2019b), there was a high percentage of the adult population for Colombia and Mexico that used mobile phones in 2018 for activities such as messaging apps, watching videos, playing games, mobile banking and for map services. According to that survey, 72% of Mexicans and 75% of Colombians use smartphones daily, being higher than Laptop users.

There are some relationships between the grade of influence and the type of media used for accessing an E–Commerce web page (Table 12). For both countries, there are significant correlations of the influence of Parents and Friends and access to Ads on Social Media, Google Ads, Web Banners and Banners of Apps. Work Colleagues influence is more related to Web Banners in as well as with Ads on Social Media and Banners of Apps. Couple impact is only significant in the case of Mexico and is related to Ads on Social Media and Google Ads. Expert opinions in Colombia is mostly related to Web Banners, Banners of Apps, typing the Web Page address and the Retailer App or QR Code, but has no significant relationship in the case of Mexico.

Table 11. Type of media- most preferred for access to an e-commerce site by country and level of significance

Type of Media, % Most Preferred and Significance	Colombia			Mexico			X2 Significance
	0	1 y 2	4 y 5	0	1 y 2	4 y 5	
Social Media Ads	3%	22%	51%	4%	28%	44%	0,265
Google Ads	3%	30%	41%	4%	39%	41%	0,118
Web page Banners	5%	53%	19%	6%	56%	19%	0,19
Apps Banners	5%	56%	19%	7%	57%	20%	0,096
Tipping the Web Page	3%	18%	64%	6%	17%	57%	0,198
Retailer / Brand App	4%	25%	49%	4%	25%	53%	0,824
E Mails	5%	47%	25%	5%	49%	30%	0,061
QR Code	5%	65%	13%	7%	68%	11%	0,306

Type of Preferred Media: Likert Scale, 0 = Not answer, 1 = low influence, 5 = high influence
Source: the authors

Table 12. Significant correlation coefficients between type of mean of access to the e-commerce webpage and type of group of persons by grade of influence

Mean of Access to the Web / Type of Advice by Country		Friends	Parents	Couple	Work Colleagues	Social Media, Internet Buyers	Experts Opinion
Colombia	Ad on Social Media	,192**	,128*	0,018	-0,009	,119*	0,096
	Google Ads	0,052	,121*	0,111	0,099	0,039	0,048
	Banners on the Web	,197**	,150**	0,072	,183**	0,078	,126*
	Banners of Apps	,236**	,120*	0,109	,279**	0,091	,150**
	Typing the Web Page	0,105	0,104	0,040	0,031	,146*	,223**
	App of Retailer	0,077	,122*	0,111	0,029	0,075	,198**
	Emails	0,054	-0,047	0,044	0,109	0,036	0,107
	QR Code	0,026	0,033	0,008	0,057	,123*	,156**
Mexico	Ad on Social Media	,301**	,183**	,170**	,123*	0,120	0,036
	Google Ads	,151*	,163**	,124*	0,083	0,065	0,026
	Banners on the Web	,173**	,191**	0,117	,182**	0,110	0,112
	Banners of Apps	,185**	,199**	0,041	,227**	0,089	0,111
	Typing the Web Page	-0,067	0,008	0,065	-0,086	-0,009	0,109
	App of Retailer	0,112	-0,004	0,104	0,024	-0,014	0,041
	Emails	0,083	0,088	0,042	,128*	0,116	0,101
	QR Code	,147*	,189**	0,098	,167**	0,056	0,085

Source: the authors

Is interesting how both countries behave differently. Despite both have relationships between friends and parents and some of the means of access, social media is more related for Mexicans with a higher range of influencers. On the other hand, in Colombia there is a higher relationship between expert's opinion and different types of means of access. Children influence is related to several factors of access but is only significant for Mexico but not for Colombia. It's possible then to establish that there is a relationship between different groups of influence and the type of mean of access to an E- Commerce page, that should be used by advertisers taking the variable group of influence into account.

Relation Between Means of Access

There are some other interesting facts about the means of access to a webpage (Table 13). For both countries, there is a strong significant positive relationship between Google Ads and Ads on Social Media. These Banners has a strong relationship

Table 13. Relationship between different means of entering to an e – commerce webpage

Type of Mean of Access to the Web / Type of Advice		Ad on Social Media	Google Ads	Banners on the Web	Banners of Apps	Typing Web Page	E-Mails
Colombia	Google Ads	,325					
	Banners on the Web		,403				
	Banners of Apps			,602			
	App of Retailer					,404	
	QR Code			,345	,335		,389
Mexico	Google Ads	,428					
	Banners on the Web	,364	,384				
	Banners of Apps		,375	,689			
	App of Retailer					,355	
	QR Code			,506	,524		,530

* Only correlation coefficients significant at 0.01 and higher than 0.3 were included in this table.
Source: the authors

with Google Ads and QR Codes. Besides, QR Codes has a strong relationship with the Banners of Apps. Typing the Web Page is related with App of the Retailer and E-Mails are related to QR Codes. These results imply that advertisers should plan the type of investment, taking into account that the usage of a specific mean of access is related to using another one. There are then three groups: those who access through ads: through banners, through the retailer (App or Web) or trough E-Mails and QR Codes.

Usefulness of the Advertisement for Knowing About the Product or Service and Making a Decision

The use of different types of advertisement was also evaluated. The most useful advertising to knowing about the product, in both countries, are Social Media Posts, Retail Store App, Digital Videos and Banners. Regarding making a decision, the same categories are essential as well. For both countries, knowing more about the product and making a decision, the significant differences are banners and social media posts, being both more critical for Colombians than for Mexicans (Table 14).

Not necessary the mean of access to a web page is related to the use of particular advertising or the preference of given advertising. According to Table 15, the persons that prefer to access using Google Ads perceived useful and is preferred in both

Table 14. Type of advertising and level of importance by country for knowing more about the product or service and for making a decision and X2 level of significance

Type of Advertising	Knowing about the Product					Making a Decision				
	Colombia		México		X2	Colombia		México		X2
	1 y 2	4 y 5	1 y 2	4 y 5		1 y 2	4 y 5	1 y 2	4 y 5	
Social Media Banners	28%	48%	38%	35%	0,037	36%	39%	51%	26%	0,014
Digital Videos	18%	51%	22%	49%	0,229	25%	44%	28%	47%	0,597
Advertising in Music (streaming)	36%	32%	38%	30%	0,252	46%	26%	41%	26%	0,187
Online Advertorials	34%	37%	37%	31%	0,533	36%	34%	34%	32%	0,975
Google Ads	22%	48%	30%	42%	0,087	27%	43%	32%	36%	0,038
Social Media posts	10%	68%	23%	51%	0,000	13%	61%	25%	48%	0,021
Web Banners	34%	30%	42%	24%	0,332	40%	25%	49%	21%	0,071
Apps Banners	46%	23%	49%	23%	0,502	46%	22%	50%	21%	0,284
Retail Store App	32%	45%	27%	42%	0,251	30%	41%	33%	38%	0,320
E-Mail	46%	28%	44%	31%	0,562	45%	27%	44%	30%	0,992
QR Code	56%	14%	60%	18%	0,091	51%	13%	48%	14%	0,290

Usefulness questions: for knowing about the product (1= less important, 5=most important), for choosing a product (1= less important, 5=most important).

Source: the authors

countries. In the case of Mexico, persons that access using Google Ads also prefer advertising in music and consider useful web banners.

There is some support for saying that the main of access is most of the times a reflection of the perceived usefulness of the mean of access used, and in some cases specific means of access are related with others.

Level of Preference for Advertisement

The level of preference for specific advertising shows that the less preferred types of adds are those that come from Banners (Web and Apps), from the Retail Store and QR Codes.

The most preferred sources of advertisement are Social Media Posts, Google Ads, Digital Videos and Social Media Banners, and significant differences by country are present in Google Ads, Social Media Posts and Web Banners (less preferred by Mexicans), and QR Codes (less preferred by Colombians), shown in Table 16.

Table 15. Relationship between different means of entering an e – commerce webpage (columns) and perceived usefulness for knowing about the product, for making a decision and perceived degree of preference (rows)

Type of Means of Access Vs Usefulness and Degree of Preference		Colombia							Mexico						
		Google Ads	Web Banners	Banners of Apps	Typing Web Page	App of Retailer	E-mail	QR Code	Google Ads	Web Banners	Banners of Apps	Typing Web Page	App of Retailer	E-mail	QR Code
Banners	Knowing										,302				
	Choice Making									,342	,323				
	Preference										,283				
Ads in Music	Knowing			,318											
	Choice Making			,334											
	Preference			,306					,333						
Google Ads	Knowing	,358	,312						,534		,304				
	Choice Making	,359							,413		,302				
	Preference	,457	,305						,412						
Web Banners	Knowing		,344						,334	,360	,410				
	Choice Making		,394	,323					,328	,382	,423				
	Preference		,382	,362						,331	,419				
Banners in Apps	Knowing		,323	,385						,328	,430				
	Choice Making			,362		,307				,331	,452				
	Preference		,326	,439		,300					,389				,315
Retail App	Knowing					,590						,307	,566		
	Choice Making				,319	,511							,486		
	Preference					,555							,528		
E-Mails	Knowing						,533							,523	,345
	Choice Making						,574							,499	,333
	Preference						,512							,541	,343
QR Code	Knowing							,611							,551
	Choice Making							,355							
	Preference							,326							

* Only correlation coefficients significant at 0.01 and higher than 0.3 were included in this table

Usefulness questions for knowing about the product and choosing a product: 1= less important, 5=most important. Preference question: 1= less preferred, 5= most preferred.

Source: the authors

Table 16. Level of preference by type of advertising and country

Type of Advertising and Country	Colombia			México			X2 Significance
	0	1 y 2	4 y 5	0	1 y 2	4 y 5	
Social Media Banners	1%	38%	40%	4%	48%	32%	0,069
Digital Videos	2%	30%	42%	4%	34%	42%	0,283
Advertising in Music (streaming)	3%	51%	23%	3%	45%	25%	0,265
Online Advertorials	2%	37%	33%	4%	39%	33%	0,514
Google Ads	2%	28%	41%	4%	34%	39%	0,005
Social Media posts	3%	19%	55%	4%	28%	44%	0,021
Web Banners	3%	43%	31%	4%	47%	24%	0,007
Apps Banners	2%	49%	24%	4%	51%	19%	0,485
Retail Store App	2%	40%	36%	5%	37%	39%	0,522
E-Mail	3%	47%	28%	4%	50%	29%	0,342
QR Code	15%	56%	12%	21%	53%	14%	0,031

Level of Preference: 1= less preferred, 5= most preferred
Source: the authors

Perceived Usefulness of Advertisement, Preference for a Specific Advertising Mean and Some Demographics

By gender, the usefulness for Music and Video Advertising is significant and different between men and women for both countries. Women find more useful Advertising in Music than men but are the opposite in Colombia. Advertising in Music is also significantly different by gender in both countries, is perceived more useful by men compared to women.

Preferred Ads also varies by gender for both countries. In the case of Colombia, these ads are more preferred by women compared to men and are the same in the case of Mexico.

In terms of age, for Colombia, there is a significant correlation between age and access through Google Ads and E-Mail, also with Usefulness of Email for Knowing about the product. Is also related to Usefulness for Making a Decision with E-Mails and Google Ads, and finally is related to the level of preference for E-Mail. That means that the higher the age, the more the usefulness and/or preference of Google Ads and E-Mails as advertising means.

In the case of Mexico, the situation is very different. Age is negatively related with Web Banners and Banners on Apps as means of access, with Advertising on Music, Web Banners, Banners on Apps and QR Codes as considered useful for Knowing About the Product and also negative for preference with Banners of Apps.

That means mainly that the higher the age, the less relevant are banners for persons in this country.

Education level also has a relationship with the means of access to an E-Commerce place. For Colombia, the higher the Education Level, the higher the access to Google Ads and E-Mail, the more Useful is the E-Mail for Knowing about the Product, the more Useful is Google Ads for Making a Decision and the more preferred are Google Ads and E-Mail. In the case of Mexico, education is only relevant for E-Mail as a mean of access. The higher the education level, more important became Google Ads for Colombia and Email for both countries.

Finally, in terms of monthly purchase, for Colombians, higher monthly expenses are related with Typing the Webpage and E Mail as a mean of access and is more useful the E-Mail for Knowing about the Product, and the Preference in Ads is higher for Google Ads. In the case of Mexico, the higher the monthly purchase, the more Useful means of advertising for Knowing About the Product are Adds Inside News or Infomercials, Google Ads, Posts in Social Media and Web Banners. In terms of Usefulness for Making a Decision, increases with higher purchases in the case of Music Advertising, Google Ads, Posts in Social Media, Web Banners, and Retail App. In terms of preference, this increases with higher purchases in the case of Infomercials, Google Ads, Posts in Social Media, and Web Banners.

Summarizing, some means of advertising are more preferred than others, mainly social media posts and Google Ads. Also, there is a relationship between some demographics and perceived usefulness of some specific media, especially for Education, Age, and Monthly purchases, mainly for Google Ads and E-Mail. Again, the necessity to direct the advertising to specific demographic groups is established; however, the relationships are not that stronger, so future studies with more heterogeneous samples should be made for confirming that results.

SOLUTIONS AND RECOMMENDATIONS

Online purchase is a potent tool in Latin America and for marketing managers. It has demonstrated that it could help to increase their sales, market share, brand loyalty, and so on. Nevertheless, online strategies still face security challenges (among others), as well as an increasing competitor's presence, which led to a very crowded market. As it happens in traditional markets, when a new niche is discovered and profitable, it attracts more companies.

Studies have shown that there is a relationship between advertising and sales results and other intermediate measures (as purchase intentions, interest, brand awareness, and attitudes, among others). Nevertheless, the results depend on the type of media, also on the design, the type of customers, past behaviors, among other complex variables. In the cases, advertising changes these intermediate measures is not clear in some studies how this change reflects in changes in a purchase.

Further, companies would never stop making efforts to improve its performance, make high amounts of investment in new and more sophisticated-efficient technologies, as well as electronic communications, advertising, and promotions. As it happens in traditional markets, when a unique niche is discovered and profitable, it attracts more companies.

Not so many comparative studies have been developed, especially for emerging markets, that analyses the relationships between advertising, attitudes, and effectiveness. Considering that, it's interesting to compare two countries such as Mexico (127 MM) and Colombia (48 MM) that represents close to 28% of Latin American population (CEPAL, 2016).

Categories such as Clothes and Accessories, Airplane Tickets, Apps and Games, Events and Entertainment, Hotel Reservations, Public Services, Streaming, and Loans Payment are the most commonly used in online purchase. There are some specific differences among the two countries studied that could be used by marketers to adapt strategies to each one. In some cases, those categories (for example in the case of Airlines and Hotels), are related between each other. Moreover, some demographics appears to have relationship with the categories, specially age, gender, education or monthly expenditure, with differences depending the country of study.

There is a similar time to purchase online for both countries, especially after lunch and before midnight. The groups that influence the most channels used to purchase, are Internet experts and family.

The main media to access an E-Commerce site are social media and google ads. Some of them are related with the influence of different types of groups, which suggest the need to target the advertising, not only the customer but their main influencers. Nevertheless, the mean of access to a web page is not necessary related with the preference for advertising. Regard preferences, the main ads for knowing more about the product and making an informed decision are the digital videos, social media posts and the retail store app. As in other cases, there are some differences between countries.

Despite the increasing trends of online purchase and technology adoption, traditional markets remain important in medium-income countries like those studied here. It seems that people like to be listened, attended, or have any personal contact when purchasing online. This means for marketing managers; they have to find ways to, simultaneously, hire people with specialized skills to attend those needs (investment in training their personnel for online customer service, online follow up surveys, marketing intelligence, etc.). Online sales do not work "by themselves", customers still face doubts, complains, uncertainty, so human responses become necessary. Therefore, is recommended to continue combining both purchase strategies, taking the best for each one according to the income level, diversity of items and people´s profiles, behaviors, as well as region's needs (rural-urban).

FUTURE RESEARCH DIRECTIONS

It would be interesting in future researches to include in the sample people from public universities, as well as a diversity of population (for example lower -income people), and explore how vital is their use in rural areas. Additionally, using a probability sample in both countries would enhance these results. More comparisons in medium-income countries vs. low- income countries, in order to understand the online influence in their well-being, their quality of life, economic development contribution, and other effects on social-environmental causes, are recommended.

REFERENCES

Asociación de Internet. (2018). *Estudio de Comercio Electrónico en México 2018 Diciembre, 2018.*

BlackSip. (2017). *Reporte de Industria: El E-Commerce en colombia 2017.* Retrieved from http://content.blacksip.com/reporte-de-industria-el-e-commerce-en-colombia-2017

Boon-Long, S., & Wongsurawat, W. (2015). Social media marketing evaluation using social network comments as an indicator for identifying consumer purchasing decision effectiveness. *Journal of Direct Data and Digital Marketing Practice*, *17*(2), 130–149. doi:10.1057/dddmp.2015.51

Bruner, G. C. II, & Kumar, A. (2000). Web commercials and advertising hierarchy-of-effects. *Journal of Advertising Research*, *40*(1–2), 35–42. doi:10.2501/JAR-40-1-2-35-42

Castro, A. (2015). *Futuro Digital Colombia 2015.*

CEPAL. 2016, Latin America population will reach 625 million inhabitants by 2016, according to ECLAC estimates. Retrieved from https://www.cepal.org/en/news/latin-america-population-will-reach-625-million-inhabitants-2016-according-eclac-estimates

Chaffey, D. (2016). Definitions of emarketing vs. internet vs. digital marketing. Retrieved from https://www.smartinsights.com/digital-marketing-strategy/online-marketing-mix/definitions-of-emarketing-vs-internet-vs-digital-marketing/

Clarke, T. B., Murphy, J., Wetsch, L. R., & Boeck, H. (2018). Teaching search engine marketing through the Google ad grants program. *Marketing Education Review, 28*(2), 136–147. doi:10.1080/10528008.2018.1448282

Dehghani, M., Niaki, M. K., Ramezani, I., & Sali, R. (2016). Evaluating the influence of YouTube advertising for attraction of young customers. *Computers in Human Behavior, 59*, 165–172. doi:10.1016/j.chb.2016.01.037

Dehghani, M., & Tumer, M. (2015). A research on effectiveness of Facebook advertising on enhancing purchase intention of consumers. *Computers in Human Behavior, 49*, 597–600. doi:10.1016/j.chb.2015.03.051

Forbes. (2018). Global digital commerce sales to near $6 trillion by 2022. Retrieved from https://www.forbes.com/sites/jordanmckee/2018/09/11/global-digital-commerce-sales-to-near-6-trillion-by-2022/#868b6e54c5a0

Hootsuite. (2019a). *Digital 2019 - Colombia*. Retrieved from https://www.slideshare.net/DataReportal/digital-2019-colombia-january-2019-v01

Hootsuite. (2019b). *Digital 2019 Colombia*.

Hootsuite. (2019c). *Digital 2019 Mexico*.

Internet Live Stats. (n.d.). Google search statistics - internet live stats. Retrieved from https://www.internetlivestats.com/google-search-statistics/

Jun, S. P., & Park, D. H. (2016). Consumer information search behavior and purchasing decisions: Empirical evidence from Korea. *Technological Forecasting and Social Change, 107*, 97–111. doi:10.1016/j.techfore.2016.03.021

Kaczorowska-Spychalska, D. (2017). Consumer perspective of omnichannel commerce. *Management, 21*(2), 95–108. doi:10.1515/manment-2017-0007

Kuisma, J., Simola, J., Uusitalo, L., & Öörni, A. (2010). The effects of animation and format on the perception and memory of online advertising. *Journal of Interactive Marketing, 24*(4), 269–282. doi:10.1016/j.intmar.2010.07.002

Laudon, K. C., & Traver, C. G. (2019). E-Commerce 2019: Business, Technology and Society (14 ed.). Pearson.

Lohtia, R., Donthu, N., & Hershberger, E. K. (2003). The impact of content and design elements on banner advertising click-through rates. *Journal of Advertising Research, 43*(4), 410–418. doi:10.2501/JAR-43-4-410-418

Manchanda, P., Dubé, J.-P., Goh, K. Y., & Chintagunta, P. K. (2006). The effect of banner advertising on internet purchasing. *JMR, Journal of Marketing Research, 43*(1), 98–108. doi:10.1509/jmkr.43.1.98

Marchant, I. (2015a). *Futuro Digital México 2015.*

Marchant, I. (2015b). *Medición Multiplataforma en México.*

Marchant, I., & Valencia, F. (2015). *Medición Multiplataforma en Colombia.*

Reimers, V., Chao, C.-W., & Gorman, S. (2013). Permission email marketing and its influence on online shopping. *Asia Pacific Journal of Marketing and Logistics, 28*(2), 316. doi:10.1108/APJML-03-2015-0037

Sen, R. (2005). Optimal search engine marketing strategy. *International Journal of Electronic Commerce/Fall, 10*(1), 9–25.

Shaouf, A., Lü, K., & Li, X. (2016). O que é o R? *Computers in Human Behavior, 60*, 622–634. doi:10.1016/j.chb.2016.02.090

Statista. (2019). Number of e-mail users worldwide 2023 | Statistic. Retrieved from https://www.statista.com/statistics/255080/number-of-e-mail-users-worldwide/

Stewart, D. W., & Pavlou, P. A. (2002). From consumer response to active consumer: Measuring the effectiveness of interactive media. *Journal of the Academy of Marketing Science, 30*(4), 376–396. doi:10.1177/009207002236912

Stokes, R. (2018). *The essential guide to marketing in a digital world* (6th. Ed.). Retrieved from www.creda.co.za

Szymanski, G., & Stanislawski, R. (2018). Research online-purchase offline-a phenomenon among the young generation in the e-commerce sector. *Journal of International Scientific Publications, 12*(January), 185–192.

The-Cocktail-Analysis. (2013). La compra online en Colombia. In The Cocktail Analysis.

The World Bank. (n.d.). Individuals using the Internet (% of population) | Data. Retrieved from https://data.worldbank.org/indicator/it.net.user.zs

Tutaj, K., & van Reijmersdal, E. A. (2012). Effects of online advertising format and persuasion knowledge on audience reactions. *Journal of Marketing Communications, 18*(1), 5–18. doi:10.1080/13527266.2011.620765

Ur, B., Leon, P. G., Cranor, L. F., Shay, R., & Wang, Y. (2012). Smart, useful, scary, creepy: Perceptions of online behavioral advertising. *SOUPS 2012 - Proceedings of the 8th Symposium on Usable Privacy and Security, 2012*. doi:10.1145/2335356.2335362

Wang, Y., & Sun, S. (2010). An online advertising model: comparing China and the U.S. *Journal of Current Issues and Research in Advertising*, *32*(2), 101–115. doi:10.1080/10641734.2010.10505288

Zeng, F., Huang, L., & Dou, W. (2013). Social factors in user perceptions and responses to advertising in online social networking communities. *Journal of Interactive Advertising*, *10*(1), 1–13. doi:10.1080/15252019.2009.10722159

Zhang, X., Kumar, V., & Cosguner, K. (2017). Dynamically managing a profitable email marketing program. *JMR, Journal of Marketing Research*, *54*(6), 851–866. doi:10.1509/jmr.16.0210

KEY TERMS AND DEFINITIONS

Digital Marketing: Digital marketing is the marketing of products or services using digital technologies, mainly on the Internet, but also including mobile phones, display advertising,and any other digital medium. Digital marketing channels are systems based on the internet that can create, accelerate, and transmit product value from producer to the terminal consumer by digital networks.

E-commerce: E-commerce is the activity of buying or selling of products on online services or over the Internet. Electronic commerce draws on technologies such as mobile commerce, electronic funds transfer, supply chain management, Internet marketing, online transaction processing, electronic data interchange (EDI), inventory management systems, and automated data collection systems.

Interactivity: Interactivity is the communication process that takes place between humans and computer software.

Omnichannel Commerce: Omnichannel commerce is a multichannel approach to sales that seeks to provide customers with a seamless shopping experience, whether they're shopping online from a desktop or mobile device, by telephone, or in a brick-and-mortar store.

Online Advertising: Ad targeting refers to the selection of potential customer groups to which an advertisement will be displayed. This specification of the ad's audience is done using targeting parameters including demographic and geographic information, interests, and device preferences.

Point of Purchase: Ad targeting refers to the selection of potential customer groups to which an advertisement will be displayed. This specification of the ad's audience is done using targeting parameters including demographic and geographic information, interests, and device preferences.

Social Media Marketing: Ad targeting refers to the selection of potential customer groups to which an advertisement will be displayed. This specification of the ad's audience is done using targeting parameters including demographic and geographic information, interests, and device preferences.

Value Proposition: Ad targeting refers to the selection of potential customer groups to which an advertisement will be displayed. This specification of the ad's audience is done using targeting parameters including demographic and geographic information, interests, and device preferences.

Chapter 6
Optimization Models in Google Ads Campaigns

Sérgio Barreto
https://orcid.org/0000-0002-6532-3623
University of Aveiro, Portugal

Ricardo José Videira Barbosa
University of Aveiro, Portugal

Belem Barbosa
https://orcid.org/0000-0002-4057-360X
University of Aveiro, Portugal

ABSTRACT

Google Ads is a powerful tool for companies wishing to gain visibility on Google searches, as it offers impression privileges for advertisers, by featuring the ad above the organic results listing. This chapter contributes to the optimization of Google Ads campaigns. It includes an empirical study with a sample of marketing professionals exploring their views on the challenges of Google Ads as a digital marketing tool. According to the participants in this study, Google Ads campaign profitability depends, largely, on the ability to choose a keyword pool that achieves the company's goals. Moreover, the complexity of these pay-per-click decisions, the costs involved, and its business implications demand more reasoned, quantified, and, if possible, optimized solutions. The chapter develops linear programming optimization models based on impressions, clicks, conversions, and billing. The models are tested on a real example using Excel optimization add-ins.

DOI: 10.4018/978-1-7998-1618-8.ch006

Copyright © 2020, IGI Global. Copying or distributing in print or electronic forms without written permission of IGI Global is prohibited.

INTRODUCTION

The emergence and development of the Internet revolutionized all business communication and dramatically changed global commerce. The digital content produced by organizations, businesses and individuals, are consulted daily by millions of people who seek information, search products, compare prices, and make purchasing decisions. Companies apply new methodologies and digital features to reach potential customers. Search Engine Optimization (SEO), Search Engine Marketing (SEM), Google Ads, Content Marketing, Social Media Marketing, Newsletters and Online Stores are part of a panoply of digital resources that companies exploit in order to gain some competitive advantage (Mehta, Saberi, Vazirani, & Vazirani, 2005; Reddy, 2016).

In this scenario, the highlight goes to the search engines that play an increasingly important role, both for businesses and consumers, in the purchase decision process. Among them, Google is clearly the most used worldwide, with very few exceptions (e.g., Russia, China) and therefore deserves special attention from companies. Advertising campaigns on Google Ads promise visibility and are the focus of this chapter, which is divided into two parts.

In the first part of the chapter, a current and historical contextualization on digital marketing, Google search engine and Google Ads is presented. This overview is enriched by the clarification on the real expectations and concerns of digital marketing professionals, especially the Google Ads campaign managers, unveiled through an opinion survey that was conducted by the authors. The second part offers mathematical models for optimization of Google Ads campaigns. The models provide optimal solutions for choosing keywords in Google Ads campaigns, taking into account the goals and constraints of the organization. Future perspectives and conclusion complete the chapter.

The primary purpose of this chapter is to show how optimization models can be used to plan Google Ads campaigns, with obvious savings of time and money and gains in objectivity. The models, illustrated by the application to a simplified real data campaign, demonstrate a great potential for evolution and integration.

BACKGROUND

The Web has turned into one of the major world markets for the acquisition of goods and services. With an average growth of 113 million a year, the number of digital buyers was 1.66 billion in 2017. It is estimated that by 2021 they may reach 2.14 billion (Statista, 2019a). Digital buyers are not only very numerous but also spend a lot on money in online sales. Online turnover has been growing at a rate of 291 billion euros per year. Sales were 2,074 billion in 2017 and are expected to more than double in coming years, reaching 4,390 billion euros in 2021 (Statista, 2019b).

The rapid evolution of the digital society and buying experiences forced companies to a massive online presence, confronting them with new technological and social dynamics (DeCastro, de Bittencourt, Chaves, Barreiro, & Reis, 2015). At the global level, new digital markets have flourished, immersed in an increasing complexity and in the abundance of information. In this scenario, business decision making becomes more difficult and diffuse, requiring new methodologies and a constant updating by professionals and companies (Miranda & de Oliveira Arruda, 2004). Despite this, the evolution of communication and of new forms of business is unstoppable, creating stimulating interactions, and definitely bringing sellers and buyers closer together (Gielens & Steenkamp, 2019).

Not surprisingly, the biggest e-commerce companies take on gigantic proportions. Amazon leads with a turnover of 96.3 billion euros per year and Google ranks second with revenue of 67.5 billion euros (Dunlop, 2019). They are enthusiastic metrics that augur a promising future for this new form of business.

Digital infrastructures and equipment have also adapted and evolved. The emergence of tablets and smartphones revolutionized once again the whole strategy of communication and image of companies. Consumers can now search, view, and purchase from anywhere, anytime, with their smartphones. Companies respond to this voracious curiosity by rapidly and massively loading their digital channels with new products, new stories, new content and multiple curiosities (Okada & Souza, 2011; Torres, 2010). The new equipment, with full image and permanently connected, potentiate the expansion of digital strategies, leading to a more personalized, dynamic and cheap communication (Miranda & de Oliveira Arruda, 2004; Reddy, 2016; Torres, 2009). In addition to the evident ability to segment the message, the new online communication tools allow to measure and control the results, granting a greater return on investment and a more assertive strategy structure (Benge, 2014).

Hence, it is a true revolution in the way of doing marketing, driven by the need to interconnect technology with marketing (Kotler, 1999). It is the era of digital marketing, which uses all mechanisms connected to the Internet and that have the functionality to spread the business message (Miranda & de Oliveira Arruda, 2004).

The Emergence of Search Engines

In 1989 the Gross brothers, Bill and Larry, introduced Magellan, later known as Lotus 1-2-3, which consisted of hard disk search software running on MS-DOS. At the same time other competitors appeared on the market but Magellan was the simplest and fastest (Scott, 1989). A year later, the first web search engine was created. Its author was Alan Emtage, a student at McGill University in Montreal. Throughout the 1990s, other proposals emerged, Veronica and Excite in 1993, Yahoo and Lycos in 1994, Altavista in 1995 and Ask Jeeves in 1997.

In 1996, Bill Gross, creator of Magellan and founder of the company GoTo.com, Inc., was interested in an idea presented by a colleague, Scott Banister. It consisted of charging search advertisers by the click with ads tied to the searched keyword. The GoTo.com, Inc., meanwhile Overture Services Inc., was the first to provide an Internet search engine that relied on sponsored search results and pay-per-click ads (Wall, 2017).

In 1997, two Stanford University students, Larry Page and Sergey Brin, launched the BackRub, a search engine that ranked pages using citation notation. In the PageRank algorithm links count as votes, but some votes count more than others do. A year later, they officially launched the Google search engine (Wall, 2017). With no cost to the user and an impressive simplicity and performance (in terms of speed and quality), Google achieved immediate success and has not stopped growing to this day.

About Google's operating algorithms, little or nothing was known until 2012, when its creators Brin and Page decided released some information to help managers and web developers improve the content they produced. The search is based on a ranking of web pages through an index, the Page Rank, which can be defined as the probability of a random user visiting the page. So, a web page will have a high PageRank if there are many pages that point to it, or if there are some pages that point to it and which, in turn, have a high PageRank. The underlying principle is that it will be worth visiting the most interesting pages (most cited in quantity and quality). The calculation algorithm is iterative and, according to the authors, allows to determine the PageRank of 26 million web pages in a few hours (Brin & Page, 2012).

As the creators themselves acknowledge, Google's search engine goes beyond PageRank (Brin & Page, 2012). Globally, there is no central record for web pages, so Google uses Googlebot to continuously crawl new pages by adding them to its database. This process is called crawling. The Googlebot crawler system is a search robot that collects information from all the websites that are available online. Online platforms are ranked based on the quality of the external links, the content on the various pages and the relevance of the content. In addition, a mechanism checks website that deal with the same subject and analyzes the most searched platforms. Determining how often a keyword appears is a very important criterion in the placement of the page and website (Pereira, 2008).

In 2000, Google launched its own pay-per-click model, calling it Google Adwords. This first approach by Google was based on a CPM (Cost-Per-Mille) philosophy, where payment was indexed to the number of impressions. Google relaunched AdWords in 2002, selling ads in an auction similar to Overture's, but also adding ad click through rate as a factor in the ad rankings. In this new business model, advertisers only pay when they receive traffic, completely altering the whole organizational mentality and encouraging participation. The minimum spend was $ 1 a day, which end up being very attractive to businesses and highly profitable to Google.

Google Ads Campaign Optimization

Planning Google Ads (formerly known as Adwords) campaigns requires making decisions about a broad set of variables and parameterization options that impact campaign performance. These decisions include the general campaign template, keywords, maximum bid, geographic limitation, negative words, ad format, budget, and so on. Decision complexity, inherent costs, impact on organizations, and market competition are all sufficient reasons to challenge researchers to develop methodologies that lead to campaign optimization. For a general knowledge concerning Google Ads, the reader can refer to the book "Advanced Google Adwords" by Brad Geddes (2014).

It is important not to confuse Search Engine Marketing (SEM), where paid ad campaign is inserted, with Search Engine Optimization (SEO), which refers to organic, unpaid optimization. SEO develops a set of techniques to act on page content and links in order to increase google indexing and hence organic page traffic (Ledford, 2015; Patil & Patil, 2018).

The offer of advertising places by Internet Search Engine Providers (ISEP) is impressive compared to the small number of bidders, sometimes one or two. Based on a two-place and two-bidder model, Zhang (2007) concludes that winning-pay auctions are preferred over all-pay auctions. In addition, Zhang demonstrates that ISEP earns more revenue from a single ad-place scenario than from a two-auction scenario.

Optimization models are mentioned as one effective strategy to plan Google Ads by extant literature, which provide some interesting contributions on the topic. Mehta and colleagues developed models to achieve optimal matching between a set of search keywords and a set of bidders with limited daily budgets, suggesting generalized algorithms to maximize total ISEP revenue. They called it Adword Allocation, in which queries are to be assigned to bidders with budget constraints (Goel & Mehta, 2008; Mehta, 2007; Mehta et al., 2005).

From the advertiser's point of view, Daniela and Anca (2008) analyzed the buying process and devised a set of techniques to optimize campaigns. Without getting involved in mathematical models, they discuss long tail keywords, landing pages, objectives and ad construction in order to emotionally capture the customer (Anca & Daniela, 2008; Dănciulescu, Daniela & Anca, 2008).

Thomaidou et al. (2012) used genetic algorithms to optimize campaigns in Google Adwords. They propose the AD-MAD System which, according to the authors, is capable of automatically generating keywords, advertising text, and managing the advertise campaign. It consists of a statistical process and optimization routines to select and refine keywords. They also refer to an additional forecasting module for estimating impressions from historical data and regression models to relate impressions to other variables. In an article published in 2012, they briefly describe the modules that make up the system (Thomaidou, Leymonis, Liakopoulos, & Vazirgiannis, 2012). A more developed version of the previous article was published in 2014, with detailed description of the AD-MAD architecture, the mathematical model (Knapsack Problem) and heuristic algorithm resolution (Genetic Algorithm) (Thomaidou, Liakopoulos, & Vazirgiannis, 2014).

Madera et al. (2017) exploited a Fuzzy Inference System to control the bidding price of the campaigns from the current bidding price of the campaign and the current CTR. According to the authors, the results are more favorable than those proposed by Google mechanisms (Madera, Castillo, Garcia, & Mancilla, 2017).

Zhou et al. (2008) study sponsored search auctions by proposing automatic revenue-maximizing bidding strategies with a limited campaign budget. The problem is modulated as an online Knapsack problem and is solved using deterministic and heuristic algorithms (Zhou et al., 2008).

Borgs et al. (2007) considered an integrated approach to the budget-limited ad auction system, proposing a heuristic methodology to optimize advertiser utility, explaining the return on investment (ROI). They conducted simulation-based testing by considering various parameters and evaluating revenue and efficiency (Borgs et al., 2007).

Szymanski and Lipinski (2018) proposed a model in order to achieve the effectiveness of Google Adwords advertising activities. The comprehensive template considers several steps: keyword selection, extension design, excluded keywords, geolocation, site design and optimization, and continuous optimization of campaign parameters. They address each of the model's components but leave optimality for future work. (Szymanski & Lininski, 2018).

The growing complexity of Adwords investment decisions leads many advertisers to seek expert help from a third party. Wang et al. (2016) optimized third-party profit while minimizing customer CPC. They proposed an interesting methodology for automatic keyword selection through Twitter and consequently a model that optimizes the balance between maximizing ROI and minimizing risk, in line with the classic Markowitz economic model (Wang, Li, Xie, Kaafar, & Salamatian, 2016).

GOOGLE ADS

The revolution of information and communication technologies has been accompanied by changing buying habits, the growth of new online markets, and even the replacement of physical stores by large online distributors. E-commerce success is due in large part to the search engines that match consumer desires with online stores (Mehta, 2007). In fact, online search engines have not only changed the way the consumer uses the internet, but also the way companies present their ads (Weusthof, 2015). With a 90% market share, Google assumes a nearly hegemonic role among search engines (Statista, 2019a). Consequently, Google Ads, the Google's business model platform, occupies a dominant position in the market. Overall, it allows companies to secure the impression of ads on the Google search engine. A well-planned investment in Google Ads can lead to greater awareness of the company and a significant growth of the business in a short time.

So, what is Google Ads? Google Ads is the Google search engine pay-per-click (PPC) program, by which an advertiser chooses the words that will activate your ad. It consists of an algorithm that positions the ad in order to make the link to the website (Pereira, 2008). The position of the ad in the search engine depends on how much the advertiser is willing to pay for each word when the user clicks on the ad. The cost that comes with it is called cost-per-click (CPC). This business model ensures the visibility of the message with a cost dependent on the number of clicks made by the search engine users. For advertisers, the main goal is to make the link between consumer searches on Google and a certain product / company to foster customer acquisition and sales. Google Ads represents an opportunity for businesses to intercept their target markets the moment someone searches for the products they sell. For this, an appropriate selection of keywords is essential in order to narrow the search and reduce the rejection rate (Oxer, 2008). Keywords are defined as phrases or sentences the user writes on the Google search box in order to initiate a search. Often, these keywords represent consumer desires, wishes, and questions associated to different phases of the buying decision process. By targeting relevant keywords with search engine advertising, companies want to identify and convert leads.

Google Ads is also a user-friendly and relatively simple tool to operate. The advertiser bids a set of keywords based on the position they want to reach for their ads on the Google search engine. In addition to setting a daily and / or monthly budget and tracking the unit cost of each clicked ad, the user has access to a set of tools to measure results, select keywords, and embed multiple ads, or ad groups (Araújo & Santos, 2017).

Google Ads Structure

Google Ads is a tool that must be handled after acquiring some basic knowledge to avoid errors and unnecessary costs for companies (Geddes, 2014). A good grasp of the Google Ads account structure is essential for campaign design and maximizing benefits according to business goals. Google Ads is based on three levels: account, campaign, and ad group (Holdren, 2011).

Creating an Account

The first step to getting started with the various potentialities of Google Ads is to create an account by associating a Gmail email address. It is possible to create a Google account that gives access to all tools, including Google Ads. Accounts control access data, administrative information, and billing (Holdren, 2011). Once the account is created, it is possible to start designing campaigns, respecting some limits (Google, 2019b). It is essential to plan the account structure so that the choice of keywords is targeted and assertive.

Example 1

The company Frutex Lda. intends to use Google Ads to promote the sale of various types of fruit. Its ads manager decides to implement a simple structure that includes keywords with a segmentation for all Portuguese-speaking countries. The account structure should be planned to contain the various campaigns with the various types of fruit (e.g., apple, orange) and various types of ads for variations (e.g., pippin apple, red apple). The keywords should have a good quality index and should not be too numerous (Figure 1).

Figure 1. Example of an ads account structure
Source: (the authors)

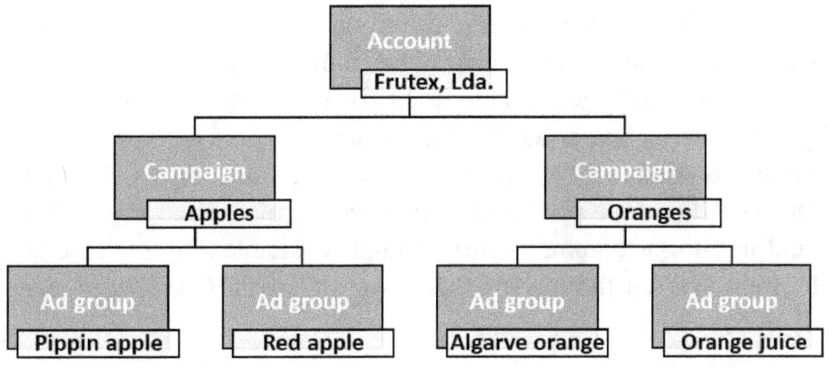

Designing a Campaign

An Ads campaign is composed of one or more ad groups, each represented by a landing page and a set of keywords (Albuquerque, Morla, Gabriel, & Campos, 2013). Campaigns control settings, daily budget, time segmentation, zone, ad type (text or display), maximum bid, and keywords (Holdren, 2011). They are subject to some limits that can be consulted in the Google Ads support page (Google, 2019b).

Example 2

Frutex Lda. wants to internationalize its fruit sales to two countries, France and Belgium. The ads manager created only one campaign, adjusting budget to ensure optimization. For each country, a different strategy should be designed, as well as the daily and monthly budget. Each country has customs that originate different types of online search. Belgium has different languages, not only French; hence, a more specific strategy is needed. The quality score for a campaign is judged from the quality of ads, keywords, and landing pages. The more relevant to the search the ads and words associated with them are, the greater the likelihood of achieving good results.

Ads Groups

The groups are the parts of the campaign that comprise multiple ads, keywords and a certain maximum click (value that the advertiser is willing to pay for each click) (Holdren, 2011). The group is the element that relates keywords, search terms and the number of conversions. They are subject to certain limits in terms of keywords and ads number (Google, 2019b).

Ads

Ads have the essential function of directing the search engine users to the company website. To be effective, the ads have to respond to the users' needs, that is, they have to match what the users are looking for in that search. If not, the ad may be a barrier to the company's sales (Geddes, 2014). There are two types of ads, search and display (banners). Search ads are text ads that appear in Google's search results and are typically used to advertise the products and / or services to search engine users. Display ads can be presented in different formats (e.g., image, video, rich media) and are allow to communicate the brand in a simple way as the user navigates through a website (Weusthof, 2015), that is, websites in the Google partner network.

Figure 2. Impression result with "porto turism" keyword search (13/05/2019)
Source: (the authors)

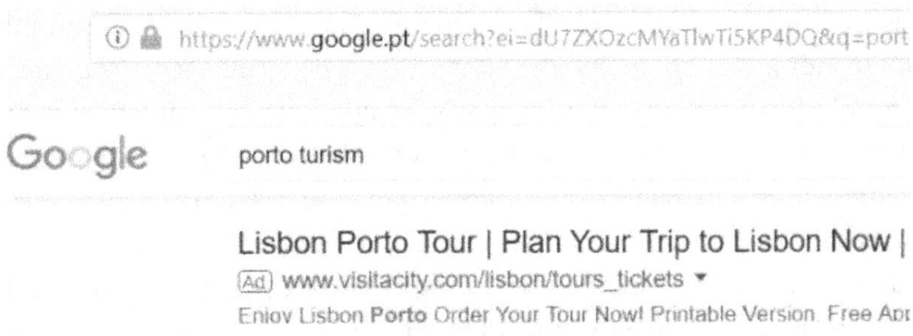

Search ads follow some rules designated by Google as "Expanded text ads". In the first line, the title (blue line) consists of two parts, plus an optional one, with a maximum of 30 characters each. The short URL domain (green second line) is automatically extracted from the final URL domain, with the possibility of couple two paths. The last two fields are for description and can have up to 90 characters each (Figure 2). It is also possible to add site link extensions; although Google does not guarantee that they appear alongside the ad (Google, 2019a).

The title is the first message that reaches the google user, sometimes the only one. It should hold the user's attention and communicate simply and immediately with him, responding to his doubts and needs. Effective communication is essential if there is to be a good click through rate and a profitable return on investment for the advertising company (Geddes, 2014).

Google's positioning system encourages companies to invest in quality ads so that they appear in the top places and in turn have more clicks (McDonald, 2014). An experiment conducted based on CPC Simulator (cost-per-click) (Clinks, 2017) shows that, the higher the quality score, the lower the cost per click (Table 1).

Table 1. Positioning test (clinks simulator)

Advertiser	Max Bid	Quality Score	AdRank	Position	Cost-per-Click
A	0,40 €	9	3,6 (0,4€x9)	1	0,23 €
B	0,65 €	3	1,95 (0,65€x3)	2	0,51 €
C	0,25 €	6	1,5 (0,25€x6)	3	Min Bid

Source: (the authors)

Keywords

Keywords are words or phrases that the campaign manager selects to the ad. Obviously, it is the main element to associate the ad with search engine users' searches, and the advertising platform matches the keywords of ads with the sentence or phrase the search engine users' type to initiate the search. The keywords price varies through an automatic auction mechanism (Albuquerque et al., 2013).

The process of keyword selection in Google Ads is particularly important so that the ad can appear in a good position in the search engines. Google launched Google Trends and Google Keyword Planner to help select keywords by providing relevant information and suggestions based on the type of business, products, or other characteristics the company wants to feature in the ads (e.g., consumer needs). The keywords may be classified according to the number of clicks and the conversion rate (Figure 3) (Monteiro, 2007).

Stars: Many clicks and an excellent conversion rate.

Question Marks: Many clicks but a low conversion rate.

Cash Cows: Few clicks but an excellent conversion rate.

Dogs: Few Clicks and a low conversion rate.

Therefore, campaigns should include the maximum of stars and exclude all dogs, in order to maximize the return on investment.

Figure 3. Keywords classification. Adapted from Monteiro (2007)
Source: (the authors)

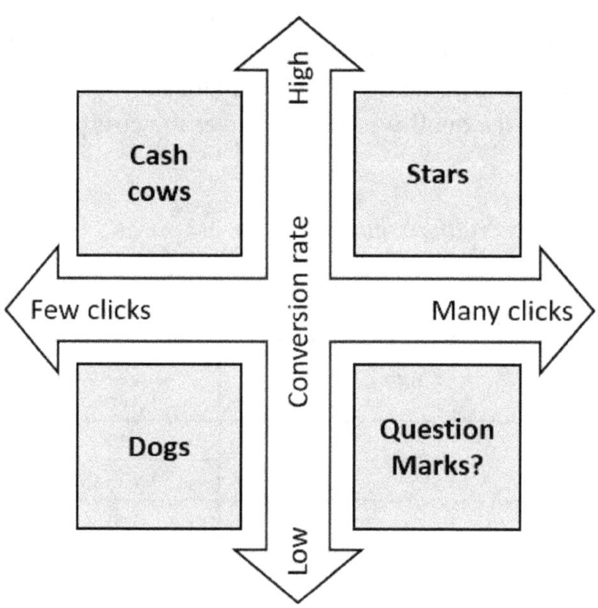

There are some cautions to note in the process of choosing the keywords, as highlighted in the following list (Fishkin, 2018; Patel, 2019).

Word grouping: Word group selection should be responsive to ad group targeting, generating a high return on investment. The higher the number of keywords in the ad, the better its placement and click through rate.

Matching words: In broad match, the ad appears through several variations of the keywords that the user inserts into the search engine. This allows increasing the number of impressions helping to better position the ad. In smaller companies with lower budgets, keyword segmentation should be directed to a niche market, always using an exact match. By this way, it is possible to minimize the money loss. A group of words with an exact match reduces the cost of the campaign and boosts results (Weusthof, 2015).

Restrictive parameters: Restrictive parameters are mechanisms that help lower the bounce rate by preventing the ads from being routed to the wrong audiences.

Negative keywords: Inserting negative keywords prevent the ad from being shown in unwanted searches.

Location criteria: Allows targeting the campaigns for a given geographic area.

Time criteria: Align ads with the highest productivity time periods.

Keywords With Traffic: Chose keywords that have a direct relationship with the product and that have traffic.

Forecasts: The forecasts allow to better design the campaign and its development. Google Trends is a tool that helps sustain and improve forecasting management.

Word Selection: Selection of derived and plural words is discouraged, especially in campaigns with exact match. In contrast, the use of a few words with broad correspondence is suggested.

Accreditation of the Ad: Accreditation of the ad or campaign gives the quality certificate that can make a difference to Google's criteria. Google Ads gives less importance to ads for commercial purposes compared to the news.

The use of Library Science indexing techniques (specification and association) is also indicated as a methodology to support the selection of keywords (Araújo & Santos, 2017). By cross-referencing existing information about the operation of the Page Rank algorithm (Brin & Page, 2012) with Davis's search engines (Davis, 2010), and the perception of the importance of digital media (Vaidhyanathan, 2011), Google's algorithms become clearer and consequently, provide more accurate and relevant results to its users.

Google Ads Metrics

The investment in online advertising justifies tight control over campaign results. The most commonly used metrics for these tracking and validation actions are the number of impressions, number of clicks paid, visits to the website, and the number of conversions. Based on these metrics, other indicators can be computed to provide additional information. Systematic monitoring of metrics and indicators leads to the creation of better quality ads, their improvement, and the exclusion of the least profitable ones (Vaver & Koehler, 2011). Google Analytics is a tool for collecting data on website traffic. Information about the visitors' location, number of pages visited, bounce rate, and many other indicators, allow to analyze, interpret, and structure website optimization (Clifton, 2012; Guerini, Strapparava, & Stock, 2010). Monitoring, evaluating and constantly adjusting an advertising campaign is the best strategy to ensure its effectiveness (McDonald, 2014).

Impressions

The number of impressions is the number of times an ad appears on a search results page or another site on the Google Partners Network (Google, 2019e). The best way to achieve a large number of clicks is to ensure maximum clicks (Weusthof, 2015).

Clicks

Clicking happens when a user clicks on the ad that was shown to him on the search page. Google counts this action as a click even if the ad link contains a problem and does not allow the user to sign in to the website. If the user enters it is considered a visit to the website, if not, it is only considered as an ad click (Google, 2018a). The higher the number of clicks, the higher the traffic on to the website.

Conversions

A conversion happens when the researcher, after interacting with the ad, performs an action that is considered valuable to the company and that was the goal of the ad, such as an online purchase, a phone call, a chat, or a quote request via email (Google, 2019c).

Click-Through Rate (CTR)

Click-through rate (CTR) is the ratio of number of clicks by number of impressions. A good CTR (closer to 1) means that the ad is appealing to the user and that the keywords match the search targeting elements (Google, 2018b). A high performing ad has a low number of impressions and a high percentage of clicks. The normal usual click-through rates for relevant ads are around 0.5% to 1.5%, meaning that for every 100 impressions an ad is clicked on average happens approximately 1 click.

Above these values for the click-through rate, the ad is considered highly relevant (Monteiro, 2007).

To improve the CTR, the advertiser must optimize the ad so that the search engine user feels like clicking on it as soon as he sees it. If the ad is well-crafted, positioned, and captivating, the searcher will be prompted to click (Monteiro, 2007).

Cost-Per-Click (CPC)

Cost-per-click (CPC) is the amount of money that the advertiser pays for each click on the ad (Guerini et al., 2010). Can be calculated by dividing the total cost expenditure on of the ad by the number of clicks. In general, the CPC is less than the maximum amount that the advertiser is willing to pay for a click (max CPC).

The ad placement takes into account the CTR of for each keyword and the maximum CPC. The most relevant ads have a privileged status over the rest. Therefore, special attention should be given to the decision on the maximum CPC in order to ensure the highest possible profit (Monteiro, 2007).

Conversion Rate

The conversion rate is calculated by dividing the number of conversions by the number of clicks. Indicates the percentage of clicks that meet your business conversion goals (Guerini et al., 2010).

Return on Investment (ROI)

The return on investment (ROI) is defined as the number of beneficial actions for the company over the number of paid impressions. It is the index that measures the success of the campaign (Albuquerque et al., 2013). When the goal is to increase profit, then the ROI can be defined as follows:

$$ROI = \frac{Revenue - Cost}{Cost}$$

DIGITAL MARKETING IN PRACTICE

Despite the user-friendliness of the platform and the promising results, Google Ads campaigns have no guaranteed return on investment and is not free of difficulties. A simple search on the Google Ads support page reveals some of the concerns of the user community, grouping the problems into several categories (Google, 2019d).

- Ad Approval and Policy
- Billing
- Performance optimization
- Conversions and results evaluation
- Audience targeting and remarketing
- Google Shopping and Merchant Center

It seems clear that digital marketers are faced with limitations, problems, and opportunities. However, research published on the subject is scare. Some possible reasons are the fact that this is a recent topic of research, with a strong transformation dynamism, and because organizations tend to look at their digital marketing strategies as prompters of a competitive advantage, and therefore classify their information as internal and confidential.

Opinion Survey

Considering that digital marketing practitioners are the most qualified to give their opinion on the subject, a global opinion survey was conducted to analyze their opinions on the opportunities and problems arising from their daily practice in the use of applications like Google Adwords. At the same time, it was also an opportunity to validate the evolution of technology, markets and consumer habits. The opinion survey took the form of a quantitative primary research, implemented through an online survey.

Getting qualified information about the digital marketing tools and more specifically about Google Ads requires respondents to have a thorough knowledge of the subject. Therefore, the target population comprised digital marketing professionals with deep knowledge of Google Ads. It is a population with infinite dimension, not circumscribed to a place and whose distribution is unknown. The lack of a listing of the entire population (with contact information) makes it impossible to use probabilistic sampling methods. Thus, a sampling basis was selected by a mixed method of judgment and convenient sampling (non-probabilistic methods). Judgement, because they are chosen by the decision maker as representative of the population, and convenient because they are grouped in websites and can be contacted relatively easily. Three private Facebook discussion groups on Google Ads were selected. They are groups of individuals with professional practice in the field of digital marketing or are simply interested in the Google Ads tool. It is expected that the individuals belonging to these discussion groups can provide a high degree of confidence in the quality of the answers obtained. In addition, the worldwide dispersion observed in these groups gives hope of achieving a high representativeness of the population of experts. Specifically, the sampling base consists of 12135 individuals belonging to the following discussion groups:

- Google AdWords in vein (4835 followers)
- AdWords & YouTube Ad Buyers (5900 followers)
- AdWords Mastery (1400 followers)

The survey was pre-tested in order to verify if it was clear and accessible to the interviewees, to measure the response time and to correct eventual incongruities. The online questionnaire was sent to all members of this sampling base. The final sample consists of all respondents (Bethlehem, 2009).

The data collection was conducted via the Internet, a low-cost, convenient, fast medium with immediate and automatic coding of error-avoidance responses, and the only viable way to communicate with experts on a global scale. In addition, the subject in question is especially dominated by individuals immersed in digital technology, daily users of these tools and therefore especially indicated for online research. The software used to prepare and conduct the questionnaire was Google Docs. For disseminating the questionnaire, the necessary posts were made in closed groups selected on Facebook. Data was collected during the first quarter of 2018.

Sample Characterization

The final sample consists of 81 respondents, among the 12135 who were asked to collaborate through the three discussion groups. They are men (53%) and women (47%) between the ages of 21 and 45 (96%). About half are residents of South America and the rest are scattered across continents. They have a higher education level and a high academic qualification, which gives an added credibility to the results. Most are executives or employees (78%), with 19% being marketing students.

Only the individuals who work in the field of digital marketing (62) were considered in the analysis. Some opinions are lost, but the maximum credibility of the answers is guaranteed.

Results Analysis

Two-thirds of respondents assume they have difficulty keeping up with the constant changes in logarithms operated by Google, Facebook, LinkedIn and other platforms, pointing to lower conversions and higher costs. They clearly identify Google Ads and Facebook as the platforms that have implemented more changes in recent years and they try to solve these difficulties by attending thematic courses and tutorials. Advertising agencies are avoided, being considered only as a last resource.

In terms of digital marketing strategy, almost all respondents (58 out of 62) run Google Ads campaigns, and 77.4% use Facebook Ads. With the exception of mobile marketing, with only 19 users saying to adopt them, the remaining strategies are used in a balanced way. They are likely to seek to use integrated strategies to maximize their results.

Almost half of respondents say that Google Ads accounts for around 45% of their companies' business volume. For a quarter of the respondents, the return on investment in Google Ads already represents 60% of the billing. The majority (57%) considers that Google Ads is essential to position their brand in the online market, while 43% did not consider it essential and 8 of them even consider that the Ads is not important for online brand positioning.

In this study only 3 respondents always carry out keyword selection strategies to implement their strategy, 19 do it quite often and 22 with some regularity. About 30% do not use keyword selection strategies or use them with reduced regularity. It is a surprising result, considering the importance of choosing the keywords for the success of the advertising campaigns. On the one hand, it can help explain some disappointment with the campaigns and on the other, it reinforces the need to find models that help optimize keyword selection strategies.

The use of content marketing strategies is not the rule. Only half of the respondents shyly resort to this type of strategy with some frequency. Almost half of the respondents (49%) believe that companies should invest in digital platforms in order to ensure better results. Only 10 respondents say that one should absolutely invest in digital platforms to see their business grow. At the other extreme, 9 take the opposite view.

About half of the respondents (53%) analyze the results of their campaigns often or very often, 27% analyze the results with some frequency and 20% never or rarely. The lack of monitoring can also affect the effectiveness of campaigns. A large number of respondents (70%) report that the most important metrics for measuring their results are the number of clicks. It follows the number of sales (53%) and the lied's number (52%).

Marketing professionals try to implement their strategies in order to guarantee more visibility (positioning) (57%), capture a specific type of consumer (63%) or a specific type product (58%). Only 16 refer to global competition, contrary to the current idea that companies are increasingly seeking to compete in international markets. The vast majority (86%) believe that training marketers is sufficient to successfully implement their strategies. Still, 14% feel that academic training did not adequately prepare them for this task.

In summary, marketers surveyed widely use Google Ads as a digital marketing strategy and consider that Google Ads contributes a significant share of their business revenue. Still, they are somewhat hesitant about the importance of the platform for the positioning of their brands, the strategies of selection of keywords and the result of their campaigns. They also show some caution about the benefits of investing in digital marketing platforms.

OPTIMIZATION MODELS FOR GOOGLE ADS

The investment in campaigns on Google Ads has become more professional. Only a competent and quantified approach can ensure that money is well spent and yields results to the investor. Indeed, the amount of information to guide the campaign decisions is impressive. It comprises impressions, clicks, conversions, billing, visiting times, purchased products, among many other indicators. This obviously poses an additional challenge to campaign managers, and can be seen either as making it difficult to decide, or as an opportunity to build models that can help you find the best investment solutions.

The models developed in this section allow optimizing strategies for clicks, conversions, or return on investment, depending on the main goal of the campaign manager. This section uses the example of a campaign of a fruit seller company that illustrates the application of the models, in order to further demonstrate its usage and to soften its mathematical component. The examples were solved using a standard desktop computer and the OpenSolver optimizer (https://opensolver.org/), a free Excel add-in.

Google Ads Settings

The setting up of Google Ads will have as an example the Frutex, a Portuguese fruit company that intends to implement Google Ads marketing campaigns for three types of fruits: apple, orange and pear.

The design of the campaigns is conditioned by a set of options that the user must take when the campaign is setting up.

- **Weekly Budget**: Establishes the daily, weekly or monthly budget to implement the campaign.
- **Bid Strategy**: Choose a bid strategy (in this case automatic) to maximize clicks.
- **Segmentation by Region**: Directs the campaign to Portugal, where potential customers are located.
- **Time-Segmentation**: Determines the time periods in which ads are displayed, that is, business days from 8:00 am to 10:00 pm.

Table 2. Keywords for the ad group – Apples

Ad Group: Maça			
Keywords	**Average monthly searches**	**Competition**	**Estimated cost per click**
Maça	1000-10000	Low	0,10 €
maça vermelha	100-1000	Low	0,03 €
fruta maça	10-100	Low	0,12 €
maca fruta	10-100	Low	0,03 €
maça maça	10-100	Low	0,09 €
maça red	10-100	Low	0,03 €
maça amarela	10-100	Low	0,06 €
maca vermelha peruana	10-100	Mean	0,05 €
variedades de maçã	100-1000	Low	0,02 €
maçã gala	100-1000	Low	0,06 €
maça reineta	100-1000	Low	0,06 €
maça portuguesa	10-100	Low	0,03 €

Source: (the authors)

- **Negative Keywords**: The following Portuguese negative words were selected: livros (books), receitas (recipes), (saladas) salads, enlatados (canned), frutos secos (dried fruits), frutos desidratados (dehydrated fruits), feira (fair) and hipermercado (hypermarket).
- **Maximum CPC**: Creates a maximum bid barrier, lengthening budget and duration of ads.
- **Targeted Budget**: weekly budget breakdown for the three campaigns: apple, orange, and pear.
- **Extensions**: Addition of two types of extensions. 4 sitelinks (links attached at the end of ads to target specific website pages) and 1 call extension that has an additional monthly charge of € 10.

Keyword Selection

With the help of Google Keyword Planner, some keywords related to the products that Frutex intends to market were selected. As Frutex is a Portuguese company, the choice was based on the Portuguese keywords indicated in Table 2, Table 3 and Table 4, each with additional information about the average monthly searches, the level of competition and the estimated cost per click. The selection of the words

Table 3. Keywords for the ad group - Pears

Ad Group: Pera			
Keywords	**Average monthly searches**	**Competition**	**Estimated cost per click**
pera portuguesa	10-100	Low	0,20 €
pera portuguesa	1000-10000	Low	0,01 €
pera rocha	100-1000	Low	0,10 €
pêra	100-1000	Low	0,02 €
pera williams	100-1000	Low	0,12 €
pera fruta	10-100	Low	0,09 €
fruta pera	10-100	Low	0,03 €
pera rocha do oeste	10-100	Low	0,09 €

Source: (the authors)

is the result of the articulation between the results obtained by Google Keyword Planner and the analysis of the main competitors' positioning.

Historical Data and Forecasts

Building models requires predictions of the number of clicks, number of conversions, and billing for the campaign period. Predictions are calculated based on historical data collected in campaigns already implemented or in progress. In the case of the company Frutex, data on number of clicks, conversions and billing (in euros) over the first 4 weeks of 2018 are shown in Table 5, Table 6 and Table 7, respectively.

Table 4. Keywords for the ad group - Oranges

Ad Group: Laranja			
Keywords	**Average monthly searches**	**Competition**	**Estimated cost per click**
laranja	1000-10000	Low	0,03 €
laranja pera rio	10-100	Low	0,02 €
laranja do céu	10-100	Low	0,10 €
preço laranja	10-100	Low	0,90 €
variedades de laranja	10-100	Low	0,01 €
tipos de laranja	10-100	Low	0,10 €

Source: (the authors)

Table 5. Click number over 4 weeks

	Week 1					Week 2					Week 3					Week 4				
	01-Jan	02-Jan	03-Jan	04-Jan	05-Jan	08-Jan	09-Jan	10-Jan	11-Jan	12-Jan	15-Jan	16-Jan	17-Jan	18-Jan	19-Jan	22-Jan	23-Jan	24-Jan	25-Jan	26-Jan
Maça						14			1		18	1	1	5		22		5	4	
maça vermelha		50	20	84	12	55	47	23	90	15	47	50	21	77	22	44	46	23	69	15
fruta maça				23					27					24					22	
maca fruta				1		31	1		3		40	4		5		35	6		12	
maça maça				1		11			2		7	1	33	5	1	15	1	21	1	1
maça red			32				1	35	1			5	5	5	1		12	7	6	
maça amarela						10					5					12				
maca vermelha peruana		80	25				74	22		13		69	18	1	17		50	23	3	27
variedades de maçã							1					1	1				2	10		
maçã gala			30	65	10			32	62	16		1	26	68	18			34	71	23
maça reineta		60	62	59	60	54	66	62	61	67	55	71	59	60	42	62	75	61	90	45
maça portuguesa		30		42	12	15	33		50	15	20	21	1	47	24	22	26	2	53	27
pera portuguesa		17	10	21	6	3	21	7	19	5	5	19	5	21	4	11	22	6	20	1
pera		1	1	1	1			1	1		1		1	2		4		2	1	
pera rocha		15	11	20	8	11	9	11	19	10	14	11	9	15	6	6	7	6	14	12
pêra				1					1					3					1	
pera williams		2		5		1	1		1		2	2		3		7	1		1	
pera fruta		10		2		4	7		1	1	5	6		3		8	5		1	
fruta pera				1					7					2	4				2	3
pera rocha do oeste		1	11	5	9	5	2	13	11	11	7	5	12	15	13	5	6	11	13	15
laranja		11	30	34	23	24	13	32	30	27	26	16	31	27	24	11	18	25	22	21
laranja pera rio			50	23				47	26				42	29				41	24	
laranja do céu				14					15		1			20	1	1		1	13	5
preço laranja		5	1	3			4	3	4		1	4	2	1		4	1	1	2	
variedades de laranja		10	2	23	33	4	12	4	27	23	1	11	6	23	21	1	13	5	17	19
tipos de laranja		9	2	1	11		10	2	3	15		8	1	1	13		11	2	1	9

Source: (the authors)

Table 6. Conversions over 4 weeks

	Week 1					Week 2					Week 3					Week 4				
	01-Jan	02-Jan	03-Jan	04-Jan	05-Jan	08-Jan	09-Jan	10-Jan	11-Jan	12-Jan	15-Jan	16-Jan	17-Jan	18-Jan	19-Jan	22-Jan	23-Jan	24-Jan	25-Jan	26-Jan
Maça						2					3					1			1	
maça vermelha		5	1	10		1	6	2	11		5	11		3		12	5	1	9	1
fruta maça																			6	
maca fruta											7									
maça maça											1					3		5	1	1
maça red			6				2													
maça amarela																				
maca vermelha peruana		4	1				1	2		7		3		1	1					
variedades de maçã													1							
maçã gala			1	4	1			2	3	1		1								
maça reineta		2	6	1	5	1	3	5	2	6	2	12	4	23	9	2	8	1	12	4
maça portuguesa		1		3	6		1		4	2	5	4	1	3	5	1	1	2	2	7
pera portuguesa		6	4	10	1	3	11	3	9	1	1	6	1	11		1	4		7	
pera																				
pera rocha		4	1	10	2	2		9		3	4			6	1	1			4	
pêra																				
pera williams						1														
pera fruta														1					1	
fruta pera																				
pera rocha do oeste					1	1	1	1	2	1	1	5		10	1	1	1	1	3	1
laranja		4	1	3	1	5	7	1	8	1	1	7		2	1	1	4	2	9	1
laranja pera rio				1					4					2					5	
laranja do céu				1					1					1					1	
preço laranja			1	3			4	3	4			4	2	1			1	1	2	
variedades de laranja																				
tipos de laranja																				

Source: (the authors)

From the time series records, a forecast of the number of clicks, conversions and billing for the following week, period of the advertising campaign (January 29 to February 2, 2018) is made. The number of clicks provided by the word "maça vermelha" over the four weeks has a noticeable seasonality, with 4 weekly seasonal cycles, each consisting of 5 periods, corresponding to the days of the week. The

Table 7. Billing over 4 weeks in euros

	Week 1					Week 2					Week 3					Week 4				
	01-Jan	02-Jan	03-Jan	04-Jan	05-Jan	08-Jan	09-Jan	10-Jan	11-Jan	12-Jan	15-Jan	16-Jan	17-Jan	18-Jan	19-Jan	22-Jan	23-Jan	24-Jan	25-Jan	26-Jan
Maça						3,18					4,77					1,59			1,59	
maça vermelha		7,95	1,59	15,9		1,59	9,54	3,18	17,49		7,95	17,49		4,77		19,08	7,95	1,59	14,31	1,59
fruta maça																			9,54	
maca fruta											11,13									
maça maça											1,59					4,77		7,95	1,59	1,59
maça red			9,54				3,18													
maça amarela																				
maca vermelha peruana		6,36	1,59				1,59	3,18		11,13		4,77	0	1,59	1,59					
variedades de maçã													1,59							
maçã gala			1,59	6,36	1,59			3,18	4,77	1,59		1,59								
maça reineta		3,18	9,54	1,59	7,95	1,59	4,77	7,95	3,18	9,54	3,18	19,08	6,36	36,57	14,31	3,18	12,72	1,59	19,08	6,36
maça portuguesa		1,59		4,77	9,54		1,59		6,36	3,18	7,95	6,36	1,59	4,77	7,95	1,59	1,59	3,18	3,18	11,13
pera portuguesa		5,94	3,96	9,9	0,99	2,97	10,89	2,97	8,91	0,99	0,99	5,94	0,99	10,89		0,99	3,96		6,93	
pera																				
pera rocha		3,96	0,99	9,9	1,98	1,98		8,91		2,97	3,96			5,94	0,99	0,99			3,96	
pêra																				
pera williams						0,99														
pera fruta														0,99					0,99	
fruta pera																				
pera rocha do oeste					0,99	0,99	0,99	0,99	1,98	0,99	0,99	4,95		9,9	0,99	0,99	0,99	0,99	2,97	0,99
laranja		7,96	1,99	5,97	1,99	9,95	13,93	1,99	15,92	1,99	1,99	13,93		3,98	1,99	1,99	7,96	3,98	17,91	1,99
laranja pera rio				1,99					7,96					3,98					9,95	
laranja do céu				1,99					1,99					1,99					1,99	
preço laranja			1,99	5,97			7,96	5,97	7,96			7,96	3,98	1,99			1,99	1,99	3,98	0
variedades de laranja																				
tipos de laranja																				

Source: (the authors)

trend manifestation is not so pronounced, although it is possible to observe a slight downward tendency (Figure 4).

Tables with the number of clicks, conversions, and billing are sparse, meaning they have too many null entries. In this case, the use of smoothing methods to predict series with seasonality and trend, such as the Winters method (Winters, 1960), is not recommended. Like most quantitative forecasting methods, the Winters method smooths out historical data, predicting non-zero clicks for all future periods. For example, the keyword "apple fruit" only shows clicks on Thursday. It would not be

Figure 4. Number of clicks for keyword "maça vermelha"
Source: (the authors)

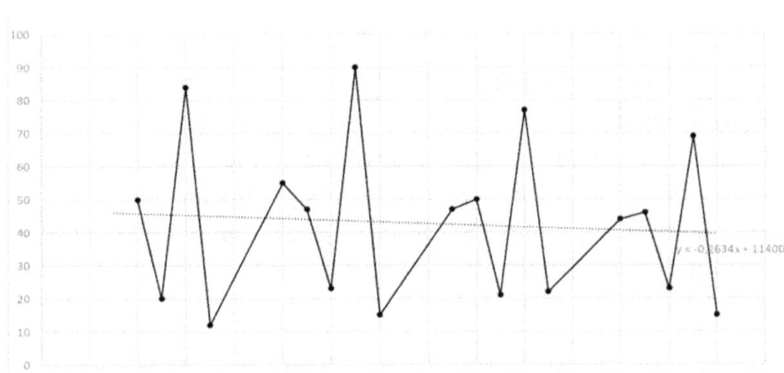

Table 8. Forecasts for week 5

CLICKS FORECAST					CONVERSIONS FORECAST					BILLING FORECAST				
29-Jan	30-Jan	31-Jan	01-Feb	02-Feb	29-Jan	30-Jan	31-Jan	01-feb	02-feb	03-feb	04-feb	05-feb	06-feb	07-feb
	1				2			1		3,18			0,4	
3	4		89	1	6	7	1	8	1	9,54	10,73	1,59	13,12	0,4
								6					2,39	
1	1		18		7					3,71				
	2	1	2		2		5	1	1	2,12		1,99	0,4	0,4
			13	1		2	6				0,8	2,39		
	3	1	11			3	2	1	4		3,18	1,19	0,4	3,18
							1					0,4		
	3		1	1		1	2	4	1		0,4	1,19	2,78	0,8
	9				2	6	4	10	6	2,65	9,94	6,36	15,11	9,54
1	4	1	21		3	2	2	3	5	3,18	2,78	1,19	4,77	7,95
	6				2	7	3	9	1	1,65	6,68	1,98	9,16	0,5
2	3		18	1	2	4	5	7	2	2,31	0,99	2,48	4,95	1,49
					1					0,33				
	1							1					0,5	
1	3		7	1	1	2	1	5	1	0,99	1,73	0,5	3,71	0,99
2	2		47	1	2	6	1	6	1	4,64	10,95	1,99	10,95	1,99
			13					3					5,97	
								1					1,99	
1	5		1			3	2	3			4,48	3,48	4,98	
	2													

Source: (the authors)

acceptable to have an algorithm that predicts the existence of clicks on other days, albeit in small numbers.

Taking into account the constraints observed in the previous paragraph, the forecasts were calculated by a 4-week simple moving average forecast method. In this way, the average number of clicks of the same word gives the forecast of the number of clicks for a particular keyword on a given day on the homologous days of the previous 4 weeks. The weekly seasonality is thus respected and it is ensured that days with zero historical entries correspond to a forecast that is also zero. Table 8 presents the forecasts for the number of clicks, number of conversions, and billing for week 5.

Mathematical Models

In the previous sections, some initial steps related to the configuration of Google Ads and the preparation of data necessary to build the optimization models were presented. As it will be explained in this section, some of the options taken provide the basis of model development and constitute themselves as parameters or constraints. Linear programming models are composed of an objective function, a set of functional constraints and binary constraints on variables.

Model 1

The objective of the first model is to choose the keywords for next week (week 5) in order to maximize the number of clicks, under the available budget.

Let K be the set of all keywords.
Let W be the set of campaign days in Google Ads.
Let G_r be the set of keywords of the ad group r.

The following parameters are defined:

c_{ij}: expected number of clicks for the word i on day j (Table 8)
CPC_{ij}: predicted cost per click for the word i on day j (Table 2, Table 3, Table 4)
B_m: budget available for the "maçã" campaign
B_p: budget available for the "pera" campaign
B_l: budget available for the "laranja" campaign

The following variables are defined:

$$x_{ij} = \begin{cases} 1 & \text{if the word } i \text{ is chosen on day } j \\ 0 & \text{otherwise} \end{cases}$$

The model presents the following mathematical formulation.

$$Max\ Z = \sum_{i \in K, j \in W} c_{ij} x_{ij}$$

Subject to

$$\sum_{i \in G_1 = \{maçã\}} CPC_{ij} c_{ij} x_{ij} \le B_m \qquad ; j \in W$$

$$\sum_{i \in G_2 = \{pera\}} CPC_{ij} c_{ij} x_{ij} \le B_p \qquad ; j \in W$$

$$\sum_{i \in G_3 = \{laranja\}} CPC_{ij} c_{ij} x_{ij} \leq B_l \qquad ; j \in W$$

$$x_{ij} \in \{0,1\}$$

The objective function indicates the total number of clicks observed in the campaign week (week 5). The constraints limit the budget available for the apple, pear and orange campaign, respectively. Note that $CPC_{ij}c_{ij}$ represents the cost of word i on day j. In the Frutex example the CPC of each keyword was considered equal every day of the week. The model supports a daily CPC variance, if applicable.

The binary constraints establish that each keyword is either chosen or not, on a given day, not admitting other alternatives.

In business terms, this template provides a daily choice of keywords throughout the week, respecting a certain budget and ensuring maximization of clicks on the company's ad.

Model 2

Model 1 can be enriched to maximize the number of conversions as well.

Let v_{ij} be the number of conversions forecasted for the keyword i in day j (Table 8)

Hence, it is possible to present a new mathematical model that allows to maximize the number of clicks and conversions.

$$Max\, Z = \alpha \sum_{i \in K, j \in W} c_{ij} x_{ij} + \beta \sum_{i \in K, j \in W} v_{ij} x_{ij}$$

Subject to

$$\sum_{i \in G_1 = \{maçã\}} CPC_{ij} c_{ij} x_{ij} \leq B_m \qquad ; j \in W$$

$$\sum_{i \in G_2 = \{pera\}} CPC_{ij} c_{ij} x_{ij} \leq B_p \qquad ; j \in W$$

$$\sum_{i \in G_3 = \{laranja\}} CPC_{ij} c_{ij} x_{ij} \leq B_l \qquad ; j \in W$$

$$\sum_{i\in K, j\in W} v_{ij}x_{ij} \geq 0{,}15 \sum_{\in K, j\in W} c_{ij}x_{ij}$$

$$x_{ij} \in \{0,1\}$$

The objective function is a linear function that represents the weighted sum of the number of clicks with the number of conversions. The weighting factors α and β allow us to assign a different weight to clicks and conversions in view of business objectives. A company that aims to make their products known or simply increase their reputation can give more weight to clicks and less to conversions. On the other hand, a company that is focused on the sale (conversion) may accentuate the value of β to the detriment of α. If α = β = 1 is given equal weight to both, clicks and conversions.

The first three constraints replicate those that were used in model 1. The fourth states that at least 15% of people who enter the company website (clicks) must generate conversions. Obviously, simply change the percentage in the model according to the business objectives.

Model 3

Consumers often turn to the web to buy low-value, low-profit items, preferring other channels to test and buy products that are more expensive. In such a case, a high number of conversions may not result in high returns for the company.

The following model maximizes not only the number of conversions, but also the profit.

Let f_{ij} be the revenue forecasted for keyword i on day j (Table 8)

$$Max\, Z = \alpha \sum_{i\in K, j\in W} \left(f_{ij} - CPC_{ij}c_{ij}\right)x_{ij} + \beta \sum_{i\in K, j\in W} v_{ij}x_{ij}$$

Subject to

$$\sum_{i\in G_1=\{maçã\}} CPC_{ij}c_{ij}x_{ij} \leq B_m \qquad ; j \in W$$

$$\sum_{i\in G_2=\{pera\}} CPC_{ij}c_{ij}x_{ij} \leq B_p \qquad ; j \in W$$

$$\sum_{i \in G_3 = \{laranja\}} CPC_{ij} c_{ij} x_{ij} \le B_l \qquad ; j \in W$$

$$\sum_{i \in K, j \in W} v_{ij} x_{ij} \ge 0,15 \sum_{\in K, j \in W} c_{ij} x_{ij}$$

$$x_{ij} \in \{0,1\}$$

The objective function, in addition to integrating the number of conversions, also represents the profit for the company, considering only the costs arising from the Ads campaign. Obviously, the choice will fall on the most profitable words and days. Note that $f_{ij} - CPC_{ij} c_{ij}$ represents the profit of the keyword i on day j.

Example of Application

In this section, the models presented will be tested considering the historical data related to the company Frutex as well as the forecasts already described (Table 8).

Frutex offers a weekly budget of 40 EUR (B = 40,00€) for the campaign, distributed as follows:

Maçã (apple)- 20,00 EUR (B_c = 20,00€)
Pera (pear)– 10,00 EUR (B_p = 10,00€)
Laranja (orange)– 10,00 EUR (B_l = 10,00€)

With this budget allocation, Frutex intends to focus on the apple campaign.

Based on the known information and using the models presented, we intend to find the best investment solutions for the next week (week 5), that is, to choose keywords for each day in order to maximize the number of clicks and / or conversions, as well as income, respecting the available budget.

For this example, the instances have been solved using OpenSolver, an add-in freeware that runs embedded in Excel software. OpenSolver solves linear and nonlinear optimization problems with continuous or integer variables. Unlike the excel solver add-in, OpenSolver does not limit the number of variables or constraints. As a linear and integer (binary) mathematical model, the choice falls on the embedded COIN-OR CBC solver routine.

Table 9. Weekly optimal keyword plan - model 1

	Weekly optimal keyword plan								
	Monday	Tuesday	Wednesday	Thursday	Friday				
	29-Jan	30-Jan	31-Jan	01-feb	02-feb	Clicks	CPC	Cost	
Maça	0	0	1	0	0	3	0,10	0,30	
maça vermelha	1	1	1	1	1	215	0,03	6,44	
fruta maça	0	0	0	0	0	0	0,12	0,00	
maca fruta	1	1	0	1	0	44	0,03	1,33	
maça maça	0	0	0	0	0	0	0,09	0,00	
maça red	0	1	1	1	1	31	0,03	0,92	19,98
maça amarela	0	0	0	0	0	0	0,06	0,00	
maca vermelha peruana	0	1	1	1	1	111	0,05	5,56	
variedades de maçã	0	1	1	0	0	7	0,02	0,14	
maçã gala	0	0	1	0	0	31	0,06	1,83	
maça reineta	0	0	0	0	0	0	0,06	0,00	
maça portuguesa	1	1	1	1	1	116	0,03	3,47	
pera portuguesa	0	0	0	0	0	0	0,20	0,00	
pera	1	1	1	1	1	7	0,01	0,07	
pera rocha	0	1	1	1	1	46	0,10	4,58	
pêra	0	0	0	1	0	2	0,02	0,03	9,96
pera williams	0	0	0	0	0	0	0,12	0,00	
pera fruta	1	1	0	0	0	13	0,09	1,14	
fruta pera	0	0	0	1	1	7	0,03	0,20	
pera rocha do oeste	1	1	1	1	1	44	0,09	3,95	
laranja	1	1	1	1	1	116	0,03	3,49	
laranja pera rio	0	0	1	1	0	71	0,02	1,41	
laranja do céu	1	0	0	1	1	20	0,10	1,95	9,97
preço laranja	0	0	0	0	0	0	0,90	0,00	
variedades de laranja	1	1	1	1	1	64	0,01	0,64	
tipos de laranja	0	1	1	1	1	25	0,10	2,48	
Clicks	140	213	207	266	144	969		39,91	
Cost	4,87	9,51	8,63	10,32	6,59				

Source: (the authors)

Model 1 Solution

Model 1 was estimated based on the number of clicks expected for week 5 (Table 8), the estimated cost per click (Table 2, Table 3, Table 4) and the available weekly budget. The solution provided by the Open Solver allowed to obtain the optimal weekly plan of keywords (Table 9).

The optimal solution is to reach the maximum number of 969 clicks by choosing each day of the week the words indicated by the cells to be shaded (numbered 1) (Table 9). The weekly budget has been respected by investing 39.91 EUR out of the 40 available. The distribution by group was as follows: 19.98 EUR for the apple campaign, 9.96 EUR for the pear campaign, and 9.97 EUR for the orange campaign. The keyword with the highest spending (6.44 EUR) is "maça vermelha" with 215 clicks, followed by "maça vermelha peruana" with 5.56 EUR and 111 clicks.

The most expensive day is Thursday, February 1, with expenses totaling 10.32 EUR for 266 clicks on all keywords chosen. The second highest expenditure is on January 30 with 9.51 EUR and 213 clicks.

Table 10. Weekly optimal keyword plan –model 2

	Monday	Tuesday	Wednesday	Thursday	Friday	β 1	α 1			
	29-Jan	30-Jan	31-Jan	01-feb	02-feb	Conversions	Clicks	CPC	Cost	
Maça	0	0	0	0	0	0	0	0,10	0,00	
maça vermelha	1	1	1	1	1	23	215	0,03	6,44	
fruta maça	0	0	0	0	0	0	0	0,12	0,00	
maca fruta	1	1	0	0	0	7	39	0,03	1,17	
maça maça	0	0	1	1	1	7	30	0,09	2,72	
maça red	0	1	1	1	0	8	30	0,03	0,89	
maça amarela	0	0	0	0	0	0	0	0,06	0,00	19,99
maca vermelha peruana	0	0	0	1	1	5	21	0,05	1,05	
variedades de maçã	0	1	1	0	0	1	7	0,02	0,14	
maçã gala	0	1	0	0	0	1	1	0,06	0,06	
maça reineta	0	0	0	1	0	10	68	0,06	4,05	
maça portuguesa	1	1	1	1	1	14	116	0,03	3,47	
pera portuguesa	0	0	0	1	0	9	20	0,20	4,05	
pera	1	1	0	0	0	0	4	0,01	0,04	
pera rocha	0	1	1	1	1	18	46	0,10	4,58	
pêra	0	0	0	0	0	0	0	0,02	0,00	
pera williams	0	0	0	0	0	0	0	0,12	0,00	9,97
pera fruta	0	0	0	0	0	0	0	0,09	0,00	
fruta pera	0	0	0	0	0	0	0	0,03	0,00	
pera rocha do oeste	0	1	0	1	0	7	15	0,09	1,31	
laranja	1	1	1	1	1	16	116	0,03	3,49	
laranja pera rio	0	0	1	1	0	3	71	0,02	1,41	
laranja do céu	1	0	1	1	1	1	21	0,10	2,05	10,00
preço laranja	0	0	0	1	0	3	3	0,90	2,25	
variedades de laranja	0	1	1	1	1	0	62	0,01	0,62	
tipos de laranja	0	0	1	0	0	0	2	0,10	0,18	
Conversions	18	23	21	56	14	133	883		39,95	
Clicks	127	129	166	346	115	1016				
Cost	3,83	4,57	6,86	20,44	4,26					

Source: (the authors)

It should be noted that 66% of the clicks are provided by only 27% of the words, with CPC between 0.03 EUR and 0.05 EUR, responsible for 54% of the total expenses (21.40 EUR). On the other hand, the most expensive keywords, with CPC above 0.10 EUR, are not part of the solution.

The user can enrich the model with other constraints. For example, the available budget can be distributed by keywords, word set, per day, or set of days. The number of clicks can be limited or weighted in the objective function assigning different weight to certain days or keywords. These are only examples of the versatility of the models that, starting from a simple basis, can be adapted, integrating other conditions.

Model 2 Solution

Considering the data already used in model 1 and the number of conversions predicted for week 5 (Table 8), an instance of model 2 was constructed, whose resolution allowed to obtain the optimal results indicated in Table 10.

The objective function indicates an optimal value of 1016, resulting from the sum of 133 conversions with 883 clicks. In this case, equal weight was attributed to conversions and clicks, with $\alpha=\beta=1$. In other circumstances, the user can weight

Table 11. Weekly optimal keyword plan - model 3

	Monday	Tuesday	Wednesday	Thursday	Friday	β 1						α 1
	29-Jan	30-Jan	31-Jan	01-feb	02-feb	Conversions	Clicks	Billing	CPC	Cost		Profit
Maça	0	0	0	1	0	1	3	4,77	0,10	0,33		4,44
maça vermelha	1	1	0	1	1	22	193	37,10	0,03	5,79		31,31
fruta maça	0	0	0	1	0	6	24	9,54	0,12	2,88		6,66
maca fruta	1	0	0	0	0	7	35	11,13	0,03	1,06		10,07
maça maça	0	0	0	1	1	2	3	14,31	0,09	0,29		14,02
maça red	0	1	1	0	0	8	26	12,72	0,03	0,77	19,86	11,95
maça amarela	0	0	0	0	0	0	0	0,00	0,06	0,00		0,00
maca vermelha peruana	0	0	0	1	1	5	21	14,58	0,05	1,05		13,53
variedades de maçã	0	0	1	0	0	1	6	1,59	0,02	0,11		1,48
maçã gala	0	1	0	0	0	1	1	11,13	0,06	0,06		11,07
maça reineta	0	0	0	1	0	10	68	43,59	0,06	4,05		39,54
maça portuguesa	1	1	1	1	1	14	116	22,66	0,03	3,47		19,19
pera portuguesa	0	0	0	1	0	9	20	21,12	0,20	4,05		17,07
pera	0	0	0	0	0	0	0	0,00	0,01	0,00		0,00
pera rocha	0	1	1	1	0	16	37	19,80	0,10	3,68		16,13
pêra	0	0	0	0	0	0	0	0,00	0,02	0,00		0,00
pera williams	1	0	0	0	0	1	3	0,99	0,12	0,40	9,59	0,59
pera fruta	0	0	0	1	0	1	2	0,99	0,09	0,16		0,83
fruta pera	0	0	0	0	0	0	0	0,00	0,03	0,00		0,00
pera rocha do oeste	0	1	0	1	0	7	15	10,23	0,09	1,31		8,93
laranja	1	1	1	1	1	16	116	31,18	0,03	3,49		27,69
laranja pera rio	0	0	0	1	0	3	26	5,97	0,02	0,51		5,46
laranja do céu	0	0	0	0	0	0	0	1,99	0,10	0,00	7,83	1,99
preço laranja	0	0	1	1	0	4	4	14,43	0,90	3,83		10,60
variedades de laranja	0	0	0	0	0	0	0	0,00	0,01	0,00		0,00
tipos de laranja	0	0	0	0	0	0	0	0,00	0,10	0,00		0,00
Conversions	19	23	17	63	12	134	718	289,81		37,27		252,54
Clicks	127	111	67	333	79							
Billing	45,03	62,33	49,43	98,45	34,57							
Cost	4,10	4,31	4,13	21,91	2,82			Z= 386,4525				
Profit	40,93	58,02	45,30	76,53	31,75							

Source: (the authors)

clicks and conversions. Like the factors α and β, also the percentage ratio between the number of clicks and conversions can be adjusted in the last restriction, taking into account the objectives of the company.

The cost of the campaign is 39.95 EUR, very close to the limit of 40.00 EUR, with 19.99 EUR for the apple campaign, 9.97 EUR for the pear campaign, and 10.00 EUR for the orange campaign. The most expensive keyword is again "maça vermelha", with 6.44 EUR, 215 clicks and 23 conversions, followed by "maça portuguese" and "laranja", almost tied in terms of cost, conversions and clicks. Thursday stands out as the most expensive day, totaling 20.44 EUR, and the highest activity, with 344 clicks and 56 conversions (Table 10).

As in model 1, this is a basic formulation to which restrictions can be added, namely related to the number of clicks, conversions and costs, by word and / or day, or every kind of functions. Hence, this feature gives the model a versatility that accommodates different business situations.

Model 3 Solution

Model 3 assumes the maximization of profit as the major business objective of the campaign. In a simplified way, profit is the difference between the total value of online sales and campaign costs in Google Ads. The objective function also integrates the number of conversions that serves as a link between variables and creates the conditions for increased billing. Unlike the somewhat hermetic language of impressions, clicks, or conversions, maximizing the profit of the campaign is something that interests the managers and immediately arrests their intention.

Considering again the forecast of the number of clicks, conversions and billing for week 5 (Table 8), the predicted cost-per-click and the available budget, an instance of the model 3, whose resolution through the Open Solver allowed to obtain the optimal results presented in Table 11.

The optimal solution provides a billing of 289.81 EUR and a profit of 252.54 EUR. The number of conversions is 134, well above the 15% minimum clicks. In this case, the optimal solution was achieved without the total budget being spent, especially since only € 7.83 was spent on the orange campaign.

The keyword "maça reineta" provides the highest profit, 39.54 EUR, although the maximum number of conversions belongs to the keyword "maça vermelha". Once again, Thursday is the day of billing and profit, with 98.45 EUR and 76.53 EUR, respectively, as well as in all other areas, with a highlight of 63 conversions.

Like previous models, this formulation can be strengthened by adding constraints on conversions, clicks, billing, cost or profit, by word or by day, depending on the goals of the decision maker. In the objective function, a small change in the first installment can replace the maximization of profit by maximizing the return on investment (ROI), the ratio between profit and cost.

$$ROI_{ij} = \frac{f_{ij} - CPC_i k_{ij}}{CPC_i k_{ij}}$$

The companies are all distinct and with very specific objectives. The proposed models have a purposely-simple structure that allows the integrated evolution to accommodate the aspirations that companies place in their campaigns.

FUTURE RESEARCH DIRECTIONS

The optimization models presented in this chapter include a great potential for future research. It offers interesting cues on the relevance of using optimization models to improve efficacy of advertising strategies, namely on Google Ads, providing interesting approaches in line with some contributions in extant literature that has demonstrated the relevance of optimizing Google Ads campaigns (e.g., (Goel & Mehta, 2008; Mehta, 2007; Mehta et al., 2005; Thomaidou et al., 2012). Being a simplified illustration, the approache proposed in this chapter enables further research and improvements. Of course, it is possible to make the time scale much finer, obtaining dynamic and permanently updated solutions. Hence, suggestions for future research include to adapt the proposed models to other sets of data, in order to further validate these findings. Moreover, this approach could also be adapted to other types of online advertising. Indeed, click through rate, conversion, and billing forecasts are critical. In this sense, they should receive special attention, seeking to make them as assertive as possible. For this, it is essential to have an extensive time series record, to test various forecasting methodologies and to evaluate its error. In addition, forecasts must be continuously updated and incorporated into models dynamically. In the case of an auction, the bid price (the cost per click) is permanently changing. New versions of the models will be able to integrate these changes dynamically, adjusting to the variations.

CONCLUSION

The available data confirm the size of e-commerce on a global scale. In 2017, it reached 1.66 billion digital buyers and a turnover of 2074 billion euros. Only two companies, Amazon and Google, currently total more than $ 160 billion a year. In the coming years, forecasts point to a growth of approximately 20% per year. They are impressive values for a technology created in the 80's and a market that only began to develop in the following decade. For this success, the search engines that match the buyer and the seller, in particular Google, with around 90% of the market share contributed a lot.

It is in this scenario that Google develops its main business model, Google Ads. A Pay-per-Click platform that allows advertisers to increase the visibility of their businesses on the Google results page and, in this way, drive more traffic to pages.

A well-planned investment strategy in advertising campaigns on Google Ads can contribute to quickly achieving organizational goals, yet it is not risk-free. The global-scale opinion survey shows how Digital Marketing professionals are apprehensive about campaign costs and declining conversions. They recognize that Google Ads contributes almost half of their turnover, but at the same time cautiously evaluate the performance of Google Ads. Most participants measure campaigns based on the number of clicks. Surprisingly, or perhaps not, this study concludes that a significant number of practitioners do not implement keyword selection strategies or even analyze campaign results. By recognizing the difficulty and the need to assist marketers to better plan and control their advertising campaigns, this chapter proposes the use of optimization models in order to improve marketing efficacy and return on investment. Hence, the chapter contributes to extant literature in several ways. It offers empirical evidence of marketers' practices that contain relevant cues for both researchers and practitioners. It also contributes to extant literature by combining a topic of marketing and online advertising with a mathematical approach that, as far as the authors' knowledge, has been absent in extant literature. Indeed, and to some extent, this chapter demystifies the use of mathematical and optimization models, demonstrating that even simplified models can offer important insights for improving marketing efforts. Moreover, the optimization models offered in this chapter can be used by both academics and practitioners to deal with efficacy challenges in Google Ads and other online advertising strategies.

In the case of Google Ads, the improvement of campaign results may involve the use of optimization models that support the decision on the choice of keywords, configuring a possible competitive advantage for the companies that decide to implement them. This chapter develops three mathematical models, in integer linear programming, that enable to optimize which keywords to choose each day, in order to maximize the number of clicks, conversions or ROI, taking into account historical data from number of clicks, conversions and billing, pre-defined budget constraints and business objectives.

The substitution of the combination of the pair (keyword, bid) variables, used by Thomaidou et al. (2014), by a single keyword variable, assuming the predicted CPC parameterization instead of bidding cost, greatly simplifies the mathematical models, dispensing more sophisticated heuristic methodologies and specific solver tools.

The elementary and modular structure of the presented mathematical formulations allows a high degree of versatility and evolution, being able to integrate other objectives, constraints, metrics or indicators. Once the model has been constructed, it is possible to test budget alternatives, bar words, add others, analyze the profit provided by each, etc.

From a theoretical point of view, this research develops new models for optimization of Adwords campaigns, demonstrating once again that relevant advances can be achieved by integrating such different areas as Marketing and Linear Programming. From a practical point of view, the simple systematization of the problem, with identification of variables, parameters and metrics, forces users to deepen their knowledge and control over the campaign. It also highlights the consequences of the decisions that are made throughout the process. Finally, under some conditions, it provides an optimal daily choice of keywords that can support campaign manager decisions.

With the use of freeware software, embedding in Excel, it was possible to run the proposed models, considering for this purpose real data, related to a Google Ads advertising campaign carried out in a fruit company. The solutions found are the optimal choice of keywords for each day, over a week, taking into account the budget available for the campaign (€ 40). Considering only CPC and billing, the optimal solution points to a maximum profit of € 252.54. The number of clicks decreases as new goals are integrated into the objective function, and the solution that maximizes billing is the one with the lowest number of clicks.

Currently the decision-making processes regarding the choice of keywords are complex, time-consuming and subjective. This research demonstrates that, with historical data on impressions, clicks, conversions, and / or billing, it is possible to build models to help design Google Ads campaigns that are objective, focused, results-oriented, short-term, error-free, and without additional costs.

Finally, the integration of optimization models with the Google Ads platform itself can be considered, providing new functionality that will facilitate the entire process of analyzing and managing advertising campaigns. Hence, new and exciting opportunities are anticipated.

REFERENCES

Albuquerque, J., Morla, R., Gabriel, D., & Campos, R. (2013). *Sugestão de palavras chave para campanhas em motores de busca em arranque*. Porto, Portugal. Retrieved from https://hdl.handle.net/10216/69731

Anca, B., & Daniela, D. (2008). Optimization and launch of a Google Adwords campaign. *Annals of the University of Oradea, Economic Science Series, 17*(4), 1289–1296. Retrieved from http://search.ebscohost.com/login.aspx?direct=true&db=bth&AN=48755865&site=eds-live

Araújo, A., & Santos, C. (2017). A contribuição da indexação no processo de seleção de palavras-chave para a Google Adwords. *Revista Brasileira de Biblioteconomia e Documentação, 13*, 109–114.

Benge, G. (2014). Why integration is key: digital marketing versus offline marketing. Retrieved from https://www.koozai.com/blog/branding/digital-marketing-versus-offline-marketing/#

Bethlehem, J. (2009). *Applied survey methods: A statistical perspective* (Vol. 558). Hoboken, NJ: John Wiley & Sons.

Borgs, C., Chayes, J., Immorlica, N., Jain, K., Etesami, O., & Mahdian, M. (2007). Dynamics of bid optimization in online advertisement auctions. In *Proceedings of the 16th International Conference on World Wide Web* (pp. 531–540). ACM. 10.1145/1242572.1242644

Brin, S., & Page, L. (2012). Reprint of: The anatomy of a large-scale hypertextual web search engine. *Computer Networks, 56*(18), 3825–3833. doi:10.1016/j.comnet.2012.10.007

Clifton, B. (2012). *Advanced web metrics with Google Analytics (3rd. Ed.)*. Canadá: John Wiley & Sons.

Clinks. (2017). Simulador de CPC (Custo Por Clique) e Posição de Anúncio no Google Ads (BETA). Retrieved from https://www.clinks.com.br/simulador-de-cpc-custo-por-clique-e-posicao-de-anuncio-no-google-adwords/

Dănciulescu, D., & Anca, B. (2008). Optimization methods for PPC campaigns. *Annals of the University of Oradea, Economic Science Series, 17*(4), 1337–1341. Retrieved from http://search.ebscohost.com/login.aspx?direct=true&db=bth&AN=48755873&site=eds-live

Davis, H. (2010). *Ferramentas de publicidade do Google* (1st ed.). São Paulo, Brazil: Novatec.

DeCastro, N. S., de Bittencourt, J. A., Chaves, F. A. V., Barreiro, J. H. L. C. D., & Reis, C. V. S. (2015). A Influência do Marketing Digital Sobre a Escolha dos Consumidores. In *XII Simpósio de Excelência em Gestão e Tecnologia - SEGeT*. Rio de Janeiro, Brazil. Retrieved from https://www.aedb.br/seget/artigos2015.php?pag=215

Dunlop, M. (2019). Top Earning Websites – How much the world's largest internet businesses make. Retrieved from https://www.incomediary.com/top-earning-websites

Fishkin, R. (2018). Why Google AdWords' keyword volume numbers are wildly unreliable - whiteboard Friday. Retrieved from https://moz.com/blog/unreliable-google-adwords-keyword-volume?utm_campaign=Submission&utm_medium=Community&utm_source=GrowthHackers.com

Geddes, B. (2014). Advanced Google Adwords. (W. Knibbe, Ed.) (3rd. Ed.). Sybex Editions.

Gielens, K., & Steenkamp, J.-B. E. M. (2019). Branding in the era of digital (dis)intermediation. *International Journal of Research in Marketing*. doi:10.1016/j.ijresmar.2019.01.005

Goel, G., & Mehta, A. (2008). Online budgeted matching in random input models with applications to adwords. In *Proceedings of the Nineteenth Annual ACM-SIAM Symposium on Discrete Algorithms* (pp. 982–991). Society for Industrial and Applied Mathematics.

Google. (2018a). Click: Definition. Retrieved from https://support.google.com/google-ads/answer/31799?hl=en

Google. (2018b). Clickthrough rate (CTR): Definition. Retrieved from https://support.google.com/google-ads/answer/2615875?hl=en

Google. (2019a). About expanded text ads. Retrieved from https://support.google.com/google-ads/answer/7056544?hl=en

Google. (2019b). About your Google Ads account limits. Retrieved from https://support.google.com/google-ads/answer/6372658?hl=en

Google. (2019c). Conversion: Definition. Retrieved from https://support.google.com/google-ads/answer/6365?hl=en

Google. (2019d). How can we help you? Retrieved from https://support.google.com/google-ads/?hl=en#topic=7456157

Google. (2019e). Impressions: Definition. Retrieved from https://support.google.com/google-ads/answer/6320?hl=en

Guerini, M., Strapparava, C., & Stock, O. (2010). Evaluation metrics for persuasive NLP with Google AdWords. *Proceedings of the 7th International Conference on Language Resources and Evaluation*, 3459–3463.

Holdren, A. (2011). *Google AdWords: Managing your advertising program*. O'Reilly Media.

Kotler, P. (1999). *Marketing para o século XXI: como criar, dominar e conquistar mercados*. São Paulo, Brazil: Atlas.

Ledford, J. L. (2015). *Search engine optimization bible* (Vol. 584). John Wiley & Sons.

Madera, Q., Castillo, O., Garcia, M., & Mancilla, A. (2017). Bidding strategies based on type-1 and interval type-2 fuzzy systems for Google AdWords advertising campaigns. In *Nature-inspired design of hybrid intelligent systems* (pp. 99–113). Springer. doi:10.1007/978-3-319-47054-2_6

McDonald, J. (2014). *Google Adwords gotchas*. San Francisco, CA: CreateSpace Independent.

Mehta, A. (2007). AdWords and generalized online matching. *Journal of the Association for Computing Machinery*, *V*(August), 1–20.

Mehta, A., Saberi, A., Vazirani, U., & Vazirani, V. (2005). Adwords and generalized on-line matching. In *46th Annual IEEE Symposium on Foundations of Computer Science (FOCS'05)* (pp. 264–273). IEEE. 10.1109/SFCS.2005.12

Miranda, C. M. C., & de Oliveira Arruda, D. M. (2004). E-produtos e variáveis comportamentais determinantes de compra no varejo virtual: um estudo com consumidores brasileiros. *Revista Eletrônica de Administração, 10*(1).

Monteiro, R. V. (2007). Google Adwords: A arte da Guerra. (S. M. Oliveira, Ed.) (2.a Edição). São Paulo, Brazil: Brasport livros e Multimídia Ltda.

Okada, S. I., & de Souza, E. M. S. (2011). Estratégias do marketing digital na era da busca. *Revista Brasileira de Marketing, 10*(1), 46–72.

Oxer, J. (2008). *Quickstart guide to Google AdWords*. Lulu Press.

Patel, N. (2019). 7 deadly AdWords mistakes that'll make you broke (and how to fix them). Retrieved from https://neilpatel.com/blog/7-deadly-adwords-mistakes-thatll-make-you-broke-and-how-to-fix-them/

Patil, V. M., & Patil, A. V. (2018). SEO: on-page off-page analysis. *2018 International Conference on Information, Communication, Engineering, and Technology (ICICET)*. doi:10.1109/ICICET.2018.8533836

Pereira, J. (2008). Google: Ferramenta de Busca de informação na web pereira. *Revista Eletrônica Do CESVA*, *1*(1), 18–32.

Reddy, G. (2016). *Digital marketing impact on the consumer decision making process in Nike's customer retail operations in South Africa*. University of Pretoria.

Scott, G. (1989). Magellan: Information Retrieval Software from Lotus. *U-M Computing News*, *17*(4), 10–12.

Statista. (2019a). Number of digital buyers worldwide from 2014 to 2021 (in billions). Retrieved from https://www.statista.com/statistics/251666/number-of-digital-buyers-worldwide/

Statista. (2019b). Retail e-commerce sales worldwide from 2014 to 2021. Retrieved from https://www.statista.com/statistics/379046/worldwide-retail-e-commerce-sales/

Szymanski, G., & Lininski, P. (2018). Model of the effectiveness of Google Adwords advertising activities. In *2018 IEEE 13th International Scientific and Technical Conference on Computer Sciences and Information Technologies (CSIT)* (Vol. 2, pp. 98–101). IEEE. 10.1109/STC-CSIT.2018.8526633

Thomaidou, S., Leymonis, K., Liakopoulos, K., & Vazirgiannis, M. (2012). AD-MAD: Automated development and optimization of online advertising campaigns. In *2012 IEEE 12th International Conference on Data Mining Workshops* (pp. 902–905). IEEE.

Thomaidou, S., Liakopoulos, K., & Vazirgiannis, M. (2014). Toward an integrated framework for automated development and optimization of online advertising campaigns. *Intelligent Data Analysis*, *18*(6), 1199–1227. doi:10.3233/IDA-140691

Torres, C. (2009). *A Bíblia do marketing digital Novatec*. São Paulo, Brazil.

Torres, C. (2010). *Guia Prático de Marketing na Internet para Pequenas Empresas: Dicas para Posicionar o seu Negócio e Conquistar Novos Clientes na Internet*. Retrieved from https://www.cairu.br/biblioteca/arquivos/Marketing/

Vaidhyanathan, S. (2011). *A Googlelização de tudo*. Editora Cultrix.

Vaver, J., & Koehler, J. (2011). Measuring ad effectiveness using geo experiments.

Wall, A. (2017). History of search engines: from 1945 to Google Today. Retrieved from http://www.searchenginehistory.com/

Wang, D., Li, Z., Xie, G., Kaafar, M.-A., & Salamatian, K. (2016). Adwords management for third-parties in sem: An optimisation model and the potential of twitter. In *IEEE INFOCOM 2016-The 35th Annual IEEE International Conference on Computer Communications* (pp. 1–9). IEEE.

Weusthof, E. (2015). Adwords Optimization (No. 2056674). Amsterdam, The Netherlands.

Winters, P. R. (1960). Forecasting sales by exponentially weighted moving averages. *Management Science*, *6*(3), 324–342. doi:10.1287/mnsc.6.3.324

Zhang, E. (2007). A study on ad-place quantity optimization in Adwords auction. In *2007 International Conference on Wireless Communications, Networking and Mobile Computing* (pp. 3339–3342). IEEE. 10.1109/WICOM.2007.827

Zhou, Y., Chakrabarty, D., & Lukose, R. (2008). Budget constrained bidding in keyword auctions and online knapsack problems. In *International Workshop on Internet and Network Economics* (pp. 566–576). Springer. 10.1007/978-3-540-92185-1_63

KEY TERMS AND DEFINITIONS

Ad Placement: Ad placement include all advertising spaces, mostly paid, offered by online publishers, websites, and social networks to advertisers to display their advertisements. The individual placements have different potential for reaching the users and perform differently when it comes to the type of content chosen for the advertisement.

Ad Targeting: Ad targeting refers to the selection of potential customer groups to which an advertisement will be displayed. This specification of the ad's audience is done using targeting parameters including demographic and geographic information, interests, and device preferences.

Analytics: Consumer behavioral data related to their platform usage behaviors such as the number of visits to a platform, time spent on the platform, and actions when using the platform. Using these behavioral data, advertisers and marketers are able to segment target audience to increase their experiences and to improve campaign effectiveness.

Big Data: A term that defines a large dataset that produces in the size of collected data over time. It refers to the size of dataset that surpasses the capturing, storage, management, and analysis of traditional databases. The term refers to the dataset that has huge, more diverse, and multifaceted structure, accompanies by difficulties of data storage, analysis, and visualization. Big Data are characterized with the commonly known attributes: high-volume, -velocity, and –variety information assets.

Conversion: Conversion refers to a desired action performed by a consumer as a reaction to an advertisement or other marketing effort. The desired action can take many forms including the purchases, membership registrations, newsletter subscriptions, and application downloads.

Digital Advertising: Used interchangeable with Internet or online advertising. This term covers a wide variety of online advertising formats, ranging from email, social media applications, search engine advertising, mobile advertising, video advertising, etc.

Search engine: A web search engine or Internet search engine is a software system that is designed to carry out web search (Internet search), which means to search the World Wide Web in a systematic way for particular information specified in a textual web search query.

SEO: Search engine optimization (SEO) is the process of increasing the quality and quantity of website traffic by increasing the visibility of a website or a web page to users of a web search engine. SEO refers to the improvement of unpaid results (known as "natural" or "organic" results) and excludes direct traffic/visitors and the purchase of paid placement.

Chapter 7
Reaching Your Customers Using Facebook and Google Dynamic Ads

Tereza Semerádová
https://orcid.org/0000-0002-9123-5782
Technical University of Liberec, Czech Republic

Petr Weinlich
Technical University of Liberec, Czech Republic

ABSTRACT

Dynamic Product Ads (DPAs) and Dynamic Search Ads (DSAs) represent a type of online advertising primarily used for remarketing purposes. However, more and more advertisers can use DPA for acquisition campaigns as well. Dynamic ads are an integral part of the marketing strategies of all large e-shops and companies that have a product or service catalog. Dynamic advertising reduces the time and effort put into the creation of online advertisements and provides the highest level of personalized targeting possible. With a product catalog and a properly set pixel or tracking code, it is possible to create individually customized ads within seconds. This chapter tests the effectiveness of DPAs and DSAs within the context of the two greatest advertising platforms, Facebook and Google ads, and compares their performance against the manually optimized ad sets.

DOI: 10.4018/978-1-7998-1618-8.ch007

Copyright © 2020, IGI Global. Copying or distributing in print or electronic forms without written permission of IGI Global is prohibited.

INTRODUCTION

Dynamic search ads (DSAs) and *dynamic product ads* (DPAs) help advertisers reach potential customers by displaying content that is tailored specifically for them. According to WordStream (2019), multichannel marketing strategies lead to an 80% higher visit rate of a target e-store. Moreover, 37% of online shoppers look for shopping inspiration on social media, and 96% of B2C marketers agree that Facebook and Google ads have a significant impact on their marketing revenues. The WordStream statistics also claim that 65% of advertisers agree that dynamic content is effective. On average, only approximately 4% of website visitors make a conversion, that directly generates income, before leaving a website (GrowthBadger, 2019).

The driving force behind marketing automation is the ability to send personalized messages tailored to a specific customer. The content is delivered to the customer in the ideal moment, i.e., when needs and searches for information arise during a browsing session. Marketing automation tools affect shoppers at the most important stage of the purchasing process–before reaching a selected merchant. Implementation of these tools greatly increases the chance that demand will eventually be placed with the merchant and not with the competition. Marketing automation systems can be used to raise customer awareness about the brand or present them the required product information to build their trust and significantly shorten the purchasing process. Experienced marketers and advertisers confirm that potential customers are not ready to respond immediately to their first contact with the company. To do so, the customer needs to be captivated, convinced, and acquired. This process is called *lead nurturing*.

A basic function of all marketing automation tools is delivering pre-selected content to potential customers, always based on their specific actions. For example, when a user visits a new car website, the system automatically responds by sending him/her an e-mail with a detailed product line offer. Similarly, when a customer leaves the shopping cart before the purchase is completed, the system can send him/her an e-mail or a special offer message for a particular item that was left behind. Thus, marketers create different automation rules in the system environment to cover the entire purchasing process or a product life cycle. When a customer makes action X, the system performs action Y. System marketing automation tools enable accurate tracking and evaluation of campaign responses to contacts in the marketing database. A full history of responses to past campaigns is available to marketers and merchants. Through lead nurturing, the campaign audience gradually becomes familiar with the brand, their relationship with the company is established, and the desired purchase is made.

In this chapter, we test the effectiveness of dynamic content ads during the entire conversion process. For the purposes of this experiment, we are going to combine search and product dynamic ads provided by the advertising platforms Facebook and Google ads. The performances of the dynamic campaigns are judged based on the standard metrics such as reach, click-through rate, number of conversions, and profitability. To get reliable results, a reference group of manually optimized ads are set up and used for the comparative analysis of the advertising performance.

THE EFFECTS OF PERSONALIZED ADS ON ONLINE USERS

Personalization is the key to individual marketing and targeting. The essence of personalization in the online environment is to offer the user services and products that are based on the information in the user's profile or behavior on the website. The necessary prerequisites for creating a personalized offer of products and services by the provider identifies the user (based on his/her registration in the system or based on the use of cookies and tracking codes), sufficient information about the user and his/her preferences, and subsequent processing of the data manually or by the system.

Research relating to the study of how personalization affects the behavior of the consumers is very extensive (Tran, 2017). Many researchers have already tested the impact of exclusively tailored advertising in traditional media (Baek and Morimoto, 2012; Yu and Cude, 2009), in the online environment including social media and websites (Bleier & Eisenbeiss, 2015; Li, 2016; Gironda & Korgaonkar, 2018) and in the context of mobile devices (Grewal et al., 2016; Lu et al., 2019). The up-to-date findings prove that the impact of personalized advertising is ambiguous and may lead to very opposite responses from the targeted users.

Yu et al. (2019) created a conceptual model of customer reactions on personalized ads and their click-through intentions. Their results from a survey of 446 WeChat users indicate that higher product involvement, brand familiarity, visual attractiveness, and information quality increase the user's intention to proceed with further interaction with the brand. Shanahan et al. (2019) came to similar conclusions. Their analysis of 242 responses from Amazon Mechanical Turk suggest that personalized content positively influences brand engagement, attachment, and, by extension, the loyalty to the brand. Bang and Wojdynski (2016) analyzed the effects of personalized banner ads on the visual attention of users using eye-tracking technology. Personalized ads generated longer fixations and users were more attracted to them. Contrastingly, the effects were moderated by the level of cognitive load during tasks the testers were asked to perform.

Setyani et al. (2019) explored intrinsic motivations of users to react to social media ads. The authors identified four types of added customer value: informativeness, credibility, creativity, and entertainment. They also distinguish two basic browsing dimensions: utilitarian and hedonic. Li and Liu (2017) claimed that simple, personalized adjustments of the ads may not be enough to produce the desired effects. To maximize the positive outcomes, a high level of involvement with the brand is necessary. However, effects of personalization may differ depending on not only the products presented but also the intensity of recommendations and the characteristics of the target segment (Schreiner et al., 2019). Chen et al. (2019) postulated that customer reactance may be significantly affected by both rational choice factors and affective choice factors such as ownership or vulnerability.

In a meta-analysis of 166 studies involving 75,269 participants from 34 countries, Baruh et al. (2017) found a contradictory relationship between users' beliefs about privacy in the digital space and their real behavior. The authors referred to this phenomenon as to the *privacy paradox*, which describes a conflicting relationship between high user concerns about the misuse of personal data and the low level of protective measures taken, especially in the social networking field. Users expressing concern about data protection in social networking environments tend to be more inclined to deliver such data recklessly–for example, accessing large volumes of their own digital footprints and allowing unauthenticated external applications to access personal data. One possible explanation for such behavior is the detachment of the user from the possible negative effects of ill-considered provision of his/her data and from any potential data misuses to which he/she does not relate. Another possible clarification includes the so-called reward risk. Most users would feel more secure in anonymity, but making available free services, applications, or content in exchange for personal data is tempting. The perceived risk of abuse is so low that they would accept such an exchange without further consideration.

Finally, it is important to note that ill-considered provisions of personal data and concerns about its misuse are not defined exclusively by information literacy and by previous experiences with internet services. Zorn et al. (2013) argued that aspects of the cultural and political environment are also involved in the form of regulations and cultural values.

Estrada-Jiménez et al. (2017) analyzed the online advertising infrastructure and the underlying privacy risk. The authors listed and classified the privacy mechanisms that allow for an increase in a sense of online privacy for its users. They described the data collection model applied by many advertising entities as the attacker model, which is characterized as having access to any personal user data. Most of the advertising services gather information such as the clickstream, browsing history, preferences, location, gender, age, and agent string in a standard manner. The agent string is data that remain traceable, even if the user deletes his browsing history including the cookies (Eckersley, 2010).

Nowadays, users have many options for protecting themselves from unwanted advertising. It has been proven that ad blocking browser extensions such as Adblock Plus or Ghostery are able to effectively prevent user tracking and prevent the online ads from displaying (Danova, 2014; Redondo & Aznar; 2018). However, by blocking all ads, users may even miss ads that could be useful to them (Parra–Arnau et al., 2017). The popularity of ad blockers has grown to such an extent that even Google considered implementing it into their Chrome browser; they are a tool that would allow all the users to moderate the kind of advertisements they want to receive (Lee, 2019; Sánchez & Viejo, 2018).

Regarding the effectiveness of online advertising, there is also another phenomenon that is necessary to mention. *Advertising blindness* is the phenomenon when users consciously or subconsciously neglect the spaces on a website where they expect advertisements to appear. Hsieh and Chen (2011) tested how different information types and their representations within the web structure affect users' attention. They focused mainly on the four most common content types that can be found on a website: only text entries, text, and pictures, mostly pictures, and mostly video. According to their results, the avoidance of advertisements depends on placement, context, and visual design. Koshksaray et al. (2015) described the influence of e-lifestyle on the ad reactance. The authors identified seven e-lifestyle categories with different attitudes toward advertising: need-driven, interest-driven, entertainment-driven, sociability-driven, importance-driven, uninterest-driven, and novelty-driven. However, their results are inconclusive.

The effects of personalized ads can thus produce a double effect. On the one hand, in most cases, ad relevance increases the potential to capture users' attention and produce the desired conversions. On the other hand, the accuracy and targeting precision of an ad may contribute to higher privacy concerns (Jung, 2017). Therefore, all aforementioned factors should be included when the experiment is set up and when the advertising results are interpreted. Based on this background research, we pose the following research questions:

RQ1: How does placement affect the effectiveness of dynamic ads?

RQ2: How does the format of an ad contribute to the overall advertising performance?

RQ3: What are the effects of dynamic ads during different stages of a user becoming familiar with a brand?

RQ4: Do dynamic, highly personalized ads perform better than "static", manually created ads with a lower level of personalization?

WHAT IS THE MECHANISM BEHIND DYNAMIC PRODUCT ADS AND DYNAMIC SEARCH ADS?

Using machine learning and artificial intelligence in PPC advertising systems, such as Facebook and Google ads, is certainly how modern marketing and advertising systems will move in the future. Regardless of online advertising tools used, the success of each automation is always proportional to the quality of the product or service data source provided. Typically, the data source is an XML file with a structure determined by the advertising system. This data source is called *feed*, which should be created with precision, even with optional parameters. Most systems have algorithms that can improve the performance of the ads over time, thanks to the advanced machine learning. However, if the original feed is insufficient or mediocre, there is no automatic correcting mechanism to fix it.

Dynamic Google Ads

The Google advertising platform offers four types of automatized advertisements. The lowest level of personalization and automatization is represented by *smart ads*, followed by DSAs, which are mostly used for acquisition campaigns, DPAs that are automatically generated based on the product feed supplied by the company and *dynamic remarketing ads*.

Unlike the other two types of ads, *smart content advertisements* do not use extensive data feed uploaded by the advertiser. The automatization is done on the level of the ad delivery with very limited personalization options. The system displays the option to create this type of campaign if the advertisers have at least 50 conversions from the *content network* over the past 30 days or at least 100 conversions from the *search network*. The targeting of a smart campaign is done by the internal mechanism of the advertising system. Google decides which sites and placements display the ad. Likewise, the advertiser does not set the cost-per-click (CPC) bids but enters only a target cost per conversion or return on investment. The creation of the smart ads is also slightly different from the standard process. The advertiser uploads up to five images, five headings, and five descriptions, and Google selects the final appearance of the ad based on user preferences and the historic ad performance data.

Dynamic Search Ads provide an easy method of targeting Google search ads to all the content on a website, without the need to look for keywords and set up ads manually for every relevant search query. DSAs have a great potential, especially for larger websites and e-shops that have to work with thousands of products, to advertise as quickly as possible in the Google search results. Manually creating these ads one by one could take months. If the advertiser chooses to set up a new DSA campaign in the Google AdWords interface, he/she can launch it quickly and easily without having to fill out a single keyword. In fact, dynamic search ads are not keyword targeted but based on the content of the advertised website. Search queries are automatically targeted on the websites if Google finds its content relevant to the user requirements. The keywords and ad title are then dynamically generated based on the content of the landing page.

The ad title is a combination of a search phrase and a landing page title. It is common practice for companies to customize their site titles specifically for DSA optimization. The important thing is that the web is written in a language that is natural for customers and that the headings of the web pages are attractive for the target audience. Since Google allows longer titles for the dynamically generated ads than for the standard ones, dynamic ads typically look more distinctive in the list of the search results. The advertiser may influence the visible URL address and descriptive text related to the website.

The distribution and placement of *DPAs* is not determined by keywords but by product data from the *merchant center*. The data feed submitted through this service contains details about the marketed products such as name, size, price, and color. Using this information, user queries are then matched with the automatically created ads so that the most relevant products are always displayed. DPAs can appear in Google Shopping selection, search results, and the content network. Since Google is trying to provide the customers with the most information available, ads on Google Shopping can appear alongside text-based ads. Customers can find the product that best fits their requirements, even before they reach the website where a purchase can be made. Product feed must be updated at least every 30 days, and the data must meet Google quality standards.

With dynamic remarketing ads, advertisers can display ads to users who have previously visited their website or used their mobile apps. This advertising format represents the highest level of personalization since it uses pictures of the products the users viewed on the web. Before using the remarketing ads, the advertiser implements a remarketing tag in all pages of the website. The tag includes all website visitors to remarketing lists and assigns them to unique item IDs in the feed they viewed. Although dynamic search ads are more suitable for the acquisition of new customers, dynamic remarketing aims to maximize the value of the existing customers. However, it may be connected with dynamic customer search. *Dynamic customer search* uses machine learning to estimate what online users are looking for. When the system detects what a user might need, the algorithm combines the user's possible intention of buying with available demographic data, such as age, gender, and household income, to find the right product for the user in the advertiser's feed. Products in the source feed are ranked based on their performance, relevance, and other factors that determine which ones have the best chance to get the user's attention and lead to a conversion.

Dynamic Facebook Ads

DPAs represent the only dynamic format Facebook offers to advertisers at this moment (May 2019). Facebook DPAs are primarily used for remarketing purposes. However, more and more advertisers also use DPA for acquisition campaigns with Facebook Marketing Partners. Facebook DPAs dynamically link the users' IDs with the product ID and the information listed in the supplied product feed. The information available in the feed is subsequently imported in the advertising system, and a personalized ad with the product he/she previously viewed on the web is delivered to the user. Facebook DPAs are applicable across all devices and placements, including Instagram.

To work with DPAs, a Facebook pixel with appropriate conversion events must be implemented on the advertiser's site. This pixel connects to the user's Facebook ID when he/she visits the website and carries the information about which product the user viewed and how he/she behaved on the web (for example, if one of the products was added to the cart, searched for, bought, etc.). As in Google dynamic ads, the marketer is able within minutes to create hundreds of variations of one ad,

Figure 1. The delivery mechanism of Facebook dynamic ads
Source: (the authors)

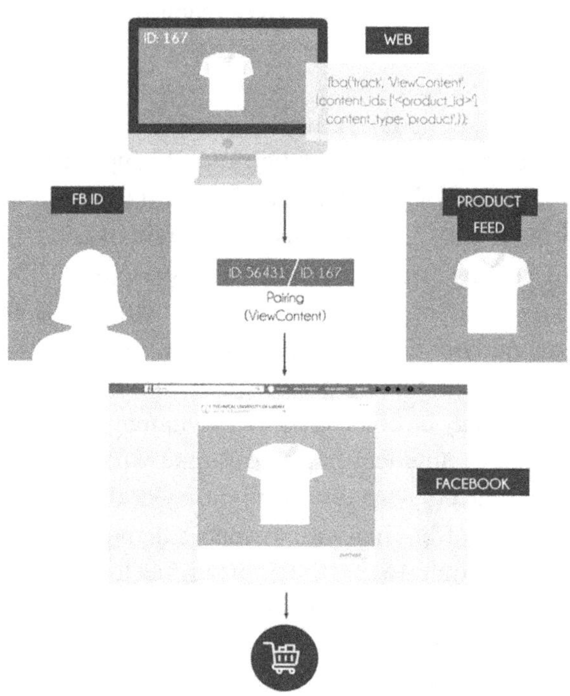

whose content is dynamically personalized using the product feed information. The fact that Facebook does not use cookies to track the user, but the Facebook profile, has many advantages. The most important advantage being that the users are easily traceable across different devices they use. User activity history cannot be deleted; thus, customer information is more accurate and historically continuous. The mechanism behind the dynamic Facebook ads is described in Figure 1.

The slightly different matching mechanisms applied by Google ads (cookies) and Facebook ads (user ID) raise another question related to the effectiveness of automatized dynamic advertising:

RQ5: What advertising platform (Facebook or Google) provides more effective dynamic ads?

We will explore this and the previously stated four research questions using the results from the following experiment. Emphasis will be put on the analysis of the variability factors that could influence the performance of the dynamic ads.

COLLECTING PERFORMANCE DATA

For the purposes of this research, the entire online conversion process was marketed parallelly with the help of dynamic and manually optimized Facebook and Google ads. Since both platforms respect the same three level structures of customer acquisition, we created ads covering all three marketing stages of customer acquisition: brand awareness, consideration, and conversion. Facebook ads copy this goal structure exactly as described and the main campaign objectives are classified into these three categories. The category awareness includes *brand awareness* and *reach*. Consideration groups optimizing goals such as traffic, engagement, app installations, video views, lead generation, and messages. The final category contains conversions, product catalog sales, and store visits. Dynamic ads can be found in the product catalog sales. However, Facebook catalog-based ads may also be used to acquire new customers since the ad-managing system allows for choosing an audience with custom and lookalike audiences, which can mimic the general advertising campaign goals. Google ads provide seven categories of targeting goals: sales, potential customers, web traffic, product and brand consideration, brand awareness and reach, app installations, and campaign without a specified goal. In our experiment, we used all the categories except app installations.

In addition, to fully testing the advertising potential of the dynamic ads, we set upped at least one ad set for each advertising placement available for DSAs and DPAs. Following the similar logic, we also experimented with the available format combinations. For the graphic ads, we used picture and interactive GIF animation on the Google platform and different picture variations supported by Facebook that

Table 1. The characteristics of the dynamic and static advertisements for the Google AdWords platform

	Smart ads	Dynamic search ads	Dynamic product ads	Dynamic remarketing ads	Dynamic customer search ads
Campaign without goal	Photo Interactive	Textual	Photo Interactive	Photo Interactive	Photo Interactive
awareness	-	-	Photo Interactive	Photo Interactive	Photo Interactive
Consideration	-	-	Photo Interactive	Photo Interactive	Photo Interactive
Web traffic	-	Textual	Photo Interactive	Photo Interactive	Photo Interactive
Potential customers	-	Textual	Photo Interactive	Photo Interactive	Photo Interactive
Sales	-	Textual	Photo Interactive	Photo Interactive	Photo Interactive

Source: (the authors)

included one photo (P), Carousel (Ca), and a collection of multiple photos (Co). In total, 168 dynamic ads and 1,575 static ads were implemented. The combinations of the campaign, ad set, and ad parameters used for the two ad groups are described in Tables 1 and 2.

The manually optimized Google ads were implemented for each of the above-described combinations. To maintain at least a moderate level of personalization and test the abilities of the delivery algorithm, each of the ad sets contained 20 product ads. To increase the chances of captivating users' attention, we chose only the best performing products from the given e-store category. The product catalog used for the dynamic ads contained all of the products from the same category (432 products in total). If the type of campaign allows the use of both photos and interactive content, the number of ads within an ad set increases to 40 (20 product ads using photo and 20 ads using the interactive content. Thus, we ran 42 dynamic and 840 static ads on the Google advertising platform.

We used the same product catalog for the Facebook dynamic ads as we did for the Google ads. The static ads were created for every targeting goal available in the Facebook Ads Manager except app installations, video views, and store visits, which were not relevant in the context of the e-store that allowed us to carry out our experiment. To keep the results comparable with the dynamic ads, we chose the same placements and same formats. The distribution of the ad characteristics is described in Table 3. Contrary to the static Google ads, only the five best performing products were used in ads within each ad set. The number of products was in this

Table 2. Characteristics of the dynamic Facebook advertisements

	Custom audience awareness			Custom audience consideration			Custom audience conversions			Lookalike audience awareness			Lookalike audience consideration			Lookalike audience conversions		
Facebook newsfeed	P	Ca	Co	P	Ca	Co	P	Ca	Co	P	Ca	Co	P	Ca	Co	P	Ca	Co
Right column	P	Ca	Co	P	Ca	Co	P	Ca	Co	P	Ca	Co	P	Ca	Co	P	Ca	Co
Marketplace	P	Ca	Co	P	Ca	Co	P	Ca	Co	P	Ca	Co	P	Ca	Co	P	Ca	Co
Instagram channel	P	Ca	Co	P	Ca	Co	P	Ca	Co	P	Ca	Co	P	Ca	Co	P	Ca	Co
Instagram stories	P	Ca	Co	P	Ca	Co	P	Ca	Co	P	Ca	Co	P	Ca	Co	P	Ca	Co
Audience network	P	Ca	Co	P	Ca	Co	P	Ca	Co	P	Ca	Co	P	Ca	Co	P	Ca	Co
Messenger	P	Ca	Co	P	Ca	Co	P	Ca	Co	P	Ca	Co	P	Ca	Co	P	Ca	Co

Source: (the authors)

Table 3. Characteristics of the static Facebook advertisements

	Brand awareness			Reach			Web traffic			Engagement			Lead generation			Messages			Conversions		
Facebook newsfeed	P	Ca	Co	P	Ca	Co	P	Ca	Co	P	Ca	Co	P	Ca	Co	P	Ca	Co	P	Ca	Co
Right column	P	Ca	Co	P	Ca	Co	P	Ca	Co	P	Ca	Co	P	Ca	Co	P	Ca	Co	P	Ca	Co
Marketplace	P	Ca	Co	P	Ca	Co	P	Ca	Co	P	Ca	Co	P	Ca	Co	P	Ca	Co	P	Ca	Co
Instagram channel	P	Ca	Co	P	Ca	Co	P	Ca	Co	P	Ca	Co	P	Ca	Co	P	Ca	Co	P	Ca	Co
Instagram stories	P	Ca	Co	P	Ca	Co	P	Ca	Co	P	Ca	Co	P	Ca	Co	P	Ca	Co	P	Ca	Co
Audience network	P	Ca	Co	P	Ca	Co	P	Ca	Co	P	Ca	Co	P	Ca	Co	P	Ca	Co	P	Ca	Co
Messenger	P	Ca	Co	P	Ca	Co	P	Ca	Co	P	Ca	Co	P	Ca	Co	P	Ca	Co	P	Ca	Co

Source: (the authors)

case reduced due to the high number of possible permutations. Overall, 126 dynamic and 735 static Facebook ads were created for the purposes of this experiment.

The experiment was performed in real-life conditions with authentic users and thus with authentic motivations behind the browsing and purchasing behavior. The advertisements were created in accordance with the marketing strategy of the Czech e-store specializing in the furniture, home accessories, and kitchen equipment. Because of the authenticity of the testing conditions, there were, however, some restrictions. First, regardless of the experimental nature, all of the above-described ads still had to fulfill the business objectives of the company and generate the desired conversions. Since the purpose of the individual ads differed according to the acquisition phase, the effectiveness of the ads was evaluated based on different metrics. Regarding awareness, the number of reactions and average price per reaction were monitored, and for the consideration stage, we focused on the click-through rate (CTR) and average cost per click. Finally, the performance of the last group of ads was evaluated based on the profitability the ads were able to produce.

Other restrictions defined by the e-store were related to some of the targeting parameters. We were allowed to target our testing ads only on women aged 25 to 44 years since it represented the most efficient customer segment of the e-store. This target was identified by the company as having the most potential from which to acquire new customers. Moreover, the bidding strategy was appointed and was non-negotiable. The e-store used a limited bidding strategy with a fixed maximum bid that was applied also on our ads. The dynamic and static ads were delivered for at least two days and at a maximum of 22 days. The main reason for the shorter delivery period of the ads was their suboptimal performance, which was judged using the maximum accepted average cost per reaction (0.19 EUR), average cost per CTR (0.24 EUR), and a minimum profitability per ad (12 EUR). The last restriction consisted of the limitation of interference of the dynamic and static ads to avoid an instance where a user is targeted by both sets. This prerequisite was achieved through the local positioning of the ads. Dynamic ads were delivered exclusively in Prague, Central Bohemian Region, South Bohemian Region, Plzeň Region, Karlovy Vary Region, Ústí nad Labem Region, and Liberec Region. The manually optimized ads targeted the remaining seven regions of the Czech Republic.

All Facebook and Google ads were connected with the Google Analytics using the UTM parameters. Thanks to this connection, we were able to monitor not only the CTR but also further behavior on the website, including the number of conversions and average profitability even for the awareness campaigns. The creative content for the dynamic ads was generated from the product catalog feed that was aligned with the uniform aesthetics of the e-store and contained both photo-based and video-based representations of the offered products. The static ads contained also photo and video content; however, a limited set of visuals was chosen and used for all the ads from this group.

RESULTS

All the collected data were exported from Google AdWords and Facebook Ads Manager as .xlsx files and imported into SPSS Statistics 24. Since the main objective of the presented research was to examine the effectiveness of dynamic ads across advertising platforms and placement, cross tabulation was chosen as the most suitable statistical method. Because of the different algorithms and tracking tools applied by Google and Facebook, any other form of statistical analysis would provide very inaccurate results. The effectiveness of all advertisements is, in the following paragraphs, judged always with regard to the stage of the customer acquisition process and the campaign goals.

According to some authors (Bang & Wojdynski, 2016; Yu et al., 2019), the phenomenon of advertising blindness heavily depends on the position of the ads, as suggested earlier in this chapter. To answer our first research question (RQ1), we focused on the results from the dynamic and static Facebook ads, since the dynamic ads on Google used variable placement.

Looking more closely at the results in Table 4, we identified that the worst performing placements in terms of reaching the desired audience were Instagram stories with 15 reactions (0.19 EUR average cost per reaction) for the dynamic ads and 21 reactions (0.17 EUR average per reaction) for the static ads and an audience network with 16 reactions (0.11 EUR) for the dynamic ads and 27 reactions (0.09 EUR) for the static ads. The right column placement generated a higher number of reactions than the previous two placements. However, the average cost per conversion was also rather high (0.13 EUR for dynamic ads and 0.12 for static ads). By contrast, the best results were achieved for the Facebook newsfeed and marketplace.

Within the campaign goal "consideration", newsfeed with 3.01 CTR for dynamic ads and 3.18 CTR for static ads and marketplace with 3.32 CTR for dynamic ads and 3.65 CTR for static ads performed significantly better than other placements.

Table 4. The impact of placement on the performance of Facebook ads

	Brand awareness and reach				**Consideration**				**Conversions**	
	Dynamic ads		Manually optimized ads		Dynamic ads		Manually optimized ads		Dynamic ads	Manually optimized ads
	Av. Num. of reac.	Av. cost per reac. (EUR)	Num. of reac.	Av. cost per reac. (EUR)	Av. CTR	Av. cost per CTR (EUR)	Av. CTR	Av. cost per CTR (EUR)	Av. profit. (EUR)	Av. profit. (EUR)
Facebook newsfeed	132	0.09	187	0.11	3.01	0.12	3.18	0.10	38.46	42.87
Right column	54	0.13	63	0.12	1.82	0.18	1.74	0.15	19.21	17.12
Marketplace	145	0.07	208	0.06	3.32	0.11	3.65	0.09	45.01	64.88
Instagram channel	89	0.09	142	0.08	2.29	0.14	2.45	0.14	17.23	10.27
Instagram stories	15	0.19	21	0.17	1.12	0.17	1.14	0.17	9.18	5.12
Audience network	16	0.11	27	0.09	1.56	0.17	1.48	0.16	12.32	7.94
Messenger	31	0.09	71	0.09	2.56	0.13	2.85	0.11	22.34	36.03

Source: (the authors)

Messenger and Instagram channels also stood out by reaching CTR values higher than 2.2. The average profitability confirms previous results. Facebook newsfeed, marketplace, and messenger have the biggest potential to captivate users' attention. This higher performance is most likely the result of the central placement of the ads in the main part of the browsing area. Contrarily, the right column and banners on the websites within audience network represent side placements that are susceptible to advertising blindness. Instagram channel and Instagram stories are considered to be straightly visual, and the users mostly do not anticipate to shop on the Instagram network. Our results indicate that Instagram users are more inclined to react than participate in any advanced conversions.

Overall, we may confirm that the choice of placement has an important effect on the performance of Facebook ads, although this effect was equally prominent for both dynamic and manually optimized ads.

Our second research question (RQ2) examined the influence of advertising formats such as text and variations of picture-based and interactive content on the performance of dynamic and static ads. The analysis included data from both Google ads and Facebook ads (Table 5). However, some factors must be considered when the data are interpreted. Since some of the formats are specific only to the respective social networks, the costs may differ across the platforms. *Carousel* and Collection represent only Facebook native formats, while Text and Interactive content were used only for the Google ads. Advertisements containing one photo of a product were set up for both ad systems. The results from the 168 dynamic and 1,575 static ads indicate that text-based advertisement in the Google search network generate the best outcomes when created as dynamic ads, regardless of the customer acquisition stage and campaign goals. Textual ads had the best CTR out of the all advertising formats. Interactive ads performed the best in terms of profitability and the number of reactions; however, their cost was higher (average cost per CTR of 0.21 EUR for the dynamic ads and 0.24 EUR for the static ads). Among the Facebook advertising formats, Carousel generated the most results at the lowest cost. According to our data, the collection of multiple product photos appears to be the least effective advertising format. As it is evident from Table 5, the choice of advertising format may significantly affect the performance of the dynamic ads and that of the manually optimized ads.

The main focus of our research agenda was examining whether dynamic ads can successfully answer the marketing needs of advertisers while cutting the time-demanding effort of creating individual ads. To answer our three remaining research questions (RQ3, RQ4, and RQ5), we first compared the advertising results of dynamic and static ads within each advertising platform. Subsequently, we performed a cross-platform comparative analysis between Facebook and Google.

Table 5. The impact of the advertising format on the performance of static and dynamic ads

	Brand awareness and reach				Consideration				Conversions	
	Dynamics ads		Manually optimized ads		Dynamics ads		Manually optimized ads		Dynamics ads	Manually optimized ads
	Av. Num. of reac.	Av. cost per reac. (EUR)	Num. of reac.	Av. cost per reac. (EUR)	Av. CTR	Av. cost per CTR (EUR)	Av. CTR	Av. cost per CTR (EUR)	Av. profit. (EUR)	Av. profit. (EUR)
Photo	85	0.11	98	0.10	1.89	0.12	1.75	0.14	12.44	12.42
Carousel	167	0.09	178	0.08	2.32	0.09	2.34	0.09	17.67	16.95
Collection	106	0.19	121	0.15	1.95	0.17	1.95	0.17	13.87	12.32
Interactive	131	0.25	167	0.18	3.28	0.21	3.10	0.24	20.12	19.21
Text	186	0.19	121	0.23	3.48	0.19	2.89	0.25	12.86	10.21

Source: (the authors)

What are the effects of dynamic ads during the different stages of getting familiar with a brand? Results displayed in Tables 6 and 7 present the stage by stage comparison of all types of dynamic ads and the grouped average values for the static ads. With regard to Google ads, smart ads performed sub-optimally in the awareness and consideration stages, but the final average profitability (22.38 EUR) can be considered rather moderate than weak. Moderate performance in all acquisition phases was typical for dynamic customer search ads and dynamic product ads. Dynamic search ads led to the lowest profitability; however, on the other hand, they produced the best CTR (3.48) in the consideration phase and a moderate number of reactions (186). The best overall performance was achieved for the dynamic remarketing ads that generated CTR of 3.21 and the highest average profitability (35.35 EUR).

The performance of Facebook dynamic ads across the individual acquisition stages also differed. Table 7 contains the aggregated results for all types of dynamic Facebook ads, including the equivalent of customer search Google ads. Lookalike ads represent a tool for finding new customers with characteristics similar to the current audience. The advertising results reflect the connection between the campaign goal optimization and the customer acquisition stage. Dynamic ads optimized for awareness performed the best in the first stage of the acquisition process (206 reactions at 0.12 EUR average cost), but their effectiveness decreased over time and failed to obtain the desired profitability. Similarly, dynamic consideration ads generated the best CTR (3.24 at the lowest cost of 0.12 EUR), whereas the conversion ads generated the best profitability (35.90 EUR). Dynamic customer search ads (lookalikes)

Table 6. Effects of dynamic and static Google ads during the different stages of the customer acquisition process

	Brand awareness and reach		Consideration		Conversions
	Av. Num. of reac.	Av. cost per reac. (EUR)	Av. CTR	Av. cost per CTR (EUR)	Av. profit. (EUR)
Smart ads	166	0.21	1.99	0.21	22.38
Dynamic search ads	186	0.19	3.48	0.19	12.86
Dynamic product ads	193	0.15	2.12	0.19	22.18
Dynamic remarketing ads	254	0.12	3.21	0.21	35.35
Dynamic customer search ads	189	0.21	2.54	0.29	28.89
Static product ads (combined)	205	0.20	2.15	0.18	25.10
Static search ads (combined)	215	0.18	3.39	0.19	15.54

Source: (the authors)

performed consistently well across all the acquisition stages and generated medium profitability (23.45 EUR).

The effectiveness comparison of dynamic and static ads was also one of the research topics (RQ4) we defined at the beginning of this chapter. If we look more closely at the results related to the Google platform (Table 6), we may conclude that the dynamic ads represent a very effective tool of marketing automatization. All of the dynamic ads brought similar or superior results to the manually optimized ads, whereas the dynamic remarketing ads were the most effective of all for the campaign we set up (average profitability: 35.35 EUR). Regarding the Facebook advertising system, the results are less conclusive. It appears that manually optimized ads work more efficiently than their dynamic versions for the first two stages: brand awareness and consideration. In the conversion stage, Facebook catalog ads outperformed the static ads (average profitability of 35.90 EUR and 29.34 EUR, respectively).

Finally, if we compare the advertising outcomes across the two platforms (RQ5), Facebook and Google, we may conclude that both types of dynamic advertising produce similarly desirable results. However, it is important to mention the necessity of evaluating ad performance with regard to the different user contexts of the platforms. Our findings indicate identical behavioral patterns when it comes to remarketing ads. The high level of personalization provided by these automatically generated ads helps to convert users that have already exhibited interest into

Table 7. Effects of Facebook ads during the different stages of the customer acquisition process

	Brand awareness and reach		Consideration		Conversions
	Av. Num. of reac.	Av. cost per reac. (EUR)	Av. CTR	Av. cost per CTR (EUR)	Av. profit. (EUR)
Custom audience awareness	206	0.12	1.95	0.15	12.00
Custom audience consideration	189	0.14	3.24	0.12	20.19
Custom audience conversions	107	0.14	2.36	0.18	35.90
Lookalike audiences (combined)	183	0.13	2.56	0.21	23.45
Facebook Static ads awareness	308	0.09	1.77	0.14	13.72
Facebook Static ads consideration	206	0.18	3.01	0.15	19.92
Facebook Static ads conversions	197	0.19	2.02	0.21	29.34

Source: (the authors)

becoming customers. In addition, our experiment proves that Facebook and Google dynamic ads may be successfully used for acquiring new customers. By contrast, the best option for addressing new customers appears to be Facebook awareness ads, which generated the most reactions at the lowest cost. Dynamic Google search ads also performed well during the first stage of customer acquisition. We suppose that the lower performance of Facebook dynamic ads in other, except remarketing, situations may be caused by the nature of the content that users are used to seeing on the social network. To capture users' attention on this medium, originality is a necessity. Hence, automatically generated content using a standardized template does not provide enough convincing power.

CONCLUSION

Communicating a marketing message to the right potential customers is a major challenge in today's marketing arena. Internet and related technologies have enabled consumers to gain more control of information gathering than before. Therefore, traditional marketing campaigns have lost their effectiveness, and more sophisticated marketing automation campaigns are taking their place. Marketing automation tools are now part of many comprehensive business systems that integrate and process data from a variety of other enterprise applications and external resources. Generally, business systems work with data from CRM, ERP, warehouse systems, or accounting and integrate large data analysis systems. The main purpose of these business systems is to gain the detailed knowledge of the customer and his/her needs. Automation then allows the advertisers to offer products and services that match the customer's interests and reach him/her at the right time and in the right place or through a suitable business channel. Finding the right combination of all parameters increases the likelihood of a successful purchase and the overall customer satisfaction and loyalty.

This chapter presented the results of 168 automatically generated dynamic and 1,575 manually optimized ads from Google AdWords and Facebook Ads Manager. In our experiment, we focused on the analysis of the effectiveness of the dynamic ads while considering the parameters that could influence the advertising performance, such as the campaign goal, placement, and the format of the creative content. Our findings indicate that marketing automatization using artificial intelligence offered by advertising systems can be successfully used to convert online users into paying customers and to acquire new customers based on the information about the current customer base. Thanks to their ability to provide highly personalized content and track the users' preferences, dynamic ads are the most beneficial when used for remarketing purposes. However, they might perform sub-optimally in situations where the browsing context requires originality. Users' participate in social networks for entertainment and not to browse through product advertisements. Making first contact with a user might require more innovative content than a dynamically generated product catalog. By contrast, dynamic Google ads are mostly displayed in a context where the user has already showed interest in the product or a similar category of products. The system thus makes recommendations based on the user's previous entries and helps him/her to find what he/she is looking for. Advertisers on social networks are generally trying to convince the users to try products that they have never directly asked for. This contextual duality might be the main factor that influences the performance of the dynamic ads.

In conclusion, dynamic ads are definitely a very helpful and effective tool for e-stores that wish to advertise many products at any time. This type of automatized and personalized advertising is very suitable for reminding online users of the products that have caught their attention in the past and for recommending suitable solutions to their search queries. Nevertheless, marketing automatization still has limitations, and artificial intelligence cannot completely replace the human factor in marketing communication. Original and creative content remains the most important prerequisite for establishing and maintaining long-term and engaged relationships.

ACKNOWLEDGMENT

This research was supported by the Technical University of Liberec, in a grant titled "Competitiveness of the company in the digital environment", registered as SGS-2019-1068, and by the Technology Agency of the Czech Republic under the Program of applied research ZETA within the framework of project "Developing the skills necessary for the digital business transformation" (registration number TJ02000206).

REFERENCES

Abedini Koshksaray, A., Franklin, D., & Heidarzadeh Hanzaee, K. (2015). The relationship between e-lifestyle and Internet advertising avoidance. [AMJ]. *Australasian Marketing Journal*, *23*(1), 38–48. doi:10.1016/j.ausmj.2015.01.002

Baek, T., & Morimoto, M. (2012). Stay away from me. *Journal of Advertising*, *41*(1), 59–76. doi:10.2753/JOA0091-3367410105

Bang, H., & Wojdynski, B. (2016). Tracking users' visual attention and responses to personalized advertising based on task cognitive demand. *Computers in Human Behavior*, *55*, 867–876. doi:10.1016/j.chb.2015.10.025

Baruh, L., Secinti, E., & Cemalcilar, Z. (2017). Online privacy concerns and privacy management: a meta-analytical review. *Journal of Communication*, *67*(1), 26–53. doi:10.1111/jcom.12276

Bleier, A., & Eisenbeiss, M. (2015). The importance of trust for personalized online advertising. *Journal of Retailing*, *91*(3), 390–409. doi:10.1016/j.jretai.2015.04.001

Chen, Q., Feng, Y., Liu, L., & Tian, X. (2019). Understanding consumers' reactance of online personalized advertising: A new scheme of rational choice from a perspective of negative effects. *International Journal of Information Management*, *44*, 53–64. doi:10.1016/j.ijinfomgt.2018.09.001

Danova, T. (2014). For mobile-social apps, advertising is winning as the money-making revenue model. Retrieved from http://www. businessinsider. com/advertising-is-the-most-lucrative-revenue-modelfor-growing-mobile-social-apps-2014-1

Eckersley, P. (2010). How unique is your web browser?. *Privacy Enhancing Technologies*, 1-18. doi:10.1007/978-3-642-14527-8_1

Estrada-Jiménez, J., Parra-Arnau, J., Rodríguez-Hoyos, A., & Forné, J. (2017). Online advertising: Analysis of privacy threats and protection approaches. *Computer Communications*, *100*, 32–51. doi:10.1016/j.comcom.2016.12.016

Gironda, J., & Korgaonkar, P. (2018). iSpy? Tailored versus invasive ads and consumers' perceptions of personalized advertising. *Electronic Commerce Research and Applications*, *29*, 64–77. doi:10.1016/j.elerap.2018.03.007

Grewal, D., Bart, Y., Spann, M., & Zubcsek, P. (2016). Mobile advertising: a framework and research agenda. *Journal of Interactive Marketing*, *34*, 3–14. doi:10.1016/j.intmar.2016.03.003

GrowthBadger. (2019). *Remarketing: the ultimate guide for 2019.* Retrieved from https://growthbadger.com/remarketing/

Hsieh, Y., & Chen, K. (2011). How different information types affect viewer's attention on internet advertising. *Computers in Human Behavior*, *27*(2), 935–945. doi:10.1016/j.chb.2010.11.019

Lee, T. (2019). Google is the internet's largest ad company. So why is it building an ad blocker? Retrieved from https://www.vox.com/new-money/2017/6/5/15729688/google-chrome-ad-blocking

Li, C. (2016). When does web-based personalization really work? The distinction between actual personalization and perceived personalization. *Computers in Human Behavior*, *54*, 25–33. doi:10.1016/j.chb.2015.07.049

Li, C., & Liu, J. (2017). A name alone is not enough: A reexamination of web-based personalization effect. *Computers in Human Behavior*, *72*, 132–139. doi:10.1016/j.chb.2017.02.039

Lu, C., Wu, I., & Hsiao, W. (2019). Developing customer product loyalty through mobile advertising: Affective and cognitive perspectives. *International Journal of Information Management*, *47*, 101–111. doi:10.1016/j.ijinfomgt.2018.12.020

Parra-Arnau, J., Achara, J., & Castelluccia, C. (2017). MyAdChoices. *ACM Transactions on the Web*, *11*(1), 1–47. doi:10.1145/2996466

Redondo, I., & Aznar, G. (2018). To use or not to use ad blockers? The roles of knowledge of ad blockers and attitude toward online advertising. *Telematics and Informatics*, *35*(6), 1607–1616. doi:10.1016/j.tele.2018.04.008

Sánchez, D., & Viejo, A. (2018). Privacy-preserving and advertising-friendly web surfing. *Computer Communications*, *130*, 113–123. doi:10.1016/j.comcom.2018.09.002

Schreiner, T., Rese, A., & Baier, D. (2019). Multichannel personalization: Identifying consumer preferences for product recommendations in advertisements across different media channels. *Journal of Retailing and Consumer Services*, *48*, 87–99. doi:10.1016/j.jretconser.2019.02.010

Setyani, V., Zhu, Y., Hidayanto, A., Sandhyaduhita, P., & Hsiao, B. (2019). Exploring the psychological mechanisms from personalized advertisements to urge to buy impulsively on social media. *International Journal of Information Management*, *48*, 96–107. doi:10.1016/j.ijinfomgt.2019.01.007

Shanahan, T., Tran, T., & Taylor, E. (2019). Getting to know you: Social media personalization as a means of enhancing brand loyalty and perceived quality. *Journal of Retailing and Consumer Services*, *47*, 57–65. doi:10.1016/j.jretconser.2018.10.007

The influence of perceived ad relevance on social media advertising: An empirical examination of a mediating role of privacy concern. *Computers in Human Behavior*, *70*, 303-309. doi:10.1016/j.chb.2017.01.008

Tran, T. (2017). Personalized ads on facebook: An effective marketing tool for online marketers. *Journal of Retailing and Consumer Services*, *39*, 230–242. doi:10.1016/j.jretconser.2017.06.010

WordStream. (2019). *31 Advertising statistics to know in 2019*. Retrieved from https://www.wordstream.com/blog/ws/2018/07/19/advertising-statistics

Yu, C., Zhang, Z., Lin, C., & Wu, Y. (2019). Can data-driven precision marketing promote user ad clicks? Evidence from advertising in WeChat moments. *Industrial Marketing Management*. doi:10.1016/j.indmarman.2019.05.001

Yu, J., & Cude, B. (2009). Possible disparities in consumers' perceptions toward personalized advertising caused by cultural differences: U.S. and Korea. *Journal of International Consumer Marketing*, *21*(4), 251–269. doi:10.1080/08961530802282166

Zorn, S., Bellman, S., Robinson, J., & Varan, D. (2013). Cultural differences affect interactive television advertising. *Journal of Marketing Communications*, *22*(1), 3–17. doi:10.1080/13527266.2013.833539

ADDITIONAL READING

de Haan, E., Wiesel, T., & Pauwels, K. (2016). The effectiveness of different forms of online advertising for purchase conversion in a multiple-channel attribution framework. *International Journal of Research in Marketing*, *33*(3), 491–507. doi:10.1016/j.ijresmar.2015.12.001

Estrada-Jiménez, J., Parra-Arnau, J., Rodríguez-Hoyos, A., & Forné, J. (2019). On the regulation of personal data distribution in online advertising platforms. *Engineering Applications of Artificial Intelligence*, *82*, 13–29. doi:10.1016/j.engappai.2019.03.013

Gijsenberg, M., & Nijs, V. (2019). Advertising spending patterns and competitor impact. *International Journal of Research in Marketing*, *36*(2), 232–250. doi:10.1016/j.ijresmar.2018.11.004

He, J., & Shao, B. (2018). Examining the dynamic effects of social network advertising: A semiotic perspective. *Telematics and Informatics*, *35*(2), 504–516. doi:10.1016/j.tele.2018.01.014

Ji, S., Choi, Y., & Ryu, M. (2016). The economic effects of domestic search engines on the development of the online advertising market. *Telecommunications Policy*, *40*(10-11), 982–995. doi:10.1016/j.telpol.2016.05.005

Kireyev, P., Pauwels, K., & Gupta, S. (2016). Do display ads influence search? Attribution and dynamics in online advertising. *International Journal of Research in Marketing*, *33*(3), 475–490. doi:10.1016/j.ijresmar.2015.09.007

White, G., & Samuel, A. (2019). Programmatic Advertising: Forewarning and avoiding hype-cycle failure. *Technological Forecasting and Social Change*, *144*, 157–168. doi:10.1016/j.techfore.2019.03.020

Yoldar, M., & Özcan, U. (2019). Collaborative targeting: Biclustering-based online ad recommendation. *Electronic Commerce Research and Applications*, *35*, 100857. doi:10.1016/j.elerap.2019.100857

KEY TERMS AND DEFINITIONS

Ad Placement: Ad placement include all advertising spaces, mostly paid, offered by online publishers, websites, and social networks to advertisers to display their advertisements. The individual placements have different potential for reaching the users and perform differently when it comes to the type of content chosen for the advertisement.

Ad Targeting: Ad targeting refers to the selection of potential customer groups to which an advertisement will be displayed. This specification of the ad's audience is done using targeting parameters including demographic and geographic information, interests, and device preferences. **Conversion:** Conversion refers to a desired action performed by a consumer as a reaction to an advertisement or other marketing effort. The desired action can take many forms including the purchases, membership registrations, newsletter subscriptions, and application downloads.

Dynamic advertisements: Dynamic advertisements describe a dynamic delivery of specific products that visitors viewed on the website of an online retailer. Their primary advantage is dynamism that allows one to create one advertising template and use it for all products from an uploaded data feed. Information from the data feed is automatically being implemented into the template based on user preferences. **Facebook Ads Manager:** The Facebook Ads Manager was developed by Facebook to manage advertisements on this social network, Instagram, and ads displayed in the audience network. This application allows the advertiser to create and target the ads, set campaign budget, view history, and collect data about previous and ongoing ads.

Marketing automatization: Marketing automation is represented by the introduction of software tools that automate some of the key processes of customer data collection, evaluation, acquisition, and customer retention. Among these automated activities, we may undoubtedly include e-mail marketing, web analytics, the evaluation of potential leads, online forms, consumer research, tracking of ongoing marketing campaigns, and many others.

Product feed: A product XML feed is a collection of all selected products available in an online store containing all the necessary data for full import and synchronization with product search engines, price comparators, aggregators, or advertising systems. It is required to implement dynamic product campaigns.

UTM Parameters: Text fragments that are attached in the specified format to the web link. Attaching these textual segments allows the analytical software to exactly identify from what source, campaign, or advertisement the users came to the website. UTM parameters generally contain the following five elements: utm_source, utm_medium, utm_campaign, utm_content, and utm_term.

Chapter 8
The (In)Effectiveness of In-Stream Video Ads:
Comparison of Facebook and YouTube

Tereza Semerádová
https://orcid.org/0000-0002-9123-5782
Faculty of Economics, Technical University of Liberec, Czech Republic

Petr Weinlich
Technical University of Liberec, Czech Republic

ABSTRACT

Video represents the most shared type of online content. The ability of this media to capture and convey a message in an interactive and informationally rich format has captivated both users and advertisers. Advertising platforms are trying to expand the offer of the tools that would help the advertisers to reach their potential customers. Therefore, many new video-based advertising formats are being introduced including ads with experimental length or dimensions. However, the increasing quantity of online advertisements the users have to face is raising questions about their actual marketing effectiveness. To provide relevant answers, authors examined the performance of 13 types of video ads that were implemented for a 30-day period and that generated 1 155 EUR overall profit. The advertising results are analyzed from three perspectives: financial, behavioral, and reactional. The main emphasis is put on the study of the video effectiveness depending on different viewing contexts with respect to the potential phenomenon of advertising blindness.

DOI: 10.4018/978-1-7998-1618-8.ch008

Copyright © 2020, IGI Global. Copying or distributing in print or electronic forms without written permission of IGI Global is prohibited.

INTRODUCTION

Video marketing is currently one of the most popular online marketing tools. Video content is more engaging, memorable, and popular with consumers than any other type of content. According to the predictions, by 2020, online videos will account for more than 80% of all consumer Internet traffic (85% in the US). YouTube is the second most visited website after Google. On a daily basis, users view more than 500 million h of video on YouTube; further, 78% of people watch online videos every week, and 55% watch online videos every day. Viewers memorize up to 95% of the message while watching the video, compared to 10% when reading a text. As more social networks have been inspired by Facebook's decision to prioritize video content, the prominence of video across all platforms has grown. Facebook videos have a 135% higher average organic reach than photos. Nearly 50% of Internet users search for videos related to a product or service before they visit the store. Implementing a video on a landing page can increase the average conversion rate by 80%. Four times as many consumers would rather watch a video on a product than read about the product. Companies that use marketing videos have a 27% higher click-through rate and a 34% higher conversion rate than those that do not. Video ads have an average click-through rate of 1.84%, which is the highest of all digital ad formats. Brands that use video marketing grow 49% faster than brands that do not use videos. Nonetheless, although video marketing is a powerful tool, there are a few factors that merchants should be aware of regarding potential customer preferences. More than 15% of viewers believe that video advertising should not last longer than 15 s. In addition, 85% of Facebook videos are watched without sound. Conversely, 82% of consumers close a browser or leave a web page due to popup video advertising and 33% of viewers stop watching video after 30 s, 45% after 1 min, and 60% after 2 min ("33 Fascinating and useful statistics about video marketing in 2019", 2019).

There can be no doubt that video has gained traction in popularity over the past years with both users and advertisers. Social networks, video listing websites, and advertising systems provide a large number of video or mixed (video and photos) formats that can be used to deliver a desired message to the potential customers. The most common formats include Facebook native newsfeed video, YouTube video and YouTube ads, stories, banner video ads, and in-stream commercial breaks. Although previous research has proven that video ads generate better results in terms of number of reactions, reach, and profitability overall (Semerádová & Weinlich, 2018), scientific evidence related to the effectiveness of the individual video formats is still insufficient. Studies on advertising blindness suggest that the placement of the marketing message may be a key variable influencing the final effectiveness of a particular video spot (Muñoz-Leiva et al., 2019; Wang & Hung, 2018; Bang & Wojdynski, 2016). Recent research results indicate that the central part of the browsing space is the most suitable placement since it represents a native environment for web pages and social network feeds (Zimand-Sheiner et al., 2019; Aslam & Karjaluoto, 2017; Alalwan, 2018). According to these studies, in-stream and newsfeed ads should be the most effective type of video marketing. However, surveys and experiments that tested viewers' attention during TV commercials indicate that users develop a certain advertising blindness over time, even for marketing content in the central area of attention (Kim et al., 2017; Joo et al., 2016; Beuckels et al., 2017).

In this chapter, we will test the ability of online video ads to capture user's attention and generate the desired conversions. The effectiveness of this advertising format will be tested on two major video content platforms: YouTube and Facebook. To obtain objective results, we will perform a comparative analysis of the available advertising video formats on both of the aforementioned platforms. The main objective of the proposed study is to examine user reactions to commercial breaks of different lengths and analyze their attitudes toward online video advertising in general. In the following sections, based on previous research in the area of online advertising, we will outline factors that may potentially influence user perception of video content. Furthermore, we will describe current video advertising options and explain the complexity of the metrics used to assess the video performance. The theoretical findings will be used to set up an online experiment implemented in the native user environment of social networks and on YouTube. The experimental data will be collected via actual advertising content implemented by a Czech online shop.

USER REACTANCE TO VIDEO CONTENT

Video is a global phenomenon that offers many new marketing opportunities. When used correctly, it represents a powerful tool that can help influence user behavior. Brands focus on two main goals: the long-term building of brand awareness and engagement and short-term increases in sales. Emotion-enhanced video supports long-term customer relationships with the brand, whereas strong-communicated videos help to achieve short-term goals. The perfect video campaign should combine both long-term and short-term goals (Lee et al., 2013). There are two basic questions, i.e., how does the emotional side affect our behavior, and what is the role of video in creating an emotional response? According to the economist Daniel Kahneman, people think far less than they perceive themselves as having done and rely on a great deal of subconscious decisions. There are two systems that run in parallel. A system where the brain makes decisions quickly with little effort and a second system where the brain makes decisions based on data (Mowat, 2018, p. 27). Video content contributes to a brand's recognition. If the customers remember the video they saw, they also remember the brand and are more likely to make a purchase. In addition, a satisfied customer likes to share a video that is in accordance with their preferences. Preserving colors, fonts, logos, and the same tonality in both video and web articles helps enhance the memorability of the video (Wu et al., 2018).

A key advantage of video lies in its functionality across different devices; responsive design plays a considerable role in digital marketing. If an advertisement does not display properly, the ads lose effectiveness, thereby leading to a decrease in conversions. Video has the advantage of displaying, although not optimally, on all devices, from computers to mobile phones, consequently allowing for a greater reach in terms of potential customers. Video is also associated with a user-friendly environment (Sidaty et al., 2017). By using videos as a marketing strategy, brand identity can be strengthened to ensure that customers become more engaged and to promote brand loyalty. It is estimated that 92% of mobile video consumers also share videos. Moreover, video is shared 1200% more than a combination of text and a link ("33 Fascinating and useful statistics about video marketing in 2019", 2019).

Currently, users are surrounded by advertising content, and it is difficult to attract and keep their attention. Often, a video is placed in the wrong place at the wrong time. Information communicated through the video must be properly targeted and relevant; otherwise, it may result in a negative impact (Van den Broeck, Poels & Walrave, 2018). There are countless competing brands on the market. The customer is often overwhelmed with advertising messages and overlooks brands' communication campaigns (Yang et al., 2015). To increase the probability of delivering an advertised message, advertisers need to get the maximum amount of information possible about the target group they wish to address and tailor the message in accordance with specific customer needs. The more details the advertiser has on the psychographics of a target group, the higher the chance of creating effective advertisements. Advertising is considered effective if the recipient is exposed to it, memorizes it, and has a change in attitude due to the interaction with the ad, leaving a positive emotional footprint, as well as when the ad results in a change in behavior or when it provides the information needed for rational decision making by the recipient (Tran, 2017).

Music can be seen as a key dimension in creating an effective marketing message. It can influence the users on three levels i.e., the psychological, social, and semantic. The psychological level refers to the ability of music to influence a person's mood, memories, and feelings. As a result, advertising message creators working via this medium can refer to selected emotions or ideas to connect them with a product. The social level is related to the preference of music according to certain demographics (e.g., gender and age), socio-graphics (e.g., social class and vocation), and characteristics (Liikkanen & Salovaara, 2015). Thus, in the context of marketing communication, we may assume that a certain target group that favors a certain type of music will prefer a particular product. If the message is carried by a sung text (song), it can be considered as a factor working on the semantic level wherein the music encodes a certain message. In connection with music and emotions, it is worth mentioning the so-called circular model, which considers two dimensions, i.e., activation × not activating and pleasant × unpleasant. Experiments have shown that music that is perceived as both activating and unpleasant appears to be aggressive, activating and pleasant as exciting, inactive and unpleasant as boring, and inactivating and pleasant as reassuring. When selecting the music for an advertising message, three basic questions should be considered: which is the best music for the product, what music fits the advertising itself, and what music will attract the audience (Martín-Santana et al., 2015)?

Another important factor influencing the user perception of an advertisement is the use of color. The correct color rendering of audiovisual compositions is equally important as other variables since colors are processed emotionally. Dominant elements may be emphasized with rich colors; however, saturated elements should occupy a minor part of the image. It is necessary to consider the fluency of the entire video spot and maintain a uniform color sequence. If each scene was colored differently, it would be distracting for the viewer. We distinguish three main functions of colors: impressive, expressive, and constructive. Impressive color function refers to the sensory perception of the image. The expressive function describes a mental or emotional response. For the constructive function, we determine what colors will prevail in the frame, what the foreground and background will be, and what the overall character of the scene will look like (Kareklas et al., 2014).

Many videos contain textual elements. Generally, it is the final claim, i.e., the main statement that the advertiser wants to emphasize with accompanying or introductory text used to promote the advertising message or even the headlines. Text can also affect the overall atmosphere. An improperly chosen or placed font can destroy the overall impression of the ad. If a company decides to add text to the video, the content creator must keep in mind that the text has to be of a reasonable length. Long texts are rather discouraging to the viewer. The text must have an appropriate color, ideally complementary to the background to be clearly legible, and also be of a sufficient size (Huang et al., 2018). Further, selecting the appropriate font requires taking the aesthetic and technical requirements and the main goal of the ad into account. The font type must correspond to the main message (Amar et al., 2017).

Having a high-quality video that corresponds to the preferences of the target group is a key prerequisite for attracting user attention. The aforementioned characteristics will be accounted for during the creation of the advertising video for the purposes of this experiment. The attractiveness of the video will be subsequently verified by using a focus group made of the typical representatives of the target customer segment.

ADVERTISING VIDEO FORMATS

Online video advertising, including YouTube, Facebook, or other video formats, represents an ideal tool for building brand awareness, capturing user's attention, and generating conversions. Unlike static content, video advertising is able to deliver emotions to the viewer quickly. The emotional dimension can be a decisive factor when converting online users into paying customers. Although video on TV is rather unidirectional and non-interactive, video in an online environment activates the user and generates direct feedback. It also allows the advertiser to track the response of the target audience quickly and acquire data for follow-up campaign optimization.

The visibility time is 1 s for classic display advertising, whereas it takes between 5 and 30 s for video advertising. In addition, videos generate three times as many click-through rates. However, there are some specific differences when it comes to online video advertising. Since it is possible to skip most online advertisements, it is essential to attract and retain the attention of the user who originally came for another type of content. A typical TV spot works with a longer story and gradation toward the end. In the digital environment, because of shorter footage and ad placement, the gradation follows a reverse pattern. Among the most popular formats are classic pre-rolls ads (displayed before the video) and individual spots on social networks and video-banner areas. In addition to the pre-roll option, the advertisers may choose a mid-roll (in-stream) ad that runs during the video or a post-roll video that is characterized by lower effectiveness. Mid-rollers are now a common part of YouTube and Facebook videos (Munnukka et al., 2019).

When preparing the video, it is important to consider the dramatic increase in the consumption of video content by users with mobile devices and adjust the content for multiple formats including vertical video with shorter footage. For example, 72% of younger users today use mobile phones only in portrait mode. In the context of social networks, the videos appear among the posts of other brands and users in the newsfeed of the customers. The video should thus fit into the visual and communication style of the given social network while simultaneously maintaining enough originality to captivate the user. Content creators should keep in mind that most video-banner areas are primarily a silent format and turn on sound only when the user moves the cursor over the video or clicks on the ad to start the sound. The absence of sound can be replaced by quick footage alternations that would attract the attention of the viewer more effectively. In addition to the video, there are usually other graphical elements in the banner area that are static and accompany the message of the video (Yang et al., 2017).

It is advisable to combine multiple footage for each video format. The classic television length of 30 s is allowed by most advertising platforms, but more often advertising systems prefer a shorter footage of 10–15 s. The bumpers of 6 s, originally introduced by YouTube, are now also a common format and function as an effective addition to longer videos, mainly for re-marketing purposes. Videos of all footage lengths should be tailored specifically for online environments and not represent merely shortened version of television ads. In Instagram Stories, the advertising time is limited; the advertiser has 1.5 s on average to captivate the user. Video is a dynamic format that is constantly evolving. A major innovation in video content is the launch of IGTV, an Instagram platform for longer videos. It generates customized content for every viewer and has ambitions to become a serious rival to YouTube. IGTV video is strictly vertical, corresponding to the trend of video consumption by means of mobile devices (Kim & Kim, 2019).

Video Ads on YouTube

YouTube currently offers six advertising formats that differ in the placement of the ads and the length of the commercial break. With Google Ads, advertisers may create impressive video campaigns with a variety of video ad formats that appeal to customers on YouTube and video partner websites. Video ad formats include skippable in-stream ads, in-stream non-skippable ads discovery ads, out-stream ads, and bumpers. Although video ad content must be placed on YouTube, video ads themselves may appear on YouTube and video partner sites as well as on applications across the entire Google Content network. Depending on the format and settings used, they may also appear on tablets and mobile devices. All advertising placements supported by YouTube are displayed in Figure 1 ("Video advertising formats – YouTube help center", 2019).

Figure 1. Available advertising formats on YouTube
Source: (the authors)

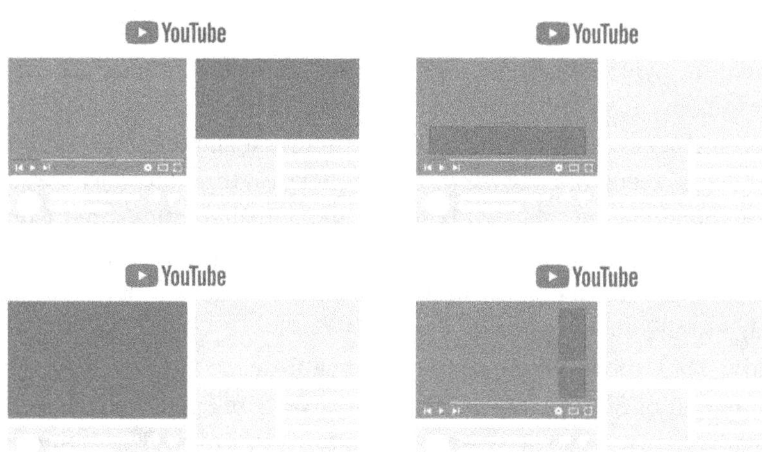

Skippable in-stream ads are designed to promote video content between other videos on YouTube or in the Google Content Network. A video ad will be played before, after, or during other videos. After 5 s, the user can skip the ad. Skippable in-stream ads can appear on YouTube watch pages, videos on partner sites, and content network applications. For cost per view bids, the advertiser pays when a user watches at least 30 s of video (or an entire video, if it is less than 30 s) or performs some interaction (whichever comes first). Another way to express advertising costs is costs per thousand (CPM), which is based on impressions. Advertising micro-spots use CPM bids, and the advertiser pays for every 1,000 ad impressions.

Non-skippable in-stream ads represent an advertising format allowing advertisers to share the full message with their customers. A non-skippable in-stream ad takes up to 15 s to play before, during, or after another video. Viewers do not have the option to play the video prior to these ads. The non-skippable ads may be used on the same placements as the previous format, and the billing is also based per every 1,000 impressions.

Discovery ads are used to navigate the users to the desired content displayed in YouTube related videos, YouTube search results or YouTube mobile home pages. Discovery ads comprise a video thumbnail and a short text. Although the exact size and appearance of video discovery ads may vary depending on where they appear, they always invite users to click to play the promoted video. The video will then be played on the YouTube watch page. The advertising costs are recorded only if the user chooses to view the ad and clicks on the thumbnail.

Bumpers represent a short video ad format allowing advertisers to reach more customers and enhance brand awareness. This format can be used to address a wide range of viewers with a short message that will keep them tuned for more information. Bumpers take up to 6 s and can be placed before, in and after a video on all YouTube pages, partner video sites and applications across the Google Content network. Viewers do not have the option to skip these ads. As in the previous cases, the advertiser pays for every 1,000 impressions.

Out-stream ads are mobile only (phones and tablets) video ads that appear on partner sites and in apps. Out-stream ads will start playing with the audio turned off. The user can click the ad to turn on the sound. An advertiser is only charged if more than half of the ad area is displayed for at least 2 s. This format is designed to increase video ad impact at an affordable price. One video template can be displayed on a variety of mobile placements. On the mobile websites, out-stream ads appear in banners, whereas in mobile apps, they appear in banners, feeds, and in both portrait and full screen modes. However, this ad format is not yet available on YouTube.

Video Advertising on Facebook and Instagram

Facebook video ads may be used for many purposes including post boosting, promoting Facebook fan pages, sending users to the advertiser's website, increasing conversions and app installations, fostering stronger engagement, and generating more user reactions. Although video ads may be distributed in various formats in all the above-mentioned purposes, their delivery will always be determined by the campaign goals and not primarily by the number of views. The same video may be used for the generation of likes as well as for the promotion of app installations. However, Facebook will always optimize the campaign for the selected purpose. Therefore, if the goal is to increase the number of views of the video, the campaign goal Video Views should be selected. Using video format for purposes other than Video Views is highly recommended, although it is necessary to adjust the message of the video to the chosen campaign objective. Facebook advertising platform offers six types of video ads including the following: short videos and GIFs, vertical videos, Instagram videos, carousel format, collection, and in-stream video ("Facebook video ads", 2019).

Short videos and GIFs may be used in all placements on Facebook, Instagram, and Audience Network. GIFs play in loop, similarly as short videos. In addition, they have the same file size requirements (4GB). To achieve the best results, the advertisers should opt for high-quality images with gentle movements. The files should always be uploaded in .gif format. According to the general Facebook advertising guide, images smaller than 8 MB and with more than 20% of text should be avoided. However, GIF-based ads may appear only as static images on some mobile devices.

The rise of ***vertical video*** presents both opportunities and challenges. The vertical orientation of the video inevitably requires a more refined look that takes full advantage of the immediacy and interactivity of the format. Vertical videos should be shot in 9:16 aspect ratio from the outset; if the advertiser shoots horizontally, they should be considering the implications for vertical formatting throughout the process. The optimization of vertical videos should always be done on a smartphone to verify that all the elements are recognizable and readable. Vertical video is not limited to the 9:16 ratio alone. Advertising platforms also allow for the aspect ratio of 3:2, which is more suitable for social network feeds and provides more space for additional text elements that make the video feel more authentic, fitting in a visual pattern that users are accustomed to seeing in the newsfeed.

Instagram Stories ads can contain both video and photo content and can be created from already existing material or form vertical videos tailored specifically for this format. Speed is typical for Stories. Every post in stories is limited only to 15 s. Therefore, the video needs to be timed correctly and transmit the main message quickly. Each individual story can consist of several short chapters, or scenes.

According to Facebook, 60% of the stories are viewed with the sound turned on. It is thus possible to add dialog or sound effects to the video. Facebook recommends placing the product, brand, and message at the beginning of the story a reminder of the brand along with a call to action before the story ends.

A ***carousel format*** is suitable for displaying two or more images or videos, headings and links, or call to action in one ad. The users who come across this ad may scroll through the individual entries by swiping, when on a mobile device, or by clicking on the arrows when on computer screens. Carousel format is used to display an array of products, services, applications, and related details or to tell a story in a creative manner. Carousel ads may be created in Facebook Ads Manager or by using the API environment. They appear on Facebook and Instagram on selected posts on mobile devices and computers.

One of the primary methods through which users discover new products is mobile video. However, when they want to get more information regarding an offer, they expect a clean and fast mobile environment. ***Collection ads*** allow people to move from the discovery stage to shopping in an effortless way. Every collection ad primarily comprises a video or an image. The advertisers may choose from four accompanying image-based grid-like layouts. Customers who click on your collection ad to browse or find out more information go smoothly into a fast-loading, fast-moving visual environment without leaving Facebook or Instagram.

In-stream videos are displayed only to users who watch video content form publishing partners approved by Facebook. Facebook in-stream video ads are included among the automatic placements offered by Facebook. However, if the advertiser desires to use only the in-stream video ads, they may adjust the placements and exclude other options except the desired one. Content creators (publishing partners) work closely with the Facebook Media Partnership team to ensure the quality of the video hosting ads. In-stream ads can be hosted only in at least 3 min long videos of the approved publishing partners. Publishing partners decide when advertising breaks occur. The first available advertising break for in-stream video is one minute. All in-stream video ads should contain an audio track. The lengths and requirements for in-stream videos differ depending on the chosen placement. In-stream ads for Facebook should be 5–15 s long and in the vertical (9:16), horizontal (16:9), and square (1:1) aspect ratios. In the Audience Network, videos can last up to 120 s when the advertiser opts for automatic placements; however, when only in-stream videos are selected, the video time is limited to 30 s. Vertical videos are not allowed in the Audience Network.

Both advertising platforms combined offers in a total of 10 different video-based advertising formats that may be further diversified by choosing specific targeting and distribution options. In our experiment, we will test the effectiveness of all the described formats: skippable and non-skippable ads, discovery ads, bumpers, out-stream ads, Facebook short videos, Instagram Stories, carousel format, collection, and Facebook in-stream ads.

HOW TO MEASURE THE PERFORMANCE OF VIDEO ADS?

The main objective for many users and advertisers is often only the number of views. They judge video and video advertisements as effective if said ads are able to generate as many views of their videos as that of their competitors. Inexperienced content creators typically do not analyze who the viewers of the video are, where they come from, or how the viewing curve fluctuates during the video. It can be argued that an ordinary user, an amateur creator, does not need this information. However, if this data is not tracked by advertisers, the amount of money invested into video advertising can be spent without achieving the desired result. Video metrics represent a considerably important step for creating video strategies and marketing campaigns. When companies or creators aim to determine the impact of their videos, they must first decide their goal and the relevant metrics for expressing said goal. Metrics, not just in the online environment, represent the individual dimensions of an object or an event that can be measured and recorded as a number or ratio. For example, for the dimension of video sharing, there are metrics such as the total number of shares or the number of shares in relation to a chosen timeframe. Video analytics can help the advertisers and content creators examine the real impact of their advertisements and evaluate the quality of the video in relation to the preferences of the viewers. In addition to achieving high ratings, the transmission of the marketing message should be included in the evaluation (Li et al., 2019).

There are two main approaches to measuring video impact. The first approach consists in the combination of web and social media tracking and the analytical tools that are applied to acquire a more detailed data track reflecting user online behavior. These tools function on the basis of a so-called site-centric measuring method (sometimes referred to as server-centric) that is implemented at the level of web pages, servers, web browsers using cookies, snippets of JavaScript measuring code inserted into the HTML code of a web page, or directly into a video player. The second approach (user-centric) focuses on an analysis of user behavior. This second set of methods includes user tracking and qualitative data collection techniques such as surveys and user evaluation panels (Liu et al., 2018; Ding et al., 2019).

Specialized video analytics tools collect the most information on the level of the video player. The JavaScript code inserted in the video player sends the information to the measuring server that then evaluates user behavior and analyzes a series of metrics, such as the percentage of the video the user actually saw, what frames the user intentionally skipped, and more information about the technical quality of the distributed video. The main major platforms that allow video advertising such as YouTube, Facebook, Google, and Instagram provide a large variety of metrics implemented directly within the administration interface. The analytical tools used by the advertising systems are comprehensive and combine both of the aforementioned perspectives. Since the user interacts not only with the video but also with the website where the video is placed or with the landing page that they visited by clicking on the video, advertising systems partially or fully integrate website analytics. Advertising systems collect analytical information about video views, user behavior and interaction with the video, user demographics, viewing device and browser, activity on social networks, etc. However, advertising systems do not typically provide technical information regarding the video distribution since such systems are conceptualized even for amateur users (Berry et al., 2015).

Although each advertising system and each video platform use their own specific metrics, we generally identify three basic categories of video performance indexes: performance metrics, behavioral metrics, and mixed metrics.

Performance Metrics

Performance metrics are applied to describe a company's business performance. They include business segment metrics as well as the user requirements or management metrics. In the case of online video content, performance metrics provide data for quantitative analysis of the user's video viewing process. The metrics are computed based on the hard, up-to-date data related to reach, the number of views, and the length of the viewing sessions per individuals or per groups of users.

Many online video content creators aim to achieve as many views as possible. However, this basic metric does not allow an analysis of the quality of the information shared in the video, audience composition, and other data that is vital for campaign targeting and customer segmentation. Although viewing metrics represent a value that can be compared to other videos on a given platform, measuring the number of views between multiple platforms is a major problem because different analytical tools use different definitions of a view. David Burch from Tubemogul, an online marketing and analytics company, says that most people in the online marketing industry do not know exactly what a single view means or how it is calculated ("What Counts as a Video View? - David Burch, Tubemogul", 2019; "Understanding How Your Videos Perform on Facebook", 2019). Facebook defines the view metric as the number of times the video has been viewed for at least 3 s. However, it does not indicate how views are counted when a user automatically (and non-intentionally) runs a video in the News feed without audio for 3 s. This type of view could happen by accident while viewing a completely different post on Facebook that happened to be close to the video, causing the users to place a mouse cursor on it.

YouTube, in the description of the view metric, states that the index describes a total number of views in a selected period, area, and within the range of the selected filters ("About video ad metrics and reporting", 2019). Youtube repeatedly mentions, in its help center, that the calculation of this metric includes only real users and analyzes each view for whether it was done by a robot or a human. However, as far as we know, there is no detailed explanation what sort of user behavior is recorded as one view. Unofficial sources claim that YouTube counts one view after viewing at least 30 s of the video. Unfortunately, there is no information about how the YouTube algorithm works if the video is less than 30 s long. The YouTube view counter stops at a value of 301. When playing the video content, the user downloads video from the nearest distribution node, and the view entry is sent to the analytical center when a video request is made. Based on the aforementioned definitions, viewing metrics may be misleading as a measure of video's popularity when compared across platforms. The definitions differ not only in the proportion of video that a user has to see but also in assessing whether it is necessary to evaluate a user as an individual or count the view by each click. These differences in the calculation of the metrics can result in distortion when setting up the marketing campaigns and deciding where to place the ads according to the average costs per view.

Quartile reporting represents a more objective method of measuring the ability of a video to capture user attention. It is used by video analytics tools in both Google AdWords and Facebook. This metric determines the number of times a certain percentage of the video has been viewed, in this case, whether the viewer has played 25%, 50%, 75%, or 100% of the video content per one viewing session. Owing to the relative, proportional nature of the quartile reporting, it is possible to use this metric to compare the video performance across both advertising platforms. The only factor of distortion is the varying average time of the viewed fraction of the video that depends on the total length of the video. For longer videos, the viewer must spend more active time to see an equal quartile as for the shorter videos. Therefore, shorter videos will reach a higher percentage much faster. Surprisingly, only a few videos reach the full 100% quartile because most videos contain intro and outro sequences that are often skipped by the users. In addition to the views and quartile reporting, we may also come across other more detailed performance metrics such as the ***viewing time*** and ***average percentage viewed***.

Behavioral Metrics

For video creators and marketers, the active viewer's interaction with the video content has the greatest value. Content creators try to embed a certain message in their videos. It can be either a joke, a question, or, in the case of online video marketing, a sales promotion or a brand name, etc. It is the thorough analysis of user responses and their attitudes toward the video they have watched that generates feedback regarding the creator on its quality. The interaction of the viewer with the online video content can take several forms. Basic user interaction options include the following: commenting, liking, adding a video to favorites, following the content creator, recommending or sharing the video with others, interacting with text annotations and overlays ads, or downloading the video.

However, not all these interactions are applicable on all platforms. Each platform allows different viewer interactions with the video and also different rating scales ranging from likes and dislikes to emojis. From a sociological perspective, users are more likely to react on thematically controversial videos, videos showing exceptional abilities or containing amusing content. Furthermore, users are more likely to respond to negative stimuli and express their dislikes than to praise good quality. Moreover, users respond to ads less frequently than to videos of interest. For video ads, in addition to standard engagement options, the analytical tools can identify click-throughs to the advertised product and the follow-up conversions. In the long term, the growing of viewer engagement indicates increasing popularity and fidelity vis-à-vis the fan base. Conversely, in the short term, monitoring viewer interactions with a single video informs the creator of the quality of the video.

One of the most important behavioral metrics is ***engagement rate***, which is calculated as the ratio of video views to the number of interactions (comments, shares, and likes / dislikes). Therefore, the metric determines the number of interactions per one view, but it does not distinguish between multiple views by one individual. The engagement metric may be then broken down to partial metrics such as the ***number of comments***, their development in time, or the demographics of the users who commented. Following the same logic, the online platforms also derive other metrics such as the indexes for ***new followers***, ***shares***, etc.

An essential aspect in measuring video content on the Internet is exploring the interaction of the viewer with the video content. While watching, users can control individual parts of the video, pause, replay, or repeat the entire video. Behavior monitoring methods are based on the same metrics as the quartile reporting metrics with the difference that user behavior when viewing video content is more accurately and qualitatively reflected in these detail indexes. In YouTube Analytics, this behavioral metric is called ***audience retention***. The metric is displayed in the form of a graph that shows the percentage of users who have seen the given second of the video. If the audience retention increases over the course of the video, it indicates that the viewers have repeatedly watched the given segment of footage. Conversely, when the retention rate is declining, it suggests that there might be an incentive in the video that discourages the viewers from watching. In addition, these metrics are also able to distinguish whether viewers came from organic or paid traffic. The ***play***

rate metric refers to the ratio of the number of times a video content was played to the number of webpage visits. The play rate metric helps website developers to choose the optimal position for the player on the website, correct the thumbnail to attract the visitors, and create the right textual context.

In addition to the above described categories of metrics, we may distinguish a special group of indicators that is related to paid advertising. Most online video ads allow the user to click through and visit the advertiser's website. The click-through rate represents the ratio of clicks to the total number of ad impressions, which is another important ad impact indicator. Other advertising metrics include advertising costs per various actions, conversions, and finally, revenues. In the case of in-stream ads that allow skipping after 5–10 s of playing, the ratio of skips to total number of views is also crucial.

The different interpretation of the video performance metrics makes the comparative analysis of the individual video formats across the two studied platforms considerably difficult. Moreover, because of the unavailability of some of the metrics for all the advertising formats, the number of comparable indicators is limited.

DATA COLLECTION

The experiment was divided into two stages. The first stage consisted in the creation of the optimized video spot. During the second stage, Facebook and YouTube advertisements were set up. First, three video spots marketing the main concept of the e-store, its offer of products, and its website were created. The three spots differed in the songs used, the fonts and the size of the titles, and the alternation speed of the scenes. A focus group of 30 individuals, profiled according to the characteristics of the e-store's most profitable customer segment, was created. The testers from the focus group gave a subjective evaluation of the videos using a 10-point Likert scale. They were asked to assess the visual characteristics, the sound profile, and the readability of the text on a smartphone as well as to describe the message and feeling the videos evoked in them and provide an overall rating. In addition, as a complementary evaluation, we organized a short eye tracking session with each tester, during which they viewed the three videos. Based on the combined results, both conscious and subconscious evaluations, we chose the advertising spot that was judged as the most optimal by a majority of the users (25 out of 30). Subsequently, the length and the dimensions of the video were adjusted for all the available video advertising formats that we decided to use for the purposes of this research. The video formats with respective footage lengths, along with the distribution on the two advertising platforms, are described in the Table 1.

Table 1. The characteristics of the advertising video spots

YouTube			Facebook and Instagram		
Type of the ad	**Length (s)**	**Dimensions**	**Type of the ad**	**Length (s)**	**Dimensions**
Skippable in-stream ads	35, 85	1920×1080	**Short videos**	35, 85	1920×1080
Non-skippable in-stream ads	15	1920×1080	**Instagram Stories**	15	1080×1920
Discovery ads	85	1920×1080	**Carousel format**	35	1080×1080
Bumpers	6	1920×1080	**Collection ads**	85	1920×1080
Out-stream ads	35, 85	1920×1080	**In-stream videos**	30	1920×1080

Source: (the authors)

The video dimensions were selected according to the recommendations given by Facebook and Google in their respective online support centers. The lengths of the videos were chosen within the time limits of each advertising format. Obviously, bumpers with only 6 s represented the shortest video that consisted only of one scene and one final text title. Ads placed in Instagram Stories and as non-skippable spots on YouTube lasted 15 s; however, their dimensions differed. For YouTube, we used horizontal video, whereas for Instagram, we used a vertical video. Carousel and collection ads represented combined video formats. In the case of the carousel, the first item we used was the video that was 35 s long, and the other items were completed with photos. For the collection ad, a longer video (85 s) was chosen as the main item of the composition, and similarly to the Carousel ad, it was completed with photos. We used the same photos for both formats. Where possible, we created ads with a short (35 s) and a longer (85 s) video in order to get more detailed information about user reactions to online advertising in terms of dependence on the length of the advertised content.

Overall, we created 13 video ads on Facebook and YouTube. To keep the setting as unbiased as possible, we chose automatic placement and bidding strategies everywhere the advertising systems permitted it. The only restrictions were thus related to the targeting characteristics and profiling of the target group of customers. Since the e-store, which agreed to let us perform the above described experiment, was specialized in selling furniture, home accessories, and kitchen equipment, we used these general categories as interest qualifiers. In addition, the delivery of ads was geographically limited to the Czech Republic, and the ads were displayed only to women aged 25 to 44. The video ads were implemented for 30 days. All the advertisements were standardly marked with Urchin Tracking Module (UTM) parameters, which also allowed us to track viewer behavior on the website after clicking on the ad and visiting the e-store. The data from YouTube and Facebook ads were thus connected with the company's account in Google Analytics. After the advertising campaigns ended, we exported all the relevant performance data from Facebook Ads Manager, Google Ads, and Google Analytics and merged the information into an Excel file using the SPSS Statics 24 software.

RESULTS

In total, 13 video ads generated an overall profit of 1,155 EUR. Nevertheless, not all the advertisements were effective in terms of profitability since their costs exceeded the revenues from the purchases activated by these ads. However, the interpretation of online advertising performance is more complex and goes beyond direct financial effectiveness (Semerádová & Weinlich, 2019). For this reason, we will compare the results from our experiment from three perspectives: financial (the average profitability and average cost per conversion), behavioral (click-through rate and the average time spent on the website), and reactional (the number of reactions and average viewing percentage).

First, we focus on the financial dimension. Looking more closely at Table 2, we see that in terms of the advertising costs, YouTube non-skippable in-stream ads may be considered the most expensive form of placement, followed by Instagram Stories and Facebook In-stream videos. However, YouTube non-skippable ads generated the second highest profitability of all the ads. According to our data, the best performance was achieved for the Facebook newsfeed video (0.08 EUR average cost and 306 EUR average profitability). Conversely, YouTube discovery and out-stream ads generated loss (−25 EUR and −31 EUR, respectively). This distribution of advertising costs and revenues suggests that the advertising performance of the video may be directly connected to its ability to fit in the browsing context of the online user. Facebook newsfeed represents a central browsing space that may be considered as the native environment of the application. If the advertising video manages to blend naturally with the other content, the chances of being seen by potential customers are higher. By contrast, if the video more closely resembles an advertisement, it tends to trigger the advertising blindness phenomenon. This may explain the lower performance of in-stream video. In-stream videos are perceived as commercial breaks and may thus produce negative effects despite the nature of their content.

As our results indicate, there is a significant difference in the performance of Facebook and Google in-stream ads. The Facebook in-stream ads generated rather low profits, whereas Google ads produced top profitability. This difference also points toward possible contextual influences. Facebook users are accustomed to viewing shorter video content whose main purpose is to provide quick entertainment and therefore do not expect to come across advertisements within the videos they

Table 2. The effectiveness of the video ads based on their average profitability and average cost per conversion

YouTube			Facebook and Instagram		
Type of the ad	**Average cost per conversion (EUR)**	**Average profitability (EUR)**	**Type of the ad**	**Average cost per conversion (EUR)**	**Average profitability (EUR)**
Skippable in-stream ads	0.12	199	**Short videos**	0.08	306
Non-skippable in-stream ads	0.20	234	**Instagram Stories**	0.15	12
Discovery ads	0.06	−25	**Carousel format**	0.13	24
Bumpers	0.1	85	**Collection ads**	0.10	289
Out-stream ads	0.10	−31	**In-stream videos**	0.15	62

Source: (the authors)

are used to seeing. On YouTube, the video creators generally post longer content that has the qualities of an online show and generally ranges between 10 to 20 min on average. YouTube users are thus more likely to react to commercial breaks positively. Instagram Stories and Instagram videos represent a special category whose profitability may be influenced by the context of the Instagram application; Instagram users do not primarily browse in search of purchasable items but rather use the application for a quick visual experience.

The metrics related to the behavioral perspective confirm our aforementioned assumptions. As illustrated in Table 3, browsing environment pre-defines user intentions to make a purchase. For example, users who were redirected to the e-store's website from the Instagram Stories spent only 16 s on the website on average, indicating a high tendency to bounce back and leave the webpage immediately. The low average time may indicate accidental click-throughs. The users who spent more than 30 s on the website may be considered to be users who were attracted by the offered product but did not find sufficient motivation to stay. Moreover, the collected data indicated a direct dependence between the average profitability and average time spent on the website. The click-through rates reflect the willingness of online users to respond to online video advertisements. The discovery ads had the lowest CTR (0.21%) and were the least effective of all the video ads. The ineffectiveness of this advertising format may be accounted to the main purpose these ads were designed for. The primary objective of discovery ads is to promote the videos of many content creators that want to grow their fan base and want their channel to be in the YouTube search results. Therefore, this format is a priori inappropriate for product advertising.

Table 3. Results related to the behavioral dimension of the video ads

YouTube			Facebook and Instagram		
Type of the ad	**CTR (%)**	**Average time spent on the website (s)**	**Type of the ad**	**CTR (%)**	**Average time spent on the website (s)**
Skippable in-stream ads	7.31	93	**Short videos**	9.08	98
Non-skippable in-stream ads	6.58	99	**Instagram Stories**	1.20	16
Discovery ads	0.21	15	**Carousel format**	3.29	42
Bumpers	2.43	32	**Collection ads**	6.21	95
Out-stream ads	2.11	37	**In-stream videos**	5.43	56

Source: (the authors)

Table 4. Number of reactions and the average viewing percentage

YouTube			Facebook and Instagram		
Type of the ad	**Number of reactions**	**Average viewing percentage**	**Type of the ad**	**Number of reactions**	**Average viewing percentage**
Skippable in-stream ads	Unavailable	27%	**Short videos**	487	65%
Non-skippable in-stream ads	Unavailable	100%	**Instagram Stories**	225	Unavailable
Discovery ads	0	5%	**Carousel format**	78	14%
Bumpers	Unavailable	100%	**Collection ads**	321	53%
Out-stream ads	Unavailable	25%	**In-stream videos**	Unavailable	78%

Source: (the authors)

The performance of the video ads with respect to the reactional dimension was examined by using the number of reactions and the average viewing percentage. Unfortunately, owing to the unavailability of the metrics for some placements, this part of the analysis may be perceived only as supporting evidence. However, as the results in Table 4 indicate, Facebook video ads have the greatest potential to be viewed fully from beginning to end (65% of the video viewed). The results from collection ads (53%) confirm this hypothesis. By contrast, YouTube skippable in-stream ads reflect the negative attitude of the users toward forced commercial breaks (only 27% of the video viewed). In contrast to the previous results, Instagram Stories performed well in terms of the number of reactions. Both the high number of reactions and the high viewing percentage of the video confirm the ability of our video spot to attract new potential customers. The lower performance of some of the placements may therefore be accounted by the negative effects of unwanted advertisements.

CONCLUSION

The present study aimed to examine the effectiveness of existing advertising video formats on Facebook and YouTube. The data presented are a result of a series of experimental online ads whose performance was tested in an authentic environment with real users. Owing to the collaboration with a Czech e-store, we had the opportunity to implement 13 selected video ads for 30 days. Our results confirmed the general expectation that video advertising represents an effective advertising tool. Most of the experimental ads were able to generate profit. However, profitability cannot be used as the only indicator of advertising effectiveness. Although the profitability of the Instagram ads was on the lower side, they managed to generate the third highest number of reactions from all the tested formats.

The findings indicate the strong influence of the browsing context on video performance. It appears that the closer the resemblance of the video to other contents in the browsing environment, the higher the chances that users will react to it. Moreover, the browsing context where the online ads appear may also have impact on the subsequent user behavior. For example, Instagram video placements performed better as a means for raising brand awareness than for triggering direct purchases. Conversely, Facebook and YouTube users were more open to shopping suggestions. The highest viewing percentage was achieved by Facebook in-stream ads, followed by Facebook newsfeed videos. Skippable ads on YouTube were viewed significantly less. Although YouTube users had a greater tendency to skip ads, if given the opportunity, they reacted to the ads rather positively and proceeded to make the desired conversions. In addition to the browsing context, the results also differed depending on the length of the video ad. Based on the collected data, the majority of online users prefer videos shorter than 1 min, since of the 85 s for our longer video, the users viewed only 65% (55.25 s). Conversely, it appears that there is also a minimum video length limit. In the aforementioned experiment, bumper ads performed moderately well. We believe that the 6 s period does not provide sufficient time to convey the full message to a potential customer. We support this assumption by the results gathered from the non-skippable ads that lasted 15 s and generated significantly more positive outcomes.

To consider the further implications of these findings, the unobtrusiveness of an advertisement determines its potential to be effective. In conclusion, advertisers should spend more time creating high-quality and personalized video content that is tailored not only to the potential customer but also to the advertising environment in which it will be distributed. Each advertising placement is characterized by specific viewing conditions and typically requires significant adjustments of the original video.

ACKNOWLEDGMENT

This research was supported by the Technical University of Liberec, in a grant titled "Competitiveness of the company in the digital environment", registered as SGS-2019-1068, and by the Technology Agency of the Czech Republic under the Program of applied research ZETA within the framework of project "Developing the skills necessary for the digital business transformation" (registration number TJ02000206).

REFERENCES

About video ad metrics and reporting - YouTube Help. (2019). Retrieved from https://support.google.com/youtube/answer/2375431?hl=en

Alalwan, A. (2018). Investigating the impact of social media advertising features on customer purchase intention. *International Journal of Information Management*, *42*, 65–77. doi:10.1016/j.ijinfomgt.2018.06.001

Amar, J., Droulers, O., & Legohérel, P. (2017). Typography in destination advertising: An exploratory study and research perspectives. *Tourism Management*, *63*, 77–86. doi:10.1016/j.tourman.2017.06.002

Aslam, B., & Karjaluoto, H. (2017). Digital advertising around paid spaces, E-advertising industry's revenue engine: A review and research agenda. *Telematics and Informatics*, *34*(8), 1650–1662. doi:10.1016/j.tele.2017.07.011

Bang, H., & Wojdynski, B. (2016). Tracking users' visual attention and responses to personalized advertising based on task cognitive demand. *Computers in Human Behavior*, *55*, 867–876. doi:10.1016/j.chb.2015.10.025

Berry, N., Prugh, W., Lunkins, C., Vega, J., Landry, R., & Garciga, L. (2015). Selecting video analytics using cognitive ergonomics: a case study for operational experimentation. *Procedia Manufacturing*, *3*, 5245–5252. doi:10.1016/j.promfg.2015.07.598

Beuckels, E., Cauberghe, V., & Hudders, L. (2017). How media multitasking reduces advertising irritation: The moderating role of the Facebook wall. *Computers in Human Behavior*, *73*, 413–419. doi:10.1016/j.chb.2017.03.069

Ding, S., Qu, S., Xi, Y., & Wan, S. (2019). A long video caption generation algorithm for big video data retrieval. *Future Generation Computer Systems*, *93*, 583–595. doi:10.1016/j.future.2018.10.054

Facebook video ads – Facebook help center. (2019). Retrieved from https://www.facebook.com/business/ads/video-ad-format

33. Fascinating and useful statistics about video marketing in 2019 - Videocake. (2019). Retrieved from http://videocake.cz/statistika-o-videu-v-marketingu/

Huang, Y., Wu, J., & Shi, W. (2018). The impact of font choice on web pages: Relationship with willingness to pay and tourism motivation. *Tourism Management*, *66*, 191–199. doi:10.1016/j.tourman.2017.12.010

Joo, M., Wilbur, K., & Zhu, Y. (2016). Effects of TV advertising on keyword search. *International Journal of Research in Marketing*, *33*(3), 508–523. doi:10.1016/j.ijresmar.2014.12.005

Kareklas, I., Brunel, F., & Coulter, R. (2014). Judgment is not color blind: The impact of automatic color preference on product and advertising preferences. *Journal of Consumer Psychology*, *24*(1), 87–95. doi:10.1016/j.jcps.2013.09.005

Kim, B., & Kim, Y. (2019). Facebook versus Instagram: How perceived gratifications and technological attributes are related to the change in social media usage. *The Social Science Journal*, *56*(2), 156–167. doi:10.1016/j.soscij.2018.10.002

Kim, J., Ahn, S., Kwon, E., & Reid, L. (2017). TV advertising engagement as a state of immersion and presence. *Journal of Business Research*, *76*, 67–76. doi:10.1016/j.jbusres.2017.03.001

Lee, J., Ham, C., & Kim, M. (2013). Why people pass along online video advertising: from the perspectives of the interpersonal communication motives scale and the theory of reasoned action. *Journal of Interactive Advertising*, *13*(1), 1–13. doi:10.1080/15252019.2013.768048

Li, X., Shi, M., & Wang, X. (2019). Video mining: Measuring visual information using automatic methods. *International Journal of Research in Marketing*, *36*(2), 216–231. doi:10.1016/j.ijresmar.2019.02.004

Liikkanen, L., & Salovaara, A. (2015). Music on YouTube: User engagement with traditional, user-appropriated and derivative videos. *Computers in Human Behavior*, *50*, 108–124. doi:10.1016/j.chb.2015.01.067

Liu, Y., Zhu, C., Mao, M., Song, F., Dufaux, F., & Zhang, X. (2018). Video analytical coding: When video coding meets video analysis. *Signal Processing Image Communication*, *67*, 48–57. doi:10.1016/j.image.2018.05.012

Martín-Santana, J., Muela-Molina, C., Reinares-Lara, E., & Rodríguez-Guerra, M. (2015). Effectiveness of radio spokesperson's gender, vocal pitch and accent and the use of music in radio advertising. *BRQ Business Research Quarterly*, *18*(3), 143–160. doi:10.1016/j.brq.2014.06.001

Mowat, J. (2018). *Video marketing strategy: harness the power of online video to drive brand growth* (1st ed.). Kogan Page.

Munnukka, J., Maity, D., Reinikainen, H., & Luoma-aho, V. (2019). "Thanks for watching". The effectiveness of YouTube vlogendorsements. *Computers in Human Behavior*, *93*, 226–234. doi:10.1016/j.chb.2018.12.014

Muñoz-Leiva, F., Hernández-Méndez, J., & Gómez-Carmona, D. (2019). Measuring advertising effectiveness in Travel 2.0 websites through eye-tracking technology. *Physiology & Behavior*, *200*, 83–95. doi:10.1016/j.physbeh.2018.03.002 PMID:29522796

Semerádová, T., & Weinlich, P. (2018). Assessing banner ads effectiveness based on the type of the creative content. In *Proceedings of the 31st International Business Information Management Association Conference, IBIMA 2018: Innovation Management and Education Excellence through Vision 2020* (pp. 1439-1446). Milan, Italy: IBIMA.

Semerádová, T., & Weinlich, P. (2019). Calculation of Facebook marketing effectiveness in terms of ROI. *Leveraging Computer-Mediated Marketing Environments*, 286-310. doi:10.4018/978-1-5225-7344-9.ch014

Sidaty, N., Larabi, M., & Saadane, A. (2017). Toward an audiovisual attention model for multimodal video content. *Neurocomputing*, *259*, 94–111. doi:10.1016/j.neucom.2016.08.130

Tran, T. (2017). Personalized ads on Facebook: An effective marketing tool for online marketers. *Journal of Retailing and Consumer Services*, *39*, 230–242. doi:10.1016/j.jretconser.2017.06.010

Understanding how your videos perform on Facebook. (2019). Retrieved from https://www.facebook.com/facebookmedia/blog/understanding-how-your-videos-perform-on-facebook

Van den Broeck, E., Poels, K., & Walrave, M. (2018). An experimental study on the effect of ad placement, product involvement and motives on Facebook ad avoidance. *Telematics and Informatics*, *35*(2), 470–479. doi:10.1016/j.tele.2018.01.006

Video advertising formats – YouTube help center. (2019). Retrieved from https://support.google.com/youtube/answer/2375464?hl=cs

Wang, C., & Hung, J. (2018). Comparative analysis of advertising attention to Facebook social network: Evidence from eye-movement data. *Computers in Human Behavior*. doi:10.1016/j.chb.2018.08.007

What counts as a video view? - David Burch, TubeMogul. (2019). Retrieved from https://www.youtube.com/watch?v=qpANKRZJ8Ks

Wu, C., Wei, Y., Chu, X., Weichen, S., Su, F., & Wang, L. (2018). Hierarchical attention-based multimodal fusion for video captioning. *Neurocomputing*, *315*, 362–370. doi:10.1016/j.neucom.2018.07.029

Yang, L., Yuan, M., Chen, Y., Wang, W., Zhang, Q., & Zeng, J. (2017). Personalized user engagement modeling for mobile videos. *Computer Networks*, *126*, 256–267. doi:10.1016/j.comnet.2017.07.012

Yang, Y., Lu, Q., Tang, G., & Pei, J. (2015). The impact of market competition on search advertising. *Journal of Interactive Marketing*, *30*, 46–55. doi:10.1016/j.intmar.2015.01.002

Zimand-Sheiner, D., Ryan, T., Kip, S., & Lahav, T. (2019). Native advertising credibility perceptions and ethical attitudes: An exploratory study among adolescents in the United States, Turkey and Israel. *Journal of Business Research*. doi:10.1016/j.jbusres.2019.06.020

ADDITIONAL READING

Alalwan, A., Rana, N., Dwivedi, Y., & Algharabat, R. (2017). Social media in marketing: A review and analysis of the existing literature. *Telematics and Informatics*, *34*(7), 1177–1190. doi:10.1016/j.tele.2017.05.008

Belanche, D., Flavián, C., & Pérez-Rueda, A. (2017). Understanding Interactive Online Advertising: Congruence and Product Involvement in Highly and Lowly Arousing, Skippable Video Ads. *Journal of Interactive Marketing*, *37*, 75–88. doi:10.1016/j.intmar.2016.06.004

Dehghani, M., Niaki, M., Ramezani, I., & Sali, R. (2016). Evaluating the influence of YouTube advertising for attraction of young customers. *Computers in Human Behavior*, *59*, 165–172. doi:10.1016/j.chb.2016.01.037

Felix, R., Rauschnabel, P., & Hinsch, C. (2017). Elements of strategic social media marketing: A holistic framework. *Journal of Business Research*, *70*, 118–126. doi:10.1016/j.jbusres.2016.05.001

France, S., Vaghefi, M., & Zhao, H. (2016). Characterizing viral videos: Methodology and applications. *Electronic Commerce Research and Applications*, *19*, 19–32. doi:10.1016/j.elerap.2016.07.002

Lee, J., & Hong, I. (2016). Predicting positive user responses to social media advertising: The roles of emotional appeal, informativeness, and creativity. *International Journal of Information Management*, *36*(3), 360–373. doi:10.1016/j.ijinfomgt.2016.01.001

Quesenberry, K., & Coolsen, M. (2019). Drama Goes Viral: Effects of Story Development on Shares and Views of Online Advertising Videos. *Journal of Interactive Marketing*, *48*, 1–16. doi:10.1016/j.intmar.2019.05.001

Simmonds, L., Bellman, S., Kennedy, R., Nenycz-Thiel, M., & Bogomolova, S. (2019). Moderating effects of prior brand usage on visual attention to video advertising and recall: An eye-tracking investigation. *Journal of Business Research*. doi:10.1016/j.jbusres.2019.02.062

KEY TERMS AND DEFINITIONS

Ad Placement: All the advertising spaces, mostly paid, offered by online publishers, websites, and social networks to advertisers to display their advertisements. The individual placements have different potentials in terms of reaching the users and perform differently when comes to the type of content chosen for the advertisement.

Bumper: Bumpers represent short videos that take up to 6 s and can be placed before, in, and after a video on all YouTube pages, partner video sites, and applications in the Google Content network. Viewers do not have the option to skip these ads. The advertiser pays for every 1,000 impressions.

Conversion: Desired action performed by a consumer as a reaction to an advertisement or other marketing effort. The desired action can take many forms including the purchases, membership registrations, newsletter subscriptions, and application downloads.

Instagram Stories ads: Instagram Stories ads can contain both video and photo content and can be created from preexisting material or from vertical videos tailored specifically for this format. Every post in stories is limited to 15 s.

In-stream ads: In-stream ads are design to promote video content between other videos on YouTube or in the Google Content Network. In-stream ads can appear on YouTube watch pages, videos on partner sites, and content network applications. In-stream ads can be either skippable or non-skippable.

Play rate: The play rate metric refers to the ratio of the number of times a video content was played to the number of webpage visits. The play rate metric helps website developers choose the optimal position for the player on the website, correct the thumbnail to attract the visitors, and create the right textual context.

Quartile reporting: Quartile reporting represents a more objective method in measuring the ability of a video to capture user attention. It is used in video analytics tools by both Google AdWords and Facebook. This metric determines the number of times a certain percentage of the video has been viewed, in this case, whether the viewer has played 25%, 50%, 75%, or 100% of the video content per a single viewing session.

UTM Parameters: Text fragments that are attached in the specified format to the web link. Attaching these textual segments allows the analytical software to exactly identify the source, campaign, or advertisement from which the users come to the website. UTM parameters generally contain the following five elements: utm_source, utm_medium, utm_campaign, utm_content, and utm_term.

Compilation of References

Aaker, D. A. (1996). Measuring brand equity across products and markets. *California Management Review, 38*(3), 102–120. doi:10.2307/41165845

AB, M. F., Sharuddin, S. H., & Rajagderan, S. (2018). E-commerce adoption and an analysis of the popular e-commerce business sites in Malaysia. *Journal of Internet Banking and Commerce, 23*(1), 1–10.

Abedini Koshksaray, A., Franklin, D., & Heidarzadeh Hanzaee, K. (2015). The relationship between e-lifestyle and Internet advertising avoidance. [AMJ]. *Australasian Marketing Journal, 23*(1), 38–48. doi:10.1016/j.ausmj.2015.01.002

About video ad metrics and reporting - YouTube Help. (2019). Retrieved from https://support.google.com/youtube/answer/2375431?hl=en

Ahmed, P. K., & Rafiq, M. (2003). Internal marketing issues and challenges. *European Journal of Marketing, 37*(9), 1177–1186. doi:10.1108/03090560310498813

Alalwan, A. (2018). Investigating the impact of social media advertising features on customer purchase intention. *International Journal of Information Management, 42*, 65–77. doi:10.1016/j.ijinfomgt.2018.06.001

Albuquerque, J., Morla, R., Gabriel, D., & Campos, R. (2013). *Sugestão de palavras chave para campanhas em motores de busca em arranque*. Porto, Portugal. Retrieved from https://hdl.handle.net/10216/69731

Ali, F. (2019). US ecommerce sales grow 15.0% in 2018, Digital Commerce 360. Available at https://www.digitalcommerce360.com/article/us-ecommerce-sales/

Amar, J., Droulers, O., & Legohérel, P. (2017). Typography in destination advertising: An exploratory study and research perspectives. *Tourism Management, 63*, 77–86. doi:10.1016/j.tourman.2017.06.002

Ambler, T., & Barrow, S. (1996). The employer brand. *Journal of Brand Management, 4*(3), 185–206. doi:10.1057/bm.1996.42

Anastasiei, B., & Dospinescu, N. (2017). Facebook advertising: Relationship between types of message, brand attitude, and perceived buying risk. *Annals of 'Constantin Brancusi' University of Targu-Jiu. Economy Series, 6*, 18–26.

Anca, B., & Daniela, D. (2008). Optimization and launch of a Google Adwords campaign. *Annals of the University of Oradea, Economic Science Series, 17*(4), 1289–1296. Retrieved from http://search.ebscohost.com/login.aspx?direct=true&db=bth&AN=48755865&site=eds-live

Araújo, A., & Santos, C. (2017). A contribuição da indexação no processo de seleção de palavras-chave para a Google Adwords. *Revista Brasileira de Biblioteconomia e Documentação, 13*, 109–114.

Arlı, E. (2013). Marina işletmeciliğinde ilişkisel pazarlama uygulamalarinin tekrar satin alma niyeti, tavsiye etme niyeti ve memnuniyet üzerindeki etkisi. *Anadolu Üniversitesi Sosyal Bilimler Dergisi, 13*(1), 61–75.

Ashforth, B. E., & Mael, F. (1989). Social identity theory and the organization. *Academy of Management Review, 14*(1), 20–39. doi:10.5465/amr.1989.4278999

Aslam, B., & Karjaluoto, H. (2017). Digital advertising around paid spaces, E-advertising industry's revenue engine: A review and research agenda. *Telematics and Informatics, 34*(8), 1650–1662. doi:10.1016/j.tele.2017.07.011

Asociación de Internet. (2018). *Estudio de Comercio Electrónico en México 2018 Diciembre, 2018.*

Backhaus, K., & Tikoo, S. (2004). Conceptualizing and researching employer branding. *Career Development International, 9*(5), 501–517. doi:10.1108/13620430410550754

Baek, T., & Morimoto, M. (2012). Stay away from me. *Journal of Advertising, 41*(1), 59–76. doi:10.2753/JOA0091-3367410105

Baglione, S. L., Amin, K., McCullough, A., & Tucci, L. (2018, Winter). Factors affecting Facebook advertisements: Empirical study. *International Journal of Business, Marketing, & Decision Sciences, 11*(1), 124–140.

Bai, B., Hu, C., & Jang, S. (2007). Examining e-relationship marketing features on hotel websites. *Journal of Travel & Tourism Marketing, 21*(2–3), 33–48. doi:10.1300/J073v21n02_03

Balta, N. F. (2006). *Endüstriyel Pazarlama*. İstanbul, Turkey: Nobel Yayıncılık.

Bang, H., & Wojdynski, B. (2016). Tracking users' visual attention and responses to personalized advertising based on task cognitive demand. *Computers in Human Behavior, 55*, 867–876. doi:10.1016/j.chb.2015.10.025

Bao, H., Li, B., Shen, J., & Hou, F. (2016). Repurchase intention in the Chinese e-marketplace: Roles of interactivity, trust and perceived effectiveness of e-commerce institutional mechanisms. *Industrial Management & Data Systems, 116*(8), 1759–1778. doi:10.1108/IMDS-07-2015-0296

Barboza, D. (2010). China passes Japan as second-largest economy. *The New York Times*, 15.

Barker, S. (2017). *Why influencer marketing has become a powerful weapon for brands: Find out some of the best ways influencers can help promote your brand.* Retrieved from https://www.inc.com/shane-barker/why-influencer-marketing-has-become-a-powerful-weapon-for-brands.html

Barney, J. (1991). Firm resources and sustained competitive advantage. *Journal of Management, 17*(1), 99–120. doi:10.1177/014920639101700108

Barrow, S., & Mosley, R. (2011). *The employer brand: Bringing the best of brand management to people at work.* John Wiley & Sons.

Baruh, L., Secinti, E., & Cemalcilar, Z. (2017). Online privacy concerns and privacy management: a meta-analytical review. *Journal of Communication, 67*(1), 26–53. doi:10.1111/jcom.12276

Bauer, H. H., Grether, M., & Leach, M. (2002a). Building customer relations over the Internet. *Industrial Marketing Management, 31*(2), 155–163. doi:10.1016/S0019-8501(01)00186-9

Bauer, H. H., Grether, M., & Leach, M. (2002b). Customer relations through the Internet. *Journal of Relationship Marketing, 1*(2), 39–55. doi:10.1300/J366v01n02_03

Benge, G. (2014). Why integration is key: digital marketing versus offline marketing. Retrieved from https://www.koozai.com/blog/branding/digital-marketing-versus-offline-marketing/#

Berman, B. (2016). Referral marketing: Harnessing the power of your customers. *Business Horizons, 59*(1), 19–28. doi:10.1016/j.bushor.2015.08.001

Berry, L. L. (1983). *Relationship marketing: Emerging perspectives on services marketing.* Chicago, IL: American Marketing Association.

Berry, N., Prugh, W., Lunkins, C., Vega, J., Landry, R., & Garciga, L. (2015). Selecting video analytics using cognitive ergonomics: a case study for operational experimentation. *Procedia Manufacturing, 3*, 5245–5252. doi:10.1016/j.promfg.2015.07.598

Berthon, P., Ewing, M., & Hah, L. L. (2005). Captivating company: Dimensions of attractiveness in employer branding. *International Journal of Advertising, 24*(2), 151–172. doi:10.1080/02650487.2005.11072912

Bethlehem, J. (2009). *Applied survey methods: A statistical perspective* (Vol. 558). Hoboken, NJ: John Wiley & Sons.

Beuckels, E., Cauberghe, V., & Hudders, L. (2017). How media multitasking reduces advertising irritation: The moderating role of the Facebook wall. *Computers in Human Behavior, 73*, 413–419. doi:10.1016/j.chb.2017.03.069

Bijmolt, T. H., Leeflang, P. S., Block, F., Eisenbeiss, M., Hardie, B. G., Lemmens, A., & Saffert, P. (2010). Analytics for customer engagement. *Journal of Service Research, 13*(3), 341–356. doi:10.1177/1094670510375603

BlackSip. (2017). *Reporte de Industria: El E-Commerce en colombia 2017.* Retrieved from http://content.blacksip.com/reporte-de-industria-el-e-commerce-en-colombia-2017

Bleier, A., & Eisenbeiss, M. (2015). The importance of trust for personalized online advertising. *Journal of Retailing*, *91*(3), 390–409. doi:10.1016/j.jretai.2015.04.001

Bondarouk, T., Ruël, H., Axinia, E., & Arama, R. (2014). What is the future of employer branding through social media? Results of the Delphi study into the perceptions of HR professionals and academics. *Social Media in Human Resources Management*, *9*(5), 23–57.

Boon-Long, S., & Wongsurawat, W. (2015). Social media marketing evaluation using social network comments as an indicator for identifying consumer purchasing decision effectiveness. *Journal of Direct Data and Digital Marketing Practice*, *17*(2), 130–149. doi:10.1057/dddmp.2015.51

Borgs, C., Chayes, J., Immorlica, N., Jain, K., Etesami, O., & Mahdian, M. (2007). Dynamics of bid optimization in online advertisement auctions. In *Proceedings of the 16th International Conference on World Wide Web* (pp. 531–540). ACM. 10.1145/1242572.1242644

Born, N., & Kang, S. K. (2015). *What are best practices in the space of employer branding that enable organizations attract and retain the best talent?* Retrieved from https://digitalcommons.ilr.cornell.edu/student/86/

Braatz, L. A. (2017). *#Influencer marketing on Instagram. Consumer responses towards promotional posts: The effects of message sidedness and product depiction* (Unpublished Master's Thesis). University of Twente, The Netherlands.

Brin, S., & Page, L. (2012). Reprint of: The anatomy of a large-scale hypertextual web search engine. *Computer Networks*, *56*(18), 3825–3833. doi:10.1016/j.comnet.2012.10.007

Brooks, A. (2019). *A brief history of influencers.* Retrieved from https://www.socialmediatoday.com/news/timeline-a-brief-history-of-influencers/554377/

Brown, D., & Fiorella, S. (2013). *Influence marketing: How to create, manage, and measure brand influencers in social media marketing (Que Biz-Tech)*. Hoboken, NJ: Que Publishing.

Brown, D., & Hayes, N. (2008). *Influencer marketing: Who really influences your customers?* UK: Butterworth-Heinemann. doi:10.4324/9780080557700

Bruner, G. C. II, & Kumar, A. (2000). Web commercials and advertising hierarchy-of-effects. *Journal of Advertising Research*, *40*(1–2), 35–42. doi:10.2501/JAR-40-1-2-35-42

Cahill, D. J. (1995). "We sure as hell confused ourselves", but what about the customers? *Marketing Intelligence & Planning*, *13*(4), 5–9. doi:10.1108/02634509510781298

Caligiuri, P., Colakoglu, S., Cerdin, J. L., & Kim, M. S. (2010). Examining cross-cultural and individual differences in predicting employer reputation as a driver of employer attraction. *International Journal of Cross Cultural Management*, *10*(2), 137–151. doi:10.1177/1470595810370890

Cappelli, P. (2001). Making the most of on-line recruiting. *Harvard Business Review*, *79*(3), 139–148. PMID:11246921

Carter, B. (2014). *The like economy: How businesses make money with Facebook* (2nd ed.). Indianapolis, IN: QUE Publishing.

Cascio, W. F., & Graham, B. Z. (2016). New strategic role for HR: Leading the employer-branding process. *Organizational Management Journal, 13*(4), 182–192. doi:10.1080/15416518.2016.1244640

Castanias, R. P., & Helfat, C. E. (1991). Managerial resources and rents. *Journal of Management, 17*(1), 155–171. doi:10.1177/014920639101700110

Castillo, M. (2017, Oct. 13). Facebook is under fire from advertisers, highlighting a wider industry issue. *CNBC*, Retrieved from https://www.cnbc.com/2017/2010/2013/facebook-under-fire-from-advertisers.html

Castro, A. (2015). *Futuro Digital Colombia 2015.*

Cedeno, E. B. (2018, May). Formative model to determine intention to adopt mobile commerce. In *Proceedings of the 2018 International Conference on E-business and Mobile Commerce* (pp. 17–21). ACM. 10.1145/3230467.3230474

Celsi, M. W., & Gilly, M. C. (2010). Employees as internal audience: How advertising affects employees' customer focus. *Journal of the Academy of Marketing Science, 38*(4), 520–529. doi:10.100711747-009-0173-x

CEPAL. 2016, Latin America population will reach 625 million inhabitants by 2016, according to ECLAC estimates. Retrieved from https://www.cepal.org/en/news/latin-america-population-will-reach-625-million-inhabitants-2016-according-eclac-estimates

Chaffey, D. (2016). Definitions of emarketing vs. internet vs. digital marketing. Retrieved from https://www.smartinsights.com/digital-marketing-strategy/online-marketing-mix/definitions-of-emarketing-vs-internet-vs-digital-marketing/

Chatman, J. A., & Jehn, K. A. (1994). Assessing the relationship between industry characteristics and organizational culture: How different can you be? *Academy of Management Journal, 37*(3), 522–553. doi:10.5465/256699

Chen, Q., Feng, Y., Liu, L., & Tian, X. (2019). Understanding consumers' reactance of online personalized advertising: A new scheme of rational choice from a perspective of negative effects. *International Journal of Information Management, 44*, 53–64. doi:10.1016/j.ijinfomgt.2018.09.001

Chow, G. C. (1994). *Understanding China's economy.* World Scientific Publishing Company. doi:10.1142/2430

Christopher, M., Payne, A., & Ballantyne, D. (1991). *Relationship marketing.* Oxford, UK: Butterworth-Heinemann.

Clarke, T. B., Murphy, J., Wetsch, L. R., & Boeck, H. (2018). Teaching search engine marketing through the Google ad grants program. *Marketing Education Review, 28*(2), 136–147. doi:10.1080/10528008.2018.1448282

Clifton, B. (2012). *Advanced web metrics with Google Analytics (3rd. Ed.)*. Canadá: John Wiley & Sons.

Clinks. (2017). Simulador de CPC (Custo Por Clique) e Posição de Anúncio no Google Ads (BETA). Retrieved from https://www.clinks.com.br/simulador-de-cpc-custo-por-clique-e-posicao-de-anuncio-no-google-adwords/

Coff, R. W. (2002). Human capital, shared expertise, and the likelihood of impasse in corporate acquisitions. *Journal of Management*, *28*(1), 107–128. doi:10.1177/014920630202800107

Cohen, D. (2015, April 20). Study: Global social media ad spend to reach nearly $36b in 2017. Retrieved from http://www.adweek.com/digital/emarketer-global-social-media-ad-spend/

Conner, T. S., Barrett, L. F., Bliss-Moreau, E., & Lebo, K. (2003, February). A practical guide to experience-sampling procedures. *Journal of Happiness Studies*, *4*(1), 53–75. doi:10.1023/A:1023609306024

Content Agency. (2018). Content Agency - Influencer marketing. Retrieved from https://contentagency.sk/

Coon, M. (2010). *Social media marketing: successful case studies of businesses using Facebook and Youtube with an in-depth look into the business use of Twitter* (Unpublished Master's thesis). Stanford University, Stanford, CA.

Criteo. (2014, September). *Cross-device advertising: How to navigate mobile marketing's next big opportunity*: Retrieved from http://www.criteo.com/media/1036/cross-device-advertising-criteo-sep-2014.pdf

Crook, T. R., Todd, S. Y., Combs, J. G., Woehr, D. J., & Ketchen, D. J. Jr. (2011). Does human capital matter? A meta-analysis of the relationship between human capital and firm performance. *The Journal of Applied Psychology*, *96*(3), 443–456. doi:10.1037/a0022147 PMID:21244126

Csikszentmihalyi, M., Hektner, J. M., & Schmidt, J. A. (2006). Experience sampling method: measuring the quality of everyday life (1st Ed.).Thousand Oaks, CA: Sage.

CTAM. (n.d.). Multiplatform definition. Retrieved from https://www.ctam.com/strategic-collaboration/advanced-cable/pages/multiplatform-definition.aspx

Cui, Y., Niu, J., & Yu, M. (2016). Effect of relationship benefits on satisfaction with an e-commerce communication tool. *Economic Management*, *5*(1), 1–8.

Dabirian, A., Kietzmann, J., & Diba, H. (2017). A great place to work!? Understanding crowdsourced employer branding. *Business Horizons*, *60*(2), 197–205. doi:10.1016/j.bushor.2016.11.005

Daily, J. (2019). Why Chinese millennials are willing to max out their cards for luxury goods. *South China Morning Post*. Available at https://www.scmp.com/magazines/style/people-events/article/2178689/can-chinas-debt-ridden-millennial-and-gen-z-shoppers

Dănciulescu, D., & Anca, B. (2008). Optimization methods for PPC campaigns. *Annals of the University of Oradea, Economic Science Series, 17*(4), 1337–1341. Retrieved from http://search.ebscohost.com/login.aspx?direct=true&db=bth&AN=48755873&site=eds-live

Danova, T. (2014). For mobile-social apps, advertising is winning as the money-making revenue model. Retrieved from http://www. businessinsider. com/advertising-is-the-most-lucrative-revenue-modelfor-growing-mobile-social-apps-2014-1

Davis, H. (2010). *Ferramentas de publicidade do Google* (1st ed.). São Paulo, Brazil: Novatec.

De Chernatony, L., Cottam, S., & Segal-Horn, S. (2006). Communicating services brands' values internally and externally. *Service Industries Journal, 26*(8), 819–836. doi:10.1080/02642060601011616

Deal, T. E., & Kennedy, A. A. (1983). Culture: A new look through old lenses. *The Journal of Applied Behavioral Science, 19*(4), 498–505. doi:10.1177/002188638301900411

DeCastro, N. S., de Bittencourt, J. A., Chaves, F. A. V., Barreiro, J. H. L. C. D., & Reis, C. V. S. (2015). A Influência do Marketing Digital Sobre a Escolha dos Consumidores. In *XII Simpósio de Excelência em Gestão e Tecnologia - SEGeT*. Rio de Janeiro, Brazil. Retrieved from https://www.aedb.br/seget/artigos2015.php?pag=215

Dehghani, M., Niaki, M. K., Ramezani, I., & Sali, R. (2016). Evaluating the influence of YouTube advertising for attraction of young customers. *Computers in Human Behavior, 59*, 165–172. doi:10.1016/j.chb.2016.01.037

Dehghani, M., & Tumer, M. (2015). A research on effectiveness of Facebook advertising on enhancing purchase intention of consumers. *Computers in Human Behavior, 49*, 597–600. doi:10.1016/j.chb.2015.03.051

Dehui, L. (2016). A comparative analysis of B2C cross-border e-commerce platforms: the AliExpress and the DHgate. In *Proceedings of the 2016 International Conference on Education, Management, Computer and Society*. EMCS.

Dell, D., Ainspan, N., Bodenberg, T., Troy, K., & Hickey, J. (2001, April). Engaging employees through your brand. In *Conference Board Report, Number R. 1288-01-RR. Canada*. Washington, DC: Conference Board.

DeLuca, J. (2013, May 8). The new opportunity in cross-platform advertising. Retrieved from http://www.imediaconnection.com/articles/ported-articles/red-dot-articles/2013/may/the-new-opportunity-in-cross-platform-advertising/

Dibb, S., & Meadows, M. (2001). The application of a relationship marketing perspective in retail banking. *Service Industries Journal, 21*(1), 169–194. doi:10.1080/714005011

Ding, S., Qu, S., Xi, Y., & Wan, S. (2019). A long video caption generation algorithm for big video data retrieval. *Future Generation Computer Systems, 93*, 583–595. doi:10.1016/j.future.2018.10.054

DMR. (2018). 26 Amazing Taobao statistics and facts. Available at https://expandedramblings.com/index.php/taobao-statistics/

Doyle, G. (2010). From television to multi-platform less from more or more for less? *Convergence: The International Journal of Research into New Media Technologies, 16*(4), 431-449. doi:10.1177/1354856510375145

Drumwright, M. E. (1996). Company advertising with a social dimension: The role of noneconomic criteria. *Journal of Marketing, 60*(4), 71–87. doi:10.2307/1251902

Duffett, R. (2015, June). The influence of Facebook advertising on cognitive attitudes amid Generation Y. *Electronic Commerce Research, 15*(2), 243–267. doi:10.100710660-015-9177-4

Duffy, D. L. (2005). Affiliate marketing and its impact on e-commerce. *Journal of Consumer Marketing, 22*(3), 161–163. doi:10.1108/07363760510595986

Dunlop, M. (2019). Top Earning Websites – How much the world's largest internet businesses make. Retrieved from https://www.incomediary.com/top-earning-websites

Dutta-Bergman, M. J. (2010, June 7). Complementarity in consumption of news types across traditional and new media. *Journal of Broadcasting & Electronic Media, 48*(1), 41–60. doi:10.120715506878jobem4801_3

Dutton, J. E., Dukerich, J. M., & Harquail, C. V. (1994). Organizational images and member identification. *Administrative Science Quarterly, 39*(2), 239–263. doi:10.2307/2393235

Dyer, J. H., & Singh, H. (1998). The relational view: Corporative strategy and sources of interorganizational competitive advantage. *Academy of Management Review, 23*(4), 660–679. doi:10.5465/amr.1998.1255632

Eckersley, P. (2010). How unique is your web browser?. *Privacy Enhancing Technologies*, 1-18. doi:10.1007/978-3-642-14527-8_1

Edelman, D. C. (2010). Branding in the digital age. *Harvard Business Review, 88*(12), 62–69.

Edwards, M. R. (2009). An integrative review of employer branding and OB theory. *Personnel Review, 39*(1), 5–23. doi:10.1108/00483481011012809

Edwards, M. R., & Peccei, R. (2010). Perceived organizational support, organizational identification, and employee outcomes. *Journal of Personnel Psychology, 9*(1), 17–26. doi:10.1027/1866-5888/a000007

Ehrhardt, J. (2017). *A brief history of influencer marketing*. Retrieved from https://blog.influencerdb.com/brief-history-of-influencer-marketing/

Einwiller, S., & Will, M. (2008). Towards an integrated approach to corporate branding-Findings from an empirical study. In *Kommunikationsmanagement im Wandel* (pp. 231–247). Gabler. doi:10.1007/978-3-8349-9772-2_13 *eMarketer.com* . (2014, May 9). Cross-device advertising a hot topic in 2014. Retrieved from https://www.emarketer.com/Article/Cross-Device-Advertising-Hot-Topic-2014/1010824

eMarketer.com . (2015a, April 2). Mobile ad spend to top $100 billion worldwide in 2016, 51% of digital market. Retrieved from https://www.emarketer.com/Article/Mobile-Ad-Spend-Top-100-Billion-Worldwide-2016-51-of-Digital-Market/1012299

eMarketer.com . (2015b, April 15). Social network ad spending to hit $23.68 billion worldwide in 2015. Retrieved from https://www.emarketer.com/Article/Social-Network-Ad-Spending-Hit-2368-Billion-Worldwide-2015/1012357

eMarketer.com . (2016, Oct. 11). *Multiplatform video ad buying is emerging as the new normal.* Retrieved from https://www.Emarketer.Com/article/multiplatform-video-ad-buying-emerging-new-normal/1014576

eMarketer.com. (2018a, Feb. 12). Facebook losing younger users: But not all are migrating to Instagram. *eMarketer.com*, Retrieved from https://www.emarketer.com/content/facebook-losing-younger-users-at-even-faster-pace

eMarketer.com. (2018b, Nov. 20). Global ad spending update: Alibaba, Facebook and Google to capture over 60% of digital ad dollars in 2019. *eMarketer.com.* Retrieved from https://www.emarketer.com/content/global-ad-spending-update

eMarketer.com . (2019, March). Social network users, by platforms. *eMarketer.com.* Retrieved from https://forecasts-na2011.emarketer.com/2584b26021403070290f26021403070293a26021403070291a/26021405851918b26021400626310a26021403070292c26021403070186b26021403070291b

Enberg, J. (2019, June 23). Q2 2019 social trends: Facebook continues to diversify its revenue streams, Snapchat holds first partner summit, and Twitter targets political tweets. *eMarketer.com*, Retrieved from https://content-na2011.emarketer.com/q2012-2019-social-trends

Enoch, G., & Johnson, K. (2010). Cracking the cross-media code. *Journal of Advertising Research, 50*(2), 125–136. doi:10.2501/S0021849910091294

Epstein, J. (2018). *The importance of relationship marketing for ecommerce brands.* Retrieved from https://www.getambassador.com/blog/relationship-marketing-strategies-ecommerce

Erdal, I. J. (2009). Cross-media (re)production cultures. *Convergence: The International Journal of Research into New Media Technologies, 15*(2), 215-231. doi:10.1177/1354856508105231

Erdensoy, D. (2018). *What is influencer marketing?* Retrieved from https://creatorden.com/en_us/what-is-marketing-influencia/

Estrada-Jiménez, J., Parra-Arnau, J., Rodríguez-Hoyos, A., & Forné, J. (2017). Online advertising: Analysis of privacy threats and protection approaches. *Computer Communications, 100*, 32–51. doi:10.1016/j.comcom.2016.12.016

Ewing, M. T., Pitt, L. F., De Bussy, N. M., & Berthon, P. (2002). Employment branding in the knowledge economy. *International Journal of Advertising*, *21*(1), 3–22. doi:10.1080/02650487.2002.11104914

Facebook video ads – Facebook help center. (2019). Retrieved from https://www.facebook.com/business/ads/video-ad-format

Fang, Y., Qureshi, I., Sun, H., McCole, P., Ramsey, E., & Lim, K. H. (2014). Trust, satisfaction, and online repurchase intention: The moderating role of perceived effectiveness of e-commerce institutional mechanisms. *Management Information Systems Quarterly*, *38*(2), 407–427. doi:10.25300/MISQ/2014/38.2.04

Federal Trade Commission (FTC). (2012, March). *Protecting consumer privacy in an era of rapid change: Recommendations for businesses and policymakers*. Retrieved from https://www.ftc.gov/reports/protecting-consumer-privacy-era-rapid-change-recommendations-businesses-policymakers

Ference, A. (2017). 7 customer engagement strategies that marketers can't ignore. Available at https://www.outbrain.com/blog/3-golden-customer-engagement-strategies-that-marketers-cant-ignore/

Fichter, D. (2007). How social is your web site? Top five tips for social media optimization. *Onlinenmag*, 57-60.

Figueria, F. (2018). *17 incredible benefits of influencer marketing in 2018*. Retrieved from https://anova.co/blog/17-benefits-of-influencer-marketing

Fisher, L. (2019a, Jan. 22). Nine trends to know for this year's media plan. *eMarketer.com*. Retrieved from https://content-na2011.emarketer.com/digital-display-advertising-2019

Fisher, L. (2019b, April 18). Digital display ad pricing StatPack: Banner, video, mobile and native CPMs, and pricing trends to watch for in 2019. *eMarketer.com*. Retrieved from https://content-na2011.emarketer.com/digital-display-ad-pricing-statpack

Fishkin, R. (2018). Why Google AdWords' keyword volume numbers are wildly unreliable - whiteboard Friday. Retrieved from https://moz.com/blog/unreliable-google-adwords-keyword-volume?utm_campaign=Submission&utm_medium=Community&utm_source=GrowthHackers.com

Forbes. (2018). Global digital commerce sales to near $6 trillion by 2022. Retrieved from https://www.forbes.com/sites/jordanmckee/2018/09/11/global-digital-commerce-sales-to-near-6-trillion-by-2022/#868b6e54c5a0

Freberg, K., Graham, K., McGaughey, K., & Freberg, L. (2011). Who are the social media influencers? A study of public perceptions of personality. *Public Relations Review*, *37*(1), 90–92. doi:10.1016/j.pubrev.2010.11.001

Fullerton, G. (2011). Creating advocates: The roles of satisfaction, trust and commitment. *Journal of Retailing and Consumer Services*, *18*(1), 92–100. doi:10.1016/j.jretconser.2010.10.003

Geddes, B. (2014). Advanced Google Adwords. (W. Knibbe, Ed.) (3rd. Ed.). Sybex Editions.

George, W. R. (1990). Internal marketing and organizational behavior: A partnership in developing customer-conscious employees at every level. *Journal of Business Research, 20*(1), 63-70.

Gielens, K., & Steenkamp, J.-B. E. M. (2019). Branding in the era of digital (dis)intermediation. *International Journal of Research in Marketing*. doi:10.1016/j.ijresmar.2019.01.005

Gilbert, D., & Powell-Perry, J. (2002). Exploring developments in web-based relationship marketing within the hotel industry. *Journal of Hospitality & Leisure Marketing*, *9*(3/4), 141–159.

Gillin, P. (2007). *The new influencers: A marketer's guide to the new social media*. Sanger, CA: Quill Driver Books.

Gilly, M. C., & Wolfinbarger, M. (1998). Advertising's internal audience. *Journal of Marketing*, *62*(1), 69–88. doi:10.1177/002224299806200107

Gironda, J., & Korgaonkar, P. (2018). iSpy? Tailored versus invasive ads and consumers' perceptions of personalized advertising. *Electronic Commerce Research and Applications*, *29*, 64–77. doi:10.1016/j.elerap.2018.03.007

Glucksman, M. (2017). Rise of social media influencer marketing on lifestyle branding. *Elon Journal of Undergraduate Research in Communications*, *8*(2), 77–87.

Goel, G., & Mehta, A. (2008). Online budgeted matching in random input models with applications to adwords. In *Proceedings of the Nineteenth Annual ACM-SIAM Symposium on Discrete Algorithms* (pp. 982–991). Society for Industrial and Applied Mathematics.

Google. (2018a). Click: Definition. Retrieved from https://support.google.com/google-ads/answer/31799?hl=en

Google. (2018b). Clickthrough rate (CTR): Definition. Retrieved from https://support.google.com/google-ads/answer/2615875?hl=en

Google. (2019a). About expanded text ads. Retrieved from https://support.google.com/google-ads/answer/7056544?hl=en

Google. (2019b). About your Google Ads account limits. Retrieved from https://support.google.com/google-ads/answer/6372658?hl=en

Google. (2019c). Conversion: Definition. Retrieved from https://support.google.com/google-ads/answer/6365?hl=en

Google. (2019d). How can we help you? Retrieved from https://support.google.com/google-ads/?hl=en#topic=7456157

Google. (2019e). Impressions: Definition. Retrieved from https://support.google.com/google-ads/answer/6320?hl=en

Grant, R. M. (1991). The resource-based theory of competitive advantage: Implications for strategy formulation. *California Management Review*, *33*(3), 114–135. doi:10.2307/41166664

Graziani, T. (2017). 2017 single's day sales data, 39% YOY growth on Tmall. Available at https://walkthechat.com/2017-singles-day-sales-data-39-yoy-growth-tmall/

Greeven, M., Yang, S., Yue, T., van Heck, E., & Krug, B. (2012). How Taobao bested Ebay in China. *Financial Times, 12*.

Greeven, M. J., & Wei, W. (2017). *Business ecosystems in China: Alibaba and competing Baidu, Tencent, Xiaomi, and LeEco*. Routledge. doi:10.4324/9781315209142

Gretzel, U. (2018). Influencer marketing in travel and tourism. In M. Sigala & U. Gretzel (Eds.), *Advances in social media for travel, tourism and hospitality: new perspectives, practice and cases* (pp. 147–156). New York: Routledge.

Grewal, D., Bart, Y., Spann, M., & Zubcsek, P. (2016). Mobile advertising: a framework and research agenda. *Journal of Interactive Marketing*, *34*, 3–14. doi:10.1016/j.intmar.2016.03.003

GrowthBadger. (2019). *Remarketing: the ultimate guide for 2019.* Retrieved from https://growthbadger.com/remarketing/

Guerini, M., Strapparava, C., & Stock, O. (2010). Evaluation metrics for persuasive NLP with Google AdWords. *Proceedings of the 7th International Conference on Language Resources and Evaluation*, 3459–3463.

Gummesson, E. (1999). *Total relationship marketing, rethinking marketing management: From 4Ps to 30Rs*. Oxford, UK: Butterworth Heinemann.

Guo, Y., Yang, X., Ryabov, Y., & Liu, W. (2013). An empirical research on influencing factors of microblogging marketing effectiveness. *International Journal of u-and e-Service. Science and Technology*, *6*(4), 91–117.

Han, Y., Hu, C., Bai, B., & Jang, S. (2005). Marketing hospitality and tourism education on the Internet: An analysis of e-relationship marketing features. *Journal of Hospitality & Tourism Education*, *17*(1), 11–21. doi:10.1080/10963758.2005.10696811

Harker, M. J., & Egan, J. (2006). The past, present and future of relationship marketing. *Journal of Marketing Management*, *22*(1/2), 215–242. doi:10.1362/026725706776022326

Havinga, M., Hoving, M., & Swagemakers, V. (2016). Alibaba: a case study on building an international imperium on information and e-commerce. In *Multinational management* (pp. 13–32). Cham, Switzerland: Springer. doi:10.1007/978-3-319-23012-2_2

Havlena, W., Ardarelli, R. C., & Montigny, M. D. (2007). Quantifying the isolated and synergistic effects of exposure frequency for TV, print, and internet advertising. *Journal of Advertising Research*, *47*(3), 215–221. doi:10.2501/S0021849907070262

He, A. (2019, June 24). Facebook's new libra cryptocurrency helps the company diversify away from advertising. *eMarketer.com*. Retrieved from https://content-na2011.emarketer.com/facebook-new-libra-cryptocurrency-helps-the-company-diversify-away-from-advertising

Hearn, A., & Schoenhoff, S. (2016). From celebrity to influencer. In P. D. *Marshall, & S. Redmond (Eds.), A companion to celebrity* (pp. 194–211). West Sussex, UK: John Wiley & Sons/Blackwell.

Heckler, S. E., Keller, K. L., Houston, M. J., & Avery, J. (2014). Building brand knowledge structures: Elaboration and interference effects on the processing of sequentially advertised brand benefit claims. *Journal of Marketing Communications*, *20*(3), 176–196. doi:10.1080/17544750.2012.660766

Heilmann, P., Saarenketo, S., & Liikkanen, K. (2013). Employer branding in power industry. *International Journal of Energy Sector Management*, *7*(2), 283–302. doi:10.1108/IJESM-03-2012-0003

Hesse, N. (2015). *Influencer marketing: How companies can benefit from influencers to strengthen their brands.* Retrieved from http://www.brandba.se/blog/influencer-marketing-how-companies-can-benefit-from-it-to-strengthen-their-brands

Hoffman, D. L., & Fodor, M. (2010). Can you measure the ROI of your social media marketing? *MIT Sloan Management Review*, *52*(1), 41–49.

Holdren, A. (2011). *Google AdWords: Managing your advertising program.* O'Reilly Media.

Homburg, C., Wieseke, J., & Hoyer, W. D. (2009). Social identity and the service–profit chain. *Journal of Marketing*, *73*(2), 38–54. doi:10.1509/jmkg.73.2.38

Hootsuite. (2019a). *Digital 2019 - Colombia.* Retrieved from https://www.slideshare.net/DataReportal/digital-2019-colombia-january-2019-v01

Hootsuite. (2019b). *Digital 2019 Colombia.*

Hootsuite. (2019c). *Digital 2019 Mexico.*

Hsieh, Y., & Chen, K. (2011). How different information types affect viewer's attention on internet advertising. *Computers in Human Behavior*, *27*(2), 935–945. doi:10.1016/j.chb.2010.11.019

Hu, J., Marques, J., Holt, S., & Camillo, A. A. (2014). Marketing channels and supply chain management in contemporary globalism: e-commerce development in China and its implication for business. In Handbook of research on effective marketing in contemporary globalism (pp. 325–334). Hershey, PA: IGI Global. doi:10.4018/978-1-4666-6220-9.ch018

Huang, Y., Wu, J., & Shi, W. (2018). The impact of font choice on web pages: Relationship with willingness to pay and tourism motivation. *Tourism Management*, *66*, 191–199. doi:10.1016/j.tourman.2017.12.010

Hubbard, G. T., Kang, J.-A., & Crawford, E. C. (2016). Strategic communication and news disciplines. *Journalism & Mass Communication Educator*, *71*(4), 453–469. doi:10.1177/1077695815598865

Hughes, D. E. (2015). The indirect effect of advertising perceptions on salesperson effort and performance. In *Proceedings of the 2010 Academy of Marketing Science (AMS) Annual Conference* (pp. 235-235). Springer, Cham. 10.1007/978-3-319-11797-3_130

Hunt, S. D., Wood, V. R., & Chonko, L. B. (1989). Corporate ethical values and organizational commitment in marketing. *Journal of Marketing, 53*(3), 79-90.

Hunt, S. D., Arnett, D. B., & Madhavaram, S. (2006). The explanatory foundations of relationship marketing theory. *Journal of Business and Industrial Marketing, 21*(2), 72–87. doi:10.1108/10610420610651296

Hunt, S. D., & Morgan, R. M. (1995). The comparative advantage theory of competition. *Journal of Marketing, 59*(2), 1–15. doi:10.1177/002224299505900201

IAB UK. (2011, April 14). Europe commits to self-regulation; Europe's online advertising industry agrees online behavioural advertising guidelines. Retrieved from https://iabuk.net/news/europe-commits-to-self-regulation

IAB. (2009, July). *Self-regulatory principles for online behavioral advertising.* Retrieved from https://www.iab.com/wp-content/uploads/2015/2005/ven-principles-2007-2001-2009.pdf

Inflow Summits. (n.d.). *Influencers of the world.* Retrieved from http://inflowsummits.com

Influencer MarketingHub. (2017). *What is an influencer?* Retrieved from https://influencermarketinghub.com/what-is-an-influencer/

Influencer MarketingHub. (2019). *Influencer marketing report.* Retrieved from https://influencermarketinghub.com/IM_Benchmark_Report_2019.pdf

Internet Live Stats. (n.d.). Google search statistics - internet live stats. Retrieved from https://www.internetlivestats.com/google-search-statistics/

Izea. (2017). *The power of your everyday influencer is stronger than celebrities.* Retrieved from https://izea.com/2017/02/03/micro-influencers/

Joo, M., Wilbur, K., & Zhu, Y. (2016). Effects of TV advertising on keyword search. *International Journal of Research in Marketing, 33*(3), 508–523. doi:10.1016/j.ijresmar.2014.12.005

Jung, J. C., Ugboma, M. A., & Liow, A. K. (2015). Does Alibaba's magic work outside China? *Thunderbird International Business Review, 57*(6), 505–518. doi:10.1002/tie.21739

Jun, S. P., & Park, D. H. (2016). Consumer information search behavior and purchasing decisions: Empirical evidence from Korea. *Technological Forecasting and Social Change, 107*, 97–111. doi:10.1016/j.techfore.2016.03.021

Kaczorowska-Spychalska, D. (2017). Consumer perspective of omnichannel commerce. *Management, 21*(2), 95–108. doi:10.1515/manment-2017-0007

Kadekova, Z., & Holiencinova, M. (2018). Influencer marketing as a modern phenomenon creating a new frontier of virtual opportunities. *Communication Today, 9*(2), 90–105.

Kang, Y. W., & Yang, K. C. C. (2019, Aug. 7-10). Will location privacy concerns influence location-based advertising effectiveness. Presented at the Competitive Paper, Advertising Division, 2019 AEJMC Conference, Toronto, Canada.

Kaplan, A. M., & Hänlein, M. (2010). Users of the world, unite! The challenges and opportunities of Social Media. *Business Horizons*, *53*(1), 59–68. doi:10.1016/j.bushor.2009.09.003

Kareklas, I., Brunel, F., & Coulter, R. (2014). Judgment is not color blind: The impact of automatic color preference on product and advertising preferences. *Journal of Consumer Psychology*, *24*(1), 87–95. doi:10.1016/j.jcps.2013.09.005

Keller, E., & Berry, J. (2003). *The influentials: One American in ten tells the other nine how to vote, where to eat, and what to buy*. New York: The Free Press.

Keller, K. L. (1993). Conceptualizing, measuring, and managing customer-based brand equity. *Journal of Marketing*, *57*(1), 1–22. doi:10.1177/002224299305700101

Kenessey, Z. (1987). The primary, secondary, tertiary and quaternary sectors of the economy. *Review of Income and Wealth*, *33*(4), 359–385. doi:10.1111/j.1475-4991.1987.tb00680.x

Khan, V. J., Markopoulos, I., & Jsselsteijn, W. A. (2007). Combining the experience sampling method with the day reconstruction method. In *Proceedings 11th CHI Nederland Conference.*

Kietzmann, J. H., Hermkens, K., McCarthy, I. P., & Silvestre, B. S. (2011). Social media? Get serious! Understanding the functional building blocks of social media. *Business Horizons*, *54*(3), 241–251. doi:10.1016/j.bushor.2011.01.005

Kim, B., & Kim, Y. (2019). Facebook versus Instagram: How perceived gratifications and technological attributes are related to the change in social media usage. *The Social Science Journal*, *56*(2), 156–167. doi:10.1016/j.soscij.2018.10.002

Kim, J., Ahn, S., Kwon, E., & Reid, L. (2017). TV advertising engagement as a state of immersion and presence. *Journal of Business Research*, *76*, 67–76. doi:10.1016/j.jbusres.2017.03.001

Kirby, J., & Marsden, P. (2007). *Connected marketing: The viral, buzz, and word of mouth revolution*. Oxford, UK: Routledge.

Kirkby, R. J. (2018). *Urbanization in China: town and country in a developing economy 1949-2000 AD*. Routledge.

Kiss, C., & Bichler, M. (2008). Identification of influencers: Measuring influence in customer networks. *Decision Support Systems*, *46*(1), 233–253. doi:10.1016/j.dss.2008.06.007

Kosaka, K. (n.d.). *7 overlooked benefits of influencer marketing. Influencer marketing benefit #5: Connects with audiences where they spend the most time.* Retrieved from https://blog.alexa.com/benefits-of-influencer-marketing/

Kotler, P. (1999). *Marketing para o século XXI: como criar, dominar e conquistar mercados*. São Paulo, Brazil: Atlas.

Kotler, P., Bowen, J., & Makens, J. (2003). *Marketing for hospitality and tourism* (3rd ed.). Upper Saddle River, NJ: Prentice Hall.

Kotler, P., Kartajaya, H., & Setiawan, I. (2017). *Marketing 4.0: Moving from traditional to digital.* Hoboken, NJ: John Wiley & Sons.

Kotler, P., & Keller, K. L. (2012). *Marketing management.* New Jersey: Prentice Hall.

Kozinets, R. V. (2002). The field behind the screen: Using netnography for marketing research in online communities. *JMR, Journal of Marketing Research, 39*(1), 61–72. doi:10.1509/jmkr.39.1.61.18935

Kuisma, J., Simola, J., Uusitalo, L., & Öörni, A. (2010). The effects of animation and format on the perception and memory of online advertising. *Journal of Interactive Marketing, 24*(4), 269–282. doi:10.1016/j.intmar.2010.07.002

Kuşçu, A., & Yolbulan Okan, E. (2010). An exploratory study on the dimensions of employer brandıng. *Öneri Journal, 34*(9), 119-130.

Lafferty, J. (2016). *Can influencer marketing really motivate purchases?* Retrieved from https://www.adweek.com/digital/can-influencer-marketing-really-drive-conversions-study/

Lasswell, H. D. (1948). The structure and function of communication in society. In L. Bryson (Ed.), *The Communication of Ideas* (pp. 37–51). New York: Harper.

Laudon, K. C., & Traver, C. G. (2019). E-Commerce 2019: Business, Technology and Society (14 ed.). Pearson.

Ledford, J. L. (2015). *Search engine optimization bible* (Vol. 584). John Wiley & Sons.

Lee, E. (2018). The incredible rise of Pinduoduo, China's newest force in e-commerce. Available at https://techcrunch.com/2018/07/26/the-incredible-rise-of-pinduoduo/

Lee, T. (2019). Google is the internet's largest ad company. So why is it building an ad blocker? Retrieved from https://www.vox.com/new-money/2017/6/5/15729688/google-chrome-ad-blocking

Lee, J., Ham, C., & Kim, M. (2013). Why people pass along online video advertising: from the perspectives of the interpersonal communication motives scale and the theory of reasoned action. *Journal of Interactive Advertising, 13*(1), 1–13. doi:10.1080/15252019.2013.768048

Lella, A., Lipsman, A., & Martin, B. (2015). The global mobile report: How multi-platform audiences & engagement compare in the US, Canada, UK and beyond. Reston, VA: com.Score.

Le, T. D. (2018). Influence of WOM and content type on online engagement in consumption communities: The information flow from discussion forums to Facebook. *Online Information Review, 42*(2), 161–175. doi:10.1108/OIR-09-2016-0246

Le, T. D., Dobele, A. R., & Robinson, L. J. (2018). WOM source characteristics and message quality: The receiver perspective. *Marketing Intelligence & Planning, 36*(4), 440–454. doi:10.1108/MIP-10-2017-0249

Li, C. (2016). When does web-based personalization really work? The distinction between actual personalization and perceived personalization. *Computers in Human Behavior, 54*, 25–33. doi:10.1016/j.chb.2015.07.049

Li, C., & Liu, J. (2017). A name alone is not enough: A reexamination of web-based personalization effect. *Computers in Human Behavior, 72*, 132–139. doi:10.1016/j.chb.2017.02.039

Liikkanen, L., & Salovaara, A. (2015). Music on YouTube: User engagement with traditional, user-appropriated and derivative videos. *Computers in Human Behavior, 50*, 108–124. doi:10.1016/j.chb.2015.01.067

Li, L. X. (2000). An analysis of sources of competitiveness and performance of Chinese manufacturers. *International Journal of Operations & Production Management, 20*(3), 299–315. doi:10.1108/01443570010294307

Lindgreen, A., Dobele, A., Beverland, M., & Vanhamme, J. (2008). Viral marketing. In *Marketing metaphors and metamorphosis* (pp. 102–117). London, UK: Palgrave Macmillan. doi:10.1057/9780230227538_7

Linqia Company. (2017). *The state of influencer marketing*. Retrieved from http://www.linqia.com/wp-content/uploads/2017/12/Linqia-The-State-of-Influencer-Marketing-2018.pdf

Liu, C., & Xiong, W. (2018). *China's real estate market (No. w25297)*. National Bureau of Economic Research. doi:10.3386/w25297

Liu, H., & Wang, X. (2018, March). Study on the application of big data in accurate marketing of cross-border e-commerce in China. In *Proceedings of the 3rd International Conference on Big Data Analysis (ICBDA)* (pp. 24–27). IEEE. 10.1109/ICBDA.2018.8367645

Liu, Y., Zhu, C., Mao, M., Song, F., Dufaux, F., & Zhang, X. (2018). Video analytical coding: When video coding meets video analysis. *Signal Processing Image Communication, 67*, 48–57. doi:10.1016/j.image.2018.05.012

Li, X. (2018). Development of intelligent logistics in China. In *Contemporary logistics in China* (pp. 181–204). Singapore: Springer. doi:10.1007/978-981-13-0071-4_9

Li, X., Shi, M., & Wang, X. (2019). Video mining: Measuring visual information using automatic methods. *International Journal of Research in Marketing, 36*(2), 216–231. doi:10.1016/j.ijresmar.2019.02.004

Lloyd, S. (2002). Branding from the inside out. *Business Review Weekly, 24*(10), 64–66.

Lohtia, R., Donthu, N., & Hershberger, E. K. (2003). The impact of content and design elements on banner advertising click-through rates. *Journal of Advertising Research, 43*(4), 410–418. doi:10.2501/JAR-43-4-410-418

Loras, S. (2016, July 18). What do China's new online advertising rules mean for marketers? Retrieved from https://www.clickz.com/what-do-chinas-new-online-advertising-rules-mean-for-marketers/103221/

Lu, L. (2013). The Chinese market layout and influence of international luxury e-commerce. *International Journal of Digital Content Technology and its Applications, 7*(4), 991.

Lu, Y., Liu, Z., & Ma, L. (2016). Competing through logistics management: Studies on e-retailing in China. In E-retailing challenges and opportunities in the global marketplace (pp. 256–275). Hershey, PA: IGI Global. doi:10.4018/978-1-4666-9921-2.ch014

Lubecka, A. (2013). Employer branding–a dialogistic communication tool of a competitive employer. *Journal of Intercultural Management, 5*(2), 5–16. doi:10.2478/joim-2013-0007

Lu, C., Wu, I., & Hsiao, W. (2019). Developing customer product loyalty through mobile advertising: Affective and cognitive perspectives. *International Journal of Information Management, 47*, 101–111. doi:10.1016/j.ijinfomgt.2018.12.020

Macdonald, C., Chapman, M., Naik, A., Fanno, M., & Beilis, T. (2016). *Cross-channel advertising attribution: New insights into multiplatform TV*. Accenture. Retrieved from https://www.accenture.com/us-en/~/media/PDF-18/Accenture-New-Insights-Into-Multiplatform-TV.pdf

Madera, J. M. (2012). Using social networking websites as a selection tool: The role of selection process fairness and job pursuit intentions. *International Journal of Hospitality Management, 31*(4), 1276–1282. doi:10.1016/j.ijhm.2012.03.008

Madera, Q., Castillo, O., Garcia, M., & Mancilla, A. (2017). Bidding strategies based on type-1 and interval type-2 fuzzy systems for Google AdWords advertising campaigns. In *Nature-inspired design of hybrid intelligent systems* (pp. 99–113). Springer. doi:10.1007/978-3-319-47054-2_6

Mael, F., & Ashforth, B. E. (1992). Alumni and their alma mater: A partial test of the reformulated model of organizational identification. *Journal of Organizational Behavior, 13*(2), 103–123. doi:10.1002/job.4030130202

Magrath, A. J. (1986). When marketing services, 4 Ps are not enough. *Business Horizons, 29*(3), 44–50. doi:10.1016/0007-6813(86)90007-8

Ma, M., Zhang, L., Liu, J., Wang, Z., Li, W., Hou, G., & Sun, L. (2017, June). Characterizing user behaviors in mobile personal livecast. In *Proceedings of the 27th Workshop on Network and Operating Systems Support for Digital Audio and Video* (pp. 43–48). ACM. 10.1145/3083165.3083169

Manafy, M. (2014, June 6). Five tips for cross-platform advertising success. Retrieved from http://www.thedrum.com/opinion/2014/06/06/five-tips-cross-platform-advertising-success

Manchanda, P., Dubé, J.-P., Goh, K. Y., & Chintagunta, P. K. (2006). The effect of banner advertising on internet purchasing. *JMR, Journal of Marketing Research, 43*(1), 98–108. doi:10.1509/jmkr.43.1.98

Marchant, I. (2015a). *Futuro Digital México 2015.*

Marchant, I. (2015b). *Medición Multiplataforma en México.*

Marchant, I., & Valencia, F. (2015). *Medición Multiplataforma en Colombia.*

Marketing-Schools. (n.d.). *Relationship marketing: Explore the strategy of relationship marketing*. Retrieved from http://www.marketing-schools.org/types-of-marketing/relationship-marketing.html

Marks, R. (2016, May). Challenges and opportunities in cross platform media measurement. *Research World, 2016*(58), 9–13. doi:10.1002/rwm3.20366

Martín-Santana, J., Muela-Molina, C., Reinares-Lara, E., & Rodríguez-Guerra, M. (2015). Effectiveness of radio spokesperson's gender, vocal pitch and accent and the use of music in radio advertising. *BRQ Business Research Quarterly, 18*(3), 143–160. doi:10.1016/j.brq.2014.06.001

Mathew, J. (2018). *Understanding influencer marketing and why it is so effective*. Retrieved from https://www.forbes.com/sites/theyec/2018/07/30/understanding-influencer-marketing-and-why-it-is-so-effective/#1471884c71a9

Maxwell, R., & Knox, S. (2009). Motivating employees to" live the brand": A comparative case study of employer brand attractiveness within the firm. *Journal of Marketing Management, 25*(9-10), 893–907. doi:10.1362/026725709X479282

McDonald, J. (2014). *Google Adwords gotchas*. San Francisco, CA: CreateSpace Independent.

McIntyre, P. (2006). Cross-media deals expected to double to $600m a year; alliance mulls multi-platform package. *Australasian Business Intelligence*, 33. Retrieved from https://www.highbeam.com/doc/2001G2001-154865588.html

McNeal, M. (2013, Summer). Solving the multiplatform puzzle. *Marketing Insights*, pp. 41-47.

Mehta, A. (2007). AdWords and generalized online matching. *Journal of the Association for Computing Machinery, V*(August), 1–20.

Mehta, A., Saberi, A., Vazirani, U., & Vazirani, V. (2005). Adwords and generalized on-line matching. In *46th Annual IEEE Symposium on Foundations of Computer Science (FOCS'05)* (pp. 264–273). IEEE. 10.1109/SFCS.2005.12

Men, L. R., & Tsai, W. H. S. (2015). Infusing social media with humanity: Corporate character, public engagement, and relational outcomes. *Public Relations Review, 41*(3), 395–403. doi:10.1016/j.pubrev.2015.02.005

Michaels, E., Handfield-Jones, H., & Axelrod, B. (2001). The war for talent. Brighton, MA: Harvard Business Press.

Miles, S. J., & Mangold, G. (2004). A conceptualization of the employee branding process. *Journal of Relationship Marketing, 3*(2-3), 65–87. doi:10.1300/J366v03n02_05

Minchington, B. (2010). *Employer brand leadership: A global perspective*. Collective Learning Australia.

Miranda, C. M. C., & de Oliveira Arruda, D. M. (2004). E-produtos e variáveis comportamentais determinantes de compra no varejo virtual: um estudo com consumidores brasileiros. *Revista Eletrônica de Administração, 10*(1).

Monllos, K. (2016, Sept. 13). Carrie Brownstein made this brilliantly creepy short film about internet fandom for Kenzo. *AdWeek*. Retrieved from http://www.adweek.com/brand-marketing/carrie-brownstein-made-brilliantly-creepy-short-film-about-internet-fandom-kenzo-173453/

Monteiro, R. V. (2007). Google Adwords: A arte da Guerra. (S. M. Oliveira, Ed.) (2.a Edição). São Paulo, Brazil: Brasport livros e Multimídia Ltda.

Montgomery, A. L. (2001). Applying quantitative marketing techniques to the Internet. *Interfaces*, *31*(2), 90–108. doi:10.1287/inte.31.2.90.10630

Morgan, R. M., & Hunt, S. D. (1994). The commitment–trust theory of relationship marketing. *Journal of Marketing*, *58*(3), 20–38. doi:10.1177/002224299405800302

Morin, R. (2016). *The rise of niche and micro-influencers*. Retrieved from https://maximizesocialbusiness.com/the-rise-of-niche-and-micro-influencers-24286/#

Moroko, L., & Uncles, M. D. (2008). Characteristics of successful employer brands. *Journal of Brand Management*, *16*(3), 160–175. doi:10.1057/bm.2008.4

Mowat, J. (2018). *Video marketing strategy: harness the power of online video to drive brand growth* (1st ed.). Kogan Page.

Munnukka, J., Maity, D., Reinikainen, H., & Luoma-aho, V. (2019). "Thanks for watching". The effectiveness of YouTube vlogendorsements. *Computers in Human Behavior*, *93*, 226–234. doi:10.1016/j.chb.2018.12.014

Muñoz-Leiva, F., Hernández-Méndez, J., & Gómez-Carmona, D. (2019). Measuring advertising effectiveness in Travel 2.0 websites through eye-tracking technology. *Physiology & Behavior*, *200*, 83–95. doi:10.1016/j.physbeh.2018.03.002 PMID:29522796

Murphy, T., & Schram, R. (2014). What is it worth? The value chasm between brand and influencers. *Journal of Brand Strategy*, *3*(1), 31–40.

National Data. (2019). Retrieved from http://data.stats.gov.cn/english/

Neijens, J., & Voorveld., R. (2015). Cross-platform advertising: Current practices and issues for the future. *Journal of Advertising Research*, *55*(3), 55-60. doi:. doi:10.2501/JAR-2016-2042

Nielsen. (2014, May 29). *The 8% unleashing the power of cross-platform advertising*. Retrieved from http://www.nielsen.com/content/corporate/us/en/insights/news/2014/the-8-percent-unleashing-the-power-of-cross-platform-advertising.html

Nielsen. (2016a, March 22). *On-demand demographics: VOD viewing across generations.* Retrieved from http://www.Nielsen.Com/us/en/insights/news/2016/on-demand-demographics-vod-viewing-across-generations.Html:Nielsen

Nielsen. (2016b, March 24). *Facts of life: As they move through life stages, Millennials' media habits are different and distinct.* Retrieved from http://www.nielsen.com/us/en/insights/news/2016/facts-of-life-as-they-move-through-life-stages-millennials-media-habits-are-different.html

Nielsen. (2017a, Jan. 30). Nielsen launches cross-device provider verification powered by digital ad ratings. Retrieved from http://www.nielsen.com/us/en/press-room/2017/nielsen-launches-cross-device-provider-verification-powered-by-digital-ad-ratings.html

Nielsen. (2017b, March 2). Millennials on millennials: A look at viewing behavior, distraction, and social media stars. Retrieved from http://www.nielsen.com/us/en/insights/news/2017/millennials-on-millennials-a-look-at-viewing-behavior-distraction-social-media-stars.html

Odabaşı, Y. (2017). *Postmodern pazarlama: Tüketim ve tüketici (5. Baskı).* İstanbul, Turkey: MediaCatYayınları.

Okada, S. I., & de Souza, E. M. S. (2011). Estratégias do marketing digital na era da busca. *Revista Brasileira de Marketing, 10*(1), 46–72.

Osman, M. (2018). *28 powerful Facebook stats your brand can't ignore in 2018.* Retrieved from https://sproutsocial.com/insights/facebook-stats-for-marketers/

Ou, C. X., & Davison, R. M. (2009). Technical opinion. Why eBay lost to TaoBao in China: The Glocal advantage. *Communications of the ACM, 52*(1), 145–148. doi:10.1145/1435417.1435450

Oxer, J. (2008). *Quickstart guide to Google AdWords.* Lulu Press.

Parra-Arnau, J., Achara, J., & Castelluccia, C. (2017). MyAdChoices. *ACM Transactions on the Web, 11*(1), 1–47. doi:10.1145/2996466

Patel, N. (2019). 7 deadly AdWords mistakes that'll make you broke (and how to fix them). Retrieved from https://neilpatel.com/blog/7-deadly-adwords-mistakes-thatll-make-you-broke-and-how-to-fix-them/

Patil, V. M., & Patil, A. V. (2018). SEO: on-page off-page analysis. *2018 International Conference on Information, Communication, Engineering, and Technology (ICICET).* doi:10.1109/ICICET.2018.8533836

Pereira, J. (2008). Google: Ferramenta de Busca de informação na web pereira. *Revista Eletrônica Do CESVA, 1*(1), 18–32.

Peteraf, M. A. (1993). The cornerstones of competitive advantage: A resource-based view. *Strategic Management Journal, 14*(3), 179–191. doi:10.1002mj.4250140303

Pinduoduo. (2019). Pinduoduo's AI-driven duo duo farm empowers farmers, helping to alleviate poverty in rural areas. Available at http://investor.pinduoduo.com/corporate-blog/pinduoduos-ai-driven-duo-duo-farm-empowers-farmers-helping

Pinegar, G. (2018). *What is influencer marketing? (+How to identify influencers in 2019),* Retrieved from https://learn.g2crowd.com/influencer-marketing

Precourt, G. (2015, December). How does cross-platform advertising work? *Journal of Advertising Research,* 356-357. doi:10.2501/JAR-2015-2018

PWC. (2016). China entertainment and media outlook. Available at https://www.pwccn.com/en/entertainment-media/em-china-outlook-nov2016.pdf

Pymnts. (2018). JD.Com rakes in $24.6b during 618 shopping festival. Available at https://www.pymnts.com/news/ecommerce/2018/jdcom-618-shopping-festival-china/

Reddy, G. (2016). *Digital marketing impact on the consumer decision making process in Nike's customer retail operations in South Africa*. University of Pretoria.

Redondo, I., & Aznar, G. (2018). To use or not to use ad blockers? The roles of knowledge of ad blockers and attitude toward online advertising. *Telematics and Informatics*, *35*(6), 1607–1616. doi:10.1016/j.tele.2018.04.008

Reichenberg, N. (2009). Branding the government as an employer of choice. Retrieved from http://unpan1.un.org/intradoc/groups/public/documents/UN/UNPAN021819.pdf

Reimers, V., Chao, C.-W., & Gorman, S. (2013). Permission email marketing and its influence on online shopping. *Asia Pacific Journal of Marketing and Logistics*, *28*(2), 316. doi:10.1108/APJML-03-2015-0037

ResearchLive. (2017, Feb. 23). *com.Score launches multi-platform digital video measure in UK.* Retrieved from https://www.Research-live.Com/article/news/comscore-launches-multiplatform-digital-video-measure-in-uk/id/5018952

Riketta, M. (2005). Organizational identification: A meta-analysis. *Journal of Vocational Behavior*, *66*(2), 358–384. doi:10.1016/j.jvb.2004.05.005

Robertson, M. (2014, April 29). Media buyers see big value in multi-platform advertising. Retrieved from http://tubularinsights.com/media-buyers-see-big-value-in-multi-platform-advertising/#ixzz4g3oWQRKh

Rodgers, S., & Thorson, E. (2000). The interactive advertising model: How users perceive and process online ads. *Journal of Interactive Advertising*, *1*(1), 41–60. doi:10.1080/15252019.2000.10722043

Romaniuk, J. (2015, September). Coming in December: How cross-platform advertising works. *Journal of Advertising Research*, 353. doi:10.2501/JAR-2015-2014

Roper, P. (2014, Dec. 16). November best global digital marketing: Red Roof Inn's search campaign, Burger King's motel, Turkish shoppable soap opera. *Marketing*. Retrieved from http://shortyawards.com/category/2017th/multi-platform-campaign

Sánchez, D., & Viejo, A. (2018). Privacy-preserving and advertising-friendly web surfing. *Computer Communications*, *130*, 113–123. doi:10.1016/j.comcom.2018.09.002

Sawhney, M., Verona, G., & Prandelli, E. (2005). Collaborating to create: The Internet as a platform for customer engagement in product innovation. *Journal of Interactive Marketing*, *19*(4), 4–17. doi:10.1002/dir.20046

Schafer, M. (n.d.). *Word of mouth versus influencer marketing.* Retrieved from https://businessesgrow.com/2018/11/12/difference-between-influencer-marketing-and-word-of-mouth-marketing/

Schein, E. H. (1985). Defining organizational culture. *Classics of organization theory, 3*, 490-502.

Schmitt, B. (2013). The consumer psychology of customer–brand relationships: Extending the AA Relationship model. *Journal of Consumer Psychology, 23*(2), 249–252. doi:10.1016/j.jcps.2013.01.003

Schreiner, T., Rese, A., & Baier, D. (2019). Multichannel personalization: Identifying consumer preferences for product recommendations in advertisements across different media channels. *Journal of Retailing and Consumer Services, 48*, 87–99. doi:10.1016/j.jretconser.2019.02.010

Scott, G. (1989). Magellan: Information Retrieval Software from Lotus. *U-M Computing News, 17*(4), 10–12.

Semerádová, T., & Weinlich, P. (2019). Calculation of Facebook marketing effectiveness in terms of ROI. *Leveraging Computer-Mediated Marketing Environments*, 286-310. doi:10.4018/978-1-5225-7344-9.ch014

Semerádová, T., & Weinlich, P. (2018). Assessing banner ads effectiveness based on the type of the creative content. In *Proceedings of the 31st International Business Information Management Association Conference, IBIMA 2018: Innovation Management and Education Excellence through Vision 2020* (pp. 1439-1446). Milan, Italy: IBIMA.

Sen, R. (2005). Optimal search engine marketing strategy. *International Journal of Electronic Commerce/Fall, 10*(1), 9–25.

Setyani, V., Zhu, Y., Hidayanto, A., Sandhyaduhita, P., & Hsiao, B. (2019). Exploring the psychological mechanisms from personalized advertisements to urge to buy impulsively on social media. *International Journal of Information Management, 48*, 96–107. doi:10.1016/j.ijinfomgt.2019.01.007

Shanahan, T., Tran, T., & Taylor, E. (2019). Getting to know you: Social media personalization as a means of enhancing brand loyalty and perceived quality. *Journal of Retailing and Consumer Services, 47*, 57–65. doi:10.1016/j.jretconser.2018.10.007

Shaouf, A., Lü, K., & Li, X. (2016). O que é o R? *Computers in Human Behavior, 60*, 622–634. doi:10.1016/j.chb.2016.02.090

Sharma, A. (2013, July 18). 'Mad Men' tops 'House of Cards' on Netflix. *The Wall Street Journal,* p. B3.

Sharma, N., & Kamalanabhan, T. J. (2012). Internal corporate communication and its impact on internal branding: Perception of Indian public sector employees. *Corporate Communications, 17*(3), 300–322. doi:10.1108/13563281211253548

Sheth, J. N. (2002). The future of relationship marketing. *Journal of Services Marketing*, *16*(7), 590–592. doi:10.1108/08876040210447324

Sheth, J. N., Gardner, D. M., & Garrett, D. E. (1988). *Marketing theory: Evolution and evaluation*. New York: Wiley.

Sheth, J. N., Sisodia, R. S., & Sharma, A. (2000). The antecedents and consequences of customer-centric marketing. *Journal of the Academy of Marketing Science*, *28*(1), 55–66. doi:10.1177/0092070300281006

Shia, B. C., Chen, M., & Ramdansyah, A. D. (2016). Measuring customer satisfaction toward localization website by WebQual and importance performance analysis (case study on AliexPress Site in Indonesia). *American Journal of Industrial and Business Management*, *6*(02), 117–128. doi:10.4236/ajibm.2016.62012

Shukla, T. (2010). Factors affecting Internet marketing campaigns with reference to viral and permission marketing. *The IUP Journal of Management Research*, *9*(1), 26–37.

Sidaty, N., Larabi, M., & Saadane, A. (2017). Toward an audiovisual attention model for multimodal video content. *Neurocomputing*, *259*, 94–111. doi:10.1016/j.neucom.2016.08.130

Simmons, G. (2008). Marketing to postmodern consumers: Introducing the internet chameleon. *European Journal of Marketing*, *42*(3/4), 299–310. doi:10.1108/03090560810852940

Singh, S., & Sonnenburg, S. (2012). Brand performances in social media. *Journal of Interactive Marketing*, *26*(4), 189–197. doi:10.1016/j.intmar.2012.04.001

Sivertzen, A. M., Nilsen, E. R., & Olafsen, A. H. (2013). Employer branding: Employer attractiveness and the use of social media. *Journal of Product and Brand Management*, *22*(7), 473–483. doi:10.1108/JPBM-09-2013-0393

Smidts, A., Pruyn, A. T. H., & Van Riel, C. B. (2001). The impact of employee communication and perceived external prestige on organizational identification. *Academy of Management Journal*, *44*(5), 1051–1062.

Srinivasan, S. S., Anderson, R., & Ponnavolu, K. (2002). Customer loyalty in e-commerce: An exploration of its antecedents and consequences. *Journal of Retailing*, *78*(1), 41–50. doi:10.1016/S0022-4359(01)00065-3

Srirojanant, S., & Thirkell, P. C. (1998). Relationship marketing and its synergy with web-based technologies. *Journal of Market-Focused Management*, *3*(1), 23–46. doi:10.1023/A:1009790421951

Srivastava, P., & Bhatnagar, J. (2010). Employer brand for talent acquisition: An exploration towards its measurement. *Vision*, *14*(1-2), 25–34. doi:10.1177/097226291001400103

Statista. (2017). *Most famous social network sites worldwide as of January 2017, ranked by number of active users (in millions)*. Statista. Retrieved from https://www.statista.com/statistics/272014/global-social-networks-rankedby-number-of-users/

Statista. (2019). Number of e-mail users worldwide 2023 | Statistic. Retrieved from https://www.statista.com/statistics/255080/number-of-e-mail-users-worldwide/

Statista. (2019a). Number of digital buyers worldwide from 2014 to 2021 (in billions). Retrieved from https://www.statista.com/statistics/251666/number-of-digital-buyers-worldwide/

Statista. (2019b). Retail e-commerce sales worldwide from 2014 to 2021. Retrieved from https://www.statista.com/statistics/379046/worldwide-retail-e-commerce-sales/

Stewart, D. W., & Pavlou, P. A. (2002). From consumer response to active consumer: Measuring the effectiveness of interactive media. *Journal of the Academy of Marketing Science*, *30*(4), 376–396. doi:10.1177/009207002236912

Stokes, R. (2018). *The essential guide to marketing in a digital world* (6th. Ed.). Retrieved from www.creda.co.za

Sudha, M. & Sheena, K. (2017). Impact of influencers in consumer decision process: The fashion industry. *SCMS Journal of Indian Management*, 14-30.

Sullivan, S. E. (1999). The changing nature of careers: A review and research agenda. *Journal of Management*, *25*(3), 457–484. doi:10.1177/014920639902500308

Sun, X., & Bao, J. (2010, August). Research on the innovation and development of the third-party B2B e-commerce model of China. In *Proceedings of the 3rd International Conference on Advanced Computer Theory and Engineering (ICACTE)* (Vol. 4, pp. V4–317). IEEE.

Swant, M. (2016a, Jan. 19). Why cross-device programmatic advertising is ready to take off in 2016. *Adweek*. Retrieved from http://www.adweek.com/digital/why-cross-device-programmatic-advertising-ready-take-2016-169025/

Swant, M. (2016b, Feb. 24). 6 ways Netflix viewing habits vary around the world. *Adweek*, Retrieved from http://www.adweek.com/digital/2016-ways-netflix-mobile-habits-vary-around-world-169848/

Szymanski, G., & Lininski, P. (2018). Model of the effectiveness of Google Adwords advertising activities. In *2018 IEEE 13th International Scientific and Technical Conference on Computer Sciences and Information Technologies (CSIT)* (Vol. 2, pp. 98–101). IEEE. 10.1109/STC-CSIT.2018.8526633

Szymanski, G., & Stanislawski, R. (2018). Research online-purchase offline-a phenomenon among the young generation in the e-commerce sector. *Journal of International Scientific Publications*, *12*(January), 185–192.

Tajfel, H., & Turner, J. C. (1986). The social identity theory of inter-group behavior. In S. Worchel & W. G. Austin (Eds.), *Psychology of intergroup relations* (pp. 7–24). Chicago, IL: Nelson-Hall.

Tan, L., & Gao, Y. (2017). The analysis of consumer behavior of fresh-products e-business—based on research in Chengdu. In *Proceedings of the 16th Wuhan International Conference on e-Business*.

Tao, Y. (2016). Survey on e-commerce development in areas inhabited by ethnic minorities of Qujing city, Yunnan province, based on computer data analysis. *Revista Ibérica de Sistemas e Tecnologias de Informação*, (E11), 239.

Tapinfluence & Nielsen. (2016). *Sales effect study: influencer marketing*. Retrieved from https://pages.tapinfluence.com/hubfs/Nielsen_WhiteWave_Study/1009_-_Nielsen_Study_Case_Study.pdf

Team, C. I. W. (2019). China retail market overview 2018; rural areas grew by 10.1%, online retail up 24%, China Internet Watch. Retrieved from https://www.chinainternetwatch.com/28092/retail-2018/

The European Parliament and of the Council. (2002, July 2). Directive 2002/58/EC of the European Parliament and of the Council of 12 July 2002 concerning the processing of personal data and the protection of privacy in the electronic communications sector (directive on privacy and electronic communications). Retrieved from http://eur-lex.europa.eu/legal-content/EN/TXT/?uri=CELEX:32002L0058

The influence of perceived ad relevance on social media advertising: An empirical examination of a mediating role of privacy concern. *Computers in Human Behavior, 70*, 303-309. doi:10.1016/j.chb.2017.01.008

The World Bank. (n.d.). Individuals using the Internet (% of population) | Data. Retrieved from https://data.worldbank.org/indicator/it.net.user.zs

The-Cocktail-Analysis. (2013). La compra online en Colombia. In The Cocktail Analysis.

Thomaidou, S., Leymonis, K., Liakopoulos, K., & Vazirgiannis, M. (2012). AD-MAD: Automated development and optimization of online advertising campaigns. In *2012 IEEE 12th International Conference on Data Mining Workshops* (pp. 902–905). IEEE.

Thomaidou, S., Liakopoulos, K., & Vazirgiannis, M. (2014). Toward an integrated framework for automated development and optimization of online advertising campaigns. *Intelligent Data Analysis, 18*(6), 1199–1227. doi:10.3233/IDA-140691

Thorne, L. (2008). *Word of mouth advertising online and off: How to spark buzz, excitement, and free publicity for your business or organization—With little or no money*. Florida: Atlantic Publishing Group.

Tode, C. (2013, Aug. 16). Cross-device advertising commands growing portion of media spend: Report. *Mobile Marketer*. Retrieved from http://www.mobilemarketer.com/cms/news/research/15969.html

Tong, F. (2018). Online retail sales in China soar past $1 trillion in 2017. Available at https://www.digitalcommerce360.com/2018/02/08/online-retail-sales-china-soar-past-1-trillion-2017/

Torres, C. (2010). *Guia Prático de Marketing na Internet para Pequenas Empresas: Dicas para Posicionar o seu Negócio e Conquistar Novos Clientes na Internet*. Retrieved from https://www.cairu.br/biblioteca/arquivos/Marketing/

Torres, C. (2009). *A Bíblia do marketing digital Novatec*. São Paulo, Brazil.

Tran, T. (2017). Personalized ads on facebook: An effective marketing tool for online marketers. *Journal of Retailing and Consumer Services*, *39*, 230–242. doi:10.1016/j.jretconser.2017.06.010

Tsui, K. Y. (2011). China's infrastructure investment boom and local debt crisis. *Eurasian Geography and Economics*, *52*(5), 686–711. doi:10.2747/1539-7216.52.5.686

Tutaj, K., & van Reijmersdal, E. A. (2012). Effects of online advertising format and persuasion knowledge on audience reactions. *Journal of Marketing Communications*, *18*(1), 5–18. doi:10.1080/13527266.2011.620765

Twice. (2016, June 20). Millennials lead way among cord-cutters. *Twice,* p. 20.

Tzokas, N., & Saren, M. (2004). Competitive advantage, knowledge and relationship marketing: Where, what and how? *Journal of Business and Industrial Marketing*, *19*(2), 124–135. doi:10.1108/08858620410524007

Understanding how your videos perform on Facebook. (2019). Retrieved from https://www.facebook.com/facebookmedia/blog/understanding-how-your-videos-perform-on-facebook

Ur, B., Leon, P. G., Cranor, L. F., Shay, R., & Wang, Y. (2012). Smart, useful, scary, creepy: Perceptions of online behavioral advertising. *SOUPS 2012 - Proceedings of the 8th Symposium on Usable Privacy and Security, 2012*. doi:10.1145/2335356.2335362

Vaidhyanathan, S. (2011). *A Googlelização de tudo*. Editora Cultrix.

Van den Broeck, E., Poels, K., & Walrave, M. (2018). An experimental study on the effect of ad placement, product involvement and motives on Facebook ad avoidance. *Telematics and Informatics*, *35*(2), 470–479. doi:10.1016/j.tele.2018.01.006

Varey, R. J. (1995). Internal marketing: A review and some interdisciplinary research challenges. *International Journal of Service Industry Management*, *6*(1), 40–63. doi:10.1108/09564239510078849

Vaver, J., & Koehler, J. (2011). Measuring ad effectiveness using geo experiments.

Vernuccio, M. (2014). Communicating corporate brands through social media: An exploratory study. *International Journal of Business Communication*, *51*(3), 211–233. doi:10.1177/2329488414525400

Video advertising formats – YouTube help center. (2019). Retrieved from https://support.google.com/youtube/answer/2375464?hl=cs

Vohra, A., & Bhardwaj, N. (2019). Customer engagement in an e-commerce brand community: An empirical comparison of alternate models. *Journal of Research in Interactive Marketing*, *13*(1), 2–25. doi:10.1108/JRIM-01-2018-0003

Wall, A. (2017). History of search engines: from 1945 to Google Today. Retrieved from http://www.searchenginehistory.com/

Wallace, B. (2017). *A complete history of influencer marketing and what it means for the future*. Retrieved from https://socialmediaexplorer.com/content-sections/tools-and-tips/complete-history-influencer-marketing-means-future-infographic/

Wang, A. (2018). *Approaching digital marketing in the era of adblock*. Retrieved from https://medium.com/the-qchain-blog/approaching-digital-marketing-in-the-era-of-adblock-909b2a896349

Wang, D., Li, Z., Xie, G., Kaafar, M.-A., & Salamatian, K. (2016). Adwords management for third-parties in sem: An optimisation model and the potential of twitter. In *IEEE INFOCOM 2016-The 35th Annual IEEE International Conference on Computer Communications* (pp. 1–9). IEEE.

Wang, B., Li, S., & Liu, J. (2014). Assessing enterprise microblogging marketing communication effectiveness and improvement suggestions. *Journal of Chemical and Pharmaceutical Research*, *6*(6), 426–430.

Wang, C., & Hung, J. (2018). Comparative analysis of advertising attention to Facebook social network: Evidence from eye-movement data. *Computers in Human Behavior*. doi:10.1016/j.chb.2018.08.007

Wang, J. J., & Xiao, Z. (2015). Co-evolution between retailing and parcel express industry and its geographical imprints: The case of China. *Journal of Transport Geography*, *46*, 20–34. doi:10.1016/j.jtrangeo.2015.05.005

Wang, Y., & Sun, S. (2010). An online advertising model: comparing China and the U.S. *Journal of Current Issues and Research in Advertising*, *32*(2), 101–115. doi:10.1080/10641734.2010.10505288

Wentzel, D., Henkel, S., & Tomczak, T. (2010). Can I live up to that ad? Impact of implicit theories of ability on service employees' responses to advertising. *Journal of Service Research*, *13*(2), 137–152. doi:10.1177/1094670510363304

Westcott, K., Lippstreu, S., & Cutbill, D. (2017). *Digital democracy survey: A multi-generational view of consumer technology, media, and telecom trends* (11th ed.). UK: Deloitte Development.

Weusthof, E. (2015). Adwords Optimization (No. 2056674). Amsterdam, The Netherlands.

What counts as a video view? - David Burch, TubeMogul. (2019). Retrieved from https://www.youtube.com/watch?v=qpANKRZJ8Ks

Wieseke, J., Ahearne, M., Lam, S. K., & Dick, R. V. (2009). The role of leaders in internal marketing. *Journal of Marketing*, *73*(2), 123–145. doi:10.1509/jmkg.73.2.123

Wilcox, P. A., & Gurau, C. (2003). Business modelling with UML: The implementation of CRM systems for online retailing. *Journal of Retailing and Consumer Services*, *10*(3), 181–191. doi:10.1016/S0969-6989(03)00004-3

Wilden, R., Gudergan, S., & Lings, I. (2010). Employer branding: Strategic implications for staff recruitment. *Journal of Marketing Management*, *26*(1-2), 56–73. doi:10.1080/02672570903577091

Winters, P. R. (1960). Forecasting sales by exponentially weighted moving averages. *Management Science*, *6*(3), 324–342. doi:10.1287/mnsc.6.3.324

Wood, D. J. (2015, April 14). As marketers rush to programmatic, consumer-privacy rules still apply. *AdAge.com.* Retrieved from http://adage.com/article/digital/rush-programmatic-privacy-rules-apply/298060/

WordStream. (2019). *31 Advertising statistics to know in 2019.* Retrieved from https://www.wordstream.com/blog/ws/2018/07/19/advertising-statistics

Wu, C., Wei, Y., Chu, X., Weichen, S., Su, F., & Wang, L. (2018). Hierarchical attention-based multimodal fusion for video captioning. *Neurocomputing*, *315*, 362–370. doi:10.1016/j.neucom.2018.07.029

Xu, W. J. (2013). Strategy study on China e-business service in big data era. Trans Tech Publications. *Advanced Materials Research*, *798*, 983–986. doi:10.4028/www.scientific.net/AMR.798-799.983

Yang, K. C. C. (2018). Multi-platform advertising as a global phenomenon. In Yang, K. C. C. (Ed.), Multi-platform advertising strategies in the global marketplace (pp. 1-28). Hershey, PA: IGI-Global. doi:10.4018/978-1-5225-3114-2.ch001

Yang, K. C. C., & Kang, Y. W. (2016, Oct. 15-16). Real-time bidding (RTB) advertising, programmatic advertising, digital advertising marketplace: Emerging policy and regulatory issues. Presented at Direct/Interactive Marketing Research Summit, Los Angeles, CA.

Yang, K. C. C., & Kang, Y. W. (2015). Exploring big data and privacy in strategic communication campaigns: A cross-cultural study of mobile social media users' daily experiences. *International Journal of Strategic Communication, Special Issue*, *9*(2), 87–101. doi:10.1080/1553118X.2015.1008635

Yang, L., Yuan, M., Chen, Y., Wang, W., Zhang, Q., & Zeng, J. (2017). Personalized user engagement modeling for mobile videos. *Computer Networks*, *126*, 256–267. doi:10.1016/j.comnet.2017.07.012

Yang, S., Chen, Y., & Wei, J. (2015). Understanding consumers' web-mobile shopping extension behavior: A trust transfer perspective. *Journal of Computer Information Systems*, *55*(2), 78–87. doi:10.1080/08874417.2015.11645759

Yang, Y., Lu, Q., Tang, G., & Pei, J. (2015). The impact of market competition on search advertising. *Journal of Interactive Marketing*, *30*, 46–55. doi:10.1016/j.intmar.2015.01.002

Yu, C., Zhang, Z., Lin, C., & Wu, Y. (2019). Can data-driven precision marketing promote user ad clicks? Evidence from advertising in WeChat moments. *Industrial Marketing Management.* doi:10.1016/j.indmarman.2019.05.001

Yu, J., & Cude, B. (2009). Possible disparities in consumers' perceptions toward personalized advertising caused by cultural differences: U.S. and Korea. *Journal of International Consumer Marketing*, *21*(4), 251–269. doi:10.1080/08961530802282166

Zaroban, S. (2018). US e-commerce sales grow 16.0% in 2017. Available at https://www.digitalcommerce360.com/article/us-ecommerce-sales/

Zeithaml, V. A., Berry, L. L., & Parasuraman, A. (1988). Communication and control processes in the delivery of service quality. *Journal of Marketing*, *52*(2), 35–48. doi:10.1177/002224298805200203

Zeng, F., Huang, L., & Dou, W. (2013). Social factors in user perceptions and responses to advertising in online social networking communities. *Journal of Interactive Advertising*, *10*(1), 1–13. doi:10.1080/15252019.2009.10722159

Zeng, W., & Richardson, A. (2017). Using immersive virtual reality to create presence in online shopping. In *Australasian Conference on Information Systems*.

Zhang, J. (2019). Shopping festival '618' registers record-breaking numbers. Available at http://www.chinadaily.com.cn/a/201906/19/WS5d09d0cca3103dbf1432919b.html

Zhang, E. (2007). A study on ad-place quantity optimization in Adwords auction. In *2007 International Conference on Wireless Communications, Networking and Mobile Computing* (pp. 3339–3342). IEEE. 10.1109/WICOM.2007.827

Zhang, X., Kumar, V., & Cosguner, K. (2017). Dynamically managing a profitable email marketing program. *JMR, Journal of Marketing Research*, *54*(6), 851–866. doi:10.1509/jmr.16.0210

Zheng, C., Yu, X., & Jin, Q. (2017). How user relationships affect user perceived value propositions of enterprises on social commerce platforms. *Information Systems Frontiers*, *19*(6), 1261–1271. doi:10.100710796-017-9766-y

Zhou, Y., Chakrabarty, D., & Lukose, R. (2008). Budget constrained bidding in keyword auctions and online knapsack problems. In *International Workshop on Internet and Network Economics* (pp. 566–576). Springer. 10.1007/978-3-540-92185-1_63

Zimand-Sheiner, D., Ryan, T., Kip, S., & Lahav, T. (2019). Native advertising credibility perceptions and ethical attitudes: An exploratory study among adolescents in the United States, Turkey and Israel. *Journal of Business Research*. doi:10.1016/j.jbusres.2019.06.020

Zorn, S., Bellman, S., Robinson, J., & Varan, D. (2013). Cultural differences affect interactive television advertising. *Journal of Marketing Communications*, *22*(1), 3–17. doi:10.1080/13527266.2013.833539

About the Contributors

Tereza Semerádová works as a research assistant at the department of informatics at the Technical University of Liberec. Her primary research areas include online marketing strategies, user experience design and advertising efficiency. Along with her academic activities, Tereza also participates in numerous marketing projects where she operates as a consultant on Facebook ads, Google Adwords and website analytics. Tereza is a specialist at dynamic ads and remarketing.

Petr Weinlich is a research assistant at the department of informatics at the Technical University of Liberec. He specializes in multimedia, web design and creative marketing content. He has both academic and professional experience. His skills include professional sound processing, green screen production, vector graphics, photo editing, animation and optimization of video content for advertising systems. Petr participated in many marketing projects as art director and designer.

* * *

Laura Berenice Sánchez Baltasar, PhD, is a graduate of the Bachelor of Management, Master of Marketing and Doctorate in Business, has held positions at regional management level in Mexican companies, mainly in the service sector. She is the author of several publications and research presented at national and international conferences; in Mexico, Costa Rica, Brazil, Uruguay, Argentina and Colombia.

Belem Barbosa is Adjunct Professor at the University of Aveiro and member of GOVCOPP, the research unit on Governance, Competitiveness and Public Policy. She received her PhD in Business and Management Studies – specialisation in Marketing and Strategy from the University of Porto, Portugal. Her research interests lie primarily in the area of internet marketing and consumer behaviour, including word-of-mouth communication, sustainability marketing, tourism and events marketing.

Ricardo Barbosa holds a degree in Business Management (ESTGA-UA), a Master in Marketing (ISCAA-UA) and is completing a new Master in Management (IPLeiria). In recent years, it has work in digital marketing agencies, more properly in the application of Social Media Marketing campaigns, Email Marketing, e-commerce, Mobile Marketing, SEO and SEM. His interests in digital marketing strategies, ecommerce and Google ads allowed a very in-depth knowledge about business sales strategies.

Sérgio Barreto is a professor at the University of Aveiro. He holds a degree in Mathematics, a master's degree in Statistics & Operational Research and a PhD in Industrial Management. He was professor in charge of several disciplines of Mathematics and Management areas. He paid special attention to logistical problems, with emphasis on location and routing models. More recently, it has been focusing on issues related to operations-level business practices and supply chain optimization. He is a member of the Center for Research in Marketing and Data Analysis, member of the AU Graduate Monitoring Observatory and member of the Scientific Council of the University of Aveiro.

Carlos Hernán Fajardo-Toro received a PhD degree in Computer Science (Tools for developing intelligent software) and the degree of MSc in Management and Logistics and Supply Chain of the University of Vigo (Spain). He serves currently as a full time teacher at the School of Business Administration - EAN (Bogota, Colombia).

Juan Renteria García holds a BS in Industrial Engineering with Specialization Degree in Marketing from Universidad Javeriana and MBA e-Business from the University of New Brunswick (Canada). Working experience in marketing, new business development and teaching. Currently in charge of all marketing programs for Universidad EAN's Business School, and PhD student at Universidad Politécnica de Valencia (Spain).

Yowei Kang (Ph.D.) is Assistant Professor at Bachelor Degree Program in Oceanic Cultural Creative Design Industries, National Taiwan Ocean University, TAIWAN. His research interests focus on new media design, digital game research, visual communication, and experiential rhetoric. Some of his works have been published in *International Journal of Strategic Communication*, and *Journal of Intercultural Communication Studies*. He has received government funding to support his research in location-based advertising and consumer privacy management strategies.

Asli Kuscu has 9 years of multicultural work experience in marketing and sales in multinational companies. After completing her PhD in Marketing at Bogazici University, Turkey, Asli is currently working as an Assistant Professor in marketing at Yeditepe University Business Administration Department, teaching marketing courses and supervising MBA and PhD students. Her research interests and previous publications cover consumer-brand relationships and interactive marketing.

Alok Mishra is a Professor in Software Engineering at Atilim University, Ankara, Turkey. He is visiting research chair at University of Technology of Compiegne (Sorbonne Universities), France. He is also adjunct professor at GlobalNxt University, Malaysia and visiting professor at Belgrade Metropolitan University. His areas of interest and research are software engineering and information systems. He has published articles, book chapters and book-reviews related to software engineering and information system in reputed journals, books and conferences. Dr. Mishra is also editor and editorial board member of many reputed journals. Prof. Mishra has extensive experience in online education related to Computing and Management curriculums. In teaching, he had received excellence in online education award by Universitas 21Global, Singapore while in research he has been awarded by Scientific and Research Council of Turkey and Board of Management of Atilim University. He is member of research consortium which recently awarded large EU research project in health informatics. He is the recipient of various scholarships including the national merit scholarship and the department of information technology scholarship of the Government of India.

Yesica Mayett Moreno is graduated in Economics, and Ph. D. in Sciences. Member of the National Research System Level I in Mexico, she works in UPAEP University as Director of Graduate programs in Business and Agribusiness since 1998. She was a Fulbright Visiting Scholar in the Department of Agricultural Economics and Agribusiness, University of Arkansas. Other outreach experiences include Oklahoma State University, Portland State University, and EAN – Colombia as Visiting Professor in Agribusiness, Business and Marketing Schools, respectively. She has been teaching since 1994. Her professional experience, projects and papers are related to market research, consumer behavior, socioeconomic studies for vulnerable people, and its relation to economic policies in order to achieve a sustainable development.

Bülent Özsaçmaci has been woking in Çankaya University since 2002. He has been teaching marketing and business courses since 2011.He also conducting the Director position of Çankaya Vocational School since 2016.

Mauricio Sabogal Salamanca is an economist (Universidad Nacional de Colombia), Master in Marketing (Universidad de los Andes, Colombia), and Doctorate student at WU University (Vienna, Austria). Worked for financial institutions and retail companies for seven years and since 2013 is full time professor at Universidad EAN in Colombia, with a research and teaching oriented to marketing

Kenneth C. C. Yang (Ph.D.) is Professor in the Department of Communication at the University of Texas at El Paso, USA. His research focuses on new media advertising, consumer behavior, and international advertising. Some of his many works have been published in *Cyberpsychology*, *Journal of Strategic Communication*, *International Journal of Consumer Marketing*, *Journal of Intercultural Communication Studies*, *Journal of Marketing Communication*, and *Telematics and Informatics*. He has edited or co-edited three books, Asia.com: Asia encounters the Internet (Routledge, 2003), Multi-Platform Advertising Strategies in the Global Marketplace (IGI Global, 2018), and Cases on Immersive Virtual Reality Techniques (IGI Global, 2019).

Liguo Yu received his PhD degree in Computer Science from Vanderbilt University in 2004. He is an associate professor at Indiana University South Bend. He received his MS degree from Institute of Metal Research, Chinese Academy of Science in 1995. He received his BS degree in Physics from Jilin University in 1992. Before joining IUSB, he was a visiting assistant professor at Tennessee Tech University. During his sabbatical of Spring 2014, he was a visiting faculty at New York Institute of Technology-Nanjing. His research interests include software coupling, software maintenance and software evolution, empirical software engineering, and open-source development.

Index

E

F

G

I

J

L

M

O

P

Q

R

S

U

V

Purchase Print, E-Book, or Print + E-Book

IGI Global's reference books can now be purchased from three unique pricing formats: Print Only, E-Book Only, or Print + E-Book.
Shipping fees may apply.

www.igi-global.com

Recommended Reference Books

ISBN: 978-1-5225-6201-6
© 2019; 341 pp.
List Price: $345

ISBN: 978-1-5225-7262-6
© 2019; 360 pp.
List Price: $215

ISBN: 978-1-5225-8003-4
© 2019; 216 pp.
List Price: $205

ISBN: 978-1-5225-5763-0
© 2019; 304 pp.
List Price: $205

ISBN: 978-1-5225-6980-0
© 2019; 325 pp.
List Price: $235

ISBN: 978-1-5225-7808-6
© 2019; 397 pp.
List Price: $215

Looking for free content, product updates, news, and special offers?
Join IGI Global's mailing list today and start enjoying exclusive perks sent only to IGI Global members.
Add your name to the list at **www.igi-global.com/newsletters.**

Publisher of Peer-Reviewed, Timely, and Innovative Academic Research

IGI Global
DISSEMINATOR OF KNOWLEDGE

www.igi-global.com Sign up at www.igi-global.com/newsletters facebook.com/igiglobal twitter.com/igiglobal

Ensure Quality Research is Introduced to the Academic Community

Become an IGI Global Reviewer for Authored Book Projects

The overall success of an authored book project is dependent on quality and timely reviews.

In this competitive age of scholarly publishing, constructive and timely feedback significantly expedites the turnaround time of manuscripts from submission to acceptance, allowing the publication and discovery of forward-thinking research at a much more expeditious rate. Several IGI Global authored book projects are currently seeking highly-qualified experts in the field to fill vacancies on their respective editorial review boards:

Applications and Inquiries may be sent to:
development@igi-global.com

Applicants must have a doctorate (or an equivalent degree) as well as publishing and reviewing experience. Reviewers are asked to complete the open-ended evaluation questions with as much detail as possible in a timely, collegial, and constructive manner. All reviewers' tenures run for one-year terms on the editorial review boards and are expected to complete at least three reviews per term. Upon successful completion of this term, reviewers can be considered for an additional term.

If you have a colleague that may be interested in this opportunity, we encourage you to share this information with them.

IGI Global Proudly Partners With eContent Pro International

Receive a 25% Discount on all Editorial Services

Editorial Services

IGI Global expects all final manuscripts submitted for publication to be in their final form. This means they must be reviewed, revised, and professionally copy edited prior to their final submission. Not only does this support with accelerating the publication process, but it also ensures that the highest quality scholarly work can be disseminated.

English Language Copy Editing

Let eContent Pro International's expert copy editors perform edits on your manuscript to resolve spelling, punctuaion, grammar, syntax, flow, formatting issues and more.

Scientific and Scholarly Editing

Allow colleagues in your research area to examine the content of your manuscript and provide you with valuable feedback and suggestions before submission.

Figure, Table, Chart & Equation Conversions

Do you have poor quality figures? Do you need visual elements in your manuscript created or converted? A design expert can help!

Translation

Need your documjent translated into English? eContent Pro International's expert translators are fluent in English and more than 40 different languages.

Hear What Your Colleagues are Saying About Editorial Services Supported by IGI Global

"The service was very fast, very thorough, and very helpful in ensuring our chapter meets the criteria and requirements of the book's editors. I was quite impressed and happy with your service."

– Prof. Tom Brinthaupt, Middle Tennessee State University, USA

"I found the work actually spectacular. The editing, formatting, and other checks were very thorough. The turnaround time was great as well. I will definitely use eContent Pro in the future."

– Nickanor Amwata, Lecturer, University of Kurdistan Hawler, Iraq

"I was impressed that it was done timely, and wherever the content was not clear for the reader, the paper was improved with better readability for the audience."

– Prof. James Chilembwe, Mzuzu University, Malawi

Email: customerservice@econtentpro.com

www.igi-global.com/editorial-service-partners

IGI Global
DISSEMINATOR OF KNOWLEDGE
www.igi-global.com

Celebrating Over 30 Years of Scholarly Knowledge Creation & Dissemination

InfoSci®-Books

A Database of Over 5,300+ Reference Books Containing Over 100,000+ Chapters Focusing on Emerging Research

InfoSci®-Books Database

The **InfoSci®-Books** database is a collection of over 5,300+ IGI Global single and multi-volume reference books, handbooks of research, and encyclopedias, encompassing groundbreaking research from prominent experts worldwide that span over 350+ topics in 11 core subject areas including business, computer science, education, science and engineering, social sciences and more.

Open Access Fee Waiver (Offset Model) Initiative

For any library that invests in IGI Global's InfoSci-Journals and/ or InfoSci-Books databases, IGI Global will match the library's investment with a fund of equal value to go toward **subsidizing the OA article processing charges (APCs) for their students, faculty, and staff** at that institution when their work is submitted and accepted under OA into an IGI Global journal.*

INFOSCI® PLATFORM FEATURES

- No DRM
- No Set-Up or Maintenance Fees
- A Guarantee of No More Than a 5% Annual Increase
- Full-Text HTML and PDF Viewing Options
- Downloadable MARC Records
- Unlimited Simultaneous Access
- COUNTER 5 Compliant Reports
- Formatted Citations With Ability to Export to RefWorks and EasyBib
- No Embargo of Content (Research is Available Months in Advance of the Print Release)

**The fund will be offered on an annual basis and expire at the end of the subscription period. The fund would renew as the subscription is renewed for each year thereafter. The open access fees will be waived after the student, faculty, or staff's paper has been vetted and accepted into an IGI Global journal and the fund can only be used toward publishing OA in an IGI Global journal. Libraries in developing countries will have the match on their investment doubled.*

To Learn More or To Purchase This Database:
www.igi-global.com/infosci-books
eresources@igi-global.com • Toll Free: 1-866-342-6657 ext. 100 • Phone: 717-533-8845 x100

IGI Global
DISSEMINATOR OF KNOWLEDGE
www.igi-global.com

IGI Global
DISSEMINATOR OF KNOWLEDGE
www.igi-global.com

Publisher of Peer-Reviewed, Timely, and Innovative Academic Research Since 1988

IGI Global's Transformative Open Access (OA) Model:
How to Turn Your University Library's Database Acquisitions Into a Source of OA Funding

In response to the OA movement and well in advance of Plan S, IGI Global, early last year, unveiled their OA Fee Waiver (Offset Model) Initiative.

Under this initiative, librarians who invest in IGI Global's InfoSci-Books (5,300+ reference books) and/or InfoSci-Journals (185+ scholarly journals) databases will be able to subsidize their patron's OA article processing charges (APC) when their work is submitted and accepted (after the peer review process) into an IGI Global journal.*

How Does it Work?

1. When a library subscribes or perpetually purchases IGI Global's InfoSci-Databases including InfoSci-Books (5,300+ e-books), InfoSci-Journals (185+ e-journals), and/or their discipline/subject-focused subsets, IGI Global will match the library's investment with a fund of equal value to go toward subsidizing the OA article processing charges (APCs) for their patrons.

   Researchers: Be sure to recommend the InfoSci-Books and InfoSci-Journals to take advantage of this initiative.
2. When a student, faculty, or staff member submits a paper and it is accepted (following the peer review) into one of IGI Global's 185+ scholarly journals, the author will have the option to have their paper published under a traditional publishing model or as OA.
3. When the author chooses to have their paper published under OA, IGI Global will notify them of the OA Fee Waiver (Offset Model) Initiative. If the author decides they would like to take advantage of this initiative, IGI Global will deduct the US$ 1,500 APC from the created fund.
4. This fund will be offered on an annual basis and will renew as the subscription is renewed for each year thereafter. IGI Global will manage the fund and award the APC waivers unless the librarian has a preference as to how the funds should be managed.

Hear From the Experts on This Initiative:

"I'm very happy to have been able to make one of my recent research contributions, 'Visualizing the Social Media Conversations of a National Information Technology Professional Association' featured in the *International Journal of Human Capital and Information Technology Professionals*, freely available along with having access to the valuable resources found within IGI Global's InfoSci-Journals database."

– **Prof. Stuart Palmer**,
Deakin University, Australia

For More Information, Visit: www.igi-global.com/publish/contributor-resources/open-access or contact IGI Global's Database Team at eresources@igi-global.com

www.ingramcontent.com/pod-product-compliance
Lightning Source LLC
LaVergne TN
LVHW061537290926
849162LV00004B/824